D1567000

Mazarin's Quest

Mazarin's Quest

The Congress of Westphalia and the Coming of the Fronde

Paul Sonnino

HARVARD UNIVERSITY PRESS

Cambridge, Massachusetts

London, England

2008

Library of Congress Cataloging-in-Publication Data

Sonnino, Paul.
    Mazarin's quest : the Congress of Westphalia and the coming of the
Fronde / Paul Sonnino.
        p.   cm.
    Includes bibliographical references and index.
    ISBN 978-0-674-03182-1 (alk. paper)
    1. Mazarin, Jules, 1602–1661—Influence.   2. Peace of Westphalia
(1648)   3. Thirty Years' War, 1618–1648—Diplomatic history.   4. Fronde.
5. France—Foreign relations—1643–1715.   6. France—History—Louis XIV,
1643–1715.   7. Statesmen—France—Biography.   I. Title.
DC130.M4S66   2008
940.2'42—dc22   2008017653

Map 1. Europe: 1618–1648 (Tryntje Helfferich and Paul Sonnino). Archives of
the author.

Map 2. The Holy Roman Empire: 1618–1648 (Tryntje Helfferich and Paul
Sonnino). Archives of the author.

Contents

Illustrations follow page 90

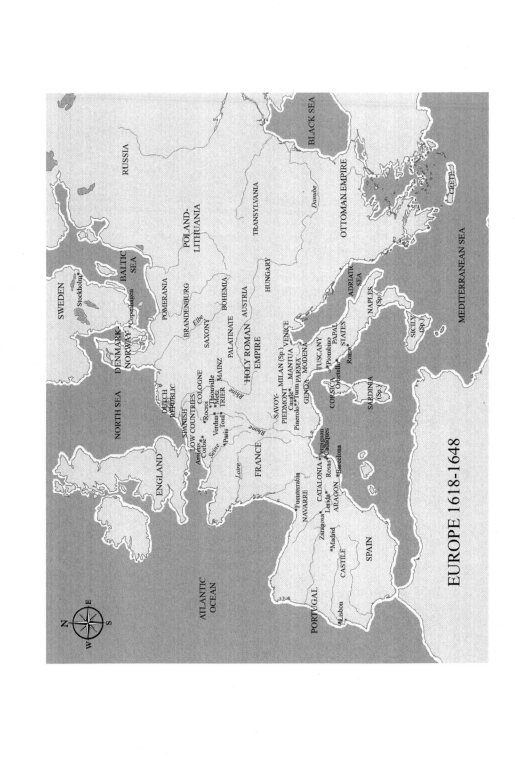

EUROPE 1618-1648

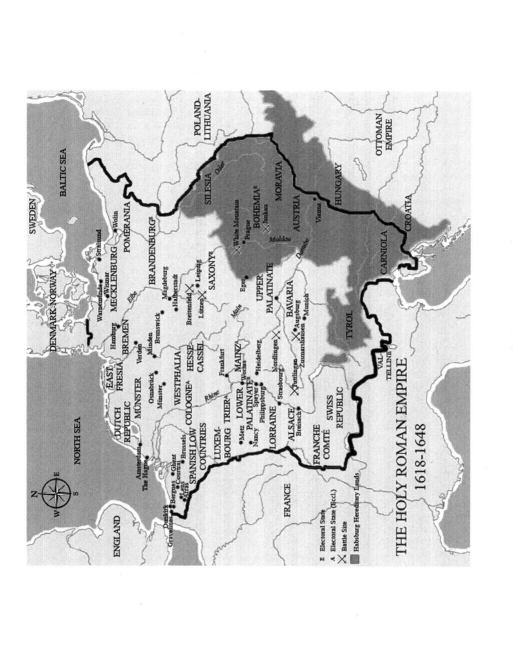

THE HOLY ROMAN EMPIRE
1618-1648

E Electoral State
A Electoral State (Eccl.)
X Battle Site
Habsburg Hereditary Lands

SWEDEN

BALTIC SEA

POLAND-LITHUANIA

OTTOMAN EMPIRE

DENMARK-NORWAY

NORTH SEA

ENGLAND

POMERANIA

BRANDENBURG

SILESIA

MORAVIA

HUNGARY

CROATIA

Oder

Warnemünde • Stralsund
Wismar
Wolin

MECKLENBURG

Hamburg
BREMEN

Verden
EAST FRESIA

Minden
MÜNSTER
Osnabruck
Münster

Brunswick
Magdeburg
Halberstadt

Elbe

Breitenfeld X • Leipzig
Lützen X

SAXONY

White Mountain X
Prague
BOHEMIA
Jankau X

Eger

Moldau

AUSTRIA
Vienna
Vienna

CARNIOLA

DUTCH REPUBLIC

Amsterdam
The Hague

WESTPHALIA

HESSE CASSEL

Frankfurt

MAINZ

Main

UPPER PALATINATE

BAVARIA
Augsburg
Munich

Danube

TYROL

VAL TELLINE

SPANISH LOW COUNTRIES

Brussels
Ghent
Bergues
Courtrai
Arras

Dunkirk
Gravelines

COLOGNE

LUXEM-BOURG

TRIER

Metz
Nancy

LORRAINE

LOWER PALATINATE

Heidelberg
Worms
Speyer
Philippsburg
Strasbourg

Nördlingen X

Rhine

ALSACE
Breisach

FRANCHE COMTÉ

SWISS REPUBLIC

Rottingen
Zusmarshausen X

FRANCE

Mazarin's Quest

Introduction

Giulio Mazarini, who became Cardinal Mazarin, was a man who made his mark both on his contemporaries and on the collective memory of posterity. An obscure and wily Italian who assumed the role of prime minister of France just prior to the death of Louis XIII, Mazarin even gained the confidence of the king's widow and guided the monarchy through the tumultuous minority of the young Louis XIV. Inheriting a costly and controversial war against the greatest Catholic powers of Europe, Mazarin pursued it with tenacity and eventually brought a portion of it to an end with considerable gains for the French monarchy at the Congress of Westphalia, one of the great diplomatic gatherings of all time. In the midst of this apparent success, he was confronted in France itself by a domestic revolt, the Fronde, which succeeded in forcing him into exile until such time as the rebellion collapsed of its own weight, paving the way for his triumphal return to the administration of the state. That is the rough recollection of Giulio Mazarini.

A more precise recollection, however, is complicated by the fact that Mazarin happened to be living in one of the first ages in the history of Europe for which the historian is drowned by a flood of sources. From the analysis of one, two, or maybe three accounts of any particular person or event, the professional researcher is suddenly inundated with a multiplicity of documents, and this is especially true of Mazarin's connection with this famous congress. In the seventeenth century, the ponderous tomes with documents on the congress began to accumulate. In 1650 Lieuwe van Aitzema produced his *Verhael van de Nederlandsche Vrede-Handeling,* concentrating on the Dutch documentation. Then in

1

1668 Michael Londorp published his *Der Römischen Kayserlichen Majestät und des Heiligen Römischen Reichs . . . Acta publica,* a gold mine of public German documents. But perhaps the most remarkable of the seventeenth-century collections was Vittorio Siri's *Il Mercurio.* Cardinal Mazarin himself had provided Siri with his own secret correspondence with the French plenipotentiaries in Westphalia, and Siri put the best possible complexion on it in order to demonstrate that Mazarin had been deprived of the full fruits of his genius by the foolish rebellion of the Fronde.[1]

During the eighteenth century, more and more materials emerged to the light of day. In 1710, during the War of the Spanish Succession, an anonymous editor in Amsterdam published two volumes of correspondence, centering on the year 1646. The editor put the worst possible complexion on it in order to castigate Cardinal Mazarin and the French monarchy, which, after years of disturbing the peace of Europe, was finally receiving its comeuppance. Then, some fourteen years later, Jean Le Clerc, a Genevan Protestant living in the Dutch Republic, published a four-volume collection of letters, *mémoires,* and assorted documents, still showing a touch of hostility toward Mazarin. Both of these publications were derived from compendiums which combined correspondence originating in the department of Loménie de Brienne, the French secretary of state for foreign affairs during the entire span of the negotiations, and more public documents collected by Théodore Godefroy, the archivist who accompanied the French delegation to the peace conference. Next, from the court of Saxony came Carl Wilhelm Gärtner, who, in nine volumes, combined many of these same sources with correspondence from the Imperial delegation. These revelations were supplemented soon thereafter by Johann Gottfried von Meiern, who, in the tradition of Londorp, constructed his collection with the mountains of documents made public by the parties as they went along. None of these publications were complete, but they raised a lot of questions and constituted an informational revolution, almost too much for a single historian to handle.[2]

In this same century Guillaume-Hyacinthe Bougeant, a French Jesuit who had obtained access to the papers of the Count d'Avaux, one of the three French plenipotentiaries at the conference, attempted something of a synthesis. Bougeant tended to see the negotiations as an attempt to limit the ambitions of the Hapsburg house of Austria and describe them from a French perspective, but even he noted that toward the end of the year 1646, the French found themselves, by virtue of too much military success, in danger of being abandoned by their own Dutch allies and that Cardinal Mazarin, "instead of opening his eyes to the approaching peril, preferred to pursue his vast enterprises and his glory." But the great Voltaire ignored such reservations and, like Siri, combined the eventual signing of the peace in 1648 with a vindication of the cardinal. "Mazarin was held in horror, even though, at this very time, he consummated the great work of the Peace of Münster."[3]

The nineteenth century, with its discovery of nationality as well as archives, elevated the Peace of Westphalia into a manifestation of the Divine plan. To Ranke, the putative German father of "scientific history," it was the not-so-scientific "guiding genius" which had been instrumental in maintaining the balance of power in Europe, and the workings of this beneficent "genius" were no better evident—which is where the "scientific" comes in—than through the analysis of diplomatic documents. These convinced him that "between 1636 and 1646 one of the greatest changes in the position of a great state that had ever occurred in Europe took place in the relationship between France and its neighbors." France made immense gains and Spain came very close to succumbing. But Cardinal Mazarin, according to Ranke, was not satisfied with these conquests. Mazarin also wanted the Spanish Low Countries, and more. In his excessive zeal, therefore, he brought the Fronde upon himself, and so the budding nations of modern Europe, the Protestant Reformation, and the destiny of mankind were thereby saved by the hand of God.[4]

The French had their Ranke too, and he was Adolphe Chéruel, who undertook to publish the *Lettres du Cardinal Mazarin*. This correspondence, along with Mazarin's *Carnets,* led Chéruel to conclude, in his *Histoire de France pendant la minorité de Louis XIV,* that Mazarin had been much maligned. "It has been claimed that Mazarin did not seriously want peace, but he responded in his letters that the *Spanish* (italics mine) had never wanted peace." This was good enough for Chéruel. As to the accusation that Mazarin wanted to annex the Spanish Low Countries, Chéruel asserted that it was the *Spanish* (italics mine) who had floated a marriage and exchange proposal, but "it did not take Mazarin long to recognize that this was a trick." And as to the conclusion of the Peace of Westphalia in 1648:

Mazarin had not only given France the frontier of the Rhine, he had established French preponderance in all of Europe without alarming the princes and the people. He was able to reconcile national greatness with the European equilibrium and the consolidation of the old German constitution. This is his claim to immortality.

Concurrent with the efforts of Chéruel was the publication of the *Coleccion de documentos inéditos para la historia de España,* three of whose volumes cover the negotiations at Westphalia and, not surprisingly, tend to describe the intentions of Cardinal Mazarin in a more negative light. However, these sources received relatively little attention from nineteenth-century Spanish historians, who preferred not to squander their labors on a great event that seemed to mark the culmination of their own golden age.[5]

No matter whose side one is on, however, there seems to be little debate that the Peace of Westphalia was a pivotal moment, and modern historiography has only added to its reputation. Modern historians have embraced passionately the notion that one of the most noteworthy developments in the history of Europe was the rise of the nation-state, to which they have associated the concept of "sovereignty," and the Peace of Westphalia seems to hold a place of honor in this uplifting drama. Take, for example, what Palmer and Colton's *History of the Modern World,* one of the most prestigious textbooks ever to have circulated in the American university, says of the treaty:

> Not only did the Peace of Westphalia block the Counter Reformation, and not only did it frustrate the Austrian Hapsburgs and forestall for almost two centuries any movement toward German national unification, but it also marked the advent in international law of the modern European system of sovereign states. Europe was understood to consist in a large number of unconnected sovereignties, free and detached atoms, or states, which moved about according to their own laws.

Palmer was certainly right about the end of the Counter Reformation, but he is so enthusiastic about the Peace of Westphalia that he goes on to assert that, after the peace, the Atlantic peoples—French, English, and Dutch—began to take the lead in European affairs while the cities of Berlin and Vienna went into eclipse.[6]

Neither the *Annaliste* movement, which takes little notice of events, nor the systems theorists, who attempt to reduce them to algebraic equations, nor the *nouvelle histoire,* which subsumes them into self-contained discourses, has had much of an impact on the theory of the rise of the state, which is repeated over and over again as a received truth. But this patriotic theory is extremely questionable, and the motives for advancing it are extremely suspect. How can we, I would ask, claim to measure the strength of a state at any given moment when we have in our own time seen any number of such leviathans disappear in a day? Machiavelli, who was no mean political analyst, observed that hereditary principalities were much more durable than some of the greatest of empires, and Montesquieu, no less of a pundit, would certainly have agreed. And if we go to the notion of sovereignty, it is an idea, as opposed to a term, which is at least as old as Sargon of Akkad and which has no necessary connection to a state's capacity to enforce its will. If, therefore, we wish to maintain an accurate recollection of the Peace of Westphalia, it might behoove us not to associate it with developments which, if they occurred at all, occurred over a long span of time, and to devote ourselves to better-posed questions still in contention, such as the exact intentions and interactions of the participants.[7]

I myself have chosen in this book to concentrate on the intentions and interactions of Cardinal Mazarin and his entourage as they attempted to achieve a peace, and this narrower focus has permitted me to navigate more safely between the methodological shoals. I presume to recreate their mind-set, follow its transformations, and compare it with that of the other participants. I may occasionally get a little testy with my protagonists, but I do not presume to second-guess their decisions. Moreover, I make no claim to assess the impact of these decisions, other than to describe the way that the other participants reacted to them. Finally, I do not attempt to employ these decisions in order to construct any system, preferring to leave these loftier concerns to those who have a better insight than I into the intentions of Providence, the indifference of the *longue durée,* or the power of abstractions.

In the study of history, there is something about the original document that no published version, no matter how scrupulous, can reproduce. The hand in which it is written, the corrections, cross-outs, or insertions, the version which has come down to us, the number of persons it went through, the number of copies which were made, the collections in which they were initially preserved, all these considerations weigh heavily in the effort to establish contact with the author and the recipients at the most direct possible level of their experience. This is why I have attempted in this book to consult the original sources whenever possible, even when they have subsequently appeared in print. This is also why I have tapped many of the indispensable original sources which are still unpublished. My conclusions, therefore, are based on a reevaluation of a number of old and on the integration of a number of previously unused original sources.

The first of these sources is the *Carnets* of Cardinal Mazarin. They are hardly unknown. In the course of the nineteenth century, excerpts were published by Cousin, Chéruel, and others, Chéruel acknowledging that they were something of a psychological treasure, but the fact that we still do not have a complete edition of the *Carnets* is a testament to the reluctance of historians to let their characters speak for themselves. At the same time a calendar, a diary, an account book, and a justification for posterity, the *Carnets* reveal to us many aspects of Mazarin's inner life of which we do not normally take notice. For example, we discover that Mazarin was a man who thought, spoke, and wrote in Italian, at least until the end of the year 1647. Thus he must have dictated in Italian his eloquent letters of this period and it was his secretaries, notably Hugues de Lionne, who turned them into readable French and give us the impression of a polyglot. But we also discover Mazarin's ups and downs, his interpersonal relations, and his eccentricities, which I would tend to interpret not quite as charitably as did his admirer Chéruel.[8]

The second of these sources is Mazarin's correspondence, which might at first sight appear to have been disposed of in the nine massive volumes of his *Lettres,* begun by Chéruel and finished by D'Avenel. However, on even cursory comparison with the original sources in the archives, one discovers that this collection omits all of the diplomatic instructions that Mazarin composed, whose subsequent publication in the *Recueil des Instructions données aux ambassadeurs et ministres de France* only begins *after* the Peace of Westphalia. Even more serious, the collection almost completely ignores the *Mémoires du Roi,* which may also be found alongside many of these same letters in the archives of the French ministry of foreign affairs. A glance at these *mémoires* will show that they were written in the same hand, that of Lionne, which had put most of Cardinal Mazarin's letters into French, and a close reading will show that it is these *mémoires,* much more than the letters, which carry the burden of his thought. It is true that some of these *mémoires* had already been uncovered in the eighteenth century and that, since the publication of the *Acta Pacis Westphalicae,* many more of them have seen the light of print, but it is still necessary to consult the originals in order to realize that they come from the same source and are of considerably greater weight than the letters.[9]

A third group of sources is the papers of the French plenipotentiaries. We have already seen that Bougeant utilized the papers of the Count d'Avaux, which are today interspersed within certain volumes in the archives of the ministry of foreign affairs. To these, however, need to be added the papers of the Count de Servien, which constitute twenty-four entire volumes and are also inserted throughout other volumes in this same archive. The papers of Servien are particularly valuable in that he carried out a pithy and secret correspondence with his nephew Lionne as well as with Mazarin. It has taken the excellent publication of the *Acta Pacis Westphalicae* to bring many of these papers to light. Unfortunately the chief of the French delegation, the Duke de Longueville, did not leave us a personal collection, but still, by identifying and separating the correspondence of each of the French plenipotentiaries, we are in a position to see clearly how three individuals belonging to the same delegation could develop different perspectives and viewpoints.[10]

Then there is the correspondence of the other plenipotentiaries at the conference with their courts. The correspondence of the Spanish plenipotentiaries, much of it in the Archivo General de Simancas, is invaluable. I have obtained it in the original, supplementing the already mentioned publication in the *Coleccion de documentos inéditos para la Historia de España.* I have followed a similar procedure with the correspondence of the Imperial plenipotentiaries, supplementing its magnificent presentation in the *Acta Pacis Westphalicae,* still unfortunately incomplete at the time of this writing. I have profited from some individual originals in the Swedish Riksarkiv with due appreciation of the fact that the publication in the *Acta Pacis Westphalicae* is now complete. The greatest lacunae in the availability of the documents, however, lie in the writings of the two mediators, the papal nuncio Fabio Chigi and the Venetian ambassador Alvise Contarini. The earlier portions of Chigi's correspondence, from 1640 to 1645, were published in Rome between 1943 and 1946, but the later portions, which cover the climax of the congress, have never appeared. Contarini's correspondence has been even more neglected. I have thus profited immeasurably from a full run of Chigi's correspondence in both the Biblioteca Apostolica and the Archivio Segreto del Vaticano, and of Contarini's in the Archivio di Stato di Venezia. Nor have I failed to consult the correspondence of the Dutch, Savoyard, and Hesse-Cassel delegations, all unpublished, from each of their respective archives.[11]

Finally, I have made measured use of the *mémoires* of contemporaries. France, for the seventeenth century, was one of the most prolific countries in Europe in the production of such recollections, and has to some extent suffered from this abundance of riches by not exploiting it to its limit. The putative *Mémoires de Monsieur D.*, for example, which came out in 1674, have until recently been attributed to the Count d'Avaux, even though they refer to events that occurred after his death. This is why I have not cited them as his, in case a learned reader may wonder at my omission. They are, in all probability, the *Mémoires* of Henri de La Court, the French resident in Osnabrück, and a priceless source if evaluated for what they are. This is, again, a sad reflection on the reluctance of historians to listen to the voices from the past or to distinguish one from the other.[12]

All these sources tell me that we are dealing here with the concerns of men who were laboring, each in his own way, for the termination of a terrible war. They had no idea of progress. The word "innovation" was anathema to them. The last thing on their minds was the creation of a new system of sovereign states. If we consider, for example, the debates which went on between Cardinal Mazarin and his own plenipotentiaries on whether France should acquire Alsace in full sovereignty or as a fief of the Holy Roman Empire, we will see that while one plenipotentiary felt that sovereignty was more dignified, another felt that feudalism was more useful, and that the issue was settled, for purely practical reasons, by leaving it vague. If the Peace of Westphalia gave to the princes of the Holy Roman Empire the right to carry on their own foreign policy, this demand was advanced by these princes themselves as a confirmation of their traditional rights, and, on the contrary, the peace limited this right by specifying that they could make no alliances against the Empire. The peace also constricted their rights to seize church lands or change the established religion in their territories. If, by his treaty with the Dutch, the King of Spain recognized the sovereignty of the United Provinces, he recognized the sovereignty of the most decentralized states in all of Europe, with the possible exception of the Kingdom of Poland. The

Peace of Westphalia may or may not have been the seedbed of the modern system of state sovereignty, but I would be hard pressed to prove it by consulting its participants.

It may be objected that the attempt to get into the thinking of another human being is a fool's errand, no matter how inviting the sources, but I am tempted to retort that this is what we do every day as we cope with our friends, our enemies, or our loved ones, and I am bemused by the fact that this objection to mind reading is frequently made by scholars who believe that they have managed to penetrate into the mind of the universe. I believe that the assertions I have made about Mazarin and his contemporaries, while they may not always be complimentary, are borne out by the evidence. They do not, of course, include everything that can possibly be said, but this is a limitation of all language which does not negate the correctness of the individual assertions. On the other hand, these same states of mind are, or should be, easily recognizable in ourselves. How easy it is for us to believe that we are in control, that God is with us, and that we can push our luck! How easy it is for us to misread the conceptualizations of others and see them as expressions of ambition, malice, or national character! How easy it is for us to suppress the memory of our own embarrassing actions! I am not presumptuous enough to talk about a universal human nature, or to pass judgment on the efficacy of human actions, but I am presumptuous enough to suggest that insofar as we can recognize these impulses in ourselves, in others, and in those who seek to direct our public policy, we can attempt, at least, to make more conscious decisions. History teaches no lessons, and what did not work yesterday may well work tomorrow. Still, I think it may be of some value to keep recalling that the world has always been populated, and probably always will be, short of some miraculous medication, by human beings not much different from ourselves.

1

The Legacies

When Louis XIII died on May 14, 1643, leaving as his successor the four-year-old Louis XIV, it looked to many observers as if the government of France was about to change dramatically. During the preceding nineteen years the late king, with the aid of Cardinal Richelieu and most recently of Cardinal Mazarin, had been carrying out a policy which was, to say the least, controversial. It was not even that Richelieu had ruled France with an iron hand, for after the civil wars of the sixteenth century and after the clamorous minority of Louis XIII any minister who could restore some sort of order to the French monarchy was not likely to be disapproved. What divided people, or at least the small minority who had opinions about such things, was that Louis XIII and Richelieu seemed to have picked up where Louis XIII's father Henry IV had left off. Henry, who was a Catholic of convenience if there ever was one, had left behind a legacy of religious toleration and enmity against Spain. He had issued the Edict of Nantes in 1598, granting toleration to his Calvinist subjects, the Huguenots, and he had permitted them to garrison about fifty fortified towns in France itself. He had gone to war against Spain and, even after making peace, he had supported the Calvinist provinces of the Low Countries, which were in rebellion against it. The King of Spain belonged to the senior branch of the house of Austria, the Hapsburgs, which was the most powerful dynasty in Europe, and the most Catholic to boot. He also controlled what was left of the Low Countries, portions of Italy, all of Portugal, plus the treasures of the New World. His junior cousins ruled Austria, Bohemia, Moravia, Silesia, and a little bit of Hungary, and regularly got themselves elected Holy Roman

Emperor. Henry's putative "grand design" had been to establish a system of collective security under which the Hapsburgs would agree to abandon their holdings in central Europe and be satisfied with the Iberian peninsula and the New World.[1]

Whatever his design, his widow, Marie de Medici, acting as regent for the young Louis XIII, would have none of it. She enriched her Italian favorites, the Concinis, and she went so far in her pro-Spanish, pro-Catholic sympathies as to pursue for her son the hand of an Infanta of Spain, Anne of Austria, a line of conduct which aroused the ire of the French aristocracy, led by the Prince de Condé, the Huguenots, and the Estates-General of 1614. It was in this assembly that Armand du Plessis, Bishop of Luçon—the future Cardinal Richelieu—made his first appearance on the stage of history with an eloquent, if self-serving, speech in favor of more clergymen in government and of the Spanish marriage. This speech and his close friendship with a Capucin monk, Father Joseph du Tremblay, whose principal passion in life was to organize a crusade against the Turks, attracted the attention of the queen mother, who, after pushing ahead with the marriage, rewarded the right-thinking bishop with a seat in the council. But he was no saint. Even at this early point he expressed the opinion that "the interest of a state and the interest of religion are two entirely different things." His political career, however, was interrupted in 1617, when the young king rebelled against his mother, took terrible revenge upon the Concinis, and replaced her other favorites with his own.[2]

These domestic squabbles in France were soon overshadowed by international ones. In 1618 a group of Calvinist nobles in Bohemia overthrew Ferdinand of Styria, their king of the house of Austria, and set off the Thirty Years War. They offered the throne to the Calvinist Elector Palatine Frederick V, who accepted it, thus challenging the religious *status quo* in the Holy Roman Empire. In 1620, Ferdinand—now Ferdinand II, Holy Roman Emperor—aided by a league of Catholic princes led by Maximilian, the Duke of Bavaria, drove Frederick and his supporters out of Bohemia and in the following year drove him out of his own Palatinate. It was now the Hapsburgs who proceeded to rock the Imperial ship of state when, as a mark of his gratitude as well as of his power, Ferdinand II transferred the title of elector and the territory of the Palatinate to his ally Maximilian. The very same year, a truce between Spain and its Calvinist provinces in the Low Countries, the Dutch

Republic, expired, and Ferdinand's cousin Philip IV of Spain energetically resumed the Spanish effort to reconquer them. In the short span of three years, therefore, the resurgent house of Austria and resurgent Catholicism were on the march all over Europe.[3]

The Bishop of Luçon had in the meanwhile managed to bring about a reconciliation between Louis XIII and his mother, earning for himself both his cardinal's hat and, in 1624, a return to the council. He had no sooner regained his seat, however, than the French monarchy began to show some of its old hostility against the Hapsburgs, much to the surprise of the queen mother. In June of that year France entered into a treaty to subsidize the Dutch Republic in its struggle against Spain, and the more Richelieu emerged as the king's principal minister, the more he did to oppose the interests of the Hapsburgs everywhere. In November 1624, a French army entered the Val Telline and chased out the papal garrisons which were occupying it. All Europe took notice. The Val Telline was an important link in the line of communication between the Spanish possessions in Italy, the Austrian hereditary lands in central Europe, and the remaining Spanish provinces in the Low Countries. It was owned by the Grisons, old allies of the French and Protestants to boot, but inhabited by Catholics. The papal garrisons were guarding it on behalf of Spain. By driving out these garrisons, Richelieu could not have given a clearer signal of his hostility toward the Hapsburgs. His only problem was that he could not sustain it. In January 1625, a Huguenot noble began an uprising in France. Richelieu, under pressure from those members of Louis XIII's council who thought it wiser, not to mention more pious, to destroy the Huguenots at home while the Hapsburgs disposed of them abroad, opted for a compromise on both fronts. He withdrew the French troops from the Val Telline and had to spend the next four years coping with his domestic problems.[4]

He had no shortage of them. In the first place, Marie de Medici was furious at him for abandoning her. The instrument of her vengeance was the king's brother, Gaston, the Duke d'Orléans, otherwise known as Monsieur, an obstreperous and easily swayed young man who quickly became the magnet for every conspiracy against Richelieu. The worse part of it was that if Louis died childless, it was Gaston who would succeed to the throne, and the king, who was cold, sickly, and alarmingly indifferent to the charms of his wife, was well on the way to dying childless. While the Spanish captured Breda from the Dutch and the Lutheran

Christian IV of Denmark, who had gone to the aid of the Protestants in the Empire, was defeated by the Bavarians, Richelieu had to contend with the first of the plots against him. He managed to squash it, but all he could do in retribution was to execute the least prestigious of the conspirators and require the apologetic Monsieur to marry one of France's richest heiresses. It was under these kinds of pressures that Louis XIII and Richelieu devoted themselves to their next most immediate problem, the Huguenots. In 1627 they undertook an ambitious siege of their principal stronghold, the seaport of La Rochelle, this as the Emperor's armies under Wallenstein were mopping up the Protestants in the Empire and Ferdinand II was redistributing their lands among his supporters. It may have appeared as if Richelieu had fallen in line with the pro-Spanish, pro-Catholic party within France, the *dévots,* but superficial observers did not know the kind of man with whom they were dealing.[5]

Louis XIII and Richelieu were still before La Rochelle when, on December 27, 1627, the Duke of Mantua died, leaving as his heir his French relative Charles de Gonzague, Duke de Nevers. The Duchy of Mantua, with its two key fortresses of Mantua and Casale in the heart of the Italian peninsula, was a rich prize and the succession did not go unchallenged. Charles Emmanuel, the Duke of Savoy, claimed a portion of the inheritance for his granddaughter. Spain supported the claim of the Duke of Guestalla to the entire succession. And since the territories were a fief of the Holy Roman Empire, the Holy Roman Emperor was the final arbiter. In February 1628, the Savoyards and the Spanish invaded, with the Spanish besieging Casale. Richelieu had to bide his time until the fall of La Rochelle, but once it capitulated on October 28, 1628, he had no doubt about what Louis XIII should do, namely to relent on the offensive against the Huguenots—depriving them of their fortified strongholds but allowing them to continue to practice their religion—while concentrating on the threat of the Spanish monarchy. This was the thrust of his long *mémoire* of advice to the king and the queen mother of January 13, 1629:

> It is necessary to stop the progress of Spain, and contrary to this nation, which has as its goal to augment its domination and extend its limits, France must think only of fortifying herself and obtaining portals from which to enter into all of its neighboring states and protect them.

These words could hardly have been music to Marie de Medici's ears, and Richelieu's goals were far from modest. He now envisioned an eventual French advance to Strasbourg on the Rhine, even fantasizing about the ultimate reconquest of Navarre and Franche-Comté from Spain. In March 1629, while Louis XIII and Richelieu campaigned in Italy against the Duke of Savoy and scared the Spanish away from Casale, the triumphant Ferdinand II issued the Edict of Restitution for the Holy Roman Empire, ordering the return to their original proprietors of all Catholic lands taken by Protestants since the Peace of Passau in 1552. Never before had the Holy Roman Emperors exercised such arbitrary power, and Richelieu did not like it. In spite of the fact that in the course of 1629 Gaston, now a widower, decided to run away and create more mayhem, Richelieu now went so far as to solicit Gustavus Adolphus, the Lutheran King of Sweden who had spent the previous six years in Catholic Poland sharpening his skills as a warrior, to intervene on behalf of the aggrieved princes of the Holy Roman Empire. It was with the encouragement of the French that Gustavus Adolphus concluded a truce with the Poles so that he could give his attention to the affairs of Germany.[6]

Richelieu was now contending with both branches of the house of Austria, although he was carefully avoiding going to war against either. In July 1630, with Louis XIII again campaigning against the Duke of Savoy and the Spanish again besieging Casale, Gustavus Adolphus landed in northern Germany. He forced the Protestant Duke of Pomerania to become his ally, and he collected more Protestant princes— Mecklenburg, Brandenburg, and Hesse-Cassel—as he went. This was Richelieu's most difficult year. The Imperialists took Mantua; the king fell seriously ill; at the Reichstag in Regensburg a panicky Father Joseph signed a treaty with the Emperor over the Mantuan succession that Richelieu found humiliating; and, to top it off, the queen mother and the *dévots* in the council made their most direct effort to get rid of him. The result of this effort, however, proved to be the memorable Day of Dupes (November 11, 1630) in which Louis XIII defied all expectations by supporting his prime minister and disgracing his enemies. Richelieu could now apply his policies with greater freedom, and he did. French diplomats proceeded to sign a subsidy treaty with Gustavus Adolphus, designed to keep him and his armies in Germany for the next five years. This diversion had one immediate benefit, in spite of the fact that the

pesky Monsieur picked this moment to run away again. By one of two secret treaties at Cherasco with Victor Amadeus, the new Duke of Savoy,
Louis XIII acquired the first of his portals, the stronghold of Pinerolo,
deep in Savoyard territory, and by a public treaty with the Emperor, who
was now facing more serious problems, Louis assured the Mantuan succession to Charles de Gonzague and was able to establish a French garrison in Casale. The frustrated queen mother now also left the country,
taking up residence in Brussels, the capital of the Spanish Low Countries.
It seemed to many that Richelieu, in order to gain these advantages, had
made a bargain with the devil, and the devil was Gustavus Adolphus,
who, after coercing Saxony into his alliance, won a decisive victory over
the Imperialists and the Catholic League at Breitenfeld and, instead of
dutifully moving on to Vienna and forcing the Emperor to come to terms,
moved on to the Rhine, occupying one Catholic diocese after another:
Mainz, Speyer, Worms, and Mannheim. The direst predictions of the
dévots were coming to pass.[7]

Intertwined with these policies were the bizarre relations between
Louis XIII and his childhood playmate, Charles IV, Duke of Lorraine.
About the only thing the two princes had in common was their religion.
Charles was a fun-loving, handsome rake who refused to be humble and
enjoyed a good rumpus. His sympathies, in so far as he had any, were
with the Hapsburgs. He had, on their behalf, participated in the reconquest of Bohemia, gaining much respect for his heroism. Between 1624
and 1626 he had established himself on the ducal throne, and he was
often mentioned as a potential crusader against the Turks. He seemed to
derive particular pleasure, however, from meddling in French affairs.
When the Duke d'Orléans had first run away, he had stopped at Charles's
capital of Nancy. The second time, Gaston also stopped there and
Charles, who had a beautiful sister named Marguerite, mischievously encouraged Monsieur's passion for her. Louis XIII and Richelieu were furious. They launched an invasion of Lorraine and obliged the duke to
sign a treaty ceding his stronghold of Marsal to France. But the crafty
Charles got the better of them, for, at the very same moment that he was
signing the treaty in January 1632, the Duke d'Orléans was secretly mar-
rying Marguerite and then proceeding, with the blessing of the queen
mother and the help of the Spanish, to foment still another plot against
Richelieu, this one headed by the Duke de Montmorency, Governor of
Languedoc. In 1632, therefore, there were two bullets for Richelieu to

dodge, the Montmorency rebellion and the extraordinary successes of the King of Sweden. Fortunately for Richelieu, he dodged them both. Montmorency was executed in the public square of Toulouse. As to Gustavus Adolphus, Richelieu was even more fortunate. In the midst of another victory at Lützen which might have made him the master of the Holy Roman Empire, Gustavus Adolphus was killed, his throne passing to his five-year-old daughter Christina and his policies to his embattled chancellor, Axel Oxenstierna.[8]

Between 1633 and 1634, as the Swedish war machine sputtered, Louis XIII and Richelieu settled their scores with the Duke of Lorraine by occupying his entire duchy. It was another notable acquisition for the French monarchy. They also brought Monsieur back into the fold. Not that Charles seemed to mind. He found it more profitable to lead the life of a condottiere at the head of his troops. But, for all of Charles's potential as a troublemaker, Richelieu's principal worry was that the Emperor, once freed from the pressures of the Swedes, would be able to lend his undivided support to the Spanish. The Dutch feared exactly the same thing, and they energetically solicited the King of France to do something he had never done before, namely to enter into an open alliance with them and to declare war against the King of Spain. They were so eager that they went to the extent of offering to partition the Spanish Low Countries with the French. Richelieu was by no means averse to the alliance, but he showed extraordinary reticence in regard to the bait. He did not want to partition the Spanish Low Countries. "It could happen soon afterwards," he advised the king, "that there being no barrier between us and the Dutch, we would get into the same war that the Spanish are in now." The eventuality, however, did not seem very likely. On September 6, 1634, the Spanish and Imperialists, with the Duke of Lorraine doing his bit, inflicted a catastrophic defeat on the Swedes and their Protestant allies at Nördlingen. Richelieu was terrified. "It is certain," he advised Louis XIII, "that if the party is entirely ruined, the brunt of the power of the house of Austria will fall on France" and, he might have added, on his own person. He rushed to make his treaty with the Dutch, including the provision for partition, and on April 28, 1635, France declared war against Spain. As the Protestants in the Empire hurried to subscribe to the Peace of Prague with the Emperor, Richelieu proceeded to assemble a huge army and conscript the Dukes of Savoy and Parma with as many other Italian princes as possible into the

French alliance. Richelieu also rushed to contract with the condottiere Bernard of Saxe-Weimar for the services of his private Protestant army in Germany, while the Emperor retaliated by declaring war against France. Richelieu had crossed his Rubicon. At the very moment when the Emperor seemed to have brought the war to a close in Germany, Richelieu had opted for an open alliance with Protestants in order to turn the tide against the Hapsburgs.[9]

If Louis XIII and Cardinal Richelieu had any qualms about their policies—and it appears as if the king was a little more squeamish than his minister—they had no shortage of either justifications or justifiers. Richelieu assembled an entire team of polemicists, headed by his "grey eminence" Father Joseph, who had developed a special talent for integrating Richelieu's most anti-Hapsburg policies with the loftiest of Christian motives. Richelieu and Father Joseph were well aware that not everyone shared their opinion, and they felt a compelling need, not only to confirm for themselves that they knew what they were doing, but also to justify themselves before the "public." Early- seventeenth-century Europe was already well into the age of printed propaganda and Richelieu exploited the medium to the fullest. He had the printers of Paris, the *Mercure François,* and, after 1631, the *Gazette de France* at his beck and call. And he did not limit himself to influencing the public opinion of his own time; he was intent upon justifying himself before posterity. Starting in 1631 or 1632 he supervised the compilation of an ambitious *Histoire,* otherwise known as his *Mémoires,* a massive work of self-justification which eschewed the classical and renaissance bombast of rhetoric in favor of the equally venerable traditions of ecclesiastical history, sharpened by the polemics of the Reformation. It was, in other words, an apologia based on documentary and, in this case, the best, evidence, the very *mémoires* and correspondence which he had himself composed in order to shape the policies of the French monarchy.[10]

The first justification that Richelieu and his propagandists advanced for their controversial politics was that the Hapsburgs—and even before the Hapsburgs, Ferdinand of Aragon—had started it. After all, hadn't the evil Ferdinand grabbed Naples and Navarre, which the Spanish were still holding? Hadn't Maximilian of Hapsburg married Mary of Burgundy and refused to return Franche-Comté? Hadn't Philip II meddled in French affairs during the civil wars? No wonder Henry IV had been obliged to support the Calvinist Dutch rebels! In sum, Richelieu and his propagandists accused the Spanish of being a bunch of hypocrites, who, under the pretext of advancing the Catholic religion, were aiming at universal monarchy and had enrolled the Austrian Hapsburgs into their conspiracy. It is not clear whether, when they lambasted the Spanish, Richelieu and his supporters had in mind the Spanish race, the Spanish kings, or the Spanish Queen of France, Anne of Austria, but it is clear that in order to justify their policies even in their own minds, the king and his minister felt the need to demonize the enemy and, in so doing, appropriate for themselves the most idealistic of motives, such as the search for perpetual peace and the suppression of heresy. To Father Joseph, moreover, it was the Hapsburgs who, in their insane pursuit of world domination, were preventing the Christian princes from engaging in his crusade against the Turks. To him, at least, all of Richelieu's policies were directed toward this visionary goal.[11]

On a slightly more abstract level, Richelieu and his advisors justified every one of their actions on the basis of maintaining legality, the principle of the just war, and they always made an effort in their treaties to protect the interests of the Catholic religion. The French justified their intervention in the Val Telline as defense of the legal rights of the Protestant Grisons, but they also made provision for the religious freedom of the Valtellinian Catholics. The intervention in Mantua was a classically just war in favor of the legitimate successor, who had the added virtue of being a champion of Father Joseph's favorite project. The justification for alliance with Gustavus Adolphus was the defense of the liberties of the German princes, and the French tried to salve their consciences by getting the King of Sweden to direct his efforts against the Emperor while treating the Duke of Bavaria and the Catholic princes as neutral. The French also insisted on a specific provision in their treaty with Gustavus Adolphus that he would make no change in religion in the territories he conquered. When he began to act like a loose cannon, the French first of all took some of the Catholic princes of the Rhine, such as the Elector of Trier, under their protection—which conveniently combined their interest with their faith—and then they began to contemplate turning against the King of Sweden, *if* they could get the Duke of Bavaria and his Catholic League to abandon the Emperor. This, of course, was an extremely big *if*, and only Gustavus Adolphus's death saved them from their dilemma. The occupation of Lorraine was justified both by the fact that part of Lorraine was a fief of the French monarchy and by the mis-behavior of the duke. The French explanation for their declaration of war against Spain in 1635 was strictly legal: the arrest by the Spanish of the legitimate Elector of Trier.[12]

On the most theoretical level, Richelieu and his apologists supported their position with an appeal to historical precedent, to medieval scholastic philosophy, and to the more recent theological science of casu-istry. His experts came up with a whole avalanche of examples, starting with David and Solomon, of kings who stood well with God having made alliances with infidels. This was perfectly all right, commented the recent casuists, as long as the *intention* was not to harm the true religion. The most traditional scholastic argument of all, however, was that God had created a natural order in the world, which functioned through *secondary* causes. It was this principle that sounded the death knell for the Sermon on the Mount. Whoever turned the other cheek or gave no thought for the morrow did so at his own peril. A king who sacrificed his state to his faith was exposing himself to losing both. The natural world, in other words, held up the supernatural one. If the interests of the state and the interests of religion coincided, as they usually did, so much the better, but the ultimate law was the law of necessity. Richelieu, Father Joseph, and their collaborators all fervently believed this. The only difference, and it sometimes showed up among them, was precisely where they were prepared to locate this necessity and how much gladness of heart they were prepared to put into implementing it.[13]

Few of Richelieu's collaborators put as much gladness of heart into it as Abel Servien. This product of a judicial family from Dauphiné, de-prived of the sight of his right eye, was as ambitious as he was indefati-gable, and he put almost all of his faith in the omnipotence of the car-dinal. With most everyone else with whom he came in contact, Servien was, to say the least, difficult. In 1627 and 1628, as intendant in Guyenne, he fought bitterly with the *parlement* of Bordeaux. The next year Richelieu made Servien one of the intendants of the army that in-vaded Savoy, and he was constantly quibbling with his colleague, Michel Particelli d'Hémery. It was in this same year, possibly, that Servien first came into contact with someone who may even have surpassed him in gladness of heart, the papal envoy Giulio Mazarini. Mazarini, or Mazarin, was a nobody. He had risen by dint of his capacity in the service of Francesco Barberini, nephew of Pope Urban VIII, who was extremely concerned about a war breaking out in Italy and was, at that moment, particularly fearful of the Spanish. In contrast to Servien, however, Mazarin had charm, and he had his first occasion to employ it upon Cardinal Richelieu in January 1630 at Lyon, where he tried to convince the cardinal, on behalf of the Pope, to sign a suspension of arms in Italy. He did not succeed immediately, but with his energy he prevailed upon the French generals to agree to a truce. Even before Servien and Mazarin became intimately acquainted, their minds seemed to function in unison. When each of them heard about the treaty that Father Joseph had concluded at Regensburg, each concluded independently that Richelieu would not approve it, and assuming that the treaty would not hold, continued with their own efforts to mediate the truce. Even as a mediator, however, Mazarin displayed a certain hostility to the Spanish, but at the last moment he obtained their accord to the truce, and on October 26, 1630, as the French and Spanish armies were about to do battle in front of Casale, he made a memorable appearance before the armies and prevented the outbreak of a full-scale war.[14]

In 1630 Servien rose to the position of secretary of state for war, and the following year, both he and Mazarin appeared at Cherasco, Servien as one of the French plenipotentiaries and Mazarin on behalf of the Pope, to negotiate a final settlement of the Mantuan succession and a final revision of the Treaty of Regensburg. There Mazarin, for all practical purposes, acted as a French envoy, being privy to all the skullduggery which secured Pinerolo to France while keeping his own master, Urban VIII, completely in the dark about it. Servien and Mazarin could not have performed a more agreeable service for Cardinal Richelieu nor done more to discredit Father Joseph, even though the fiasco at Regensburg did not prevent Richelieu from nominating Father Joseph for a cardinal's hat in 1633. It was at Cherasco, too, that Servien and Mazarin established a bond of friendship and mutual admiration that they maintained for the rest of their lives. They saw each other as hard-nosed men of the world, good Catholics, but unencumbered by the sanctimonious veneer of a Father Joseph. After Cherasco, Servien eventually returned to resume his secretaryship for war. Mazarin, thinking more and more of putting his hostility toward the Spanish in the service of France, appeared there in 1635 in the capacity of nuncio extraordinary from the Pope.[15]

The sanctimonious veneer of Father Joseph, however, had not lost all of its luster. It was kept shining by another of Richelieu's favorite diplomats, Claude de Mesmes, Count d'Avaux. The scion of a distinguished Parisian family of jurists, the young Claude, who remained a bachelor throughout his life, quickly exhibited the most ideal virtues of the French nobility of the robe: capacity, piety, and purity of Latin. His legal training endowed him, like so many judges in the *parlements,* with an enduring faith in the compatibility of law with absolute monarchy. Father Joseph adopted him as one of his creatures, and in 1627 Richelieu sent him on a mission to Venice, where D'Avaux did his best to get the Venetians to come to the aid of Charles de Gonzague. D'Avaux did well enough so that in the crisis of 1634, Richelieu entrusted him with a mission to Denmark, Sweden, and Poland in an effort to shore up the sagging opposition to the Hapsburgs. Here was a more delicate mission from a religious perspective, since the first two powers were Lutheran, but D'Avaux rose to the occasion. He built a diplomatic network, his Latin stood him in good stead, and, while in Stockholm in 1634, he found his own special way of illustrating the distinction between the interests of the state and those of religion by ostentatiously having one of his secretaries buried with all the rites of the Catholic Church. After the Hapsburg victory at Nördlingen the distinction became even more pertinent, and D'Avaux's great achievement the following year was to mediate a new truce between Sweden and Poland which permitted the Swedes to concentrate their energies on the Empire. His star was in such ascendance that Father Joseph proudly informed him that Cardinal Richelieu intended to employ him in the peace congress, if it were ever held.[16]

But Richelieu's critics, with the exception of a few wild-eyed theology students, were not enthusiasts either. The questions of blame and legality aside, most *dévots* in France took the position that any state had to begin by establishing religious unity at home in order to prosper. They could even point with envy to the example of the Spanish, whose proscription of the Jews and Muslims had inaugurated Spain's golden age. The Spanish, for their part, would have denied blame for anything, insisting that their monarchy was simply asserting its own unimpeachable legal rights. As the Count-duke de Olivares, principal minister of Philip IV, wrote to him in 1625 celebrating the twin Spanish victories of Bahia de Todos los Santos and Breda: "These are successes in which it is seen that God assists his own cause, and as the ends of His Majesty address themselves purely to defending it, without any other human pretension . . . we can hope that He intends to favor and support this monarchy everywhere." The Spanish thus looked at the French just as the French looked at them—hypocritical, insatiable, and out of step with the Almighty. But perhaps the most embarrassing argument against the policies of Richelieu was made by Cornelius Jansen, the penetrating Bishop of Ypres in the Spanish Low Countries. In his *Mars Gallicus* Jansen made the telling point that even if the Spanish were advancing their own interest along with that of Catholicism, it didn't make any difference. "Would the Most Christian King dare say to God: Let the religion that teaches men to adore you be destroyed, provided my state is protected?" Jansen was not abandoning the principle of necessity; he was simply raising it to a higher level.[17]

There is a tendency for modern historians to accept the premises of Richelieu in regard to the house of Austria or, less frequently, those of his critics in regard to him, but it is quite possible to look at these premises from a different perspective and to see them as extremely questionable. Even if the Hapsburgs had been able to achieve universal monarchy in Richelieu's time, would it have been possible, given the powers of enforcement at the hands of any early modern state, for them to sustain it? The ancient Roman emperors had found it advisable to divide the administration of their empire among themselves. Charles V of Hapsburg had found it desirable to divide his own empire within his family. The problem with modern historiography, obsessed as it is with the rise of the state, is that it tends to conceive of the states of the seventeenth century as prototypes of nineteenth- and twentieth-century ones, as blocks of people, wealth, and power functioning as units in relation to each other. They were more like family enterprises, with a lot of connections admittedly, but with an extremely limited ability to harness large elements of their populations to their purposes. The capacity of any adventurer who could maintain an army, any condottiere like Wallenstein, Bernard of Saxe-Weimar, or an exiled Duke of Lorraine to do better at extorting from a population than at ruling over it, amply illustrates the limited resources of the territorial states. If any family had achieved universal monarchy in the seventeenth century, its members would just as likely have begun competing against each other after one generation. As to the Christian church, it had managed to spread in the ancient Roman Empire without any assistance either from a politically sovereign state or from a politically independent pope. It had also managed, in the later empire, to thrive under a whole line of universal

Christian emperors. It was even managing to survive in the time of Riche-lieu under the Turks in the Ottoman Empire. Not that it would have been possible for these considerations to have made any impact either on Riche-lieu, Olivares, or Urban VIII, who moved from supporting the French to supporting the Spanish with the turn of events. Self-righteousness was the overriding principle of their thought.[18]

Entering openly into the war had not solved Richelieu's problems; it had exacerbated them. The costs of the war constituted a crushing burden on the population and necessitated all sorts of financial expedients. An army of some 180,000 soldiers—hastily recruited, badly led, and fighting on numerous fronts—was no match for the experienced Spanish and Impe-rial troops. One of the earliest casualties was Servien, whose colleagues jumped on his deficiencies in supplying the army. By February 1636 they had enrolled Louis XIII and Father Joseph into their conspiracy and Richelieu, with some reluctance, exiled him. Richelieu was feverishly trying to collect allies, managing to obtain expensive treaties with Sweden and with the Calvinist Landgrave of Hesse-Cassel, and was just as eager for a peace congress which would assemble in Cologne. But the reverses continued. Most embarrassing was the Spanish invasion of France and their taking, on August 15, of the stronghold of Corbie, which guarded the passage of the Somme. The services of a diplomat like D'Avaux were all the more valuable under the circumstances. On his re-turn to France later that month, the king rewarded him with the greffier-ship of the Order of the Holy Spirit. By November the French had retaken Corbie, but they were barely holding their own. In fact, Richelieu was so eager for peace that toward the end of that year he was already com-posing his first instruction for the conference. It appears that he was less concerned with what the Spanish had occupied in France than coming out of the war with Pinerolo and Lorraine. The King of France was even willing to leave Casale, with proper assurances that it would not fall into Spanish hands. But there was also a call in the instruction reminiscent of the "grand design," namely for the establishment of two great leagues, one in Italy and one in Germany, as the only possible means to contain the ambitions of the house of Austria. To this same noble end, the French showed a particular partiality toward the Duke of Bavaria, being quite prepared to leave him in possession of the electoral dignity and the Upper Palatinate. The way that Richelieu summed it up: "The king wants to assist disinterestedly the princes of Italy and Germany and to maintain the balance."[19]

Whether the princes of Italy and Germany appreciated this assistance was another matter. In February 1637, the Duke of Parma, under pressure from both the Pope and the Spanish, abandoned the French alliance. In Germany, where Ferdinand II had been succeeded by his son Ferdinand III as King of Bohemia, Hungary, and Holy Roman Emperor, the Swedes and Hessians were perpetually tempted to do likewise. In April Richelieu sent D'Avaux there as ambassador extraordinary for the purpose of holding on to the Swedes and preparing the peace congress. The tasks required all of his agility and coolness. A few French military successes, like the taking of Landrecies, were invariably offset by frustrations of equal or greater proportions. On the death of Charles de Gonzague, for whom the French had done so much, his daughter-in-law, acting as regent for her minor son, began gravitating toward the Spanish. On the death of Victor Amadeus of Savoy, his widow Christine became regent for her minor son, and even though she was the sister of Louis XIII, under pressure from her brothers-in-law, she too began to waver in her loyalty to France. It was a poignant suggestion that even a universal Hapsburg monarchy might not hold together any better, but not poignant enough for Cardinal Richelieu, who even survived, at this juncture, an effort by the *dévot* party to capture the conscience of Louis XIII. In Richelieu's mind, nothing was so terrifying as losing the Swedes, and the diplomatic skill of the pious D'Avaux became all the more important, this at a time when Mazarin, though rising steadily in Richeleu's affections, was still in papal service though increasingly out of favor with Urban VIII. And D'Avaux, who was convinced that the Swedes needed France, held the fort in Germany, managing in March 1638 to renew the alliance with Sweden for three years. Richelieu may have breathed another sigh of relief when, on September 5, 1638, Anne of Austria gave birth to a son, the future Louis XIV, thus putting one more body between the throne and the specter of Monsieur, but the frustrations continued. The Duchess of Mantua went so far as to conspire with the Spanish—unsuccessfully, as it turned out—to massacre the French garrison in Casale. The Spanish routed the Prince de Condé before Fontarabia. The Duchess of Savoy was faced with the open revolt of her brothers-in-law, who were in alliance with Spain. The one notable military success of 1638, Bernard of Saxe-Weimar's taking of the great stronghold of Breisach on the right bank of the Rhine, was clouded by the fact that this condottiere wanted to keep it for himself. Father Joseph, whose unfulfilled nomination to cardinal Richelieu passed on to none other than Giulio Mazarini, died at the end of 1638. Through all of these vicissitudes, Louis XIII may have showed some occasional signs of flinching, but Richelieu showed none.[20]

Early in 1639, Richelieu was thinking of abandoning his courtship of the German princes by allowing them to declare their neutrality, while France and Sweden pursued the war pretty much on their own. He asked D'Avaux for his opinion and received a stern warning against doing such a thing:

> So many princes and states of the same nation, sharing the same customs, language, and family relationships, are jealous of any foreign power, even if they had called it to their aid. On this the Catholics and Protestants are strongly united. If they saw the King of Hungary humbled and the two crowns getting a foothold in Germany, they might well take up arms. I remember what happened to Charles VIII, who passed through Italy by arms. All the princes declared themselves neutral, but after his victories, they all combined against him, and he lost all his conquests.

D'Avaux, in other words, was implying that in early modern Europe the force of arms, no matter how intimidating, was no match for a dormant national feeling if it were awakened, and he was also afraid that if France and Sweden gave the impression of being out for their own interests, the princes of Germany might well put aside their differences and exploit this impression for their own advantage. Richelieu, for the time being, took D'Avaux's advice.[21]

Things got no better during the rest of 1639. Although in that year the death of Bernard of Saxe-Weimar rid France of another troublesome friend, and Amalia Elizabeth, the stalwart widow of the Landgrave of Hesse-Cassel, renewed her alliance with Louis XIII, the situation in Italy deteriorated as the rebels and the Spanish occupied large portions of Piedmont, including all of Turin except for the citadel. Richelieu was still very eager for peace, and Mazarin having opted to become a French subject and to return to France, Richelieu announced early in the following year that Mazarin would be the second plenipotentiary at the peace conference. Richelieu needed peace. By 1640, out of the 80 million *livres* that the government collected annually in taxes, more than 45 million went into servicing the debt. But as the year advanced, the military situation began looking up. A great victory by Harcourt over the Spanish in front of Casale on April 29 secured the French position in north central Italy, after which Harcourt went on to besiege Turin. Closer to home, Marshals de Chaunes, Châtillon, and La Meilleraye, under the watchful eye of Louis XIII, undertook a two-month siege of Arras, which capitulated on August 9 and opened the way to further French progress into the Spanish Low Countries. The birth of Louis XIII's second son on September 21 provided Richelieu with one more layer of reassurance. Finally, Harcourt had taken Turin on September 18, reestablishing the duchess as a French puppet and permitting the French to entrench themselves all over Piedmont. In comparison to the first stages of the war, these successes were dazzling.[22]

It should not be surprising, therefore, if the year 1640 marked a psychological turning point for Richelieu. Conscious of his own mortality, but beginning to perceive a light at the end of the tunnel, we find him interrupting his massive *Histoire* in order to devote himself to a new, more personal, and shorter memorial, his *Testament politique*. In this work, he repeatedly took the amazing position that peace was at hand. He seemed to envisage that by this peace, France would keep some of its outposts in Italy, chiefly Pinerolo, and, apparently in the hope of separating Charles IV from the Hapsburgs, only some outposts in Lorraine. He predicted that Louis XIII would by the peace return some of his conquests for the benefit of his allies, cautioning him against engaging in any more wars and exhorting him to undertake an ambitious program of peacetime domestic reforms. And in a second text of the same work, written in the course of the same year, Richelieu even expressed the hope that he might be able to complete the task in his own lifetime.[23]

After Richelieu composed these two texts, the prospects for peace became even brighter. By the end of 1640, the Spanish monarchy, which was carrying the principal financial burden for the Hapsburg cause, began to disintegrate. In October Catalonia revolted. This was followed almost immediately by the revolt of Portugal, which rallied under the leadership of John de Braganza. The Emperor was not doing much better. In 1641, in the midst of a Reichstag which he had called at Regensburg in order to assert his position as the spokesman for the princes of the Empire, he found himself abandoned by the new Elector of

Brandenburg, and his efforts to conciliate the Protestant princes by means of an amnesty came to naught. Richelieu's excitement in the face of these developments was unbounded, his moderation unshaken. Even though the Duke of Lorraine had hardly corrected his prankish ways—indeed, in 1637 he had divorced his wife without papal approval and married a beautiful camp follower—Richelieu invited him to Paris in 1641 and made a treaty with him by which the French restored him to most of his duchy. Once again the duke did not cooperate, which made Richelieu all the more fearful of losing the Swedes and eager for a peace conference. He decided that it would be most convenient to hold it at Münster and Osnabrück, and, once more D'Avaux came through. By June 26 he had renewed the alliance with Sweden and by July 18 he had gotten the Swedes to accept the new site for the conference. The infidelity of the Duke of Lorraine was easily overcome. By October, the French simply reoccupied his duchy.[24]

Lest we be tempted to credit Richelieu with a surplus of moderation, we need to analyze the three texts of the instruction that he prepared for Mazarin and D'Avaux toward the end of 1641 and the beginning of 1642. At his time, Richelieu was also composing an addition to his *Testament politique,* while D'Avaux was negotiating the preliminaries for the peace conference and Mazarin was finally getting his cardinal's hat. In this instruction, the standard accusation against the house of Austria for aiming at universal monarchy, the usual protestations of public spiritedness on France's part combined with some territorial gains, and the call for collective security after the peace were all carried over from its predecessor. But in this new one it becomes clear that Louis XIII and Richelieu—with a little help, perhaps, from Mazarin—had raised their expectations. They were once more dead set on keeping Lorraine. They wanted to hold on to their conquests in Artois, Flanders, and Alsace, get more assurances about Casale, and even revive their claims on Navarre. On the first draft of the instruction, in one of the most heavily reworked segments, we find the statement: "It must be indicated that if France in negotiating with the house of Austria which ordinarily keeps everything that it conquers were to make peace without doing the same, the peace would truly be insecure." And on the margin Richelieu, or maybe Mazarin, commented, although a secretary was doing the writing: "This reason seems so important, that I do not consider that it can be neglected without being responsible to God." There is a sense throughout this instruction, that, when push came to shove, France still did not intend to keep all of its conquests. Certainly it did not intend to fight for the independence of Catalonia and Portugal, and it appears from an accompanying *mémoire* that Louis XIII and Cardinal Richelieu would have settled for any number of alternative packages. But the principle of holding on to the conquests, once pronounced, was extremely difficult to violate, especially since God, apparently, was on the side of the big battalions. There are other remarkable changes of outlook in this instruction. From the very first text, there is much less anticipation of a forthcoming peace. On the contrary, in the accompanying *mémoire,* we find the explicit expectation that the Spanish would not come to terms as things then stood. Also, in this instruction Richelieu began to advance the amazing theory, which he most certainly did not apply to his own monarchy, that princes had the right to go to the aid of other princes' subjects who rightfully revolted. But the most revolutionary feature of this instruction is what it does not say. In contrast to the previous instruction of 1636–1637, in this new instruction, the word "balance" has disappeared.[25]

The Swedes were not anticipating peace either. By 1641 their Queen, Christina, was fourteen going on fifteen. She was assertive, intellectual, and displayed some aversion to the war, but she was still a minor and was almost entirely in the hands of her father's old minister, Axel Oxenstierna, a crusty hard-liner who held firm control over the regency council, or Senate. The Swedes occupied the entire Duchy of Pomerania along the Baltic as well as key posts in Brandenburg, Mecklenburg, and Westphalia, including the city of Osnabrück. They also occupied a line of strongholds along the Elbe stretching into Silesia and Moravia, from where they constantly threatened the hereditary lands of the Emperor. They possessed Zweibrücken and Bielefeld in southern Germany. With their subsidies from the French, with the contributions they exacted from the occupied territories, and with their armies made up mostly of Germans, the Swedes were the only belligerents, aside from the condottieri, who had come anywhere close to making a paying proposition out of the war. In October 1641, in anticipation of the peace conference, they appointed their plenipotentiaries, the experienced diplomat Johan Adler Salvius, Axel Oxenstierna's son Johan, and the Senator Ture Bielke, drawing up some vague instructions for them. The Swedes had three principal demands: amnesty and compensation for all of their adherents,

satisfaction, and pay for their army, but the biggest of these was satisfaction, by which they meant that they wanted to keep their control
over the seacoast of Pomerania along the Baltic. this in spite of the fact
that, since the death of the last duke in 1637, the Elector of Brandenburg had the best claim on the duchy. Their solution was that he would
just have to get his compensation elsewhere, presumably at the expense
of their enemies. The Swedes constituted a terrible dilemma for all of
their allies. With no particular incentive to make peace, if they got too
strong, they would become a menace; if they got too weak, they would
be irreplaceable.[26]

It was never easy for Richelieu. His health was failing and in recent
years Louis XIII had developed a passion for a younger man, the Marquis de Cinq-Mars. It was about this same time that Mazarin began to
record his own life in his *Carnets*. Richelieu tolerated the marquis until,
in June 1642, the cardinal discovered that the Cinq-Mars was at the
center of one more conspiracy against himself, involving Spain and,
needless to say, Monsieur. Once more Richelieu escaped by the skin of
his teeth. The marquis was arrested and later executed with one of his
accomplices. Louis XIII took Perpignan, adding the County of Roussillon to the catalogue of possible French annexations, and Richelieu
confronted his last hours. He died on December 4, 1642. On his recommendation, Louis XIII made Cardinal Mazarin prime minister. Mazarin
began immediately to build up his own clientele by installing Michel Le
Tellier, an army intendant whom he had met in Italy, as secretary of state
for war, but the king's own health was failing. If he died, the prospects
for the future were alarming. His queen was a Spanish Hapsburg, who
had only since the birth of her children shown the slightest sign of sympathy for her husband's cause. The Duke d'Orléans had just given another demonstration of his unreliability. The Prince de Condé, first
prince of the blood, was a man of unbounded self-interest. None of
these individuals could be excluded from any regency government, yet
none, with the possible exception of Condé, had demonstrated any de-
votion to Richelieu's policies. The only thing that the king and his ministers could do was to issue a declaration that upon his death, the queen
would be regent, Monsieur Lieutenant-General, and Condé chief of the
council, where they would be assisted (and outvoted) by Mazarin, by
the Chancellor Séguier, by the Superintendant of Finances Bouthillier,
and by Bouthillier's son Chavigny, the secretary for foreign affairs. This

arbitrary arrangement could not help but be overturned by the *parlement* of Paris, and everyone knew it. As Louis XIII lay dying, he expressed some regrets about not having been able to conclude a peace, but he must also have been wondering whether all of his wars had been for naught.[27]

2

The Queen's Beloved

The death of Louis XIII threw the entire policy of the previous nineteen years into question and sent everyone at the French court scrambling for position. The central person in this upheaval was Anne of Austria. Here was a pious princess, forty-one years old, sister of the King of Spain, ignored by her husband and isolated by Richelieu, with every opportunity to pay them back in full measure. The previous regency of Marie de Medici came immediately to mind. She had enriched her favorites, reversed her husband's policies, and run afoul of the aristocracy, but, after Cardinal Richelieu, this did not look half bad. Would Anne do the same? It appeared as if she might. Her first act was to recall two of her ladies in waiting, who had been exiled by Louis XIII. If she were to get rid of Richelieu's creatures, however, she had to find a minister who could keep the government going and, at the same time, deal with the two princes of the blood, the Duke d'Orléans and the Prince de Condé, who had, like her, been thrust into prominence. Ready to serve her was her chaplain Augustin Potier, the Bishop of Beauvais, but she concluded from the very first that he was not up to the task. Then there was Giulio Mazarini, for whom she had always had a hankering, with whom she could converse in Spanish, and who was doing his best now to reinvent himself. Finally, there was the Marquis de Châteauneuf, an elderly former keeper of the seals who had been imprisoned by Richelieu. She consulted two of her closest intimates, the President de Bailleul and the Count de Brienne. Bailleul urged her to get rid of Mazarin, but Brienne, sensing her inclinations, suggested she hold on to him, at least for a while, and merely hinted at the recall of Châteauneuf. She opted for Mazarin.[1]

Mazarin hastened to pledge his loyalty to her. Just as he was doing so, however, she was conspiring behind his back with the Duke d'Orléans and the Prince de Condé to overturn the late king's declaration. They had the same interest as she did in getting rid of the extended council which the declaration had imposed upon them. So did the *parlement* of Paris, eager to assert its claims to be the guardian of the fundamental laws of the monarchy. On May 18, 1643, four-year-old Louis XIV held his first *lit de justice* before it, accompanied by his mother, Monsieur, the Prince, dukes, marshals, and the Chancellor Séguier. The Chancellor spoke and asked for the revision of the late king's declaration. The judges hastened to confirm the regency in her "full, entire, and absolute authority," with the Duke d'Orléans as lieutenant general and the Prince de Condé as chief of the council. This was hardly what Mazarin had bargained for, but she invited him to continue as her principal minister. He allowed himself to be persuaded.[2]

Mazarin's *Carnets* permit us to be with him at this critical junction as he attempted to establish his position and formulate his plans for the regency. Anne, he jotted down, was not to be generous with her favors. She was to temporize with the Huguenots. She needed a superintendant of finances who was her man. She was to watch out for the Prince de Condé, whom Mazarin feared the most, and she was to keep the *parlement* of Paris in check. She was not to do anything without Mazarin's advice, and she was to make it evident to the public that he enjoyed her support. To counter Condé, Mazarin believed she should combine with the Duke d'Orléans, notwithstanding the benefits to the house of Lorraine. Last but not least, she needed to "preserve the title of mother of the king, so that no one ever speaks of her as the sister of the King of Spain." Whether she would follow his advice was another matter.[3]

The best Mazarin could do was to try to build a circle of collaborators on whom he could rely. One of his first thoughts was to recall Servien from exile, along with Servien's nephew Hugues de Lionne, who was on a mission to Italy, but in the midst of this bureaucratic shuffling, the court received exhilarating news. A motley French army of some 23,000, under the command of the twenty-one-year-old Duke d'Enghien, had surprised and completely routed a veteran Spanish army of some 25,000 attempting to besiege Rocroi in Champagne, killing some 7,000 and taking some 6,000 prisoners, including the flower of the Spanish infantry. It was the greatest victory for France since the war had begun, but it was a mixed blessing for Mazarin because the Duke d'Enghien was the son of the Prince de Condé. And the recall of exiles continued! The queen freed Châteauneuf and then recalled one of Richelieu's oldest enemies, the Duchess de Chevreuse, who had devoted her banishment to building connections in Spain and in the Low Countries. Mazarin feared that his days were numbered. The Duke de Vendôme, an illegitimate son of Henry IV, was demanding to be made Governor of Brittany and was making overtures to the increasingly prestigious Condé.[4]

Mazarin did not begrudge the Duke d'Enghien his victory. On the contrary, he wanted to exploit it by having the duke besiege Thionville, in the direction of Trier. He had to overcome the hesitation of the Prince de Condé, who did not want further to expose his son, and the Duke d'Orléans, who did not want to give him any more triumphs, before Anne finally approved the plan. But Mazarin was becoming increasingly isolated, either unable or unwilling to support his former cohorts. On June 6, the superintendant of finances, Bouthillier, seeing the handwriting on the wall, resigned. The queen immediately replaced him with two superintendants—Bailleul, who, it will be remembered, had advised her to get rid of Mazarin, and D'Avaux, the paragon of pious diplomacy. The best Mazarin could do was to put in his own man, Particelli D'Hémery, under them as controller-general to do the dirty work. Bouthillier's resignation was followed on June 14 by that of his son Chavigny, whom Anne replaced as secretary of state for foreign affairs with the Count de Brienne, hardly the man Mazarin would have chosen. Mazarin managed to preserve Bouthillier's and Chavigny's seats in the council, designating the latter for an embassy to Rome, but they remained there as little more than ornaments. On that same day the Duchess de Chevreuse arrived, and the queen greeted her like a long-lost friend. And Châteauneuf was waiting in the wings! The queen was criticized in some quarters for her piety and in others for too much intimacy with Mazarin. And the most dangerous people—Condé, the Bishop of Beauvais, the Duchess de Chevreuse, Châteauneuf—were openly advocating a separate peace with Spain and intimating to Anne that Mazarin was another Richelieu.[5]

But Mazarin was not simply fighting for his survival; his was no ordinary ego. He had chosen to devote himself to the French monarchy—his dignity, his reputation, and, last but not least, his vanity required that he serve it well. The better he thought of himself, the more passionately he loved the monarchy; the more willing the queen was to share in his passion, the more passionately he adored her; the greater the obstacles in his path, the greater the achievement in the eyes of posterity. This adventurer who had risen from obscurity was fully convinced that he was the only person, out of 20 million Frenchmen, who knew what was good for the state. He noted in his *Carnet:*

> The French of every class are interested in weakening the king's authority . . . and this is why the *parlement,* the Princes, the Governors of Provinces, the Huguenots, and others want to undo . . . what was done in the time of the late king for the establishment of his absolute authority . . . and want to reduce things to the time that France, even though in appearance governed by a king, was in fact a republic. Once the king comes of age, he can have no greater complaint than if, because of bad government . . . he returns to being dependent on his subjects. Her Majesty must have more regard for this point than for any other, and for this she can not trust any Frenchman . . . and a great minister who has true faith and passion for the king can only be abhorred by the French.

He thus continued steadfastly to place his supporters in key posts, moving Chavingy from the embassy to Rome to the peace conference at Münster, where he could keep an eye on D'Avaux, and designating Servien for the Rome embassy.[6]

The most important battle of all, the battle for Anne's heart, Mazarin was winning. She approached him, one day, with that most suggestive of all questions, whether there was any way to make him happy when he was with her. He exploited her advance not for carnal but for political purposes. Since, he lectured, his sorrows and afflictions came from his not seeing her served as he wished and from the bad turn that affairs would take if this were not remedied, his affliction was all the greater when he was with her because he could see all the more closely her great merit, his obligations to her, and the ingratitude of those who did not do their duty toward her. He added that if she could see how much he wanted to serve her and the extreme passion he had for her greatness, she would complain about how little he accomplished, even though she claimed to appreciate it. It was a bizarre relationship, built upon sexual frustration and moral exhortation, and one wonders how the queen could possibly have found pleasure in it, but apparently she did and so did he. After proudly recording this unequal exchange in his *Carnet,* he punctuated it with a cryptic and meaningful "§." They were in love.[7]

Philip IV of Spain was watching. His monarchy may have been in bad straits, but he and his council were holding firm, and they were observing the change of regime in France with guarded optimism. In June they sent off Don Diego Saavedra Fajardo, a fast-talking second-level diplomat who had combined attempts to massacre the French garrison of Casale with high-minded treatises for the Spanish Infante, as one of their plenipotentiaries to the peace conference. His particular instructions were to go by way of Paris, seek out Anne of Austria, and turn her into an ally. About the same time the council of Spain also drafted more general instructions for the conference. These envisioned a return to the *status quo ante bellum* including no help by the French to the Catalonian and Portuguese rebels, while, on the other hand, the French were to agree to reinstate the Duke of Lorraine. The instructions also looked forward to a renewed truce with the Dutch. When Saavedra, courtesy of a French passport, passed through Paris in July, Mazarin understood exactly what Saavedra had in mind and would not even let him approach her. Saavedra grumbled to whomever he could about the French siege of Thionville before moving on to Brussels and Münster, where he was to join up with his colleagues, Antoine Brun and the head of the Spanish delegation, Count Zapata.[8]

Ferdinand III, the Holy Roman Emperor, was also watching. He too was in bad straits, but he and his council were no less imperturbable. They were preparing to send two of their skirmishers, the Count von Nassau and Dr. Krane, to feel out the French in Münster, and two more, the Count von Auersperg and Dr. Volmar, to feel out the Swedes in Osnabrück. They were to try to discover, through the mediators, what the enemies demanded. If the French refused to explain themselves, their plenipotentiaries were to express bewilderment as to why the French had attacked the Empire in the first place. If the French still balked, Nassau and Krane were to offer, of all things, the same terms that Ferdinand II had tried to foist on Father Joseph in 1630, with the additional foisting of the restoration of the Duke of Lorraine. It was a similar approach to the Swedes. The Imperial plenipotentiaries were to find out from the mediators what the Swedes wanted. If this failed, Auersperg and Volmar were to revive some financial inducements that the Imperialists had indirectly offered to Sweden in 1635.[9]

Mazarin was still uncertain about Anne's intentions, and even the Prince de Condé, who had his own agenda, warned him that a cabal was forming against him. It was led by the Duke de Vendôme, who accused Mazarin of denying him one favor after another and of protecting Richelieu's relatives. It was supported by the Bishop of Beauvais, the champion of the prudes, and by the Duchess de Chevreuse, the champion of the Spanish. She accused Mazarin to his face of not being a good friend to the queen, and assured him that the queen would soon become aware of it. It was an acute observation on the contorted relationship and a confident prediction that it could not last. On top of all this, the financial situation was desperate. It had deteriorated to the point that by the beginning of the regency, the government had encumbered all of its revenues up to the year 1646, and, in order to borrow an additional 12 million *livres*, the government had to mortgage all of its revenues up to the year 1649, as well as borrow more money at exorbitant interest rates. That in itself seemed like an excellent argument for getting out of the war as quickly as possible.[10]

Mazarin, however, was not one for financial imperatives, as long as the superintendants came up with the money, and it was he who was running the government. The *conseil d'en haut*—which now included the queen; Monsieur; the Prince de Condé; Mazarin himself; Bouthillier; Chavigny; the chancellor; the two superintendants of finance, Bailleul and D'Avaux; and the four secretaries of state—continued to meet regularly for the reading of dispatches and the making of major decisions. But Mazarin did not care for debate, and he was especially irritated by the opinions of D'Avaux, who was adept at animating the moderation of Anne, and the Prince de Condé, who also had a conciliatory streak in him. Little by little, therefore, Mazarin managed to limit the activity of the council to the reading of incoming dispatches, listening to the replies, and to periodic displays of solidarity. For example, if the queen received a letter from one of her diplomatic representatives, Brienne would formally read it in the council, but Mazarin would dictate the answer in privacy and in Italian to one of his secretaries, who would tranform it into French and transmit it to Brienne for reading in front of the council and for expedition. If the envoys also wrote directly to Mazarin, which they often did, he would not even go through Brienne, who, as time went on, became little more than a glorified clerk. It was not a perfect solution, but it succeeded in marginalizing the council and came as close as Mazarin could to Richelieu's system.[11]

It is in this manner that the first instruction of Mazarin's ministry, and the first relating to the Congress of Westphalia, was composed. This was the instruction for Chavigny and D'Avaux, whom the queen ordered to pass by The Hague on their way to Münster so as to coordinate their goals with France's oldest ally in the war, the Dutch Republic. The instruction was apparently composed by Mazarin in conjunction with Chavigny, to the exclusion of Brienne, for the first copy that we possess is written in the hand of one of Chavigny's clerks. Certainly, it bore the mark of Mazarin. The document made a reasonable argument that since "the stronger France emerged from the peace, the less the Spanish will be in a position to break it," France should demand to keep all of its conquests, and France expected the Dutch to support that stance, just as France would support the Dutch in a similar manner. The only complication that Mazarin envisaged was that the French were going to Münster to make peace, whereas the Dutch were going there to renew their truce, but he did not consider this an insuperable obstacle as long as both powers agreed to come to each other's assistance in case the Spanish broke either of their respective treaties. If, however, the French and the Dutch made their treaties, and the Spanish, after the expiration of their truce with the Dutch, refused to renew it, the French were not prepared to go to war again. Chavigny and D'Avaux were to consult with two distinct parties: one, the States General, the assembly of the seven provinces which made up the republic; and the other, Frederick Henry, Prince of Orange, stadtholder and captain-general. The States General and the house of Orange did not always see eye to eye, and the French looked at Frederick Henry as their particular friend.[12]

For the domestic opponents of Mazarin, however, the most important consideration was their pensions, their governorships, and their influence at court, and by mid-August they were becoming increasingly frustrated by the queen's persistence in holding on to him. The Duke de Vendôme and the Duchess de Chevreuse were the most dangerous leaders of the cabal, and everyone referred to them as the "Importants." There were more complaints about the queen herself, mixed with insinuations about her relationship with Mazarin; there was much sanctimonious talk about the suffering of the people; and there were predictions that Mazarin would share the fate of the Concinis. The Duke de Vendôme's son, the Duke de Beaufort, was one of the loudest talkers. Anne still believed that she could cajole the Importants into behaving, but Mazarin was afraid that they would intimidate her into dismissing him, if not worse.[13]

Enghien's siege of Thionville was also in trouble. The Spanish managed to bring in reinforcements with which the defenders repulsed two French assaults. In another assault on August 4, a leading French officer met his death, but finally, on August 7, the duke's batteries were able to breach two bastions and the next day the stronghold capitulated. Mazarin did not take this conquest modestly. He reminded both himself and everyone else that he had been the principal proponent of the siege. The French army in Italy was also making good progress. It had taken Asti in Piedmont and was now before Trino in Monferrato. Marshal La Mothe in Catalonia was on the frontiers of Aragon. Inebriated by his own military genius, Mazarin now conceived a new plan. He would send the invincible duke to reinforce the former army of Bernard of Saxe-Weimar, now under the command of Marshal de Guébriant, in Alsace. Enghien and Guébriant would cross the Rhine and sweep downriver in the direction of Landau, Speyer, Worms, and Mainz, where they would combine with the troops of the widow of the Landgrave of Hesse-Cassel. It was an ambitious plan for the end of a campaign, but Mazarin was managing, somehow, to find money for it, and he anticipated that it would be this victory that would finally bring the Hapsburgs to heel.[14]

The fall of Thionville may have puffed up the vanity of Mazarin, but the criticisms of the regency continued. Anne sought to appease the Importants by giving Châteauneuf the governorship of Touraine. It didn't help. The Duke de Beaufort was particularly virulent, and he seemed to be the instigator of a band of thugs whose principal mission was to intimidate Cardinal Mazarin. On August 31, the queen had been invited to dine at the Bois de Vincennes by the captain of the château. On his way to join her, Mazarin's procession was stopped by a party of masked men carrying pistols, who attacked one of the carriages and then fled. That evening, when Mazarin, flanked by a bodyguard, went to the Louvre to speak to the queen, he found that palace surrounded with menacing ne'er-do-wells, who dispersed on his arrival. There was no proof as to the instigator of these pranks, but the duke was the most plausible suspect, and reason of state did not stand on legal niceties. With the support of Monsieur and the Prince de Condé, who was himself thoroughly disgusted with the Vendômes, the queen decided to act. Beaufort was as insouciant as he was rash. He still visited the queen as if nothing were amiss, and, on the night of September 2, he was arrested in her chambers by Guitault, captain of her guards. At daybreak of the following day, Beaufort was conducted to the donjon of Vincennes. The rest of the conspirators scattered. The Duke de Vendôme and his younger son were relegated to their estates. Within a few days Anne ordered the Bishop of Beauvais to return to his diocese. The Duchess de Chevreuse took it upon herself to withdraw, ending up once more with her friends in the Spanish Low Countries. The Importants had expected another regency of Marie de Medici; they had participated in another Day of Dupes.[15]

Mazarin was now in a position to move more freely. He moved into a home on the Rue Neuve des Petits Champs, which he eventually purchased and expanded into the grandiose Palais Mazarin. About the same time, the queen and court moved closer to him, leaving the Louvre for Richelieu's old residence, the Palais Cardinal, which became known as the Palais Royal. Mazarin was now constrained only by his coalition partners, the Duke d'Orléans and the Prince de Condé. They were still coming to the council, but he thought that as long as he kept them plied with favors and satisfied with his policies, he could rely on their remaining in his camp. He did a little reorganizing. He decided he could keep Chavigny at his side, while sending Servien to the peace conference in Westphalia. This reorganization had both advantages and disadvantages. On the one hand, it gave Mazarin someone completely under his control to keep an eye on D'Avaux. Moreover, when Servien's nephew, Lionne, returned in October, he became Mazarin's principal secretary and provided a direct channel to Servien. On the other hand, given D'Avaux's place in the council, his prestige with the queen, and his connections in the *parlement*, Mazarin could not avoid designating him as Servien's senior, which gave D'Avaux a number of important prerogatives. Finally, Mazarin decided to appoint the Prince de Condé's son-in-law, the blue-blooded Duke de Longueville (who was descended from a bastard of Charles VI), as head of the delegation, though the duke was to remain at court for the time being.[16]

The time had come for Mazarin to compose the instruction for Münster and to review the instruction for Holland. The one for Münster turned out to be a monument to the self-righteousness of the French monarchy. It adhered steadfastly to the thesis that nothing but the pious necessity of protecting both his kingdom and his allies had forced the previous king into the war, and it now proclaimed that his widow was, if anything, even more desirous of peace. Firmly established on this moral ground, the instruction moved on to the more practical considerations of strategy. The principal offensive strategy would still be to split the two branches of the house of Austria, which by dint of its usurpations—many against France—had aimed at universal monarchy. Conversely, the principal defensive strategy would still be to prevent the separation of France from her allies. God was already on France's side since he had shown, "by the continual blessings which he gave to their majesties, that He protected the justice of their cause." The final object, as always, would be to conclude a secure peace that would be firmly guaranteed by France's allies; and this security also required the conquerors to keep almost all their conquests. The instruction continued to place great emphasis on two regional leagues, one in Italy and one in Germany, which would unite against anyone who had the temerity to violate the peace. In demonstrating the unselfishness of the French monarchy, the plenipotentiaries were to begin by insisting on the liberation of the Elector of Trier. But the regency did not retreat an inch on France's territorial demands; instead, it augmented them. The retention of Casale (or its return to the Duke of Mantua under all sorts of restrictions) and Pinerolo, Lorraine, large portions of Alsace, and Breisach remained, and Roussillon was added. It was in connection with the French demands on Casale that Mazarin introduced what became one of his characteristic rules of thumb, namely the "law of opposites." According to this "law," if the Spanish favored something, it was good reason for the French to oppose it. Thus, if the Spanish wanted to demolish the fortifications of Casale, the plenipotentiaries should insist on keeping them standing. Like its predecessor, the regency government was embarrassed by the disposition of Catalonia and Portugal. It stuck to the policy, therefore, of reserving this issue to the end, in the full expectation that they could then make some provision for their newfound friends and in good conscience abandon them. Here, once again, the instruction showed the more confrontational presence of Mazarin, for it informed the plenipotentiaries that if they could not cut a reasonable deal on behalf of the Portuguese, they should at least make it possible for the French to assist them after the peace.[17]

It would seem as if the triumph of Mazarin also had its effect on the Emperor and his council in faraway Kaiser Ebersdorf near Vienna. They proceeded to draw up a revised instruction for their plenipotentiaries at the peace conference. The instructions dismissed the Spanish expectations of a change of government in France. The irony of this instruction, however, was that it did not direct the Austrian plenipotentiaries to make concessions to the French; instead, it directed them to attempt a secret negotiation with the Swedes, who were to be bribed with part or all of the Duchy of Pomerania. This concession would require compensating the Elector of Brandenburg with territories elsewhere in the Empire—most likely the Bishoprics of Magdeburg and Halberstadt—but Ferdinand's first concern was preserving his own hereditary lands. The Emperor may have been more desperate for peace than the Spanish, but he preferred to make his concessions to the Protestants before bowing to the dictates of the French monarchy.[18]

D'Avaux left Paris on October 8, Servien and his wife a few days later. Their processions, especially when they came together, must have resembled a small army: secretaries, archivists, servants, deputies of Portugal and Catalonia, and 300 "volunteers." They all went by land to Mézières, the edge of the French possessions, where they boarded boats waiting for them on the Meuse and then entered Spanish territory. At every stronghold that they passed, cannons fired salvos in their honor. When they reached Dortrecht, they were met by La Thuillerie, the French ambassador to the Dutch Republic. Finally, on November 23, after more than a month in transit, they arrived at The Hague, where they were honored with a magnificent reception. Soon after they arrived, however, they received some embarrassing news. The Duke d'Enghien had gone to Alsace to execute Mazarin's master plan, but the duke decided that the plan was impractical and promptly returned to court. Guébriant tried to execute as much of it as he could. He crossed the Rhine, advanced through the Black Forest, and besieged the town of Rottweil, where he was mortally wounded. Then on November 24, a portion of his army, under the drunken Rantzau, was surprised near Tuttlingen by a combined force of Bavarian, Imperial, and Lorrainian troops. The French may have lost as many as 4,000 men, mostly prisoners—not quite the proportions of Rocroi, but not the best backdrop for the negotiations at The Hague.[19]

On December 1, D'Avaux and Servien went before the States General, where D'Avaux announced the purpose of his mission. Later the same day they visited Frederick Henry and his wife, Amalia von Solms. The States General named as their commissioners Barthold van Gendt, Lord of Meynerswijck; Johan van Matenesse; Adriaan Pauw; Johan de Knuyt; Gijsbert van de Hoolck; Frans van Donia; Willem Ripperda; and Adriaan Clant, all of whom, with the exception of Hoolck, would reappear at Münster. The negotiations did not go smoothly. At their first meeting with D'Avaux, Servien, and La Thuillerie on December 10, the Dutch were not even willing to confirm their old treaties, much less add to them. They could hardly object to the idea of not making a separate peace, but they balked at the principle that France should keep all of its conquests. The King of France was too magnificent for that, they countered, combining their flatteries with their fears. They also tried to convince the French to press for a truce. If the French absolutely insisted on making a peace and the Dutch made a truce, they wanted to make sure that the French would resume the war if the Spanish refused to renew the truce. When the French tried to break the deadlock by appealing to their friend Frederick Henry, he supported the commissioners, suggesting, as a compromise, some sort of memoir of understanding that the French would renew the war. If this was not enough, the Dutch put forth the demand that France accord their plenipotentiaries to the peace conference the full royal treatment, an honor that the French monarchy reserved for the Venetian republic alone. Servien drew up the articles of a projected treaty, but the Dutch would not budge.[20]

From the very beginning of their embassy, moreover, it was evident that D'Avaux and Servien were incompatible. D'Avaux had his conceits, and he exulted in being the center of a wide circle of connections collected over his previous embassies in the North. He enjoyed playing the gentleman, and, on hearing of the defeat at Tuttlingen, he gallantly wrote to Anne of Austria, offering her the queenly sum of 300,000 *livres* interest free! Servien, on the other hand, resented his secondary spot. He felt out of place in this unfamiliar environment and he despised D'Avaux's style. Characteristically, Servien became unpleasant. He began by complaining about their method of composing their common letters to the court. D'Avaux had instituted the practice of conferring on their content, while he, as senior, actually drafted them. This was not satisfactory to Servien. He complained to the court. His complaint reached the ears of D'Avaux, who, in the interest of harmony, conceded the drafting of the letters. This conciliatory gesture, however, still did not satisfy Servien. He concluded that D'Avaux could be bullied, and continued to collect his grievances.[21]

Sweden added to the mounting troubles. Its primary interest, as we have seen, was control of the Baltic. In 1643, moreover, the Swedes discovered that Christian IV, the King of Denmark, in spite of being one of the mediators for the peace conference, was conspiring against them with the King of Poland and the Grand Duke of Muscovy. This was just the excuse the Swedes needed. They decided to turn their attention to Denmark, placing the peace conference on the back burner, simply instructing their plenipotentiaries to make sure that the Protestant princes would show up at Osnabrück. In December a Swedish army suddenly invaded Christian's territories. The invasion left only one French ally active in Germany: Amalia Elizabeth, the Landgravin of Hesse-Cassel, who had her hands full with the inhabitants of East Frisia, sick of paying contributions to her army.[22]

But Mazarin had no lack of resiliency. As to the disaster at Tuttlingen, he assured one of the survivors that "the queen is resolved to take her revenge." She named Marshal de Turenne to succeed Guébriant and set about collecting 2 million *livres*—while declining the offer of D'Avaux— for the levying of more troops. As to the Dutch insistence on a truce, Mazarin confided in a *mémoire* to the plenipotentiaries that, in point of fact, France also wanted a truce, but he warned them not to act as if they did because if the Spanish got an inkling of it, they would oppose it. It would appear, therefore, as if his "law of opposites" cut both ways. If there were a truce, he insisted that France hold on to all its conquests and that the Dutch acquiesce in this goal. "They must understand," he continued in the same *mémoire*, "that if their friendship is expedient for us, ours is extremely necessary to them." The possibility that the Dutch already feared France more than they feared Spain, he categorically dismissed. The possibility that the rest of Europe would come to fear France more than they feared the house of Austria was just as remote from his mind. He was only upset because his plenipotentiaries were wasting their time in The Hague while the Spanish were accusing them of stalling. As to the Swedish invasion of Denmark, he admitted in a subsequent *mémoire* that it it could "change the face of affairs." He offered French mediation and subsequently sent La Thuillerie as mediator.[23]

D'Avaux and Servien, meanwhile, found themselves trapped at The Hague. If they left without signing a treaty, the whole world would know that the French monarchy and the Dutch Republic were at loggerheads. The Dutch finally agreed to confirming the old treaties, but they were extremely touchy about establishing their own right to negotiate independently. It should have been clear by now that any treaty with such allies would not be worth the paper on which it was written, whatever assurances they reiterated that they would not conclude separately. Nevertheless, both sides debated the exact wording of every article as if the fate of the world depended on it. The article on which they could not agree was Article 6, the issue of peace or truce, or, to be more precise, the consequences of Article 6. But if the two sides could barely agree on working together in Münster, what was the point of arguing about the distant future, when circumstances would undoubtedly be different? There was more to it than that; it was a struggle of wills. Frederick Henry again offered the compromise of putting a French promise to renew the war into a supplementary writing, but the French, sticking by their instructions, would not budge, and the negotiations could not advance.[24]

In the absence of progress, D'Avaux and Servien vented their spleens upon each other. When Servien discovered that D'Avaux had made his offer to the queen, he claimed this was in violation of their agreement not to do anything without each other's knowledge. D'Avaux was also corresponding unilaterally with his old collaborators, the French residents in Germany. When Servien threatened to report this practice to the court, D'Avaux stood his ground, replying that if he were attacked he would defend himself. But the biggest clash between them occurred over one of Servien's greatest passions, protocol. Frederick Henry's wife, the Princess of Orange, was in the habit of not making the first visit to the wives of ambassadors, with the result that Servien had prevented his wife from visiting her. From then on the two ladies had scrupulously avoided each other. Imagine his indignation when he discovered that D'Avaux had decided to hold a lavish party to which he was inviting all the ladies. Nor would he hear of calling it off. Servien, after being calmed by La Thuillerie, attended the festivities alone, mumbling about his colleague who "thinks more of honors for himself than of those that must be rendered to the embassy." He immortalized his sorrows in an appeal to the court, which he refrained from sending.[25]

By the end of the month of February, the French plenipotentiaries had reconciled themselves to leaving The Hague without accomplishing anything. When they announced that they were departing, the States General finally agreed to go along with the article permitting the French to negotiate for a peace, and they also expressed their readiness to sign the annual subsidy treaty for the campaign. This did not mean, however, that the Dutch had given up on the compromise suggested by Frederick Henry. They came in with a piece of paper, which stated that the French would resume the war if the Spanish did not renew the truce. and tried to hand it to the French plenipotentiaries, who, of course, would not accept it. On March 1, the day of the signing of the treaties, the Dutch again showed up with the same piece of paper, which became known as Article 9. At this critical juncture, one of the French plenipotentiaries—it is not hard to guess which one—grabbed the paper from the table, and, with the words, "it's not right that a piece of paper should delay further such a good work," threw it into the fire. It was easier to throw it into the fire, however, than to sweep it under the rug.[26]

The thoughts of the plenipotentiaries now turned to Münster, where one of their first concerns would be to ensure that the Emperor, who was at that moment meeting with his supporters at Frankfurt, did not try to speak for the German princes. D'Avaux and Servien thus decided that they should concert a circular letter to these princes, inviting them to the peace conference. This was one letter that D'Avaux, who was so proud of his Latin, reserved for his own composition. Before they left The Hague, however, it was D'Avaux's responsibility to deliver a farewell speech to the States General. He had apparently decided with Servien and La Thuillerie that it should include some passing appeal on behalf on the Catholics in the Dutch Republic. D'Avaux took the occasion to stage another of his patented performances before Protestants, and this was one of his most stunning. His speech, which centered on the issue of toleration, could have been given by Voltaire. "Do you want to turn disaffected men into good citizens? . . . Diminish the severity of your ordinances!" It was, in any case, an odd appeal to a regime that was as forbearing to nonconformity as any in Europe. Servien was flabbergasted and immediately concluded that D'Avaux was angling for a cardinal's hat. The States General was outraged and immediately promulgated a new set of ordinances against the Catholics. The mission to The Hague had begun badly, it had ended badly, and it augured badly for the future.[27]

3

Dissensions in Westphalia

Having apparently come so close in the campaign of 1643, Mazarin was intent on making the campaign of 1644 the one that would win the war. His plan was for Monsieur to lead the main French army toward the Channel, besiege the Spanish strongholds of Bourbourg and perhaps also Gravelines on the coast with Dutch naval support, while the Prince of Orange would besiege Dunkirk. If Frederick Henry did not want to besiege Dunkirk, the French would, while he kept the Spanish occupied near Ghent. It did cross Mazarin's mind that the Dutch might have "considerable jealousy" at seeing the French in a post such as Dunkirk, but, he added unbelievably, "there is no appearance of it." He sent a courier to La Thuillerie, or in his absence to his secretary Brasset, with instructions to consult with the Prince of Orange on the plan, and also sent a personal emissary for good measure. It all seemed so plausible to Cardinal Mazarin. What the experience of his entire life, confirmed by his experience at the court of France, seemed to be telling him was that he was a master manipulator living in a world of fools. Yet the experience of the war, so dramatically encapsulated in the vicissitudes of the previous campaign, might have reminded him that neither battles nor sieges seemed to be able to break the enemy's will, that too many victories disaffected one's friends, and that each side with each setback could always manage to dredge up 5,000 or 10,000 more roughnecks to ravage the land. All of the elements for classical tragedy were therefore in place. Mazarin had all the hubris, and fate held all the cards.[1]

D'Avaux was the first of the French plenipotentiaries to reach Münster. He entered the city impressively on March 17, welcomed by the coaches of the Imperial and Spanish plenipotentiaries and of Alvise Contarini, the Venetian mediator; by the garrison and the bourgeois militia under arms; by crowds in the streets; and by women peering from windows. Two days later Fabio Chigi, the papal nuncio, arrived, making his entrance not so impressively in a litter. The first item of business to which D'Avaux gave his attention was the composition of the circular letter inviting the princes of Germany to send their deputies to the conference. The letter made the obvious points, and he sent a draft to Servien, who made some corrections, notably inserting the title *"Sacra Rega M."* (Holy Royal Majesty) when referring to the King of France. D'Avaux, however, ignored this correction on the grounds that it was not good Latin. In the midst of these preparations, the head of the Spanish delegation, Count Zapata, died. Servien made his own grand entry on April 5 and on the very next day D'Avaux and Servien sent their letter to the German princes.[2]

Mazarin's eyes were, as usual, bigger than his stomach. The Prince of Orange dismissed the siege of Dunkirk as too perilous an undertaking, but he did encourage the French to try their hand at Gravelines, while he would divert the Spanish by besieging the fortress of Sas near Ghent. And so they planned for war, while at Münster, the French, Spanish, and Imperial plenipotentiaries proceeded on April 16 to make the first historic gesture toward negotiating a peace, the exchange of powers through the mediators. But historic as the moment may have been, it was also a predictable ritual in which each side outdid the other in finding flaws in each other's powers. The Emperor and some of his strongest supporters at Frankfurt also took umbrage to the circular letter. In Osnabrück, where Salvius and Oxenstierna had arrived by April 6 (the third Swedish plenipotentiary never showed up), there was no exchange at all because the Swedes were currently at war with their only mediator. Everyone was waiting for the results of the campaign. The Duke d'Orléans began the siege of Gravelines, which advanced very slowly. In Spain Philip IV led his army into Catalonia, where his troops got the better of the French and laid siege before Lérida. The Dutch tried to approach the Sas of Ghent, only to be repulsed. The Swedes, occupied with the Danes, stood on the defensive throughout the Empire, hoping against hope that the Emperor would himself be immobilized by George Rakoscy, the Prince of Transylvania, in upper Hungary. Twenty-six years had passed since the war had started with the revolt in Bohemia, and the god of battles had still not declared himself.[3]

Servien picked this lull to renew his attack upon D'Avaux. This time it took the officious form of a letter which catalogued his shortcomings. Servien began with D'Avaux's behavior in The Hague, complaining about how lethargic he had been in reacting to the Danish-Swedish war and how unwise he had been in making the speech on behalf of the Catholics. He had only gone along with it, Servien now revealed, out of deference. Turning to more recent grievances, he expressed criticism of the anti-Hapsburg tone in the circular letter, which he predicted would only discourage the Emperor's supporters from participating in the congress. Servien suggested that from now on they keep a written record of their conferences with each other, and he sent a copy of the letter to his nephew Lionne, obviously meant for Mazarin's eyes. D'Avaux waited nine days and then replied sarcastically. He apologized humbly for his own ponderousness and expressed astonishment at the patience of those who had employed him up to then. He accused Servien of creating the delays, reminded him that he had given his assent to the appeal on behalf of the Catholics, and retorted that the circular letter had been a huge success. He ridiculed the idea of having to confer with his colleague in writing. And correctly guessing that the letter had not been intended for his eyes alone, he communicated the exchange to the court. Servien contained his rage for nearly a month and then exploded in 196 pages, convinced as he was that his own first letter had been a model of civility. He began to dwell on the theme that he and D'Avaux were equal in dignity, which was not entirely correct, and he maintained that he had not communicated his letter to anyone, which was an outright lie. So great was the difference between the two men that the humorless Servien was not even capable of catching D'Avaux's sarcasm. "You are only acting as if you don't think highly of yourself!" Servien scolded.[4]

The campaign began looking up for the French when on July 29 Gravelines capitulated. Mazarin immediately sent the Duke d'Enghien, who had been covering the siege with a body of some 5,000 troops, to reinforce Turenne in Germany. But in Catalonia, Lérida capitulated to the Spanish, and, in any event, Mazarin did not want to make it appear as if he were delaying the peace. He instructed the plenipotentiaries to be as accommodating as possible on the correction of the powers, and he tried to repair the ruffled feelings of the Emperor by having Louis XIV send his own, ostensibly more moderate, circular letter to the princes of Germany. The quarrel between D'Avaux and Servien was, of course, one more embarrassment. It threatened to divide the council, disgruntle the *parlement* of Paris, and wreak havoc with public opinion. Mazarin wrote eloquently to the plenipotentiaries, entreating them to make up their differences, and privately, he told Lionne that Servien "had overdone it." Since Saint-Romain, the French resident in Münster, happened to be in Paris at the time, Mazarin rushed him back with the entreaties and began thinking about sending Brasset from Holland to take charge of the correspondence temporarily until the Duke de Longueville could arrive.[5]

The campaign continued to go well for the French. While the Bavarians were besieging Freiburg on the right bank of the Rhine, the Duke d'Enghien moved out from Denzingen on the left bank with his tiny army and made a dash for Philippsburg on the other side. After a seventeen-day siege, the Bavarian commander capitulated. Speyer had already fallen, and Worms and Mainz followed in quick succession, so that in a little over three weeks the French found themselves in possession of the entire right bank of the Rhine up to Bingen. It was Mazarin's grand design of the previous year brought to fruition, and nothing like it had been seen since the days of Gustavus Adolphus. France's allies were also doing their part. The Prince of Orange finally took the Sas of Ghent, and the Swedes, gorged with spoils from their war with the Danes, were back on the offensive in Germany, threatening to join Rakocsy for an attack upon Moravia and Silesia. Yet even such consistent successes did not succeed in bringing the enemies to their knees. On the contrary, in keeping with the ironic law of early modern statecraft, the more advantageous the military situation became, the more disadvantageous the diplomatic situation. On the same day that the Duke d'Orléans took Gravelines, the relatively pro-French Pope Urban VIII died, and just as the Duke d'Enghien was sweeping down the Rhine, the conclave in Rome—including Cardinals Francesco and Antonio Barberini, nephews of the previous Pope—elected Giovanni Battista Pamfili, a cardinal of unvarnished Spanish sympathies, to the pontificate as Innocent X. The College of Cardinals, it would seem, was trying to make a statement about the balance of power, and if the College of Cardinals was making a statement, the princes of Italy would not be far behind. Who was to say if more French and Swedish victories might not alienate the Dutch and even unite the princes of the Empire behind the Emperor?[6]

During the month of September, D'Avaux and Servien did manage to send off the king's circular letter to the German princes, along with a second one of their own. They also sent one of D'Avaux's creatures, Antoine de Fouquet-Croissy, to Transylvania to negotiate a French alliance with Rakocsy, but there was still no sense of urgency at Münster and Osnabrück. By the beginning of November, the French, the Spanish, and the Imperialists had agreed on the revisions of the powers, but as the parties began discussing the wording of the agreement, Servien and D'Avaux began quarreling again. Servien objected to various formulas which, in his mind, established too much distance between the Emperor and the King of France and too much equality between the Kings of France and Spain. D'Avaux was exasperated. He reached a point where he went directly to the mediators and appealed for their help in getting rid of his colleague. Finally, on November 20, the French, the Spanish, and the Imperialists reached an agreement on the agreement, but by this time D'Avaux and Servien were barely on speaking terms, communicating with each other through their secretaries and in writing. Once the French had reached an agreement, however, the Swedes in Osnabrück followed suit.[7]

This bitter feuding between D'Avaux and Servien made it extremely difficult for them to coordinate among themselves and with their allies the next historic milestone of the negotiations, namely, the first exchange of proposals. It took place on December 4. The best D'Avaux and Servien could come up with was a brief statement in which they insisted on the coming of the German princes and the freeing of the Elector of Trier as a prerequisite to proceeding. The Swedes, who were in no hurry, limited themselves to insisting on the coming of the princes. The Spanish and the Emperor, as if oblivious to their reversals, proposed a return to the situation in 1630. They still hoped that some sort of compromise, or, failing that, some stroke of fortune, would bail them out. It was at this point that the enterprising Saavedra came up with an idea. Philip IV had recently and most conveniently been widowed. Why, Saavedra suggested to his own court, not break the stalemate with a marriage of his king to the eldest daughter of the Duke d'Orléans, promising the Low Countries to their second son?[8]

The initial exchange of proposals infuriated Cardinal Mazarin. He was furious that the plenipotentiaries had presented their position in writing, he was furious that they had gone beyond generalities, and he was incensed that by making the arrival of the German princes and the liberation of the Elector of Trier preconditions of negotiations, they had given an impression of intransigence. Yes, they had been instructed to make this demand, but they were not supposed to have made it so unconditionally. They had fallen, in other words, into an enemy trap, and Mazarin was so angry that he wrote at least a part of the draft of the *Mémoire du Roi* in his own hand and in Italian. This would not have happened, he wrote, if the plenipotentiaries "weren't giving their principal dedication to their personal differences." He was so furious, in fact, that he forgot his own rule by expanding their written proposition into two written revisions, one for the Spanish and one for the Emperor. The most remarkable thing about these revisions was that in dictating them Mazarin began to divulge his territorial ambitions. The revision for the Spanish proposed that "all things remain in the state that they are today"—i.e., the French keep their conquests. The revision for the Emperor inferred almost the same thing under cover of solicitude for the German princes. It stated that the king "would consider his own interests only for the security of the said princes"—i.e., he would demand a footing in Germany. But Mazarin was clearly interested in making some progress. About a week after sending the revised proposals, he caved in almost entirely to the Dutch on the matter of the royal treatment.[9]

It was a great humiliation for both Servien and D'Avaux to be reproached by Mazarin. They rushed to send Saint-Romain back to court with their justifications, and they also found themselves in the predicament of having to make their amended proposal in conjunction with the Swedes, who were in no hurry. Their army under Torstensen was about to enter into Bohemia, and they were still waiting for all of the German princes to show up at the peace conference so that on February 4 D'Avaux went to Osnabrück, where he and Rorté, the French resident there, spent six days trying to prod the Swedes into another proposition. Oxenstierna did not object if the French wished to clarify theirs, but he refused to move further. "What does it matter," he retorted, "if our enemies complain that we don't want peace? We want it, but first we want to fight!" D'Avaux wrote to Servien describing his frustrations, but even in the midst of their common struggle, Servien did not fail to pursue his vendetta. "With more forceful action," he grumbled to Brienne, "they would have gone along!" The next few weeks were spent in squabbling between D'Avaux, who did not want to displease the Swedes, and Servien, who did not want to displease Mazarin. The new Spanish powers had arrived, and the French still did not like them, making it even more difficult to move forward. Thus, after more squabbling between D'Avaux and Servien, D'Avaux caved in. On February 24 they transmitted the two revised proposals to the mediators, both under seal, with the stipulation that they would retain the Spanish copy in their own hands until the Spanish had once more reformed their powers. But the hostility between Servien and D'Avaux reached a point when, on March 3, D'Avaux asked for his own recall.[10]

Just as the French delegation was falling apart, Philip IV was beginning to dispatch a new head for his own delegation. It was to be Gaspar de Bracamonte y Guzman, Count de Peñaranda, an epitome of Spanish gravity with long years of experience in contending with adversity. His instructions still envisioned a return to the *status quo ante bellum,* no help to the Catalonian and Portuguese rebels and the reinstatement of the Duke of Lorraine. The Spanish, however, were showing some signs of cracking. Saavedra's suggestion of the marriage of Philip IV to the daughter of the Duke d'Orléans had not fallen on deaf ears, and the instruction elaborated on it with a number of possibilities, *e.g.,* ceding the counties of Artois or Franche-Comté until the marriage proved fruitful, even throwing in the complete cession of Gravelines, Arras, and Thionville. One of the more mischievous suggestions was for the marriage of Philip IV's eldest daughter, the Infanta Maria Theresa, to Louis XIV's brother, the Duke d'Anjou, who would then establish his own sovereign state in Franch-Comté and perhaps even in all of Burgundy. That of course would have recreated an independent Duchy of Burgundy, ready, as it had been in the Hundred Years War, to ally with the enemies of France at the slightest provocation. Finally, and perhaps most attractively, was the possibility of a marriage of the Infanta to Louis XIV, giving her Franche-Comté as her dowry. If this failed, Peñeranda was to attempt a separate arrangement with the Dutch. These sanguine speculations, however, were quickly squashed by events in Bohemia. There, on March 6, 1645, the Imperialists and the Bavarians had made a stand at Jankau against the invading Torstensen. Hoping for another Nördlingen, they ended up with another Breitenfeld—close to 10,000 dead, the Imperial and Bavarian cavalry decimated, one Imperial general killed, another captured, and the Swedes threatening to cut a swath right across the hereditary lands. Reduced to the defense of his last strongholds, the Emperor finally began to show some strain. He released the Elector of Trier and consented to the princes in Frankfurt transferring themselves to Münster.[11]

Mazarin's plans for the campaign of 1645 were simply an extension of the previous year's, with even greater expectations of bringing the enemies to their knees. The Duke d'Orléans would besiege Mardick, edging the French ever closer to the great prize of Dunkirk, and the Prince of Orange would keep the Spanish occupied with his own enterprises. Other French armies would advance on other fronts, while the Swedes and the Transylvanians would apply similar pressures on the Emperor. D'Avaux's request for his recall, however, confronted Mazarin with a dilemma. If he agreed to the recall, he would once more have to contend with D'Avaux's presence in the council, where he might turn out to be more of a nuisance than he was at Münster. Added to this was the potential impact of his return on domestic public opinion, which would conclude that he had been gotten out of Servien's way simply because Mazarin did not want peace. Then there was the reaction of the allies of France and the mediators at Münster—the more they saw of Servien, the better they liked D'Avaux. They too began putting every kind of pressure on Mazarin to keep D'Avaux at the conference. Faced with this insoluble perplexity, Mazarin simply stalled, and when he finally replied on April 6, he sent out a letter with the shuttling Saint-Romain, in which the king permitted D'Avaux to continue asking for his recall but expressed the hope that the coming arrival of the Duke de Longueville would restore some harmony.[12]

The re-revised powers for the Spanish plenipotentiaries having finally arrived, the mediators found themselves in a position, on April 1, to deliver the French proposal into the hands of the Spanish. Oxenstierna arrived in Münster a few days later with, as might be expected, some exorbitant Swedish proposals in his hands. He was welcomed by a quarrel between the coaches of Servien and D'Avaux disputing the precedence in his procession, and left a few days later in disgust. On April 17 Saint-Romain arrived from court, and the following day Saavreda and Brun made their reply to the French. It did not budge an inch from the restitution of the conquests. Notwithstanding the military situation, the negotiations were still stalled. The only movement that was occurring at Münster was in the mind of D'Avaux, who began having second thoughts about where he could do Mazarin the most harm. Even before Saint-Romain's dispatches were decoded, D'Avaux went to visit Contarini and told him in all confidence that he might possibly decide to remain if there was any chance for peace, so as to "pay the favorite back in full measure." Such a statement confirmed Contarini's suspicions that Mazarin did not want peace, and it was about this time that Contarini, in a moment of exasperation, blurted out the most fateful words that were ever uttered during the Congress of Westphalia. "It is impossible," he exclaimed to D'Avaux and Servien, "for this treaty to be concluded without a marriage between the Infanta of Spain and the king!" Meeting with silence, Contarini added, "with Burgundy and the Low Countries as a dowry!" More silence, and Servien finally responded that they had no power to negotiate such a thing. It was plausible, he added, echoing the reaction of Richelieu eleven years previously, but problematic, because it might lead to Spain gaining and France losing the friendship of the Dutch. Amazingly, however, none of these men—not Contarini, D'Avaux, or Servien—reported the conversation at the time.[13]

With D'Avaux sulking, it fell upon Servien to advance the negotiations, and his first thought was to consult with the Swedes again on a new proposal to the Emperor. He drew it up, as may be imagined, to suit himself, and he could not avoid dealing with controversial matters. In one article he tried to ensure that the Emperor could not come to the assistance of the Spanish after the peace without the Swedes promising to come to the assistance of France. In another he wanted the political situation in the Holy Roman Empire to return to 1618, "unless otherwise specified," which betrayed the French partiality for the Duke of Bavaria. Servien tried to limit the touchy religion question to one article (Article 9), which stipulated for the religious issues to be settled by the parties to the "common satisfaction." An article which called for the maintenance of the German princes in their "rights" merely reiterated the principle that future historians would find so innovative in the Peace of Westphalia, but it innovated to the extent of specifying that this principle included the right of princes to carry out their own foreign policy, as long as it did not interfere with the interests of the Empire. Most embarrassing both to France and Sweden, in view of their constant disclaimers of self-interest, was an article in which the crowns would demand "satisfactions" of an unspecified nature, and it was with this project in his pocket that on April 26 Servien went up to Osnabrück. The Swedes, needless to say, had different ideas. They had no intention of helping the French once the war was over, and, out of eighteen articles in their project, *six* dealt with religion. They wanted the 1618 date to apply both to the political and to the religious situation, without qualifications. Bowing to pressures from the Landgravin of Hesse-Cassel, they included a specific article that demanded equal status for Calvinists. The Swedes too wanted satisfaction for themselves and for their allies, and they wanted the Emperor to pay for the dismissal of all of the armies. Servien accepted a number of amendments to his initial project, but he found himself obliged to remind the Swedes that the war had never been one of religion and obtained a delay until he could once more consult with his court. The French, however, were soon embarrassed by their incapacity to keep up militarily with the Swedes. On May 5, 1645, Marshal de Turenne blundered into a stronger Bavarian army at Mergentheim and was roundly defeated.[14]

The danger of a resurgent Protestantism seemed incapable of dampening Mazarin's spirits. He did not even see why his plenipotentiaries had bothered to seek further instructions about it, but since they did, he instructed them not to stick their necks out on the matter of religion, and for the first time he explained why: "The need to make peace," he divulged, "might well oblige the Emperor, the Spanish, the Catholic electors, and princes to agree to many things, as they have done on other occasions, for which this crown cannot in any way be blamed." This is no minor insight into Mazarin's intellectual and moral universe, to which we can now add what we might call the Pontius Pilate position. In keeping with this notorious principle, if the Emperor and the Catholics turned over half of Germany to the Lutherans and Calvinists, the King of France could wash his hands entirely.[15]

By this time D'Avaux had decided to stay, and this kind of casuistry only confirmed his belief that he was the only person who could turn the tables on it. He lost no time in doing so, and by an ingenious twist of logic, he perverted Mazarin's indifferentism into the argument that it behooved the French to drop *all* mention of religion from their project. Servien, who had been so critical of D'Avaux's timidity toward the Swedes, found himself outmaneuvered. After much discussion, D'Avaux prevailed, and the two men sent Saint-Romain to Osnabrück with a revised project. The Swedes, needless to say, were very upset. The debate between Servien and D'Avaux continued until June 11, when they finally handed their proposal, omitting the article on religion, to the mediators. The Swedes, of course, also felt free to amend their proposal as they wished, and, on the same day, they handed it over to the Imperialists in Osnabrück. For the first time in the negotiation, the French and the Swedes showed signs of disunity.[16]

It is hard to understand why, but it was at this point that Servien decided to write to Lionne about Contarini's marriage and exchange proposal. He wasn't sure, he said, whether it had been inspired by the Spanish, but he thought he had better inform Mazarin about it. These casual thoughts came at a critical juncture in every respect. On May 29 Marshal du Plessis Praslin took the port of Rosas in Catalonia from the Spanish. On June 25 a huge Turkish armada invaded the island of Crete, putting the Venetian Republic, which controlled the island, and the whole of Christendom, in imminent peril. On June 30 the long-awaited Duke de Longueville arrived in Münster, making an entry that befitted an illegitimate offspring of the house of France who expected to be addressed as "highness" by friend and foe alike. On July 5 the Count de Peñaranda entered much more modestly and, with equal modesty, took up residence in a Recollect monastery. On July 10 the Duke d'Orléans took Mardick, and on August 3 the Duke d'Enghien and the Marshal de Turenne defeated the Bavarians and Imperialists at Nördlingen. If there was ever a moment to come to a face-saving peace, this was it, and suddenly Contarini's suggestion of a marriage and exchange acquired new urgency, especially for him. He repeated it a few days later in a conversation with D'Avaux, and the French plenipotentiaries were increasingly persuaded that the Spanish were behind the offer. Servien still opposed it, and this time he expressed his opinion to Lionne for the benefit of Mazarin. "The proposition of the marriage of the Infanta with the king seems to be very dangerous at this time." Contarini also made a similar proposal to Peñaranda, and did not get much encouragement from him either.[17]

At this juncture, it was the Ottoman sultan who breathed some life into the expiring Hapsburg cause. Ibrahim I, who was in the process of committing his forces against the Venetians, did not want an overmighty Prince of Transylvania extending his power into Hapsburg Hungary. Just as he was about to invade Crete, therefore, the sultan ordered Rakocsy to make peace with the Emperor, and the Prince of Transylvania had no choice but to do so. It was a glorious peace for him. Ferdinand acceded to all of his demands—full freedom of religion for the Protestants of Hungary and surrender of a number of border strongholds—but this defection liberated an Imperial army to counter the Swedes in Bohemia and gave the Emperor, as he concocted his replies to the French and Swedish proposals, a few more months to stall. To the demand for amnesty, he replied that he had already accorded it in 1641 at the Reichstag in Regensburg. To the demand for constitutional reform in the Empire, he replied that this was a matter between himself and the princes. To the demand of satisfactions for the crowns and for the Landgravin of Hesse-Cassel, he replied that he saw no basis for it. Yet there were some remarkable features in this reply. Ferdinand acquiesced without a murmur to the demand that the princes and states of the Empire be maintained in their right to make alliances—which, I insist, may or may not have been an innovation—and he agreed to the recognition of Calvinism—which most certainly was. But he also presented himself as a defender of the princes by demanding that the French restore the Duke of Lorraine to his lands. This marked a subtle shift in diplomatic strategy. The very weakness of the Emperor and the presence of a growing number of representatives of the princes at Münster and Osnabrück now gave him the opportunity to play upon their patriotism in an effort to rally them to his cause. Did they really want to share the Holy Roman Empire with the French and the Swedes? In sending his replies to his plenipotentiaries on August 23, he instructed them to present these first of all to the representatives of the princes and states, to the mediators, and to the Spanish. Desperate stabs. On that same day the Swedes made their own peace with the Danes, securing lower duties through the Sound, a number of strategic islands in the Baltic, and full disposition of the Archbishopric of Bremen and Bishopric of Verden. As the Emperor's plenipotentiaries were distributing his reply, the Swedes were the undisputed masters of northern Europe.[18]

Mazarin, meanwhile, was establishing himself as the undisputed master of France. On September 7, 1645, the seven-year-old Louis XIV—accompanied by his mother, the Duke d'Orléans, the chancellor, and a host of dignitaries—appeared before the *parlement* of Paris and held the second *lit de justice* of his reign. It was the first such *lit* held for the purpose of forcing some financial edicts down the throat of the *parlement*, and there was even some question as to whether a minor king had the authority to do such a thing, but the chancellor read the edicts, and, miraculously, the *parlement* registered them. It is not clear how much they would bring in, but it was enough, apparently, to carry Mazarin through the campaign of 1646, and he did not bother to look much further. The string of victories which had concluded the campaign of 1645, crowned by the conquest of Armentières on September 10, again convinced him that the enemies were about to crack. Nor did he see any reason to make them feel any better. On hearing of the marriage proposal which would have sugarcoated the cession of the Spanish Low Countries, his reaction was strictly in keeping with the reservations of Servien. "France," Mazarin dictated in the name of the king on September 30, "has experienced notable prejudices from similar subterfuges." One might think this would have settled the matter then and there, but it didn't, for the apparent desperation of the Spanish had also planted a seed in the mind of Cardinal Mazarin, not for a marriage between Louis XIV and the Infanta, which he continued to disparage, but for the exchange of Catalonia and the abandonment of Portugal by France in return for the great prize of the Spanish Low Countries. He was perfectly aware of the capacity of the proposal to drive a wedge between France and three of its most important allies, the Dutch, the Catalonians, and the Portuguese. But the idea of a foreign-born minister at the helm of a regency government going above and beyond the achievements of Cardinal Richelieu piqued Mazarin's vanity. If France could acquire the Spanish Low Countries, it would dominate Europe, and he, Giulio Mazarini, would go down in history as the greatest statesman of all time.[19]

Mazarin was right about the Spanish. They had reached the limits of their endurance. Indeed, just as he was beginning to accept at least one-half of the marriage and exchange proposal, they were beginning to embrace it in its entirety. It was toward the end of September that in a *consulta*—the text of which has unfortunately been lost—the Count de Monterrey recommended to Philip IV that they expand on their instructions to the Count de Peñaranda so as to make them more appealing to the French. First of all, Monterrey suggested that the projected marriage between the Duke d'Anjou and the Infanta be made more inviting by including the entire Spanish Low Countries as dowry. This offer, of course, still involved the risk of a new thorn in the side of the French monarchy, but Monterrey then went on to suggest that if this offer were rejected, they should then offer the marriage of the Infanta with the Spanish Low Countries to Louis XIV himself. This was the monumental suggestion. It meant that the Spanish, as opposed to Cardinal Richelieu, were prepared to surrender the hegemony of Europe to their rival. The implications in the religious sphere were equally far-reaching. With a Catholic and hegemonic France as a neighbor of the Dutch Republic, the Counter Reformation could pick up where the Edict of Restitution had left off. Philip IV agreed. There were even intimations that the Spanish would put the specific terms of the peace into the hands of Anne of Austria. The only thing that Cardinal Mazarin now needed in order to carry out his coup was for the Spanish to persevere in their decision.[20]

Mazarin was also right about the Emperor. Looking at the situation in the fall of 1645, Ferdinand III concluded that he had no choice but to bow to reason of state. The most he could hope for now was to hold on to his hereditary lands, preserve them as much as possible in the Catholic religion, and wait for a better day. His most trusted advisor, the Count von Trauttmansdorff, thought exactly the same way, and the Emperor decided to send him to Münster to see what he could salvage from the war. Ferdinand composed the instruction in his own hand and in the strictest secrecy, going from concession to greater concession. He ordered Trauttmansdorff to try to obtain the religious situation as of 1627, but *"in extremo casu"* to go back to 1618. The electoral vote of the Palatinate could alternate between the houses of Bavaria and the Palatinate, but *"ad extremum"* the Emperor was willing to create an eighth electorate. The instruction even contemplated the return of the entire Palatinate to its rebellious house. The crowns, too, were to be satisfied. The Swedes were to be offered half of Pomerania, plus the Archbishopric of Bremen and the cities of Stralsundt, Wismar, and Rostock—all, of course, *"in ultimo necessitatis grado."* The Elector of Brandenburg was to be compensated for the Swedish half of Pomerania with the Duchy of Grossen, the Bishopric of Halberstadt, and portions of the Bishopric of Magdeburg. The French were to be offered Alsace on the left bank of the Rhine; if that wasn't enough, the stronghold of Breisach on the right and, *"in desperatissimu casu,"* the Breisgau, the territory around Breisach. Moreover, they were to be offered these things in full sovereignty. Ferdinand not minding to see the Swedes, but fearing above all to see the French sitting in the Reichstag as princes of the Empire. The Emperor's cousins, archdukes of Innsbruck and members of the house of Austria, who held possessions in Alsace, were to receive a monetary compensation. In short, Ferdinand gave Trauttmansdorff a virtually free hand, step by step, to save the dynasty by giving away the Empire.[21]

The Dutch, like Mazarin, observed that something was happening, and in the fading months of 1645 they finally decided to send their plenipotentiaries off to Münster. It was much the same group which had negotiated at The Hague the year before, except that Hoolck was replaced by Gerhard van Reede, the Lord of Nederhorst, and their instruction, dated October 28, was in the same vein. The Dutch expected their plenipotentiaries to be treated as excellencies. They did not want them to become embroiled in other negotiations. They wanted a truce. They demanded that the King of Spain acknowledge them as "free provinces," They wanted to keep all of their conquests. The most extravagant demand of all was for the right to trade in the East and West Indies, along with other portions of the Spanish monarchy, which meant, in effect, obtaining a virtual monopoly over the commerce of that empire. Almost as extravagant was the demand for the closing of the Scheldt, thus freeing the Dutch Republic from the commercial competition of the Spanish Low Countries in perpetuity. These were bitter humiliations for the Spanish to swallow, but on the other hand, the instruction, with its precisely worded articles, sounded very much like a finished treaty, ready to be signed. And it appeared, moreover, as if the Prince of Orange was all for it.[22]

The Swedes too picked this time to define their goals. Toward the end of November the council of Sweden—or, to speak more properly, Axel Oxenstierna—finally expressed itself to its plenipotentiaries as to what, specifically, they should demand. Oxenstierna ordered them, in the name of the queen, to demand not only all of Pomerania, but also the Archbishopric of Bremen, the port of Wismar, the Duchy of Mecklenburg, and the Bishoprics of Verden, Halberstadt, Minden, and Osnabrück, enough of a prize to give Sweden virtually the entire northern coast of Germany and a good part of the interior. The displaced princes, like the Elector of Brandenburg with his claim to Pomerania, would have to be compensated by the Emperor with such areas as Silesia. What made this tall order even taller was that at that very moment the German Protestant princes, meeting under Swedish protection in Osnabrück, were working out their complaints, or *gravamina*. The Protestants objected first and foremost to the "Ecclesiastical Reservation" which they claimed that the Emperor had arbitrarily attached to the Peace of Augsburg of 1555 and which obliged Catholic ecclesiastics who converted to Protestantism to vacate their benefices. The Protestants wanted to go back to the religious situation in 1618, but they went so far as to intimate that they wanted full freedom to practice their religion anywhere in the Empire. In the hands of the Swedes, these complaints were the perfect instrument with which to continue the war in quest of their most extreme demands. But even if the Spanish and the Emperor were about to surrender immediately, which they were not, their enemies, with their own conflicting goals, had put themselves in danger of splitting apart.[23]

The Spanish plenipotentiaries in Münster were finding it harder to maintain a stiff upper lip. In November the philosophical Saavedra contrived an occasion to chat socially with Servien. "For God's sake, let's make peace," Saavedra pleaded, "we don't deny that we need it, but the affairs of the world are subject to such revolutions, that one should not press one's luck!" "By all means," Servien replied, "just accept our demands!" A short time later Peñaranda discovered that Dr. Volmar, the Imperial plenipotentiary, had begun to address the Duke de Longueville as *celcitudinis*, or "highness." That was alarming enough as a mark of the Emperor's desperation. When, however, on November 29 the Count von Trauttmansdorff sneaked into town, carrying with him Ferdinand's cornucopia of concessions, Peñaranda immediately sized up his counterpart as "faint of heart in adversity," and Peñaranda himself panicked. He was so terrified that the Imperialists would make a separate peace that very winter that he rushed to send a courier to Madrid suggesting that the Spanish offer the French Roussillon, Pinerolo, and some strongholds in Flanders. None of the Spanish plenipotentiaries, however, were as yet aware of the extent to which their own court had caved in. Peñaranda also took another decisive step at the beginning of his embassy. He asked his court for the recall of the impetuous Saavedra, preferring the collaboration of the more submissive Brun. The Spanish may have been in desperate straits, but, unlike the French, they would have a cohesive delegation at the conference.[24]

Mazarin was so certain that the Spanish were at the end of their rope that he was already thinking of what to do about it. The marriage proposal was not looking any more attractive to him, but the exchange was. He wrote in his *Carnet:*

> The affairs of Spain are going from bad to worse . . . they will send orders to Peñaranda to press for the Treaty. . . . Thought about sending D'Estrades to the Prince of Orange for the partition of the Low Countries, under the pretext of the campaign, by making him the mediator and giving him Antwerp.

Against all of his stated principles, moreover, Mazarin also attempted to entice the Spanish into a private arrangement with France. He told the Nuncio Bagni that the Spanish should stop trying to divide France from her allies and address themselves to the queen and her ministers. He made similar overtures to the new Queen of Poland and to Domenico Roncalli, the Polish resident in Paris, both of whom were going through Brussels. He held private discussions specifically over the marriage and exchange proposal with the Marquis Mattei, a Roman nobleman who was also on his way to the Spanish Low Countries. The only people to whom Mazarin did not open himself were the members of his council. In a long instruction of November 22 or 23, prepared for the plenipotentiaries at Münster, the council repeated the principle that France wished to retain its conquests and contemplated a number of options for achieving its goals: a comprehensive peace, truces, or a combination of the two. It merely touched on the marriage and exchange proposals as an afterthought. A few days later, a former Spanish soldier who had taken service with the French opened the gate and let his original employers back into Mardick, but no forewarnings about the fickleness of fate could unsettle the great cardinal.[25]

The enemies played with what weapons they had. When the new Queen of Poland reached Brussels, the Marquis de Castel Rodrigo, Governor of the Spanish Low Countries, showered praises on Cardinal Mazarin and intimated loudly within the hearing of the Dutch that the Spanish wanted to make him arbiter of the peace. Trauttmansdorff in Westphalia followed exactly the same policy. Fully intending, while fervently disclaiming, any desire to create division among his enemies, he began through the mediators by offering the French Pinerolo, the Three Bishoprics of Metz, Toul, and Verdun in full sovereigny, and the stronghold of Moyenvic, while the French in return intimated that they were also expecting Alsace and Breisach. Mazarin in Paris was amused by the flatteries of Castel Rodrigo, but the French plenipotentiares in Münster took those of Trauttmansdorff very seriously. They were so worried about arousing the suspicion of the Swedes that they insisted on the presence of Rosenhane, the Swedish resident in Münster, in their negotiations with Contarini. Then Trauttmansdorff went to Osnabrück to sound out the Swedes, who furthered his goals by excluding La Barde, the new French resident in Osnabrück, from their confidential discussions. When Oxenstierna made a trip to Münster late in December in order to concert with the French a reply to the Imperial offers, this issue of participation in each other's negotiations was still contentious between them. Even more contentious, however, was the issue of the Swedish satisfactions. Oxenstierna confided for the first time that the Swedes intended to include the Archbishopric of Bremen and the Bishoprics of Verden, Halbersadt, Osnabrück, and Minden in their demands. The French, with D'Avaux taking the lead, retorted that they could not consent to any usurpation of Church lands. Oxenstierna held out for Bremen and Verden while giving the impression that he was backing down on the rest. The French resorted to the Pontius Pilate position, namely that the Swedes were free to make this demand without French support. Once again the specter of religion raised its ugly head.[26]

Still, if Philip IV and Ferdinand III had indeed reconciled themselves to the hegemony of France, Mazarin was about to fulfill his destiny. What could the Dutch or the Swedes, not to speak of the English in the midst of their civil war, have done about it? It was not that simple, however, because the council of Spain, after having bowed to the inevitable, began to reconsider its options. Without even knowing about the recovery of Mardick, the council decided to think again about its marriage and exchange offer, and it concluded that the reintegration of Catalonia and Portugal, and the triumph of the Catholic faith, were not worth the nightmare of a universal French monarchy. The council had come ever so close to an ideological revolution, but it had returned to the same maxim that had inspired Cardinal Richelieu. The independence of the state was the fount from which all blessings flowed. Thus on December 30 Philip IV rescinded the instructions to offer the Infanta and the remaining Low Countries to France and placed his hopes, as precarious as they were, on an ingenious response to Mazarin's invitations. It was craftily worded and purely tactical. Under the pretext of concern for the Turkish menace, Philip would offer Anne of Austria and her council, *i.e.,*

Mazarin, the mediation, but with the qualification that the decision be "proper." In other words, if the French accepted the offer, they would arouse suspicions that they had come to a private agreement with the Spanish; if the French rejected it, it would look as if they did not even want peace on their own terms. Not that the Spanish expected that such an open trap would be of much more than propaganda value. They never imagined that Cardinal Mazarin was walking right into it.[27]

4

The French Show Their Hand

At the beginning of 1646, Cardinal Mazarin was faced with the delightful prospect of reaping the benefits of the separation of the Emperor from the Spanish, while threatening a new campaign which would consummate the French conquest of the Spanish Low Countries and the Franco-Swedish conquest of the Holy Roman Empire. He had a few minor problems. In his own council, and in public, the ever-troublesome Prince de Condé was speaking too enthusiastically about truces. And then there was the ironic law of early modern statecraft. The more successful France was in the Low Countries, the more this threw the Dutch into the arms of Spain. The more successful France was in the Empire, the better for the Swedes and the Protestants. Mazarin was aware of these problems, but, after all he had been through, he did not consider it beyond his capacities to continue to manipulate his council, gain most of the Spanish Low Countries for France, and still keep his allies in line.[1]

The French plenipotentiaries at Münster began to reap his harvest for him. On January 7, 1646, accompanied by the Swedish resident Rosenhane and the Hessian envoys, they went to Contarini's residence to inform him of their response to the Imperialists. They insisted on doing so verbally, with Contarini taking notes. After a bit of posturing on behalf of their allies, the French got down to business. In keeping with their instructions, they demanded Upper and Lower Alsace, including the Sundgau, the stronghold of Breisach and its surrounding Breisgau, the forest towns, and the stronghold of Philippsburg. The French expressed a willingness, however, to accept these territories as fiefs of the Empire *if* this cession would assure France a seat in the Reichstag. Significantly, the French made no mention of the Swedish demands, while expressing their full support for those of the Landgravin of Hesse-Cassel. Then, minus their Protestant allies but in the company of Contarini, the French moved to the residence of the nuncio, where Contarini read his notes to his colleague. Both Contarini and Chigi were bemused by the fact that the French, notwithstanding their denials of territorial ambitions, seemed to be demanding so much. They were confirmed in their growing suspicions that Mazarin did not want peace.[2]

On the same day the Swedes delivered their own response in Osnabrück, with the notable difference that they did not take the French resident La Barde along with them, and they delivered it directly to Trauttmansdorff at his residence. They too made their response verbally, and they too, after the *pro forma* declarations in favor of their allies, seemed to be interested in gorging themselves. In keeping with their instructions, they demanded all of Silesia and Pomerania, the ports of Wismar and Warnemünde, the Archbishopric of Bremen, and the Bishopric of Verden, all as fiefs of the Holy Roman Empire, with the princes displaced by these acquisitions to be compensated with the Bishoprics of Osnabrück, Minden, and other ecclesiastical territories. They also complained bitterly that the Imperialists had ignored the Swedish demand for payment of their soldiers.[3]

In theory these two responses were coordinated, but the cracks in the alliance were widening. The French were particularly suspicious that the Swedes had excluded La Barde from their meeting with Trauttmansdorff. Adding to the French discomfort was the Swedish insistence on including Osnabrück, Minden, and other ecclesiastical lands as potential compensation for the displaced German princes. The French jumped on it as "a new cause to complain about their way of dealing with us." When Chanut, the French ambassador in Stockholm, brought up the matter of La Barde's exclusion, Chancellor Oxenstierna not only threw it in his face that Rosenhane was being excluded from the meetings with the nuncio but also launched into a flippant defense of the Swedish ecclesiastical demands. Bremen and Minden, Oxenstierna reminded him, hadn't been Catholic for years. And weren't the French claiming areas inhabited by Protestants? Since everyone agreed that the war had not been for religion, each crown could simply promise to maintain its free exercise. The Swedes had obviously taken a page from the French demands and saw no reason to moderate their own.[4]

If contending with the Spanish, the Imperialists, the Dutch, and the Swedes were not enough, Cardinal Mazarin was also preparing to take on the Holy See. Rome was still in many ways the center of his world, and there the new Pope, Innocent X, was not displaying the proper humility. He seemed to be harboring French exiles at his court, sympathizing with the Spanish in Münster, and most recently had begun prosecuting Cardinals Francesco and Antonio Barberini, nephews of Urban VIII. Not that Mazarin had any particular love for the Barberinis at that time. Although they had been his patrons in his youth, they had been instrumental in the election of Innocent, and Mazarin had angrily deprived them of French favor. But now the situation had changed, and the persecution of his former patrons set a bad example for the rest of Italy. Thus on hearing that Cardinal Antonio had fled from Rome, Mazarin immediately took the matter personally. On January 11 Cardinal Antonio appeared in Paris to a warm welcome.[5]

The council of Spain was still desperate for peace, and the arrival of Peñaranda's courier in Madrid with the account of his first encounter with Trauttmansdorff made it even more so. In a meeting on January 8, only the knowledge of Mazarin's conciliatory comments to Roncalli gave the Count de Monterrey some glimmer of hope. He insisted that the only means to achieve peace was to separate the Swedes and Dutch from the French, but he also advised some concessions to the French, such as a truce which would permit them to hold on to Roussillon as long as they abandoned Catalonia. He was also prepared to let them keep most of what they had conquered in the Low Countries plus Pinerolo in Italy. The *sine qua non* was still the exclusion of Portugal, although it was a mark of Monterrey's panic that he went so far as to envision setting up John de Braganza as a vassal outside of Spain. The Marquis de Santa Cruz concurred and renewed his support for the appeal to Anne of Austria. One daydreamer, the Count de Chinchón, fantasized that the peace would be followed by a revolution in France, while one diehard, the Count de Castrillo, maintained that the Spanish monarchy still had another year of fight left in it. Philip IV went with the peacemakers. Indeed, the following week he sent extremely flexible orders to Peñaranda, permitting him, step by step, to make extensive concessions and even to surpass his orders if it seemed as if the Emperor was about to make a separate peace.[6]

The French plenipotentiaries in Münster were more conscious of France's diplomatic predicament than was Mazarin himself, but instead of scoffing at the rumors that the Spanish were about to designate Mazarin as an arbiter, D'Avaux capitalized on them in order to play on Mazarin's vanity. "The enemies themselves feel your strength!" D'Avaux wrote to Mazarin. "It's as if the Spanish intended to get along with Your Eminence from now on!" D'Avaux also advocated making concessions in the Empire and obviously felt that the moment had come for a grand reconciliation with the Spanish, with the Emperor, and, last but not least, with the German Catholics. Servien was not quite so sanguine. He was still fearful of alienating the Swedes and wrote to Lionne suggesting that the best way to appease them was to bypass the mediators and deal directly with the Imperialists. But Servien too was conscious of the fact that the French demands had made an extremely bad impression on the German princes, and he suggested that France offer to reimburse the displaced archdukes of the house of Austria and accept the Three Bishoprics of Metz, Toul, and Verdun only as fiefs of the Empire. Longueville, in his letter to Mazarin, underscored his colleagues' concerns, so that on this occasion, the three French plenipotentiaries were unanimous in urging Mazarin to trim his sails.[7]

Meanwhile, on January 11, the Dutch had finally arrived in Münster. Hardly affecting modesty, they placed their coat of arms, complete with a royal crown, over their door and awaited their visitors. Their French allies were the first to welcome them on January 13, but allies as they may have been, they addressed the Dutch as "Gentlemen" rather than "Excellencies." The Dutch seemed submissive enough, but there was something formal and hypocritical about the mutual protestations of friendship and support. When, on the next day, the Spanish visited the Dutch, the atmosphere was entirely different. The Spanish did give the Dutch plenipotentiaries the title of "Excellencies," and enemies though they had been, they acted like long-lost friends.[8]

The Spanish also played their cards with the mediators, approaching them on January 15 and expressing the desire to come to terms with the French as well. When, however, the mediators passed on the message, the French refused to budge from their earlier demands for all of their conquests. The mediators were disheartened, but the Spanish were not. They hinted that they would make some concessions and continued to sing the praises of Cardinal Mazarin, owning as to how eager they were to negotiate with him directly and how impossible it would be to conclude a peace without his direct participation. The flattery policy was in full swing, and Contarini commended it to his colleague in France.[9]

There was no need for further flattery. The exchange proposal was now firmly entrenched as the centerpiece of Mazarin's diplomatic policy. On January 19, 1646, he dictated two long *mémoires* to Lionne for the edification of Longueville, D'Avaux, and Servien on why France should exchange Catalonia and perhaps even Roussillon for the Spanish Low Countries. The reasons were as follows. By annexing the Spanish Low Countries, France would make the city of Paris the true center of France and impregnable from foreign attack. This acquisition would also discourage domestic revolt and make France dominant in Europe. The Dutch would be intimidated and the advantages to the Catholic religion would be immeasurable. These reasons were, of course, obvious, and that was precisely the problem. If the purpose of the agonizing war had been to prevent the Hapsburgs from establishing their sway over Europe, why would anyone now be willing to permit the Bourbons to establish theirs? Mazarin, incredibly, believed that the Dutch "would find their interests in it." In his mind a people who had struggled for over half a century to achieve their independence from Catholic Spain would now acquiesce tamely to having a Catholic France as their immediate neighbor. Most of all he believed that the ailing Frederick Henry should jump at the opportunity of improving his family's position in the republic with French support. Mazarin also believed that it was in the interest of the Spanish monarchy to rid itself of the Spanish Low Countries. "This could be the real security for the duration of the peace, which we would find in our own forces," he paused to summarize. He may well have been right, but if the exchange was so advantageous to France, wouldn't the Spanish oppose it for that very reason? His own law of opposites guaranteed that they would, but, in a third *mémoire,* he found a solution to their perversity. All his plenipotentiaries had to do was to get the Spanish to come up with the idea by themselves. He was thus creating a world in which the desperate Spanish and dull-witted Dutch would discard their own passions to suit his fancy. And he knew perfectly well that he was going beyond the aspirations of his predecessor, Mazarin adding in a brief note to his plenipotentiaries that "if it should come to it, I will sustain the king's service with more firmness and courage than the cardinal-duke ever did!" Nor had the world of

Mazarin's imagination become a better place. To D'Avaux's appeal for reconciliation between France and Spain, Mazarin snapped back that "there can never be a true and cordial friendship between the French and the Spanish!"[10]

For the same reason that Mazarin favored the marriage and exchange, Peñaranda opposed it. He too thought it would bring about French domination of Europe, but he was not averse to exploiting the proposal if the French were foolish enough to make it. Thus he concentrated his efforts on his budding relationship with the Dutch, who, on Wednesday, January 24, came to visit the Spanish for the purpose of exchanging their powers. As usual, each side had its objections, but they agreed easily on the amendments. Not only that, but the two sides decided to deal with each other directly and set the following Saturday, January 27, to begin the discussions. On that day Peñaranda proposed negotiating a truce similar to the one of 1609, and on the following day the Spanish transmitted the proposal in writing and the two delegations drank to each other's health. But during these same critical days, when Contarini dropped in on Longueville to congratulate him on the birth of a son and on another occasion when D'Avaux was also present, Contarini got the distinct impression that the French were contemplating a marriage and exchange proposal. The French plenipotentiaries reported to Mazarin as if they were dismissing Contarini's overtures, but he kept insisting in his own correspondence that it was the French who were dropping the hints. He passed them on to Peñaranda, who was only too happy to reply that "if the marriage and the dowries were to be a way of making peace, it was appropriate that the proposition be made directly so that it can be reported to our king." In other words, if the French wanted to commit suicide, he was at their disposal.[11]

The French plenipotentiaries still saw their most important function as getting the Swedes to moderate their demands. On February 12, D'Avaux went to Osnabrück and, in company with La Barde, began to confer with Oxenstierna and Salvius. The first meeting was amiable enough, but the next day the discussion became heated. The Swedes refused to make any concessions, and D'Avaux became convinced that Oxenstierna, in particular, wished to use the Protestant *gravamina* as a means of continuing the war. One more day of discussion, however, and the Swedes softened, even hinting that they would eventually back down on their demands for the Catholic bishoprics, so that after six days D'Avaux returned from Osnabrück under the illusion that he had made some progress. Servien and Longueville were equally optimistic. They had great hopes that with some minor French concessions in the Empire, possibly even giving up on Philippsburg, this would bring the Swedes into line. What was beginning to worry Servien and Longueville, however, was the marriage and exchange proposal, even though they had themselves played along with it to some extent. Thus they responded to Mazarin's enthusiasm for the proposal by reiterating its dangers, and they especially warned him against making it to the Prince of Orange. "We find it hard to believe that he could favor this design," they wrote to Mazarin with uncharacteristic bluntness.[12]

At the same time that Longueville and Servien were imploring him not to do so, Mazarin was deciding to execute his original plan of sending the Count d'Estrades to Frederick Henry. The count, under the usual cover of planning for the campaign, would inform the prince that the Spanish were about to propose the exchange, and once again Mazarin anticipated how the Dutch should react. He was now certain that if he offered Antwerp not just to the Prince of Orange, but also to the republic, this would overcome all hesitations. And just as he had ordered his plenipotentiaries at Münster to arrange things so that the Spanish would think that they had come up with the marriage and exchange proposal by themselves, so did he order D'Estrades to arrange it so that the idea of Antwerp would pop into the head of the Prince of Orange. What seemed to make Mazarin particularly impatient to execute his plan was the civil war in England. The English would never permit the French to acquire the Low Countries under normal circumstances, so the present predicament of the English monarchy provided a window of opportunity that might never again be open. He dictated a long *mémoire* for the plenipotentiaries explaining his reasoning. He did not have the slightest idea what the Spanish had concocted.[13]

Armed with their option of offering the mediation to Anne of Austria, Peñaranda, Saavedra, and Brun sprung their trap. They presented it verbally to the mediators on February 19, and the mediators enthusiastically transmitted it in like fashion to the French the next day. The French plenipotentiaries, who might have treated it as a joke, took it seriously. They retired into a room, debated among themselves about whether the offer was qualified, and concluded that it was worth exploiting. Longueville emerged from the room saying how gratified he and his colleagues were by it, and when asked by the mediators to send a courier to France, the French agreed to do so. The next morning they dutifully informed their Dutch allies, who, as might have been expected, were less than ecstatic. They had been waiting calmly for permission to proceed with their own negotiation while the King of Spain amended his power. Now they suddenly found themselves outmaneuvered, and they rushed to send two of their number, Pauw and Knuyt, to The Hague to spread the alarm. The French, however, were not particularly disturbed by this averse reaction. In spite of it, they persisted in interpreting the offer as an indication that the Spanish had given up their effort to divide France from its allies. D'Avaux took the occasion to reiterate to Mazarin that "our firmness has been very useful up to now, but if Her Majesty is just as rigorous, the King of Spain will turn all of Europe against France." Longueville exulted in the "humble and public submission of the King of Spain." Servien, as usual, was the most skeptical, but even he merely suggested that the French should exploit the offer in order to restate their original demands.[14]

Mazarin's overriding purpose was still to panic the Spanish, preferably before the beginning of the campaign, into themselves proposing the exchange, and on February 28 he threw 3 million *livres* more into replacements and new levies. It was worth the money, he was certain, whether or not the campaign would become necessary. If it did become necessary, he was all ready for it. The strength of the armies would rise to some 90,000 men, on paper at least. The Duke d'Orléans would lead one in Flanders and the Duke d'Enghien another, but what these armies would actually do depended on the decision of the generals on the spot as well as on whether the Prince of Orange would come out and press the Spanish from the other side. In Italy it would be up to Prince Thomas to decide and, in Spain, up to the Count d'Harcourt. Turenne was at court at the time, and to please the Swedes, it was decided that his Weimarian army should move out from Alsace and effect a junction with them in the Upper Palatinate for action against the Emperor and the Bavarians.[15]

Mazarin was also prepared to listen to his plenipotentiaries' suggestions for concessions in negotiations with the Emperor. Thus on March 3 he met privately with the queen, the Duke d'Orléans, the Prince de Condé, and Brienne and persuaded them (it was not difficult) to permit the plenipotentiaries to give in on their demands for Philippsburg as well as to offer compensation to the archdukes for their interests in Alsace. This was well worth it, he believed, if it would produce peace in the Empire and panic the Spanish into making peace "at any price." To the warnings of his plenipotentiaries that they should make sure of the Spanish before approaching the Dutch on the exchange, Mazarin replied that it was too late. He knew better than they what to do, and he had already sent D'Estrades to approach the Prince of Orange.[16]

Everything, therefore, was proceeding the way that Mazarin imagined it should, when later on the same day, the courier from the plenipotentiaries galloped into Paris with the Spanish offer of mediation to Anne of Austria. It threw Mazarin into a rage. How could the plenipotentiaries have taken it seriously? Didn't they realize the Spanish were desperate? Wasn't it obvious that since they had made the offer so ostentatiously, they were only making it for public consumption? The only thing he could do to repair the stupidity of the plenipotentiaries was to have the queen summon the Duke d'Orléans and the Prince de Condé and to mobilize the entire council in rejecting the offer. Mazarin himself composed the queen's response, putting his own maxims into her mouth. "The obligations of a mother and those of regent," he had her say, "do not permit me to consider the satisfaction of a brother." The duke and the prince dutifully contributed their own chastisements. But then, had not Mazarin himself invited the overtures? Forgetting his own broad hints that the Spanish should approach him, he began to display at this juncture another facet of his personality, his capacity to delude himself. He made a special point, in personally writing to Longueville, of claiming that it was Castel Rodrigo who had initiated the overtures and that "if I received them favorably, there was more appearance than there is today that they were sincere." It was a facet of his personality that was to emerge ever more prominently as the negotiations continued.[17]

The rumors were already swirling around The Hague of a secret understanding between France and Spain just as the States of Holland, followed by the States General, were debating whether they should permit the Dutch plenipotentiaries at Münster to proceed with their negotiations with the Spanish while waiting for the arrival of the amended powers from the King of Spain. The rumors were enough to hasten the deliberations, and on February 25 the States General decided to send the proposal to the individual provinces for their approval or disapproval within fifteen days. It was on that very same day that the Count d'Estrades entered into town, ostensibly to plan the campaign. The following day he went to see Frederick Henry and sought his advice on the exchange proposal, presenting all the wondrous reasons why he and the entire republic should embrace it with alacrity. We cannot enter into the Prince of Orange's mind at this moment, but coming when it did, we can assume that it must have confirmed all the rumors of a Franco-Spanish understanding that he had been hearing. What, therefore, could he do but make the best of it? Survivor that he was, he informed D'Estrades that he supported the exchange enthusiastically, but his words were belied by his deeds. He absolutely refused to write to the Duke de Longueville in support of the exchange, and on the contrary, he asked to be kept entirely out of the affair until such time as it was arranged. Even so, the conferences between D'Estrades and Frederick Henry aroused even more suspicions, and accurate ones at that. One more day, and Pauw and Knuyt arrived in The Hague with the news about the Spanish offer of mediation to the queen. D'Estrades had barely written his first report to Mazarin, when the Prince of Orange advised him to get out of town. D'Estrades then rushed to write a second.[18]

Mazarin had just finished upbraiding his plenipotentiaries when the first report from D'Estrades arrived. Frederick Henry's empty protestations changed Mazarin's mood miraculously. "I was not fooling myself," he exulted to the plenipotentiaries, "when I judged that this prince would wish the exchange of Catalonia for the Low Countries with at least as much passion as I!" Just as he was writing this, he received the second report. Even it did not worry him. Indeed, it led him to wonder whether anyone who could ever have expressed any reservations about the proposal did not have ulterior motives. He was particularly suspicious about Longueville, Lionne inquiring of Servien "if there were not in this some maxims of the great nobles of France who would not like to see the king so powerful." Contradiction being synonymous with treason, Lionne was even fearful that Servien might fall prey to similar suspicions and begged him "in your own interest and for the good of the state to push firmly for the exchange!" A few days later, still cultivating the impression that D'Estrades's mission to The Hague had been a smashing success, Mazarin ordered the plenipotentiaries to make an approach on the exchange directly to Contarini.[19]

The rumors of a Franco-Spanish understanding, the mysterious mission of D'Estrades, and the arrival of Pauw and Knuyt with news of the mediation proposal combined to light a fire in the Dutch Republic. On February 28, Frederick Henry went before both the States of Holland and the States General to inform them that he had heard from France that a marriage between Louis XIV and the Infanta had been decided upon and that the exchange of Catalonia for the Spanish Low Countries would be executed within three weeks. He suggested that, under the circumstances, the republic had better insist on the partition called for in their treaty of 1635. All hell broke loose. The crowds in the streets of the Dutch republic almost changed sides overnight. By March 5 D'Estrades was writing to Mazarin that "the sentiments of the Prince of Orange are a far cry from what they were!" By March 9 Brasset was writing to the French plenipotentiaries that "the Spanish could not have wished for anything more advantageous to arouse the suspicion of these people."[20]

The only thing Mazarin still had going for him was the desperation of the Emperor. The mood of his council had now shifted from one of pure self-righteousness to one of self-righteousness surrendering to necessity, and during the month of February the council had devoted three interminable *Gutacten* to pondering the *gravamina* of the Protestants and the satisfaction of the crowns. The house of Austria, it insisted, had done its best to maintain the Imperial constitution and to protect the Catholic religion only to be thwarted by Sweden and France. Now all it could do for the faith was to try to salvage the Ecclesiastical Reservation. Even here, however, the council was prepared to make concessions, extending it from its base date of 1552 to November 12, 1627, if not further. In the religious sphere, therefore, the Emperor was reduced to trying to stop the further progress of the Protestant religion. But the most critical issue was the satisfaction of the crowns. The council was indignant, but it candidly admitted that it had to avoid greater ills, cynically considering that since such areas as Pomerania were irretrievably Protestant, it did not matter whether they were held by the Swedes or by some other Protestant prince. Thus the council advised the Emperor that he could abandon to the Swedes part or all of Pomerania, even Wismar, Poel, Walsich, and Warnemünde, likewise the Archbishopric of Bremen, and the Bishoprics of Verden and Minden, and accept the Swedes as Imperial princes. If this created tension between the dispossessed Protestant princes, like the Elector of Brandenburg, and the

Swedes, so much the better. In short, about the only Swedish demand that the council totally rejected was for Silesia. The council was equally bountiful to the French, conceding, step by step, one part of Alsace after the other, then the Sundgau, possibly as fiefs of the Empire, merely balking at seating the King of France in the Reichstag. In apparent ignorance of the Emperor's previous instruction to Trauttmansdorff, the council refused to surrender Breisach, or, for that matter, anything on the right bank of the Rhine, leaving the final decision on Breisach to the Emperor. For his part, Ferdinand III added a section in his own hand insisting that the archdukes of his house be reimbursed for any of the territories that they ceded in Alsace, and a few days later he approved the surrender of Breisach. Thus, for all of Trauttmansdorff's maneuvering, the council was no longer even entertaining any hope of dividing its enemies. It was aiming at peace.[21]

The French plenipotentiaries were keeping a watchful eye on the affairs of the Empire, but their principal concern suddenly was with the reproaches of Cardinal Mazarin on their handling of the Spanish offer, to which each responded in his characteristic manner. D'Avaux admiringly congratulated Mazarin for having hit upon "the best means to diffuse the captious offer of the Spanish" and enthusiastically deferred to his superior genius. Servien changed the subject, while doing his best to pledge his allegiance. "Is it possible," he wrote to Lionne, "that it can be judged by any of my writings that I have not approved the party of the exchange?" But even he had the gumption to pipe up, "in truth, as to the means of achieving it, I have been of a different sentiment from His Eminence." The proud Duke de Longueville, however, came right out and said it. "If the rumors of marriage and exchange had not happened at the same time as Pauw and Knuyt arrived in Holland," he threw in Mazarin's face, "the offer of the Spanish would not have created such a stir."[22]

The Spanish gleefully fanned the flames. One of their pamphlets, *The Intrigues of Spain hidden under the Proposition to give the Infanta in marriage to the King of France,* in the guise of a warning against the Spanish, carried all the implications of a threat. It was published first in French and then republished in Dutch and German. Three other pamphlets— *The Münster Chatterbox, Answer to the Münster Chatterbox,* and *The French Chatterbox*—made the point stridently and unequivocally that it was no longer the Spanish but the French who posed the greatest threat to the Dutch Republic. The Prince of Orange did not need much convincing.

He was now hearing that the mediators had proposed the marriage and exchange to the Spanish. He wrote to D'Estrades, "this is different from what you have given me to believe, namely that you were merely sounding out my opinion. Don't think that I am so easy to fool. Please treat your friends better next time."[23]

Something had gone terribly wrong, but the only way in which Mazarin could explain it to himself was to continue to take liberties with his own memory. He thus began to cultivate a new thesis, namely that all of the commotion in the Dutch Republic was not his fault, it was not even the fault of his plenipotentiaries, but it had been due to a Spanish trick. "Never has artifice been better conducted," he wrote to the plenipotentiaries on March 16, adding, incredibly, that "I thank God for having given me the strength never to have wanted to listen [to any proposals] here." Not that he was giving up on the exchange. The next day he fantasized in a letter to Brasset that the Spanish might still become desperate enough to offer it. And having found it so easy to delude himself, he found it even less difficult to delude others, for three days later he called in the nuncio and Nani, the Venetian ambassador, to complain to them about the duplicity of the Spanish. What had they done? Well, said Mazarin, at the same time that they were offering to put the mediation in the hands of Anne of Austria, they were trying to intimidate the Dutch into making a separate peace with the threat of offering the Infanta and *all* of the Low Countries to Louis XIV. The Spanish, added Mazarin with mounting outrage, had even claimed that D'Estrades's last trip to The Hague had been for the purpose of bribing the Prince of Orange into accepting the plan. Who could imagine such a thing? The nuncio and the ambassador took it all in good stride, but then, they were not Dutchmen.[24]

Having succeeded brilliantly in undermining their enemy, the Spanish in Münster went to the mediators on March 21 and proceeded to make a more serious offer in keeping with their instructions. They now offered the French the four strongholds of Landrecies and Bapaume in Hainault, Hesdin, and Damvilliers in Artois. The French could keep Pinerolo if the Emperor approved, but everything else had to be to be returned. The Emperor, the archdukes of the house of Austria, the states of the Empire and the Duke of Lorraine were to be included in the treaty, and both sides were not to aid each other's rebels. The mediators immediately went to see the French, who acted as if they took the proposals with a grain of salt, sarcastically suggesting that if the Spanish wanted any conquered territories restored, they should be ready to restore Navarre. But the French plenipotentiaries were becoming increasingly divided among themselves. D'Avaux claimed to agree with Mazarin that the French needed to hold fast, but with this important qualification: "until they offer us advantageous conditions whose refusal could break the treaty and make France look bad." Servien insisted to Lionne without qualification: "If we hold fast and stay united at the court and here, we can hope for whatever we may desire." As to Longueville, he was getting increasingly more suspicious that Mazarin was negotiating behind his back and that Servien had secret orders to stall the peace. If the fiasco in The Hague was not enough, the divisions were widening among the French and within the French court, and the public was fully aware of them.[25]

The Imperialists, however, were still marching in lockstep with Mazarin's master plan. Thus, after some *pro forma* consultations with the representatives of the Imperial princes and states gathered at Osnabrück and Münster, they turned their attentions to wooing the French. Toward the end of March, Volmar composed a memorandum for the mediators in keeping with the Emperor's instructions and adding to it his own profound knowledge of the constitution of Alsace. They attempted most skillfully to bribe the French with the house of Austria's rights to the portion of Alsace in which these rights were most limited, *i.e.*, the lower one, particularly if the French would get the Swedes to moderate their demands. They insisted, as the Emperor had required, that the dispossessed archdukes of the house of Austria be recompensed. The memorandum pushed the wooing of the French to a considerable extreme. It contained an incredibly chimerical suggestion, namely that if the Swedes and the Protestants did not moderate their terms, the French should promise to join with the Emperor in compelling them. It also offered, with French support, to restore the Lower Palatinate to the family of Frederick V while keeping the Upper Palatinate and the electoral title in the hands of the Duke of Bavaria. The mediators, who received this memorandum on March 28, found it hopeful, likely to be extended, and possibly as opening the way to forcing the Spanish into making peace as well. They communicated it verbally to the French on April 2, who treated it with disdain, but the apparent flexibility of the Imperialists was still the biggest chink in the Spanish armor.[26]

It did not take much of a struggle for Mazarin to play tricks with his own conscience, but it took some. He wrote the plenipotentiaries on March 31 that he had no time to answer the Spanish broadsheets; yet two days later he and Lionne manufactured a six-folio letter from a fictitious Venetian gentleman in Münster to an equally fabricated friend in Turin, insisting that even though the marriage and exchange had created quite a stir in the Dutch Republic, the French had successfully exposed it. Any Dutch merchant knew better, but the imaginary Venetian had done the trick for Cardinal Mazarin. He put the marriage and exchange temporarily out of mind and concentrated for the immediate future on holding firmly to his present demands. But the principal result of this incident completely eluded him. He could not come to grips with the fact that he had made his ambitions perfectly clear to the Dutch. The negotiations at Westphalia now turned from the delightful prospect of France reaping all the benefits from the separation of the Emperor from the Spanish into a neck-and-neck race between the separation of the Emperor from the Spanish and the separation of the Dutch from the French. It was still a race, but by refusing to admit to himself that he was in one, Mazarin was putting himself in the most serious danger of losing it.[27]

5

The Emperor Gives Way

Mazarin considered the letter from Frederick Henry, which accused the French of having lied to him, as "most civil." When, moreover, Mazarin succeeded in signing a treaty with the Dutch for the upcoming campaign, he was even more elated. The Dutch were once more back in their place, and he felt up to one more effort to pound his thesis of the war into the head of the impenetrable D'Avaux. Mazarin insisted,

> You must accept it as an article of faith, that since the Spanish naturally hate us, and since this hatred has just been augmented by the losses and affronts that we have made them suffer, we have got to make them as incapable as possible to harm us, since they will never lose the urge or the occasion to do so.

Even by his logic, however, the quickest way to incapacitate the Spanish was to go back to the original plan and make peace with the Emperor.[1]

D'Avaux, on the other hand, saw the prospect of peace with the Emperor as another opportunity for himself to guide the malevolent Mazarin toward reconciliation, if not with the Spanish, at least with the Germans, thus saving the Catholic religion in the Empire and returning Christendom to the business of Father Joseph. On April 11 Count von Trauttmansdoff remarked to D'Avaux that "Cardinal Mazarin is treating us with more rigor than Cardinal Richelieu, but I don't know whether this will not turn against France itself." It was both an assessment and a prediction, and D'Avaux, who never lost an opportunity to present his own thoughts through the words of another, passed it on to his superior. Indeed, at this point, D'Avaux began to experience his own hallucinations, even more uplifting than the exchange of Catalonia for the Spanish Low Countries. He began thinking that France could solve the knotty problem of what to do with the Duke of Lorraine by giving him Alsace in compensation for his original duchy. D'Avaux did not yet dare make that proposal out loud, but he was prepared, in other words, to sacrifice Alsace and all the other French conquests in the Empire in the renewed quest for Father Joseph's utopia.[2]

Since his previous offer had been met with disdain, Trauttmansdorff had Volmar prepare another writing which was considerably more historic. The Imperialists now offered to the King of France both Upper and Lower Alsace, plus the Sundgau, along with the title of Landgrave and all rights (whatever these may have been) formerly held by the house of Austria over these lands. In recompense they asked for the return of the forest towns to the Archdukes of Innsbruck, and specified the hefty sum of 5 million *Reichsthaler* in compensation for their rights in Alsace. The King of France was to hold Alsace as a fief of the Empire. They reiterated their request that the French assist them in moderating the demands of the Swedes and the Protestant *gravamina,* but on Breisach they claimed they had to wait for further orders, appealing for a suspension of arms in the Empire until they arrived. The compromise with regard to the Palatinate remained unchanged. The French got wind of the breakthrough. On April 14 Servien wrote for himself and his colleagues: "It seems that they want to negotiate with us in earnest for the satisfaction of the king in the Empire." On that very same day Nassau and Volmar presented the Imperial offers to the mediators, who immediately transmitted them to the French. The French still held on to their full demands and would not even receive the proposal until the Imperialists deleted any suggestion of collaboration against the Swedes and Protestants. Still, the French could not entirely hide their exultation, and they promised to press the Swedes for the suspension of arms. D'Avaux was ecstatic. Could all of his dreams be coming through? "The house of Austria in Germany," he entreated Mazarin, "does not hate us in the same way as the Spanish. The Germans are good and manageable. Their friendship can be expected if the peace is concluded with some satisfaction for them." On April 20 Servien rushed up to Osnabrück to speak to the Swedes about the suspension—fruitlessly, as it turned out.[3]

Never had the prospects looked brighter, either for peace or for war, and Mazarin, who followed the old Roman maxim, continued to prepare for the latter. Once more, the centerpiece of the campaign would be the advance into Flanders with the Dukes d'Orléans and d'Enghien acting in concert with Frederick Henry. The French armies would attack Courtrai and Oudenarde the Dutch Dendermonde, and then the allied armies would unite for the siege of Ghent, which was destined for France, followed by Antwerp, which would go to the Prince of Orange. This plan was so important that Mazarin sent one of his agents, Ronette, to coordinate it with Frederick Henry. Later, toward the end of April, Prince Thomas of Savoy appeared at court to make plans for the campaign in Italy. There, Plessis Praslin would threaten Milan, while the prince would concentrate on the Spanish presidios in Tuscany, beginning with San Stefano. This was not all, however, for the ambitious Thomas also began filling Mazarin's head with prospects of fomenting a rebellion in Naples, which, the prince assured, was eager to welcome him, Prince Thomas, as its new ruler. In Catalonia, Harcourt was intending to retake Lérida, lost to the Spanish in 1644. Mazarin had some doubts about this enterprise, but he trusted in Harcourt's assurances that he could starve the stronghold into surrender. The prospects in Germany were equally rosy. Turenne would either set out from his winter quarters in Alsace for his junction with the Swedes, or, in case the Emperor caved in, bring the Weimarian army north for an attack on the Duchy of Luxembourg. The campaign in Flanders was so central, however, that to inspire the troops, as well as to demonstrate the capacity of the court of France to leave its own capital without causing a revolution, Mazarin also announced that the court itself would advance into Picardy.[4]

It was all very well and good, except that one of the principal participants in this scenario was no longer playing. In a series of conferences at The Hague between Mazarin's agent Ronette and Frederick Henry during the latter part of April, Ronette proposed to the prince the siege of Ghent. Frederick Henry countered that it was too difficult and of interest only to the French. He proposed the siege of Antwerp instead, and this only if the States General would provide funds for the campaign. The most he would guarantee was to assemble a corps of 6,000 men in the vicinity of Hulst. The diffidence and intractability of the prince exudes from Ronette's report. And yet neither he, nor Brasset, nor La Thuillerie were prepared to alarm Mazarin with the extent to which he had disaffected the Dutch. As La Thuillerie hemmed and hawed to Mazarin on April 24: "These gentlemen are calming down a little on the rumors of the marriage of the king with the Infanta of Spain, but there is still some recollection of it in the minds of the most jealous."[5]

Still, all this hurly-burly combined with the Imperial concessions was enough to panic Peñaranda. He rushed to obtain the advice of Castel Rodrigo about the unveiling of their final concessions, and the two men decided to add to their previous offer by offering to France the entire counties of Roussillon and Artois. On April 20, Peñaranda and his new colleague, Joseph Bergaigne, the newly nominated Archbishop of Cambrai, went to the mediators with this offer, camouflaging it with the request that the mediators present it as if it were their own hypothetical suggestion. The mediators immediately went to see Longueville and D'Avaux, who rejected the hypothetical proposal out of hand. Peñaranda complained to Chigi that if he had known when he accepted his embassy that he would be giving away Roussillon, he would have preferred to die, but three days later he, the Archbishop, and Brun returned to the mediators and made the proposals officially. For their part, Longueville and D'Avaux stuck to their original demands, except that they countered with offers of truces in Catalonia and Portugal, and threatened, moreover, that if the campaign proved successful their demands would increase. The mediators were becoming more and more exasperated with the French. Between the concessions of the Emperor and those of the Spanish, Contarini reflected, the French were getting the equivalent of a kingdom. "If this is not enough to make a glorious peace," he sighed, "I would say that God wants to punish us."[6]

Trauttmansdorff was under tremendous pressure from his court to reach a settlement before the campaign began, yet he was facing stiff opposition, both from the representatives of the Protestant princes gathered in Osnabrück, who were distressed by his offers of Alsace to the French, and those of the Catholic princes gathered at Münster, bolstered by the nuncio, who were scandalized at the Swedish demands for the various bishoprics. On April 24, Ferdinand, writing in his own hand, once again gave permission to cede Breisach, but Trauttmansdorff, while waiting, engaged in a number of propagandistic moves, largely designed to regain support and sympathy throughout the Empire. The first was a response to the French issued in Münster by the Count von Nassau and Dr. Volmar on May 1, 1646, which recapitulated the long-winded and self-righteous *Gutacten* of the previous February without making any further concessions. The reply was too inflammatory for the mediators, who persuaded the Imperialists to moderate and shorten it. On the same day in Osnabrück, however, Trauttmansdorff made his reply to the Swedes, shorter in length, similar in tone, but more generous in outcome. In its appendix he expressed a willingness to cede Pomerania, along with the Archbishopric of Bremen and Bishopric of Verden, as fiefs of the Empire, subject to approval by the German princes and states. The Imperialists, moreover, took this occasion to offer to the mediators an article-by-article *Instrumentum Pacis* of their proposed treaty with the French and to the Swedes a similar *Instrumentum Pacis* of their proposed treaty with them, which included, for the first time, an offer of an eighth electorate, especially created for the Elector Palatine. The French and the Swedes had thus stolen a march on the Spanish, since for the first time someone had come forth with the actual articles of the treaty. It was not much of a march, however, for Servien in Osnabrück had made no headway in moderating the Swedes and a few days later Pauw and Knuyt reappeared at Münster, ready and willing to advance their treaty with Spain. It was rumored that they had already prepared sixty-eight articles, and D'Avaux, at least, was worried.[7]

What was bothering D'Avaux most of all, however, was his conscience. The apparent readiness of the Imperialists to cave in to the most extreme Swedish and Protestant demands was not the outcome of the war with which he intended to meet his maker. The Swedes, he alarmingly concluded, had finally managed to turn the war into a war of religion, and in the best seventeenth-century tradition, he found this both spiritually and politically damning. He unburdened himself to Mazarin:

> If this is not taking off their mask and using the power of the king for the propagation of Lutheranism, and dragging us in spite of ourselves into waging a war against the Catholic religion to the great dishonor of their majesties and of a prince of the Church who is their principal minister, I don't know what is. The good of the state is at stake. If the Protestant party were to make itself so powerful in Germany, what with the parliament of England, the United Provinces, and our Huguenots, it will be found that in France and in its neighborhood there will be many enemies of the Catholic religion and of royalty.

There was even more to this remarkable letter. D'Avaux reported on a conversation with Knuyt, the Dutch plenipotentiary most closely associated with the Prince of Orange. Knuyt had suggested that in order to achieve peace between France and Spain, the French and the Dutch could agree on what terms the French should impose upon the Spanish. D'Avaux, who did not have much confidence in the good faith of the Dutch, simply passed the suggestion on to Mazarin without comment. Still, the suggestion showed that the Dutch, in spite of their instructions to the contrary, were concerning themselves with the broader negotiation and that they would have preferred not to abandon the French, if at all possible. Thus, if Mazarin opted to come to an agreement with the Dutch, he still had a chance to survive his blunders of the previous winter.[8]

He had to hurry, though, because the Spanish negotiations with the Dutch were in full swing. On May 13 they had exchanged proposals. The Spanish, doing their utmost to keep the Dutch from coming out on campaign, limited themselves to four articles, reiterating their offer to renew the truce of 1609, this time for twelve to twenty years, plus an immediate cessation of fighting while the ratifications were exchanged, a suspension of arms should they be delayed, and a promise not to assist each other's enemies. The Dutch were much more prolific. They came up with seventy-one articles, in full keeping with their instructions, dutifully expressing their solidarity with the French, as well as adding some provisions on behalf of the Prince of Orange. In contrast to the tentative treaties presented thirteen days before by the Imperialists to the mediators and to the Swedes, this one had a ring of finality to it. From the Spanish standpoint the only problems lay in the surrender of church lands, especially in the Municipality of 's Hertogenbosch, and the extensive demands for the freedom of trade, which would have subjected the entire Spanish empire to Dutch economic supremacy. The Spanish replied four days later, raising some minor objections. Still, there was a spirit of courtesy and understanding on both sides that completely obliterated the memory of over half a century of enmity. Even Servien began to worry.[9]

On May 11 the court of France moved to Chantilly, the elegant residence of the Prince de Condé. It was the first military campaign for seven-year-old Louis XIV. The next day the court moved on to Compiègne. It was in Compiègne that Mazarin composed an overview of the prospects for the coming campaign, carefully assessing the strength and plans of the French armies, for the benefit of the plenipotentiaries. He could not have drawn a brighter military picture, but, at the same time, he wrote to Turenne ordering him, if at all possible, to avoid executing his junction with the Swedes. Clearly Mazarin's intention was not merely to undermine the Swedes; it was also to achieve peace, for in a *Mémoire du Roi* to the plenipotentiaries, he ordered them, as soon as they obtained Breisach, to push for a suspension of arms in the Empire. It was a measure of his self-assurance that he could now indulge himself in his own complaints that "the exorbitant demands of the Swedes and Hessians aim at the ruin of the Catholic religion." He did not, however, carry the point to its logical conclusion, namely, that it was time to relent against the Spanish. On the contrary, in his mind the principal reason for ending the war in the Empire was simply to bring more pressure upon the Spanish to accept his terms, and, as far as these were concerned, it is now clear that he had never abandoned this goal. Yes, he added in still another *Mémoire du Roi,* it was fine for the plenipotentiaries to offer truces in Catalonia and in Portugal, but the most desirable outcome of these offers would be to make the prospect of these truces so unpalatable for the Spanish that they would, in exasperation, "fall in with exchange of the Low Countries."[10]

During the latter part of May, Trauttmansdorff excruciatingly exhibited his final concessions. First, he floated the idea through various channels that, instead of ceding Alsace to France as a fief of the Empire, the Empire might cede it outright. This was a historic distinction, although the French, for the time being, responded to it with indifference. He then empowered the mediators to try various alternatives to offering Breisach such as offering it only through the minority of Louis XIV before hinting that they might offer it outright if the French agreed to all the other Imperial conditions. The French were still not satisfied, much to the exasperation of the mediators. Finally, on May 29, Trauttmansdorff and his colleagues came to the mediators with their own writing, in which they offered Breisach in perpetuity and the Emperor's rights to Alsace "without any obligation or subjection to the Holy Roman Empire." This time the French felt that they had gotten what they wanted, as much as they attempted not to show it. They continued to insist on Philippsburg, though they were prepared to give up on it. The only remaining questions were the exact reimbursement of the archdukes, the form of the session of Alsace, and what to do with the Duke of Lorraine.[11]

During the very same period, the Spanish and Dutch were also coming together, with the Spanish, after a little soul searching, conceding the ecclesiastical lands in the Municipality of 's Hertogenbosch. Only some additional ecclesiastical lands, the commerce of the Indies, and some demands for the Prince of Orange were holding things up, and Peñaranda was getting increasingly confident that he had kept the Dutch from participating in the forthcoming campaign. Moreover, as he was conversing with one of his Dutch counterparts, either Pauw or Knuyt, there took place another one of those seemingly casual exchanges which was to change the face of the Peace of Westphalia. The Dutch once more—and for the first time, to the Spanish—began dropping hints about becoming involved in the Franco-Spanish negotiations, and unlike D'Avaux a few weeks before, Peñaranda was excited. He wanted nothing more than to involve the Dutch so that they would become disgusted with the French and make a separate peace. The French plenipotentiaries did not know the half of it, yet they were so alarmed by the rumors they were hearing that in the midst of their own negotiation over Breisach, they dispatched a courier to their court warning about the progress of the Spanish-Dutch negotiations. The Dutch, however, were dead serious about interposing their good offices, and they dropped their broad hints to the French as well. Servien and Longueville ignored them, but D'Avaux now came forward with his opinion. He did not want any help from the Dutch. "Unless I am mistaken," he wrote to Mazarin, "the Count von Trauttmansdorff would be much more useful to us."[12]

It is not that the Spanish did not prefer a general peace. They were still terrified by the progress of the Franco-Imperial negotiations, and, having heard about the French rejection of the last Spanish offers, the council of Spain bestirred itself into more concessions. It seems to have met intensively in both Madrid and Zaragoza on the question during the first three days of June. In one important *consulta* which has been preserved, the Count de Chinchón went so far as to begin contemplating a truce in Catalonia, still cherishing his fantasies that peace would bring domestic troubles within France itself. He had no hesitation about caving in on the humiliating Dutch demand that the Spanish reform their powers to qualify them as free provinces. He even suggested that they send Peñaranda some signed ratifications which would be filled in once the treaty was made. The feisty Count de Castrillo still believed that the Spanish monarchy could hold out for one more campaign, but once more he was overruled. Philip IV backed Chinchón, approving, as a last resort, a four- to six-year truce in Catalonia. It would also appear as if the council of Spain reintroduced the possibility of the marriage of the Infanta to Louis XIV's brother, the Duke d'Anjou, with the Low Countries as a dowry.[13]

The French court had meanwhile moved to Amiens, but it returned to Paris while the Duke d'Orléans, supported by the troops under Enghien and Gassion, prepared to begin his campaign. The combined French armies came to some 33,000 men, but their allies the Dutch, for all of their subsidies, were not coming out, and the duke, left to his own devices and those of his lieutenants, decided to settle for the siege of Courtrai. It began on June 13. and he was facing, in the absence of a diversion by the Dutch, a garrison of 2,000 and a potential relief army of some 30,000 under the command of the Duke of Lorraine. The issue, therefore, was in doubt, but perhaps the greatest irony in the situation, and the farthest from Mazarin's mind, was that by leaving him in the lurch, the Dutch were doing to him precisely what he intended to do to the Swedes.[14]

Even though he was in the hands of generals whom he could not control, the news of the cession of Breisach brought Mazarin to the point where he was seeing all of his plans coming to fruition. If there is any document that captures him at the height of his hubris, it is the *Mémoire du Roi,* which he dictated on June 22, 1646. He was so satisfied with the concessions that the plenipotentiaries had obtained from the Emperor that he instructed them to concede the remaining points if it became necessary. This would force the Swedes to moderate their demands, relieve the conscience of Anne of Austria, and bring a halt to the Reformation. Mazarin was so self-satisfied that he was beginning, on the surface at least, to sound like D'Avaux:

> The only reason that France has joined her arms with those of the crown of Sweden and the other Protestants has been the absolute necessity of moderating the power of the house of Austria, but today, if there is anything to fear in Germany, it is the excessive power of the Protestant party sustained as it is by the crown of Sweden.

On the surface, that is! It occurred to Mazarin that the Imperialists by offering Alsace in full sovereignty, intended to keep the King of France from participating in the Reichstag, and Mazarin began wondering if, in keeping with the law of opposites, he should not insist on obtaining Alsace as a fief. He thus asked the plenipotentiaries to send him their opinions on this matter. He also was fearful, for all of his rhetoric, of alienating the Swedes, and he ordered Turenne, if they became insistent enough, to effectuate his junction with them. But about the Spanish and the Dutch Mazarin refused to be worried. Though the Spanish may have won over Pauw and Knuyt, he thought these two men could be bribed. Though the Dutch army had not yet budged from its quarters, he was certain that it would do so. Though he had misgivings about the siege of Lérida, he presumed that it would terrify the Spanish into making peace. And the following week, he issued another set of ambiguous instructions on Portugal which seemed to set a higher price on selling it out.[15]

Not only did Mazarin believe that he was now in a position to manipulate the diplomacy of Europe, he also believed that he was in a position to become more assertive in France. The day after the Duke d'Orléans had begun the siege of Courtrai, the twenty-six-year-old Duke de Brezé, son-in-law of the Prince de Condé and Grand Admiral of France, was killed off the coast of Tuscany in a naval engagement with the Spanish. Upon receiving the news, the Prince de Condé immediately asked the queen for Brezé's offices to be passed on to Brezé's brother-in-law, the Duke d'Enghien, or to Brezé's nephew, the Duke d'Albret. But the queen, on the advice of Mazarin, refused, announcing that she intended to reserve these offices for herself. This display of independence presented quite a challenge to the house of Condé. The prince prepared to retire to his government of Burgundy without even taking leave of the queen. With rumors filling the court, Mazarin resorted to exhortations and appeals to the prince's patriotism, and the prince caved in. He visited the court before heading for his government, postponing any further action until the return of his son, the Duke d'Enghien. Mazarin had thus defied one of the principal members of his coalition, and he had gotten away with it. He was also making very little effort to maintain his relationship with Chavigny, which was deteriorating day by day. Mazarin took the other principal member of his coalition no less seriously. On June 28 the city of Courtrai capitulated, without the Duke of Lorraine making the slightest effort to relieve it. The Duke d'Orléans then moved on to lay siege to Bergues St. Vinox, and then, once again, Mardick, coming closer and closer to Dunkirk. It was not good enough. In Italy Prince Thomas suffered a setback before the Spanish presidio of Orbitello in central Italy.

PIECE ALLEGORIQUE A LA LOÜANGE DU CARDINAL MAZARIN SUR SA NOUVELLE DIGNITÉ.

Allegory praising Cardinal Mazarin on his new dignity: 1643.

(Bibliothèque Nationale de France, Cabinet des Estampes)

The French plenipotentiaries.

Bignon, F., *LES PORTRAICTZ AV NATVREL AVEC LES ARMOIRIES ET BLASONS, NOMS ET QVALITEZ DE MESSIEURS LES PLENIPOTENTIAIRES ASSEMBLEZ À MVNSTER ET OSNABVRG POVR FAIRE LA PAIX GÉNÉRALE* (Paris, 1648).

(Paris, Archives du Ministère des Affaires Etrangères)

Jean Comte d'Oxenstern
plenipotentiaire de Suede
Cum Privilegio Regis

Jean Adler Silvius
plenipotentiaire de Suede
Cum Privilegio Regis

The Swedish plenipotentiaries.

Bignon, F., *LES PORTRAICTZ AV NATVREL AVEC LES ARMOIRIES ET BLASONS, NOMS ET QVALITEZ DE MESSIEURS LES PLENIPOTENTIAIRES ASSEMBLEZ À MVNSTER ET OSNABVRG POVR FAIRE LA PAIX GÉNÉRALE* (Paris, 1648).

(Paris, Archives du Ministère des Affaires Etrangères)

The Dutch plenipotentiaries.

Bignon, F., *LES PORTRAICTZ AV NATVREL AVEC LES ARMOIRIES ET BLASONS, NOMS ET QVALITEZ DE MESSIEURS LES PLENIPOTENTIAIRES ASSEMBLEZ À MVNSTER ET OSNABVRG POVR FAIRE LA PAIX GÉNÉRALE* (Paris, 1648).

(Paris, Archives du Ministère des Affaires Etrangères)

Adrian Paw
plenipotentiaire de Hollande

Adrian Clant
plenipotentiaire de Groeningen

Godard de Reede de
Nederhorst plenipotentiaire d'Utrecht

Guillaume de Riperda
plenipotentiaire d'Oueryssel

The Dutch plenipotentiaries.

Bignon, F., *LES PORTRAICTZ AV NATVREL AVEC LES ARMOIRIES ET BLASONS, NOMS ET QVALITEZ DE MESSIEURS LES PLENIPOTENTIAIRES ASSEMBLEZ À MVNSTER ET OSNABVRG POVR FAIRE LA PAIX GÉNÉRALE* (Paris, 1648).

(Paris, Archives du Ministère des Affaires Etrangères)

The mediators.

Bignon, F., *LES PORTRAICTZ AV NATVREL AVEC LES ARMOIRIES ET BLASONS, NOMS ET QVALITEZ DE MESSIEURS LES PLENIPOTENTIAIRES ASSEMBLEZ À MVNSTER ET OSNABVRG POVR FAIRE LA PAIX GÉNÉRALE* (Paris, 1648).

(Paris, Archives du Ministère des Affaires Etrangères)

The Spanish plenipotentiaries.

Bignon, F., *LES PORTRAICTZ AV NATVREL AVEC LES ARMOIRIES ET BLASONS, NOMS
ET QVALITEZ DE MESSIEURS LES PLENIPOTENTIAIRES ASSEMBLEZ À MVNSTER
ET OSNABVRG POVR FAIRE LA PAIX GÉNÉRALE* (Paris, 1648).

(Paris, Archives du Ministère des Affaires Etrangères)

Jean Louis Comte de
Nassau plenipotentaire de l'émpereur
Cum Priuilegio Regis

Maximilian Comte de
Trautmandorff plenipotentiaire de l'émpereur
Cum Priuilegio Regis

Isaac Volmar
plenipotentiaire de l'émpereur
Cum Priuilegio Regis

The Imperial plenipotentiaries.

Bignon, F., *LES PORTRAICTZ AV NATVREL AVEC LES ARMOIRIES ET BLASONS, NOMS ET QVALITEZ DE MESSIEURS LES PLENIPOTENTIAIRES ASSEMBLEZ À MVNSTER ET OSNABVRG POVR FAIRE LA PAIX GÉNÉRALE* (Paris, 1648).

(Paris, Archives du Ministère des Affaires Etrangères)

Germany at the King's feet: 1645.

(Bibliothèque Nationale de France, Cabinet des Estampes)

The Relief of Lérida: November 21, 1646 (Peter Snayers).

(Madrid, Museo del Prado)

The exchange of ratifications between Spain and the Dutch Republic:
May 15, 1648 (Gerald Terborsch).

(London, National Gallery)

Mazarin put both of his generals in the same category. "If I had to answer for the errors of the commanders," he grumbled, "I would certainly be in a bad way."[16]

By the beginning of July, the Spanish plenipotentiaries received their new powers, along with the orders for the new concessions to the French, and came to an agreement on the satisfaction of the Prince of Orange, so that only matter of trade in the Spanish empire was holding up their treaty with the Dutch. The articles were then revised, conveniently omitting the expression of solidarity with the French, and the Spanish began to press the Dutch to sign them. The French got wind of this progress and went to the Dutch for the first time with veiled threats about what happened to people who offended a great kingdom. The threats were only partially successful. The Dutch dutifully confirmed, verbally, to the Spanish that they would not abandon the French, but this merely gave Peñaranda the opportunity to ask more urgently for their interposition, but did not delay the signing of the articles for long, since by July 8 all of the Spanish plenipotentiaries had signed seventy articles and—although it is not entirely clear when—in the absence of some of their colleagues, three of the Dutch, Gendt, Knuyt, and Pauw, also subscribed in great secrecy. Still the Dutch were trying to keep some semblance of faith. On July 9, they went to the French and announced that they, the Dutch, would soon be coming with some peace proposals on behalf of the Spanish that would meet all the French demands, with the exception of the demand on Portugal. The Dutch, in other words, were now explicitly offering to replace the Pope and the Venetians as mediators. It will be remembered that about two months previously, D'Avaux had rejected this idea, and with good reason, for whereas the Pope and the Venetians were only in a position to exert moral pressure upon the French, the Dutch were in a position to back up their mediation with the threat of a separate peace. Yet, amazingly, the French plenipotentiaries now apparently concluded that the Dutch had learned their lesson. They replied that they "could hardly refuse the intercession of their allies" and that if they could obtain the terms that they had been demanding, which now included Courtrai, the whole affair could be settled in twenty-four hours. The once skeptical D'Avaux, in particular, now became so enthusiastic that he gave Pauw a kiss! The elated French plenipotentiaries also addressed themselves to responding to the sanguine *mémoire* they had received from Cardinal Mazarin, in which he asked them whether France should acquire Alsace in full sovereignty or as a fief of the Empire. This question produced further evidence of the difference in thinking between D'Avaux and Servien. D'Avaux envisaged a king who would sit modestly as an Imperial prince in the Reichstag. Servien thought it more dignified for the King of France to acquire Alsace in full sovereignty. After stating his own view, however, D'Avaux fell in with Servien's, and the three plenipotentiaries ended up by unanimously recommending full sovereignty.[17]

It was now the Swedes who were beginning to feel left out, and during these same early days of July Oxenstierna betook himself to Münster, accompanied by a collection of Protestants, ready and willing to confer with both the Imperialists and the French. He found Trauttmansdorff somewhat cooler toward the peace—a coolness Oxenstierna attributed, in part, to the delay of the French in making their junction. Obviously, Trauttmansdorff, having settled with the French, felt less urgency about settling with the Swedes. Thus he did not move beyond his previous concessions, except that on the matter of the restoration of the religious situation—"the autonomy," as it was called—he retreated from the base date of 1627 to that of 1624. Nor did Oxenstierna find the French very forthcoming. They seemed happy enough with the Imperial concessions and did their best to put pressure on the Swedes to accept them. There was not much of a meeting of the minds. Oxenstierna left Münster not thinking that he had conceded anything, whereas the French and Contarini, with whom he also talked, thought they had gotten him to agree to the base date of 1624.[18]

By the summer of 1646 Mazarin was more than ready for peace. "It is no small skill," he wrote to D'Avaux on July 20, "to know how to quit when one is ahead." Perhaps this is why at this point he fell in enthusiastically with the Dutch offers of interposition. "Pauw and Knuyt," he continued, "are the best mediators that we could have to conclude an advantageous peace with Spain." He repeated the same point in a letter to Longueville, whose beautiful wife was about to join him in Münster, and if Mazarin's urgings were not enough, Lionne wrote authoritatively to Servien: "Make peace as soon as you can and take the Spanish offers seriously!" And indeed, if Mazarin was resolved, in keeping with Knuyt's original suggestion, to come to an understanding with the Dutch on the exact terms to impose upon the Spanish, the Dutch would have been more than happy to provide him with a peace. The only question was whether Mazarin had entirely digested his own platitude.[19]

D'Avaux had digested the platitude, but he still believed that the way to peace lay through the Count von Trauttmansdorff, whom he assiduously cultivated to that end. In a two-hour conference on July 29, Trauttmansdorff hinted that he was about to give up Philippsburg and indicated that he was merely waiting to settle the *gravamina* before broaching the subject with the princes of the Empire. He seemed to be prepared to satisfy the Landgravin of Hesse-Cassel as well, and became emotional as he pleaded that the Emperor could not honorably abandon the King of Spain. Pressed by D'Avaux on what the Spanish were prepared to offer, Trauttmansdorff confessed that they were preparing to offer all of the conquests in the Low Countries, the County of Roussillon, a two- or three-year truce in Catalonia, and *even some sort of exchange for it*. D'Avaux kept insisting on a truce in Catalonia equal to the one between the Spanish and the Dutch, and he left the meeting convinced that the Spanish would even consent to a short truce for Portugal and that the Emperor would abandon the Duke of Lorraine. In recounting this interview proudly to Cardinal Mazarin, D'Avaux praised the cardinal to the sky for "not losing the occasion to make the most glorious peace that has ever been made for the crown."[20]

Certainly, the Dutch were not being very cooperative. On July 15 the Prince of Orange suffered a stroke which deprived him of his memory, but he would not consider surrendering his command to anyone—this while his army and 6,000 French troops sent by the Duke d'Orléans to join him languished uselessly in the vicinity of Ghent. Meanwhile Knuyt and Nederhorst arrived in The Hague, followed by Gendt and Matenesse, and on July 26 they reported on the signing (or non-signing, in the case of Nederhorst) of the articles with the Spanish. The strong complaints by Brasset and especially by La Thuillerie, who got up from his sickbed on August 7 in order to discredit the signing, produced just the opposite effect. Three days later the States of Holland passed a resolution asserting that "the King of France, once he had received his satisfactions in the Low Countries, no longer had the right to keep the Union at war." The Dutch also began to consider, apparently, turning their projected truce with the Spanish into a permanent peace treaty so as not to tie themselves to the truce which the French were demanding for Catalonia. And they stood squarely behind the action of their plenipotentiaries in signing a record of what had transpired between the Spanish and them-selves. Still the States General did not discourage their plenipotentiaries from offering their interposition to the French.[21]

Chigi and Contarini were also pushing vigorously for peace. In a memorable meeting that took place on August 10, the mediators pleaded with the French plenipotentiaries to make some overtures and hinted broadly that the Spanish were prepared to make a short truce for Catalonia, as long as the French did not insist on one with Portugal. The French, who had heard nothing yet from the Dutch, let it out that if the Spanish ceded to France its conquests in the Low Countries and the County of Roussillon, including the port of Rosas, and agreed to a truce in Catalonia to last as long as the Spanish truce with the Dutch, they would not press for the Portuguese truce. Indeed, they would con-clude the peace in twenty-four hours. The Dutch were still a question mark. The Prince of Orange recovered only enough of his memory to take a small Spanish outpost, but the States General promised dutifully that they would not conclude a peace without the French, and when, on August 24, the Duke d'Orléans again took Mardick and several weeks later the Duke d'Enghien appropriated Furnes, it seemed as if the French could have the peace they claimed to want if they indeed wanted it.[22]

Meanwhile the money was running out, and the policy of financial ex-pedients was facing increasing opposition in *parlement*. Mazarin, how-ever, continued to put his faith in D'Hémery, who was clearly aiming to replace Bailleul entirely, and on the upcoming expiration, on January 1, 1648, of the *paulette*. The *paulette* was an advantageous tax paid by judges to assure passing their offices on to their heirs, and the renewal of this tax could be used to extort more millions. Mazarin thus basked in the impression that all the options in the negotiations at Westphalia were up to him as he asked himself in his *Carnet*:

> 1st whether it would be more convenient to obtain Alsace and Breisach in sovereignty or recognized by the Empire like Spain does with the Duchy of Milan and others. 2nd whether it is more convenient to treat about the affairs of Lorraine in Münster or whether it would be more advantageous to do it here at court, it being impossible for us to keep Lorraine without being constantly disturbed. Or even if it is better to insist on a two-year truce in Portugal with promises not to assist it or not to speak about it and assure ourselves of giving it assistance.

Mazarin had already jeopardized the negotiation once by advancing the marriage and exchange proposals. Now he was thinking of doing the same thing again by insisting on the truce for Portugal![23]

The Protestants were showing signs of compromise on their *gravamina*. Toward the end of August, they advanced the base date for the restoration of the religious situation from 1618 to 1621, and they generously offered to extend the freedom of conscience to their own Catholic subjects. Around the same time the Imperialists transmitted to the mediators another project for the treaty with France. They seemed to backtrack a bit on their offer of Alsace in full sovereignty, in that they were prepared to surrender the rights of the Emperor and the house of Austria to Alsace and other territories, but not those of the entire Empire. They did give in on the demand for Philippsburg, but, further backtracking on the offer of sovereignty, they explicitly retained good portions of Alsace and many of its nobles in their immediate dependency on the Empire. With the mediators shuttling back and forth between the French and the sickbed of an ailing Trauttmansdorff, the French complained that the Imperialists were only ceding a lot of air, but then, whether out of caution or out of foresight, the French agreed to a nonsensical resolution of this dispute. In one article the Emperor and the entire Empire agreed to cede *omnibus dominij* over these territories to the French crown. In another article it stated, to the contrary, that many of the same territories and their nobility would *retain* their privileges *and* their immediate dependency on the Empire. The French then insisted on compounding the contradiction in this last article by adding to it the clause "as long as this did not detract from the *supremi domini*." The meaning of such wording, of course, could only be decided in the course of time, as indeed it was. The French also got the Imperialists to accept 3 million *livres* for one Archduke of Innsbruck. The French could thus take pride in their acquisition of sovereignty and strongholds, while the Imperialists could draw some comfort from having sold the King of France a lot of empty titles and having kept him from sitting in the Reichstag. On September 13 the French plenipotentiaries, the mediators, and the Imperial plenipotentiaries came together at Trauttmansdorff's bedside. The nuncio read the articles and the plenipotentiaries signed them.[24]

The French had thus achieved their first objective in Westphalia, which was to bring the Emperor to terms, and the plenipotentiaries had obtained even more than Mazarin had expected. Moreover, it seemed like a new era of collaboration was about to begin between the French monarchy and the Holy Roman Emperor. In a secret article, the French promised to come to his aid in case of war against the Turks, and in a separate writing the French agreed to support him in bringing both the Swedes and the Protestants to a reasonable settlement. D'Avaux was so proud of his achievement that he contrived to have the articles delivered to the French court by his nephew, Herbigny. Only two issues remained: the Emperor's insistence that he would not make peace without the inclusion of Spain, and his similar insistence on behalf of the Duke of Lorraine. On the first, however, the secret interposition of the Dutch, backed up by pressures which the Emperor himself would bring upon the Spanish, suggested a quick solution. On the second, the duke's pitiful performance in the campaign spoke vehemently against him. The French plenipotentiaries were so confident of the future that their first thought was to go to Osnabrück and see if they could get the obstreperous Swedes to read the handwriting on the wall.[25]

Mazarin kept up the military pressure. In Flanders, the Duke d'Enghien closed in on Dunkirk. In Germany, Turenne belatedly effectuated his junction with the Swedes, and in Italy, undaunted by their setback before Orbitello or the death of Brezé, the French were preparing to lay siege to Porto Longone on the island of Elba. The Dutch plenipotentiaries still at Münster did not want to wait for the outcome. On September 18, just as the Duke d'Enghien was investing Dunkirk, they went to the residence of Peñaranda and reiterated the French terms: retention of all conquests and truce in Catalonia to last as long as the Spanish-Dutch truce, as well as the total silence on Portugal, and urged him to accept them. He did not need much convincing. He gave them full and complete authority to act as his mediators with the French. The French having gone to Osnabrück on the same day, Pauw, Donia, and Clant followed them there. The French were suspicious about accepting the Dutch interposition, but they reiterated their demands, glossed over the issue of Portugal, and trusted that the pressures would work. They certainly did with Innocent X. He was so frightened by French moves in Italy that he made a complete turnabout and restored the Barberinis to all their posts.[26]

In spite of Mazarin having played into the hands of the Spanish, his plenipotentiaries had regained the lead in the negotiations at Westphalia, and it seemed as if this lead were insurmountable. The Dutch, admittedly, were not the friends they had once been. Since the French were still refusing to sign the infamous Article 9 and since they were now insisting on a truce in Catalonia to last as long as the Dutch truce with the Spanish, the States General now took a major step in asserting their independence. They no longer wanted their relationship with the King of Spain to be in any way dependent on the King of France. On September 18, therefore, they passed a resolution in favor of turning their truce with Spain into an outright peace. This involved some additional demands, such as for the remaining quarter of Gelderland, but, in their eagerness for peace, they also went on to moderate their demands on the West Indian trade. Not the best candidates to take over the mediation! Still, if Cardinal Mazarin would have been satisfied with what he was telling them he wanted, they would have been good enough.[27]

6

The Defection of the Dutch

On September 11, 1646, Count Magnus de La Gardie, the extraordinary Swedish ambassador, arrived in Paris to a splendid welcome by the entire court. Mazarin assured him enthusiastically of French support for the Swedish demands—which was the consummation of all hypocrisy— but also warned him of "the risk we could run if we lose such a wonderful opportunity," adding that "the least setback in the war is capable of cooling the desire of the enemies for peace." Never had any prophet been more prophetic, nor less persuaded of his own prophesies, for only a few days after sobering his Swedish guest with these infallible predictions, Mazarin was evaluating the future in an entirely different light for the benefit of his own plenipotentiaries. In a *Mémoire du Roi* of September 28, he informed them that the Spanish were about to accede to every French demand as long as nothing was said about Portugal, and that they were hoping that the French would reject these offers and lead the Dutch to make a separate peace. He was also sure that if France did make peace, the Spanish did not intend to keep it. He therefore "reminded" his plenipotentiaries to "take all imaginable precautions to bridle the enemies so that they cannot break it." Otherwise, "their Majesties would be ill advised to consent, since they can hope to render their enemies in even worse condition by continuing the war." And, inspired by this more profitable vision, he now enlisted it in the service of his insatiability, specifying that in their demand for the County of Roussillon and the port of Rosas, the plenipotentiaries should include the port of Cadaqués; that they should figure out a way to acquire Dunkirk and Lérida, still under siege; and that they should try to extend the duration of the French occupation of Casale. He even instructed the plenipotentiaries to make every effort on behalf of Portugal before desisting. Thus after priding himself on knowing when to quit and warning the Count de La Gardie about pushing his luck, the irrepressible Cardinal Mazarin was now inciting his plenipotentiaries to push theirs.[1]

Pauw, Donia, and Clant were doing their utmost to conclude the peace before such terrible things could happen. On returning to Münster, they, along with Nederhorst, held four conferences with the Spanish—principally with Brun, since Peñaranda was ailing—in which the Dutch did not mention the issue of Portugal and the Spanish caved in on practically all of the other French demands, including the truce in Catalonia for as long as the Dutch deemed proper. Only the cession of Rosas and the inclusion of the Duke of Lorraine seemed to remain as potential sticking points. "The negotiation can be considered concluded," Peñaranda wrote to Philip IV, "but for my doubts about the French!" The French returned to Münster on September 29, and the next day the Dutch began a series of conferences with them. Little by little the Dutch disgorged the Spanish concessions, and by October 1 the French plenipotentiaries could not deny it. As they wrote to Brienne, "it came close to what we desired!" Yet, amazingly, not a single one of the French plenipotentiaries displayed any sense of urgency. They claimed to be reluctant to "affect delays" but willing to "let them come from things themselves" until they could hear from their court. They did not rush, as the Dutch had done four months before, to present an article-by-article comprehensive project for a treaty. They merely produced a courteous response which held out on Rosas; insisted, in case the Dutch went for a peace, on a duration of thirty years for the truce in Catalonia; and noted, enigmatically, that "there had been no consent in regard to Portugal."[2]

D'Avaux was so confident of peace with Spain that, after consulting with Salvius, he took this occasion to compose another one of his eloquent Latin letters, this one to the Queen of Sweden pleading for the limitation of the Swedish demands to the control of Wismar (jointly with the Duke of Mecklenburg), Lower Pomerania, the island of Rügen, the Archbishipric of Bremen, and the Bishopric of Verden—which Servien considered too menacing and refused to let pass. But D'Avaux went even further. He now summoned up the courage to lay bare his own long-simmering thoughts before Cardinal Mazarin. In a letter of October 8 that was just as revealing of its author as the *Mémoire du Roi* of September 28 was of Cardinal Mazarin, D'Avaux addressed himself to the question of what to do about the troublesome Duke of Lorraine. D'Avaux didn't think that the Spanish would agree to a mere pension or lands within France as compensation for Lorraine, but he did think that they would approve compensating Charles IV with some sovereign lands outside of France, and so D'Avaux came forward with his extraordinary recommendation that France should exchange its hard-won province of Alsace with Europe's last remaining condottiere. It was a high price, D'Avaux admitted, but "one could not pay too much for the peaceful possession of such a beautiful country." Not only was he prepared to give back Alsace, but he was also prepared to throw in Breisach for good measure. The Duke of Lorraine was not immortal and his heirs would eventually turn their attentions in the direction of Germany. "Our nation has never conserved its conquests in foreign countries," D'Avaux reflected, and clearly for him Alsace was in a foreign country. One week, therefore, after Mazarin was inciting his plenipotentiaries to grab as much as they could, D'Avaux was brazenly championing moderation and the rule of law. No wonder the two men so completely detested each other![3]

The Spanish continued to furnish the French with all of the rope they needed in order to hang themselves. The Spanish response, delivered by the Dutch on October 11, left open the question of Rosas, which meant that the Spanish would probably give in at the end; it continued to leave the duration of the truce in Catalonia up to the Dutch, which meant that the French would undoubtedly get their thirty years; it agreed to guarantees for the preservation of Casale, which is just what the French demanded; and it broadly hinted that the Spanish did not want to alienate Duke Charles at the moment but would also abandon him at the end. Silence on Portugal. All of these efforts to conclude the peace before the fall of Dunkirk, however, proved to no avail. On October 13 the stronghold capitulated to the Duke d'Enghien. France now occupied a port from which it could menace the commerce of the North Sea.[4]

By this time Mazarin had completely liberated himself from the faintest recollection of his own prophesies. He was more certain than ever of the forthcoming peace, and his state of mind emerges with absolute clarity in another milestone of Mazarinian miscalculation, the *Mémoire du Roi* of October 14. In it he made a special point of discussing for the benefit of his plenipotentiaries all of the evidence, *pro* and *con,* that the Dutch would remain faithful. The evidence *pro* was dismally thin—namely, the implausible rumor that the province of Holland wanted Frederick Henry to do something in the campaign. The evidence *con* was that he was still maneuvering aimlessly with his army, while his wife was imploring him to come home, but, as far as Mazarin was concerned, this evidence should have been sufficient "to remove the scruples of the plenipotentiaries that if France ever so briefly delays the conclusion of the peace, our allies might be capable of failing us." On the contrary, since Dunkirk was virtually in French hands (he had not yet received the confirmation that it was) and the prospects in Italy looked so bright, Mazarin was happy to envisage that the French had plenty of time to complete their conquests in the course of the coming six weeks. But just in case:

> Since Their Majesties want absolutely to profit from the rest of this campaign, they would desire that the plenipotentiaries continue to delay the signing of the treaty without affecting to do so, which it will not be hard for them to do since the nature of the thing itself will furnish them the means.

Here was an explicit order to delay the conclusion of the entire Peace of Westphalia for the sole purpose of collecting a few more strongholds in the Spanish Low Countries, a presidio or two in Italy, and, as Mazarin himself went on to admit in this same *mémoire,* of suffering a possible reversal before Lérida! What is particularly remarkable about this order is that he issued it in full confidence that it would not jeopardize the conclusion of the treaty, for he took this opportunity to come to a decision on how to deal with the Duke of Lorraine. The terms were outlined in a *mémoire* that accompanied the orders to delay. It offered to pay Charles, if he would disarm and settle elsewhere, and his brother Francis, a handsome annual pension, and then, in ten years' time, to return the original duchy to Charles or to his legitimate successors. The King of France also reserved the option of giving to these successors a sovereign state of equal value, all, of course, on the condition that in the intervening decade, the entire house of Lorraine would act in a properly submissive manner to the French monarchy. This offer was a sham—Mazarin did not have the slightest intention of ever giving back Lorraine—but it does demonstrate beyond a shadow of a doubt that he was cleaning out his files.[5]

The *Mémoire du Roi* of September 28 had already given the French plenipotentiaries a good hint of how Mazarin wanted them to proceed. Thus, even before receiving his definitive order to delay, their response on October 14 to the Spanish asked for a lot of clarifications and laid broad hints of complications ahead. For example, in insisting on an immediate answer regarding the cession of Rosas, the response specified that this cession included "everything on this side in the direction of France," which meant the port of Cadaqués as well. On the matter of returning Casale to the Duke of Mantua, the French announced that "an individual writing will be given," which implied that the restitution would not be a simple transfer of command. The Dutch "interpositors" accentuated the positive, but Peñaranda was not convinced. He was despairing of bringing the Dutch to a separate peace, as much as his colleagues did their best to keep up his spirits. He was even coming to the conclusion that the marriage and exchange proposal was better than continuing to fight in the Low Countries. One more campaign, he predicted, and they would have to send a monk to Paris begging for peace.[6]

The council of Sweden was also coming to the conclusion that with the French having gotten their way with the Emperor and with the Spanish on their last legs, Sweden had better settle up the best it could. Their meetings of September 23 and 27, 1646 produced an instruction to their plenipotentiaries which authorized them to settle, as a last resort, for Lower Pomerania, parts of Upper Pomerania, the islands of Rügen and Wollin, the port of Wismar with some nearby towns, the Archbishopric of Bremen, and the Bishopric of Verden. This was no mean satisfaction, and they were still uncertain about how to compensate the Elector of Brandenburg, but it was the first time the crown of Sweden had trimmed its sails since the dark days of 1637.[7]

Amalia Elizabeth, the Landgravin of Hesse-Cassel, reacted a bit differently. She figured that it would behoove her to ask for the moon, which included a full satisfaction in her long-standing dispute over Marburg with the Lutheran Landgrave of Hesse-Darmstadt, some Catholic enclaves within her own lands, and some 200,000 *Reichsthaler* in compensation for the territories she would be willing to evacuate, all in the hope that her allies would not want to alienate their most stalwart friend in Germany. She calculated correctly. By virtue of her army and her standing as an Imperial princess, this intrepid Calvinist had gotten herself in a position where she could back up the rights of her state and secure the status of her religion.[8]

One might think that the fortunes of Spain could not sink any lower, but on October 9, 1646, Philip IV's only son, sixteen-year-old Balthazar Carlos, died after a short illness. Strong, handsome, and intelligent, he represented the last hope for the resurgence of the monarchy. Yet as dismal as the prospects looked, they presented, in a perverse way, an exceptional opportunity. Now, if the forty-one-year-old king should die without further issue, the throne would be inherited by his eldest daughter, Maria Theresa. If he did remarry, his future wife would either cement the Hapsburg hold on the Spanish monarchy or herald the introduction of a competing dynasty. Suddenly, the eight-year-old Infanta emerged as the most powerful weapon in Europe, whether as a wife for Ferdinand III's son, the Archduke Leopold; as a wife for Louis XIV; or as the final threat in inducing the Dutch Republic to make a separate peace with Spain, with Philip IV also gaining on the marriage market. None of these considerations was lost on the council of Spain, which, in spite of the lugubrious circumstances, met on October 13 in Zaragoza and coldly deliberated on whether they should revise their instructions to Peñaranda. The Count de Chinchón made much of what the Infanta could bring to the monarchy and predicted that "in proportion as these advantages are seen in France, it follows that suspicions will arise in Holland." Not that he favored offering Maria Theresa to Louis XIV, but the count did recommend ordering Castel Rodrigo and Peñaranda to find out how the French and Dutch were taking this new development and to listen to any offers they might make in its regard. The Count de Castrillo and Don Francisco de Mello hammered on these same points, while the Bishop of Malagra combined a homily on the inscrutable judgments of God with a pragmatic plea for the quick remarriage of their present king. Philip IV was even more emphatic. "Not only will it be good to limit any order that the Count de Peñaranda has for the proposition of the marriage of my daughter, he should suspend it totally," the king added, "because the gravity of this accident could also dispose the spirits of the princes of Italy to conclude the league that we are negotiating." From the depths of his grief over the loss of his son, Philip IV placed his last glimmers of hope on the ironic law of European diplomacy.[9]

On receiving a copy of the penultimate Spanish reply, Mazarin dictated to Lionne a lengthy set of "Observations" upon it. It was Mazarin's last chance to change his ways, but it never even occurred to him to do so. On the contrary, he began by grumbling about a provision by which hostilities stopped the moment the peace was signed, preferring to wait until the exchange of ratifications so he could gobble up a few more outposts. He cautioned his plenipotentiaries not to press the demand for Cadaqués lest this give a bad impression to the Dutch, but this was the extent of his restraint. He now expected from them an ironclad guarantee for his thirty-year truce in Catalonia. He exhorted his plenipotentiaries to complicate the restitution of Casale with all sorts of precautions; he reversed himself on the long-standing French insistence on a league of Italian states to preserve the peace, since, he speculated, France had much more to gain than to lose from a renewal of hostilities in that area; and he concluded that if the Duke of Lorraine refused France's generous offers, the best way to force the Spanish to abandon him was to renew the French demand that they *recognize the King of Portugal!* Furthermore, in a separate letter written by Lionne directly to Servien, Lionne announced that Mazarin had changed his mind about taking Alsace in full sovereignty. Why? Because he had heard that this was the option that the Spanish and the Emperor feared the most. Had Mazarin gone mad? Did he actually believe that by undermining every foundation of the forthcoming treaty on the eve of its conclusion, he would still have peace? Apparently he did.[10]

The Spanish continued their desperate game. On October 15 Brun, by the usual word of mouth, gave to the Dutch "interpositors" the humble Spanish reply to the last set of French proposals. If the Spanish had caught the hint about Cadaqués, they did not let on. However, they did have suspicions about Casale and indicated that they were waiting to hear what the French had to say. "I cannot believe," Peñaranda wrote to Castel Rodrigo on October 18, "that the French want peace or that the Dutch will venture to abandon them." And, after sitting on the Spanish reply for seven days, the Dutch plenipotentiaries relayed it to the French on October 22, all in ostensible secrecy, even though the official mediators were perfectly aware that they were being circumvented and took this with good grace. The French plenipotentiaries did not have the slightest idea that they were in any kind of jeopardy. As long as Mazarin was promising them victories, all of the plenipotentiaries were willing to play their parts. On October 24 they wrote to him that everything was going perfectly and that, once the peace was signed, the

Spanish would either find themselves enfeebled by the loss of Catalonia and the continuing war against Portugal or "they will finally be constrained to leave to France what they are occupying in the Low Countries." On October 25, the French plenipotentiaries transmitted their answer to the last Spanish reply, and lo and behold, it included the explicit demand for Cadaqués.[11]

Servien was even more emphatic. "The last three *mémoires* that have been sent to us," he replied to Lionne on October 20, "are full of so many beautiful instructions that we would be remiss in our duties if we failed to study them carefully." He was especially enthralled with Mazarin's turnabout on the league of Italian princes. But, in the guise of elaborating on his patron's genius, Servien also brought out some of the inconsistencies in his patron's logic. Yes, they would try to do all they could to obtain a Dutch guarantee for the truce in Catalonia, but if it was true that a league of Italian princes would be detrimental to France, wouldn't any arrangement with the Dutch which might reinforce the peace in the Low Countries be even more so? "The Low Countries," he maintained, "have more to fear from France than France from the Low Countries . . . If one wants to aggrandize oneself, as it seems that one is obliged to do when it is possible, there is no easier way than in the direction of the Low Countries."[12]

But finally, after a month of dawdling, early in November, and with Servien holding the pen, the French plenipotentiaries proceeded to compose the "individual writing" on Casale, and it took the form of an actual article of the treaty. It began modestly enough by insisting that the Duke of Mantua had to promise not to pass the stronghold on to the Spanish, but the plenipotentiaries kept attaching more and more strings to this promise as they went along. The house of Mantua could not make any marriage alliances with the house of Austria. They had to readmit a French garrison the moment that the King of Spain violated the peace treaty in any way, and the entire arrangement was to be guaranteed by the Pope, the Venetian Republic, the Dukes of Florence, Mantua, and Modena, plus the Republics of Genoa and Lucca. Thus the desire to accommodate Mazarin's order to stretch out the negotiation seemed to override any considerations on the undesirability of an Italian league. The most destructive part of the article came toward the end, and it was a provision that the future garrison of Casale was to be paid by the King of France and the Republic of Venice, who also had to approve the governor. We may imagine what impression this made on the Dutch, who communicated it to the Spanish on November 5.[13]

When the news of Balthazar Carlos's death reached Paris, it produced the expectable expressions of grief, but, just as in Zaragoza, the lamentations quickly gave way to cold calculation. Rather than thinking, as the council of Spain did, that the event gave Philip IV some fresh ground for maneuver, Mazarin concluded that in the short run it helped while in the long run it threatened the interests of France. In the short run it helped because it would make the King of Spain even more desperate for peace; in the long run it would lead to the Infanta being married off to the Emperor's eldest son, with the prospect of eventually recreating the monarchy of Charles V. The campaign in Italy was going well. The Marshals de La Meilleraye and du Plessis-Praslin had landed on the island of Elba and laid siege to Porto Longone. While besieging this important presidio, they moved on to the mainland and besieged Piombino, which had capitulated on October 8. All the more reason, therefore, for Mazarin to squeeze out every possible advantage and demand security from his allies. In other words, after having momentarily glimpsed an inconsistency between the ideas of hegemony and collective security, Mazarin reverted to his original program of going for both. Indeed, he even pressed his plenipotentiaries to try to obtain a six-month or even a one-year truce for the Portuguese. The reason?

> Not only so that the peace that we are presently concluding will be sure and durable, but that perhaps the Spanish, seeing no other means of re-conquering Portugal and getting back Catalonia will resolve . . . to cede to us the rest of what they possess in the Low Countries, for then, as the plenipotentiaries so well remark, no other power would be capable of frightening this kingdom, which would be able to live in great security without fearing its allies.

So Mazarin had not gone mad after all! Behind all of the orders to delay, behind all of the reopening of settled issues, behind all the bombast about collective security, his *idée fixe* had never left him. The principal purpose of these superfluities was to force the Spanish into surrendering the Low Countries, and, one suspects, not merely in the course of time but now, while the iron was hot. Moreover, the iron was becoming even hotter. On October 29 Porto Longone had fallen. Even if France could not coerce the Spanish into giving up the Low Countries, she could at least place herself in an ideal position to control Italy and the Papacy. Who could resist such a temptation? No sooner was he informed of this last conquest than he ordered the plenipotentiaries to insist on a provision in the treaty permitting the French to go to the aid of Portugal! Just one more inducement to panic the Spanish into making peace at any price! He had committed himself to despoiling the Goddess of Fortune, and she seemed to be enjoying it![14]

Confined to bed in his monastery, Peñaranda could only put his hopes on a miracle or, failing that, on the diplomatic skills of Brun and the Archbishop of Cambrai. On November 8 he sent them to see the Dutch with the Spanish answer to the last French demands. They performed brilliantly, contrasting the French promises to settle in twenty-four hours with the last month and a half of procrastinations. The Spanish expressed a willingness to go along with the demand on Cadaqués, but they flatly rejected the new article on Casale as a novelty and announced impatiently that if they did not get an agreement on their offers within a week, they would retract them. They declared to the Dutch "that it was time to know if they desired to treat separately in case the French did not conclude," hinting that "His Majesty did not lack the means to continue the war against his enemies or to settle with some of them separately." This was the threat—put into their hands by Mazarin—that the Spanish never stopped repeating. The Dutch retired to consult among themselves and returned with a historic admission, namely, that the Spanish were right and that, if there were no agreement within a week, they would seek a resolution from the States General on whether they could abandon the French. The French had absolutely no idea about the bad impression they had made. They casually spent a week formulating their response, and when it came, on November 16, it contained more grist for the Spanish mill, the incendiary demand for a truce in Portugal, and a gratuitous one, raked up from a halfhearted injunction in their September 1643 instructions, for the evacuation by the Spanish of the Duchy of Sabionetta. But the Swedish plenipotentiaries were in such a panic at the conclusion of the peace that they handed over their minimum demands to the Imperialists, along with those of the Hessians. It is true that at the same moment the Swedish council decided to tighten up on these very terms—insisting once again on all of Pomerania unless they could get the approval of the Elector of Brandenburg—but, for the moment, their army, supported by Turenne's, was accomplishing very little against the Imperialists and Bavarians. The peace hung on the Franco-Spanish negotiations.[15]

As we have seen, Servien was so confident of France's preponderance in Europe that he did not see any advantage in her being defended by her allies. But since Mazarin had reverted to his own original position on the desirability of obtaining a guarantee, Servien was quick to adapt himself to his patron's wishes—Mazarin insisted on a guarantee from the Dutch, and Servien set about to obtain it. and he found a new reason to do so, namely, that it would prevent the Dutch from forming an alliance with the Spanish. The only question was how to obtain it. The answer? By bullying! As he wrote to Mazarin on November 24, "we've got to speak strongly to them here and at The Hague, without displaying that we need their friendship as much as they think." He had no doubt that they were looking for the first occasion to abandon France and make an alliance with Spain. Yet he now intended to go in person to The Hague to set them straight. That, of course, may have been all the Dutch needed, one of his interminable reprimands. Here was another slight difference between Mazarin and Servien: as opposed to Mazarin, who believed the Dutch were fools, Servien thought they were cowards.[16]

It would be more accurate to say that they were deliberate, but once the States General had finally opted for peace with Spain, Pauw, Donia, Clant, and Nederhorst came back to life, begging the French to moderate their demands and pressing them to compose the articles of the treaty. The first request, the French adamantly refused, insisting that they intended to keep every one of their conquests, including Piombino and Porto Longone. The second request, the French graciously granted, and Servien finally began to draft some articles, but he was still devoting the major portion of his time to the care and feeding of his personal rage. In a letter of December 4 to Lionne, Servien did not say a word about his drafting of the treaty, but he did hurl several tons of abuse in the direction of D'Avaux and reiterated his reevaluation of the Dutch. They had "changed the maxims of their state" and had to be handled roughly. He was certainly right about the first part. Thus, by the time that Knuyt, Matenesse, and Gendt rejoined their colleagues on December 6, the stage was set for a showdown in Westphalia. Peñaranda demanded that the Dutch sign with him then and there and agreed, at their prompting, to make a final offer to the French. Moreover, in an effort to expose French intransigence at its most transparent, he sent Brun, on December 9, to visit Servien. Servien did not disappoint him. As Peñaranda described it, the "one-eyed devil" was completely unbending on the question of Piombino and Porto Longone, but he dangled out all sorts of hopes for marriages once the peace was made, which was all Brun needed for the benefit of the Dutch. As Servien described it, Brun absolutely groveled, dangling the marriage of the Infanta and the exchange of the Low Countries and pleading for the restitution of Piombino and Porto Longone. Not that Peñaranda had much confidence in his own strategy. "Only God," he wrote, "can work with such inadequate tools!" But, without being entirely aware of it, he was doing an excellent imitation of the Almighty, and Servien of Oedipus Rex. "I am sure," Servien boasted to Lionne, "that the next time Brun comes they will concede everything." Famous last words! Servien was so sublimely overconfident that when the Dutch presented the final Spanish offer, he convinced his colleagues that, in order to gain their point about Casale, they should add the demand that the Spanish return the three towns of Charlemont, Philippeville, and Mariembourg to the Bishopric of Liège, whose overlord, the Elector of Cologne, had not even asked for them.[17]

Never was the climax of a classical tragedy so perfectly timed! Never was the denouement so quick to unravel! Never had the Goddess of Fortune come so pristinely to the defense of her chastity! On November 21, at eleven o'clock at night, as the French troops of the Count d'Harcourt were resting in their siege lines before Lérida in the mistaken belief that the Spanish troops of the Marquis de Leganés had abandoned their effort to relieve the stronghold, the marquis, in a stunning countermarch, surprised the French, overran them, and sent them flying. That least little setback, which Mazarin had so prophetically predicted, had finally taken place.[18]

The news of the relief of Lérida reached Paris on December 9. It produced a *Mémoire du Roi* for the plenipotentiaries at Münster in which Mazarin exposed the stream of his consciousness in all of its endangered course. First he tried to comfort himself that the French had fought bravely; then he tried to rationalize that the Spanish would now feel better about making peace, then he advised the plenipotentiaries that if they just acted as if the siege no longer mattered, everything would be fine. But, in the course of the writing, the idea began to occur to him, as it had occurred before on a similar occasion, that he himself had done nothing wrong. He had always known, he reminded the plenipotentiaries, that the enterprise against Lérida was chancy, but Harcourt had insisted on pursuing it. Thus its failure was Harcourt's fault. The blame game had begun. The question was, of course, if Mazarin had known that the enterprise against Lérida was chancy—which he did—why did he stake so much on his success? This was, however, hardly the time for self-searching, even assuming there ever was any. His emotions kept driving him. He felt a longing now for the signing of the peace and wished to economize on the expenses of the forthcoming campaign. Yet he wrote to Longueville not to relent on any of the demands. The great Giulio Mazarini had squandered his best opportunity to make a glorious peace and still he would not face up to it.[19]

The courier from the French court arrived in Münster on December 17. But the plenipotentiaries were less indulgent with their imaginations. They warned the court about economizing on the forthcoming campaign, "there being no certainty of peace or as to the time when it can be made." The plenipotentiaries thus found themselves in a terrible bind. They had to advance the peace, but they could make no concessions. The best solution that they could find was to clear up the confusion, once and for all, about what conquests that they wished to retain, and, for this purpose, they came up with an "article on the retention of the conquests." It included a long list of localities in the Spanish Low Countries, which the French either occupied or claimed to occupy. It reiterated the demands for Rosas and Cadaqués. It made explicit, for the first time, the demand for Piombino and Porto Longone. They presented this article to the Dutch as a great step forward in advancing the peace, but like the article on Casale, it only demonstrated the wide difference between agreeing on something in general and agreeing on it in particular. Two months before, the article on the retention of the conquests might have had some credibility. After Lérida, it looked like evidence that the French merely wished to continue the war; the Swedish plenipotentiaries certainly saw it that way. Armed with their new instructions, and taking heart from the interruption of the peace process, they again pressed for all of Pomerania, with huge compensations elsewhere for the Elector of Brandenburg, all of which carried immense religious baggage.[20]

The French still had a little bit of breathing room because of some final Dutch demands, but now that Peñaranda had acquired an instrument with which to work, he, Brun, and the Archbishop of Cambrai produced a reply to the latest French writings which was a diplomatic imitation of Leganés's countermarch. Every obfuscation that the Dutch had permitted in order to advance the negotiation and the French had exploited in order to extend it, the Spanish now turned to their advantage. They claimed they had never assented to the method of garrisoning Casale; they ridiculed the demand for Charlemont, Philippeville, and Mariembourg; they challenged the accuracy of the list of conquests; they refused to consent to the cession of Rosas and Cadaqués; and they screamed bloody murder about Porto Longone and Piombino. The Spanish promised to stand by their offers of the previous September but would go no further. They felt that in the pattern of French delays they had irrefutable proof that the French were insatiable and that all of Europe was ready to accept it.[21]

"I don't know what to tell you about the peace," wrote Servien to Lionne on December 24, "so unhappy am I that it was not concluded six weeks ago, as it was in our power to do it." We have seen that he was absolutely right, and that, six weeks before, the Spanish had been perfectly willing to settle. The question, therefore, was what had gone wrong, and Mazarin had already set the tone for the answer when he refused to blame himself for having wagered the entire negotiation on the dubious outcome of a superfluous siege. Servien hardly needed the inspiration. Now that the peace with Spain had gone amiss, he proceeded to come up with scapegoats of his own, and his prime candidate, of course, was D'Avaux. It now turns out that it was D'Avaux who had been advised by monks to hold firm, it was D'Avaux who had introduced all sorts of petty points, and it was D'Avaux who had held up the drafting of the most important articles. But if Servien was admitting to himself that France was now facing serious problems, he was feeling more and more as if he was the only person who could resolve them. He was all the more determined to march up to The Hague, where, in his inimitable style, he would "make the Dutch realize how important it is for their state to get along well with France." He also worked with his colleagues on the articles for the treaty with Spain, studded with such conditions as the truce for Portugal and a Spanish promise not to aid the Duke of Lorraine.[22]

Even the blame game, however, was not enough for Cardinal Mazarin. It was once again time to find comfort in oblivion. On December 21 he wrote privately to Servien, enlightening him, as if there were still time, on how duplicitous were Brun's intimations about a marriage of the Infanta to Louis XIV. This was the man who ten months before had been the prime mover of the marriage and exchange. And he went even further: "I have always thought, and still think, that it would be advantageous for you gentlemen to consult face to face with our opponents so as not to depend so absolutely on the caprices of the mediators, who often delay our affairs instead of advancing them." This was the man who two months before had said that Pauw and Knuyt were the best mediators France could have, and who six weeks before had given orders to delay the negotiation instead of advancing it.[23]

Mazarin could play all the tricks he wanted with his own memory, but the fates would not let up on him. During the entire month of December, the Prince de Condé had been suffering from the effects of a goiter. As Christmas approached, his condition seemed to be improving. He was even able to rise from his bed on Christmas Eve and listen to Mass in his room. On Christmas day, however, he suffered a fluxion, which reduced him to extreme agony. It took one more day for the hemorrhage to choke him, and he died on December 26 at the age of fifty-eight. The queen had little choice but to pass his offices on to his son and grandson. Mazarin was now rid of the man whom he had once feared but had learned to manage, only to replace him by a more dangerous one, who combined his father's greed with youth and military genius at a very moment when his services could not be dispensed with.[24]

Everyone was becoming truculent. From The Hague, where he had gone to strengthen his ties with the house of Orange, the Elector of Brandenburg complained bitterly about giving up any part of Pomerania, wondered why the Swedes could not get their satisfaction elsewhere, and left the door open only slightly to an immense compensation for himself. This permitted D'Avaux, who did not dare to criticize the handling of the negotiation with Spain, to criticize the handling of the negotiation with Sweden. "Our allies have found us too easy in letting them retain all of Pomerania and all of Wismar," he wrote to Mazarin on December 31. "It would have been better to have sent my letter to the Queen of Sweden. Once they saw that we didn't even dare to write to Sweden, they decided to go for everything." He predicted that the elector and the Duke of Mecklenburg would quickly make an alliance with the Emperor and renew the war in Germany. The cause of all the troubles, therefore, had been Servien.[25]

The Spanish, for their part, were not about to let Cardinal Mazarin get away with amnesia. They had been assiduously collecting all the evidence for their case, and Castel Rodrigo in Brussels had a first-rate propagandist in a certain Philippe Le Roy, who put together, in French, a *Pertinent and True Relation of the negotiation of the Peace since the Mediation of the Plenipotentiaries of the States General*. It detailed every Spanish offer and every French response, and the cumulative effect was devastating. "It is time," it concluded, "not only to explain but to publish to the whole world who is to blame for the effusion of so much Christian blood." Using a passport which he had obtained for his own private affairs, Le Roy arrived at The Hague on January 1, 1647. He had his writing translated into Flemish, and on January 7 he presented it to the States General, where it was read on January 9 and listened to "with extraordinary attention." Within a few days, it was being circulated widely throughout the Low Countries. In the part of the world where public opinion counted the most, the Spanish had made the most of it.[26]

Meanwhile, in Münster the Spanish and the Dutch were coming to an agreement on all but a few contentious matters, like some further details over the Municipaity of 's Hertogenbosch, the trade of the Indies, and the upper quarter of Gelderland, which they decided to leave open, and on the night of December 26, they were all ready to sign their agreement. The French plenipotentiaries got wind of it, managed to persuade the Dutch to suspend the signing for ten days and, just in case, wrote up a paper to protest the signing. Two days later Servien left on his quest for a treaty of guarantee, but the Dutch were not about to wait for the outcome of his mission. Pauw composed and transmitted to D'Avaux and Longueville, along with a Spanish reply, a complaint about French delays which could have been written by Le Roy. The Dutch also pressed the French to come up with the articles of their own treaty with Spain, but D'Avaux and Longueville would not do so, although they found themselves slightly embarrassed in defending a position which they felt in their hearts to be flawed. They presented not one but two official protests to the Dutch, the second one bowing to the inevitable and merely pleading with the Dutch to insert a proviso in their agreement to the effect that it would be invalid unless the French also received their satisfaction. This they accomplished, and on the evening of January 8,

1647, the Spanish and the Dutch signed what they titled their "provisional articles," this time with only Nederhorst refusing to go along. It was not that much different from what the Spanish and the Dutch had done six months before when they had signed their first agreement. In fact, it was infinitely better if one considers the proviso in favor of the French satisfaction, but it was infinitely worse if one considers the atmosphere.[27]

7

Playing the Blame Game

Cardinal Mazarin was an expert at consoling himself. In the early days of January 1647, looking out at the world from the perspective of the Palais Royal, he considered that there were still ample grounds for optimism, and, it being time to write another letter, he decided to share them with Longueville and D'Avaux. The Spanish, he had heard, were conspiring against Trauttmansdorff. Thus Mazarin thought of having Longueville and D'Avaux approach Trauttmansdorff with offers of Mazarin's friendship and for the "maintenance of the peace which is about to be concluded." He had heard that the ministers of Spain in Italy suspected that he had a personal interest in holding on to Piombino and Porto Longone. All the more reason for Longueville and D'Avaux not to relent on this demand! He had heard the Spanish feared that the French would insist on including the King of Portugal in the peace treaty. All the more reason for Longueville and D'Avaux to threaten that if the Spanish did not make peace immediately, this might well happen. The loss of Lérida? "All they did was to prevent us from taking one more stronghold." The Dutch? "There is no appearance that they will abandon us." He did not know yet that they just had.[1]

D'Avaux and Longueville also tried to put up a good front, but with considerably less success. While Servien was at The Hague, there emerged in their attitude a degree of deference in regard to the Dutch and even, one begins to sense, a degree of distance in regard to Mazarin. In their letter announcing to the court the signing of the articles between the Spanish and the Dutch, the remaining French plenipotentiaries were uncertain as to what do next, but they advanced the suggestion that, under the present circumstances, it might be best to continue the Dutch interposition. Having wronged the French, Longueville and D'Avaux fantasized, the Dutch might now be more inclined to make it up by supporting the French demands. And after D'Avaux left for Osnabrück on January 15, Longueville became even more deferential. He expressed his concern to the Dutch plenipotentiaries that they would confirm Philippe Le Roy's allegations and seemed to put up with their vague responses. Longueville went further in his efforts to be reinstated in their good graces. On January 25 he took the giant step of communicating to them the entire French project for the treaty with Spain—the first twenty articles of which they promptly transmitted to the Spanish. He went on to confide to the Dutch plenipotentiaries Mazarin's plans for the Duke of Lorraine and to present them with chapters and verses of minor French demands. Left to his own devices, Longueville seemed to have found his own voice, and it was the voice of a man who wanted to go home.[2]

It was a rough winter voyage for Servien, but his first encounters with the Dutch whom he met along the way reassured him that the situation was fluid, that the state was leaderless, and that all he had to do was to disabuse them of the impression that the French did not want peace. In other words, he promptly forgot his own insight that the Dutch had changed their maxims, and, what's more, he refused to admit to himself that the French had given them any grounds for suspicion. When he finally reached The Hague on January 8, the old Prince of Orange was dying, his young son just happened to be out of town, and the welcoming committee consisted of two obscure deputies. On January 13, moreover, he got word of the signing of the Spanish-Dutch articles at Münster. Still he did not despair. He feigned ignorance of the signing, entertained hopes of rebuilding his bridges with the Princess of Orange, and on January 14 at noon he gave a speech before the States General proposing the treaty of guarantee. It was a patronizing speech, uncompromising in its demand for an absolute guarantee, and emphasizing, both inconsistently and insultingly, how indispensable the protection of France was to a political monstrosity like the Dutch Republic.[3]

The French discomfiture and the Elector of Brandenburg's truculence had also given the Swedes exactly what they were looking for: an opportunity to stiffen. Arriving at Osnabrück on January 16, D'Avaux discovered that they had gone back to demanding all of Pomerania, while the Imperialists were exploiting this developing schism between the

Brandenburgers and the Dutch on the one hand and the Swedes on the other. D'Avaux found himself in demand by both the Dutch and the Brandenburgers to act as mediator, and he set about it with his usual dexterity. He argued to the Swedes that the elector had not yet given them his answer, to the Brandenburgers that they should moderate their demands, and to the Dutch that they needed his support against the Swedes. The Brandenburgers were willing to deal—they had no choice—and on January 19 he managed to get them to give up half of Pomerania, the right bank of the Oder, the island of Wollin, and (in return for 1.2 million *Reichsthaler*) the city of Stettin if they could get the Bishoprics of Halberstadt, Magdeburg, and Minden in compensation. It was the Swedes who would not balk, and in a memorable confrontation with Oxenstierna on January 20, D'Avaux threatened that if they demanded one more village than they had demanded the previous November, he was going to put on his hat and return to Münster.[4]

For one brief week in the middle of January, it seemed as if Cardinal Mazarin, too, was mellowing. When he found out about the signing of the Spanish-Dutch articles, his first reaction, in writing to Servien on January 18, was to express appreciation for the efforts of D'Avaux and Longueville, to encourage Servien to dissimulate so as to extract a treaty of guarantee, and to push for an agreement with the Dutch on what terms the French would impose upon the Spanish. Not that Mazarin's memory had improved. It would be easy, he went on, to counter the allegations of Le Roy, because they were "false and artificious!" A week later, however, writing to Longueville and D'Avaux, he began to change his tone. Insinuate to the Dutch, he dictated, that "kings have long hands!" And those of the King of France were particularly favored by the Almighty, for in a letter to Servien of the same date, Mazarin displayed the incredible flexibility of his theory of Providence. Whereas, back in 1643, God had ostensibly shown by his blessings that he was on the side of France, Mazarin now claimed to have noticed that, "since the beginning of the war, by a visible declaration of Heaven in favor of this kingdom, all the advantages which the Spanish have obtained have only thrown them into greater embarrassments." It is hard to imagine, therefore, how God could ever have succeeded in revealing his displeasure with the policies of Cardinal Mazarin, and one more week, encouraged by this exegesis, he was back to his old form. He grumbled to Servien that Longueville should not have turned over the project of the treaty to the Dutch, felicitated Servien on his harangue to the States General and scolded D'Avaux for revealing all of the Brandenburg concessions to the Swedes at once.[5]

The council of Spain in Madrid still wanted out of the war. The Marquis de Leganés, who had just saved Lérida, belabored the obvious in a *consulta* of January 13, emphasizing the necessity of coming to a separate peace with the Dutch and the dangers of installing the French in Italy, but he went considerably beyond commonplaces by concluding that if the Dutch refused to abandon the French, the Spanish should, as a last resort, give up Piombino and Porto Longone. The Count de Castrillo and the Duke de Villahermosa agreed, and Philip IV approved. The council had not yet heard the news about the signing of the articles with the Dutch, but several weeks later, when it did, it still held to its position. But if, after twenty-five years of war, the Spanish council was losing confidence that God was on their side, their spunky plenipotentiary Antoine Brun was not. He tried to get a passport to enter the Dutch Republic in order to consult with its leaders. When this failed, he went to Brussels from where, armed only with a previous passport, he entered the republic and began to bombard it with open letters. The first, written from Gorinchem on January 31 to the States General, thanked them profusely for their arbitration and asked for its continuation so that they could decide on the "frankness of the combatants." The second, written from Gouda on February 3 to the States of Holland, informed them of his voyage. The third, written from Deventer on February 11 to the States General, was the most pointed, contrasting the now-infamous French promise to make peace in twenty-four hours with their "new obstacles dug up from everywhere." And behind all the flattery was the threat that if the Dutch did not consummate their negotiation by signing a separate peace, the Spanish might decide to abandon the Low Countries. The printed versions of these letters and the number of manuscript copies distributed in the archives of Europe provide ample evidence as to their dissemination and their impact.[6]

Nederhorst was the first of the Dutch plenipotentiaries to rush to The Hague to provide his justifications to the States General, but it was Pauw, apparently, who composed the majority report. It made much of the Spanish threats to abandon the Low Countries to France and complained about the "rude" and "abusive" efforts of the French in trying to prevent the signing. Longueville still seemed to think he could win over the Dutch while holding firm on his own demands. When they came to inform him that four of their number—Knuyt, Matenesse, Ripperda, and Clant—would also be returning to deliver their report (they did not mention Gendt, who was also about to disappear), Longueville again beseeched them to reveal to him how they would respond to the accusations of Le Roy, and when they replied that they could not, Longueville disgracefully pressed a *mémoire* into their hands in order to make his case. Peñaranda, on the other hand, continued to exploit his advantage. Even though he had received his latest instructions, he insisted that he had no orders regarding Piombino and Porto Longone, and on February 24, he submitted his own project of the treaty, in Spanish, both to Pauw and Donia, who was also about to make himself scarce, and to the original mediators. It confirmed the cession of all the conquests in the Low Countries; the County of Roussillon; the thirty-years truce in Catalonia; Rosas; Cadaqués; and even allowed for a degree of French control over Casale. But it continued to demand the inclusion of the Duke of Lorraine and did not say a word about Piombino and Porto Longone, nor about the truce in Portugal. He was also, as a little extra bonus, beginning to receive, from someone in the circle of the Duke de Longueville, copies of his ends of the French correspondence. On receiving the Spanish project, Longueville complained bitterly that it was written in Spanish and that the Spanish had not addressed themselves to his proposal. He would have been even more upset if he had realized that his mail was being intercepted.[7]

It was not easy for Servien to hold his temper under the best of circumstances, and the inhospitable surroundings in which he found himself in The Hague made the task all the more difficult. He attempted to negotiate with the Dutch over the new treaty of guarantee and attempted to follow Mazarin's latest instructions about agreeing with them on what terms the French could impose upon the Spanish, but once the Dutch plenipotentiaries arrived and presented their report, Servien concluded that Pauw—the same Pauw in whom he and Mazarin had put all their trust—"is one of France's most dangerous enemies!" Servien considered in his correspondence whether France should not recuse Pauw and Knuyt and even go back entirely to the original mediators. And once the States General communicated to him a copy of Brun's last letter, Servien could no longer restrain himself. He composed another one of his unctuous reprimands, directed primarily at Pauw and Knuyt, whom he now accused of violating their instructions for their personal gain in collusion with the Spanish. He tried to corner the States General into disavowing them. He swore "as God was his witness" that the French had not delayed. They had never added on! Just like Mazarin, whose inspiration he always followed, Servien had taken leave of his memory—either that or he had taken leave of his religion. On March 2, he presented his writing to the States General, and on March 4 it was read before them. But the more angry, the more dubious, or the more pathological it sounded, the better it made the point for the Dutch plenipotentiaries. He published it with a cover letter, ostensibly written by a *gentilhomme français,* playing right into the hands of Brun, who, of course, wished for nothing so much as a protracted public spectacle.[8]

While Servien was alienating the Dutch with his boorishness, D'Avaux in Osnabrück was alienating the Swedes with his sanctimony. Under his pressure, on January 25, the Swedish plenipotentiaries reluctantly returned to offering the first part of the alternative, adding a few more towns on the right bank of the Oder for good measure, and finally, on the evening of February 10, the Brandenburg and Swedish deputies signed a convention. He went on forthwith to mediate a similar understanding between the Emperor and the Swedes, leaving only the issue of Minden still in contention. D'Avaux was extremely proud of his achievement. He felt that he had succeeded in containing the influence of Sweden, winning the gratitude of the Elector of Brandenburg and the Dutch, and controlling, as much as humanly possible, the damage to the Catholic religion. There was some hope, moreover, for an armistice in the Empire. The Duke of Bavaria was making strong overtures toward it, and the French and Swedish generals were collaborating by sending their delegates to Ulm to discuss it. The French plenipotentiaries also did their part by sending D'Avaux's old collaborator, Fouquet-Croissy, to participate in the negotiations. No sooner, however, was D'Avaux relishing some measure of success than the Swedish plenipotentiaries, sticking to the letter of their instructions, proceeded to champion every last demand of the Elector Palatine, the Landgravin of Hesse-Cassel, and other Protestant princes. Nor did the Swedish plenipotentiaries feel at all magnanimous toward the Duke of Bavaria. It began to dawn on D'Avaux what he had wrought. "It has never been the intention of France," he wrote to Longueville, "to carry its arms into Germany in order to destroy the Catholic religion." He confessed that he was undergoing a crisis of conscience. "It is an unfortunate thing from which one must look away in order not to be touched by it, or not to fool oneself." The Swedes and the Emperor rapidly signed their convention. Next on the agenda were the Protestant demands, and D'Avaux wrote frantically to his court, begging it to prevent "the last final ruin of the Catholic religion." He had finally become a full-fledged *dévot*. The triumph of Protestantism, he argued, would permit a lot of people "to calumny us in France, where the Protestants themselves would attribute all of their good fortune to the Swedes, who, with their ascendancy in Germany, no longer have any need of France." At the end of his own draft of this letter, he called upon Horace's *Carmina* for consolation: *Impavidum ferient ruinae.* "I will not flinch in the face of ruin."[9]

Mazarin's reaction in the face of ruin was to fall back on his most dangerous domestic rival, the new Prince de Condé, to set things straight in Catalonia. It is hard to imagine which would have been more dangerous to Mazarin, Condé's failure or his success, but since Mazarin had made a symbol out of Lérida, he had little choice but to send his best general in that direction. Indeed, Mazarin was putting the bulk of the monarchy's diminishing resources into this front, to the detriment of all the others, what with the overtures coming out of Bavaria reviving the hope for a truce with its duke, which would permit the inexpensive unleashing of Turenne's Weimarians upon the Spanish Low Countries. As the days grew longer, the better these prospects looked, the more Mazarin could vent his distempers. He began with Longueville, hinting, in a *Mémoire du Roi* of February 22, that he had made a mistake by giving the articles to the Dutch plenipotentiaries since "the pressures by which they pulled the treaty from our hands had no other end in sight than to use it against us at The Hague." The news of their actual report made Mazarin even angrier, and he had no trouble getting his more bellicose council, which now included the new Prince de Condé, to hold firm on the French demands, to approve of Servien's attack on Pauw and Knuyt, and to castigate Longueville for having communicated the articles. It was left to the embarrassed Brienne, on March 1, to convey the more explicit and more symphonic reprimand. For D'Avaux, however, Mazarin was holding back his bile. He agreed enthusiastically with D'Avaux on the danger of the Swedish threat, while cautioning him *sotto voce* not to press the Swedes too hard. A few days later, in a council meeting held before the queen, Mazarin sounded even more like he too had become a convert to the *dévot* position. If things turned out badly, of course, he could always decide which part of his advice D'Avaux had failed to follow.[10]

Longueville did not feel receptive to any hint of criticism. He replied sarcastically to the court on March 4 that the efforts of the Dutch plenipotentiaries to "pull the treaty from our hands" were in the expectation of getting a refusal and thereby justifying their own conduct. His turning over of the articles, he argued, had foiled their designs, as well as prompted the Spanish into presenting their counter project. Moreover, he excluded any idea of going back to the original mediators, who, he maintained, were so eager to conclude the peace that they would try to precipitate it. And, as the criticisms from the court became more explicit, Longueville became more rebellious. "I can hardly understand," he replied to Brienne on March 11, "what I am supposed to do!" Didn't they realize at the court that the more he insulted the Dutch, the more this played into the hands of the Spanish? There was no reason to exclude Pauw. His very friendship with the Spanish could work to French advantage. Longueville was not being very logical—why wouldn't the Dutch be just as precipitous and even more partial than the original mediators?—but he was giving it back as good as he got.[11]

Everyone knew it was imminent, and in the early morning hours of March 14 at The Hague, the Prince of Orange finally expired at the age of sixty-three. The event produced one of Servien's rare exhibitions of humor. "I think," he remarked to the Portuguese ambassador, "that the King of Spain would pay as much now to bring him back to life as he has spent over the last ten or twelve years to send him to the hereafter." It was also a bitter example of how to lose a friend, if Servien had wanted to reflect on it, but he was in no mood to do so. He was more interested in making a new one. On the following day, Frederick Henry's twenty-year-old son, now William II, Prince of Orange, was invested by the States General with all of his father's generalty offices. Servien saw his opening. "The present Prince of Orange," he wrote to Longueville, "is of an entirely different inclination than the one that his father has had for two years." In fact, Servien feared that the new prince was too hotheaded and, in his passion for continuing the war, would break openly with his mother and with the province of Holland. Still, with his collaboration and support, there was fresh hope for Dutch participation in the campaign and for the guarantee.[12]

The Swedes in Osnabrück, too, were envisaging another campaign, but hardly for the greater glory of France. D'Avaux attributed to them the desire to become dominant in Germany and to expand the practice of the Lutheran religion, and, having been through this once before, he recalled, or perhaps imagined, in a *mémoire* of March 4 to the court, that even in the heyday of Gustavus Adolphus, who was never as powerful as the Swedes currently were, "the means were beginning to be thought of in France to moderate his ambitions." Even the deputies of the Protestant princes and states in Osnabrück seemed to want to get out from under. They issued a new set of *gravamina*, which dropped the demand for the repeal of the Ecclesiastical Reservation and advanced the date of the restoration of the religious situation to 1624. But they put in a good many exceptions to that date, notably the Bishopric of Osnabrück, and they insisted on the freedom of conscience in their private homes for Lutherans as well as Catholics throughout the Empire and on the restoration of the public exercise of the Protestant religion in the Emperor's hereditary lands. It was enough to make D'Avaux suspect a Swedish plot to create a new electorate for themselves and to elect a Lutheran emperor, although not enough to make him advocate concessions to Spain in order to rush the peace. Christendom, he opined, in the best tradition of Father Joseph, needed a truce in Portugal in order to concentrate its forces against the Turks. Then there were the negotiations at Ulm, where, on March 14, the French, Swedes, Hessians, and Bavarians came to an armistice agreement. Fifteen years of French attempts to separate the Duke of Bavaria from the Emperor had finally borne fruit, and it would have been a perfect counterweight to the defection of the Dutch, if only it did not also give the Swedes a golden opportunity to finish off the Emperor. On March 15 Trauttmansdorff offered the alternative possession of Minden to the Protestants, and he was threatening to make further concessions to them unless the French were prepared to support him with more than words. D'Avaux was in no position to do so, and by the time he left Osnabrück a few days later, he was sure that the Swedes were on the verge of becoming a greater threat to France than the Hapsburgs had ever been.[13]

One tendentious document deserved another, and Longueville's spirited defense of his conduct evoked from Mazarin a point-by-point refutation. It took the form of a personal letter on March 22, and it betrayed Mazarin at his most truculent. He had looked everywhere, he jeered, but could not find anyone ever ordering that Longueville should transmit the articles to the Dutch, passing over the fact that no one had ever ordered him not to do so. In keeping with his new priorities, Mazarin began sounding as if Servien had gone to The Hague for the purpose of settling with the States General on what terms to impose upon the Spanish, failing to remember that he had gone there, first and foremost, to negotiate a treaty of guarantee. Mazarin also reprimanded Longueville for having undercut the efforts of Servien to discredit Pauw and Knuyt, which implied, both insensitively and insultingly, that Longueville should have been following the guidance of his inferior. What seems to have been most difficult for Mazarin to swallow, however, was Longueville's intimation that he had received conflicting orders. Even for Mazarin this was difficult to deny. "All the terms of patience, of moderation, and of not overreacting," he now tried to explain, "were relative to the body of the state and not to the persons who were and are still out to get us." He added: "We have never intended to give obscure orders to those who serve Their Majesties so as to impute the problems later to their conduct." Of course not![14]

In Münster, the Spanish fashioned their reply to the French project. They were becoming stickier, explicitly refusing to give up Porto Longone and Piombino, and maintaining their silence on Portugal. On March 11 they delivered it to Pauw, who passed it on to Longueville a few days later. He responded with some intractable comments on the Spanish articles and with threats to withdraw all previous agreements unless the Spanish caved in. Chigi and Contarini were gradually getting back into the negotiation, but it was, for all practical purposes, immobilized, and the sticking point was Portugal. On March 21 Longueville was rejoined by the disconsolate D'Avaux. Together, they opened the possibility of an article permitting both France and Spain to go to the defense of their respective allies in case they were attacked, with Peñaranda countering with offers of a league against the Turks which would ostensibly limit the capacity of the Spanish to attack Portugal, but this was all very theoretical, and D'Avaux was more preoccupied with the menace of Sweden. On March 27 the Duchess de Longueville bailed out of the sinking ship, and once her husband received Mazarin's reproach, he broke entirely with Pauw, who returned to The Hague, leaving the Dutch embassy in the hands of its secretary, while D'Avaux returned to Osnabrück. Chigi and Contarini did their best to pick up the pieces. On April 5 they went to Peñaranda and officially offered to resume the mediation. He made some difficulties about his commitment to the Dutch but quickly came around and indicated that he was prepared to agree to an article giving each side the right to defend its own allies. The next day Chigi and Contarini went to see Longueville, who, reeling as he was under Mazarin's reprimand, created his own difficulties over the same article, such as suggesting a confirmation in a separate writing to the effect that that article referred to Portugal. However, after shuffling back and forth between the parties and sufficiently obscuring the issue, the mediators got Longueville to say, "Voilà qui est bon!" and they began working with him on the first twenty articles of the French project for the treaty. The mediators inserted a section to the original French proposal, which permitted each king to come to the aid of his allies, but Longueville's powers prevented him from signing any treaty without the signature of a colleague, and D'Avaux, who was the closest at hand in Osnabrück, was reluctant to return. "If the Duke de Longueville were not so obsequious to orders," bemoaned Chigi, "he would certainly have made peace with Spain by now, and if M. D'Avaux was not so afraid of the Bastille they would make it even now." Privately Longueville was fuming. He was convinced that he had won over Pauw, who left on April 12, and that Mazarin had fabricated the whole Portuguese issue in order to block the peace. Chigi and Contarini worked feverishly, hoping against hope that by bringing the French and Spanish to an agreement, this would force the Swedes and Protestants in Osnabrück to moderate their demands. Longueville sent the first twenty articles, including the insertion on the allies (and he was working on adding "and friends" for good measure), back to his court, but with three French plenipotentiaries in three different locations, each intent on his own agenda, it seemed as if only a miracle could prevent still another year of war.[15]

At The Hague Servien was losing any hope that the Dutch would come out and participate in the campaign, but he was still hoping to extract some sort of guarantee out of them, not so much in order to secure their assistance in case of another war with Spain, but in order to prevent them from giving aid to the Spanish. The Dutch were moving with their usual ponderousness on this score, the province of Holland proposing to the States General on March 21 to offer a guarantee limited to the territories France possessed in 1635 and its new conquests in the Low Countries. In his humiliation, Servien could only dream of revenge, "Since God," he wrote to Longueville "has permitted to sovereigns who represent him on this earth the sweetness of vengeance, they can adroitly use it when it is useful to their state."[16]

Without much progress either in Münster or at The Hague, D'Avaux in Osnabrück had to rely almost exclusively on his own powers of persuasion, which were by no means negligible. After threatening to return immediately to Münster, he got Oxenstierna to concede the electorate and the Upper Palatinate to the Duke of Bavaria. It was a giant step toward the preservation of French influence and of Catholicism in the Empire, assuming the Swedes would not reverse themselves. He also did his best to present himself as a friend of the Protestants while privately attempting to strengthen Trauttmansdorff by assuring him of French support if they became unreasonable. Oxenstierna, however, quickly changed his tune. He began creating new difficulties over the settlement in Pomerania and insisting on the Bishopric of Osnabrück for the Protestants, as well as upholding their full demands. When D'Avaux pulled out his ultimate weapon and threatened that France would stop subsidizing the Swedes, Oxenstierna softened his tone, but only slightly. D'Avaux tried to continue his balancing act by supporting every demand of the Landgravin of Hesse-Cassel, short of the ones for ecclesiastical lands, but he left Osnabrück with the consciousness of a new European order. "If the Swedes want to tear up the Empire," he wrote, "there is no reason to let them do it without participating."[17]

At the same time, the exiled "Importants," who had been waiting impatiently for a chink to develop in the armor of Cardinal Mazarin, saw a fresh opportunity to undermine his authority. From his estate in Anet, where he had been trying to foment trouble since 1643, the Duke de Vendôme prepared to renew his contacts with the Spanish and with the Duchess de Chevreuse in the Low Countries, offering to support an invasion of France by stirring up internal uprisings, especially by the Huguenots. She was only too happy to cooperate. Even more ominously, a plot was brewing in which a person claiming to be the Baron de Raré (or Raray), a gentleman of the chamber of the Duke d'Orléans, was to approach the Spanish authorities in the Low Countries, challenging the paternity of Louis XIV and his brother and claiming the succession for the duke and the Prince de Condé.[18]

Mazarin's bluster may have returned, but it seemed to be accompanied by a touch of hysteria. In a couple of *Mémoires du Roi* written between

April 5 and 7, he seemed to be foregoing the article on the defense of the allies as long as it was replaced by a separate writing to the same effect signed by the mediators, the Dutch, and the Imperialists. He was also prepared to put most of the unsettled issues, with the notable exception of the truce for Portugal, up for Dutch arbitration, but the following week he began to fret about the possibility that the Spanish would profit from the vague wording of either the article or the writing on Portugal, and he instructed Longueville and D'Avaux to take special care that the wording not be "ambiguous or equivocal." By April 19 he had completely caved in to his anxieties. He instructed his plenipotentiaries, therefore, that it was not enough to specify in the treaty that each side could come to the defense of its friends and allies, but that the passage should add, "when they will be attacked or that they continue to be attacked." By April 26 it dawned upon him that he was adding on, and he tried to defend himself. "It is not us who have changed, it is things!" he whistled in the dark, "and we have always said that we would increase our demands in proportion to the improvement of our affairs." What is bizarre about his argument, even assuming that things had improved, is that he was now holding up the peace in front of the whole world over a dependent clause, either in cynical or in inane violation of Machiavelli's maxim that the wording of treaties was always subject to interpretation, In either case, he did not look good. For the first time since the beginning of the regency, rumors began to circulate that Anne of Austria was dissatisfied with him. There were also popular risings in Languedoc.[19]

Angry, frustrated, and isolated, Longueville gave the impression of being weak and vacillating. He tried to revive the demand for a truce in Portugal and immediately came up against the outcry of the mediators, who adamantly refused to communicate it to the Spanish. He confidentially castigated Mazarin in their presence and continued working with them on the remaining articles of the treaty, but, bombarded as he was by Mazarin's anxieties, Longueville kept adding more words on the section giving each party the right to defend its allies, which now became a new separate Article 3, and he insisted on its confirmation by a certificate from the mediators for good measure. They became exasperated. Peñaranda showed no surprise, and the long-awaited return of D'Avaux from Osnabrück on April 27 only made things worse. He was disheartened by the concessions of the Imperialists to the Protestants, and now, whether out of conviction, fear, or inclination, he held firm on the truce for Portugal.

Mazarin, in other words, had managed to tie the hands of his plenipotentiaries so effectively that the negotiation in Westphalia had become a sideshow. His own agents bore witness to it, the Spanish made capital of it, and from one end of Europe to the other, the overwhelming consensus was that everyone wanted peace with the exception of Giulio Mazarini.[20]

Servien was giving an even worse impression. He entreated the Dutch to accept a French subsidy and proceed to the guarantee, but he was no match for Adriaan Pauw, whose return pounded still another nail into the coffin of the Franco-Dutch alliance. In three secret sessions spread out over two days on April 17 and 18, he presented his report to the States General. He asserted that the Spanish had been negotiating in good faith, evoked the specter of the marriage and exchange proposal, and accused the French of trying to undermine the Protestants at Osnabrück. He concluded by expressing his outrage over the accusations of Servien, to which he reserved the right to respond publicly in defense of his own honor. His report was well received. The province of Holland went on the offensive by refusing to fund the campaign, advocating a quick resolution of the remaining articles with Spain, and sending representatives to the other provinces in order to bring them over to its point of view. Servien tried to counter the blow by sending his own circular letter to the other provinces, castigating the "passionate spirits who have the temerity to preach to you about the affection and sincerity of your enemy." Pauw was quick to respond. In an open meeting of the States General, he cited the time, hour, and place when he had been suborned by Servien. The French subsidy was refused.[21]

And for the first time in twelve years the Spanish Low Countries were no longer threatened on two fronts. On April 11 the Archduke Leopold, younger brother of the Emperor Ferdinand, made his entry into Brussels and assumed governorship of the Spanish Low Countries. The archduke was accompanied only by his staff and a small guard, but he had a reputation as an energetic, if not brilliant, soldier, and upon his arrival the military preparations for the defense of what was left of the Spanish Low Countries proceeded with renewed vigor. He was immediately greeted too by appeals from the Duchess de Chevreuse and her cronies, eager to assure him that the French people were waiting only for his invading army in order to revolt. It seemed unlikely that the Spanish could go on the offensive, but, on the other hand, the French were completely unprepared for another campaign.[22]

The best Mazarin could do was to preach to his choir about the reasonableness of the French position. "How could anyone believe," he dictated in a *Mémoire du Roi* of May 3 for Servien, "that the Spanish would want to give us the heiress of all their kingdoms and make the king absolute master of Europe?" Mazarin was now willing to submit some minor remaining issues, plus the controversial truce for Portugal, to the arbitration of the Dutch. He even informed Longueville and D'Avaux that in the last extremity they could give up on the truce entirely. But even in announcing these concessions, Mazarin still held out for the right of each side to come to the aid of its allies, complete with explanatory clauses and confirmation by the mediators. And he launched into a long sermon on how the French, by their support of the German Catholics, had proved to the world that they were better Catholics than the Spanish. This was a kind of reasoning that only violence could impose, and on May 9 the court, with the notable exception of the Duke d'Orléans, who was taking the waters at Bourbon, left Paris to join the army assembling on the frontiers of Picardy. It grew to some 40,000 men, but they were raw troops, hard to command and even harder to hold together. By the time the court reached Compiègne, news came that the Spanish were besieging Armentières. In the new war between two exhausted monarchies, the hapless Spanish, under their new governor, had struck the first blow. Mazarin's fate was now all the more in the hands of the Prince de Condé, who, on May 12, arrived before Lérida with a hastily collected army of some 13,000, facing a strong Spanish garrison of 3,000 foot and 400 horse.[23]

In Münster, Longueville and D'Avaux both felt like men who were only going through the motions, and they acted accordingly. On May 13 they presented Mazarin's latest orders to the mediators, dutifully coupling the offer to submit the remaining issues—including the truce with Portugal—to the arbitration of the Dutch Republic with a new version of the new Article 3, which now included a few lines that implicitly prevented the King of Spain from aiding the Duke of Lorraine—plus the confirmation by the mediators of the French right to aid Portugal. Not surprisingly, the mediators complained that all this merely complicated the negotiation, and, after rereading their orders, Longueville and D'Avaux decided that they could start with the arbitration. This decision was still another token of the extent to which they had stopped relying on their own intelligence, since it permitted Peñaranda to reply that he would not listen to anything which in any way mentioned Portugal. His health was deteriorating, and he announced that he would soon be going to the baths. One of the Dutch plenipotentiaries, Gendt, had returned to Münster, and Longueville and D'Avaux also made an effort to press their proposals through him with no greater success. It had come down, therefore, to the French insisting on including a point in the arbitration, even though they were prepared to abandon it, and the Spanish refusing to include it, even though they were in an excellent position to gain it. Longueville, considering himself entirely useless, asked for permission to "make a tour" in France. Meanwhile, the Swedes and Protestants were settling their affairs with the Emperor, whose plenipotentiaries were extremely accommodating. On May 18 they settled on most of the articles on the *gravamina* in the forthcoming treaty. They accepted the freedom of conscience for Lutherans and Catholics in their private homes throughout the Empire. If there was any debate, it was between the Lutherans and the Calvinists, who squabbled among themselves over the terms by which the Calvinists should be included in the treaty and even came up with a revolutionary article which prohibited Protestant rulers from establishing a different form of Protestantism in their territories. Moreover, on May 21 Trauttmansdorff received permission to offer the alternative possession of the Bishopric of Osnabrück. The Swedes now went from being intransigent to being eager for peace, and the Imperialists, who had wanted peace at any price, now felt much less urgency about accommodating the French. At The Hague, Servien, caught between the pacific Amalia von Solms and her bellicose son, finally got the energy to make some official proposals to the States General for a treaty of guarantee.[24]

Mazarin could not have been feeling very comfortable, but his capacity for daydreaming was undiminished. They need not worry about the Swedes, he assured Longueville and D'Avaux in a *Mémoire du Roi* of May 25, because he had heard that the Queen of Sweden had just ordered her own plenipotentiaries to stop stalling. At the same time, however, he was not sure whether this was a good thing, since if the Swedes continued to be difficult, the Emperor, to avoid his final ruin, would compel the Spanish to cave in to the French demands. Mazarin even managed to integrate the possibility that the Spanish would take Armentières into his scenario. Even if they were to take ten strongholds in the campaign, he consoled himself, they could not withstand the demise of the Emperor. "The means are very easy," Mazarin concluded, "and the success infallible." How the Swedes could stop stalling, continue stalling, and terrorize the Emperor in just the right proportion for the greater convenience of France, Mazarin did not specify, although his bottom line was to encourage Longueville and D'Avaux to make peace, if only with the Emperor, if they could. There were hints of dissatisfaction in the *mémoire* about the slowness of the French generals in completing their levies, but these were balanced by great hopes for the siege of Lérida and in the ability of Turenne and his Weimarians to come up from Germany and turn the tide in the Low Countries. Not a hint, however, about the fact that the regency was running out of money, or of the surly mood in Paris, where press gangs were roaming the city and Mazarin's unpopularity was reaching new heights.[25]

The truce in Portugal having run into a stone wall, the mediators went back to trying to get an agreement on the article permitting each party to defend its allies, along with the clarificatory declaration. It was the first time that the Spanish had seen either the article in its amplified form or its clarifications, and Peñaranda immediately spotted the difficulties. He objected to the right of the French to assist the Portuguese to their hearts' content, while the Spanish would be prevented from assisting the Duke of Lorraine. For the first time since its opening, it seemed as if the congress were in danger of breaking up. Under these circumstances, the last-minute concessions of Cardinal Mazarin and his rosy ruminations struck a particularly sour note in the minds of his plenipotentiaries, and on June 10 Longueville could not take it any longer. He replied to Mazarin:

It will be very easy for you to judge, why the peace is not concluded, since we have insisted on obtaining the truce in Portugal . . . and when we received letters not to let this block the peace, whether because of the precautions on the article regarding the liberty to assist Portugal have aroused the suspicions of the Spanish, or that they are using this as a pretext for dragging things out, the negotiation has been entirely interrupted.

And once the negotiations with Spain were interrupted, the peace in the Empire took on an entirely different complexion. Trauttmansdorff now cagily divided the treaty into two projects, one of the treaty with the Swedes and one of the treaty with the French, which he further divided

into two versions—one for Chigi, glossing over the religious concessions, and one for Contarini, which did not. The project for the Swedes
included the agreement over the *gravamina;* the explicit granting to the
Calvinists of all rights granted to the Lutherans, along with the provision which prohibited Protestant rulers from establishing a different
form of Protestantism in their territories; the full cession of Minden as
part of the compensation of the Elector of Brandenburg; and the alterna-
tion of the Bishopric of Osnabrück between a Catholic and a prince
of the Protestant house of Brunswick-Luneburg. Trauttmansdorff also
communicated this project to the princes and states of the Empire for
their consideration. The issues in the Empire were continuing to narrow.
With the Swedes, the only stumbling blocks were the matter of the payment of their troops and the restoration of public exercise of the Protestant religion in the hereditary lands. With the Hessians, the Landgravin
was willing to evacuate the Catholic enclaves within her own lands in
return for greater monetary compensation. With the French, however,
the open issues were much more stubborn. Even though the Emperor
was now prepared to make peace without Spain, he absolutely rejected
the idea of not being able to aid his cousins after the peace, and he still
insisted on the reestablishment of the Duke of Lorraine. There was also
the question now of whether the Empire would relinquish its right to
come to the defense of the Spanish possessions in its Circle of Burgundy,
should these be attacked by the French. Summoning all of the sangfroid
at his disposal, Trauttmansdorff now assumed a take-it-or-leave-it attitude toward his considerable concessions and prepared to return to Vienna. The French, having lost the Dutch, were now in danger of losing
the Swedes and the Hessians in the same manner.[26]

The only appeal left to Mazarin was to violence, and it failed miserably.
On June 14 the stronghold of Armentières fell to the Archduke Leopold,
from where he moved on to Landrecies, a stronghold that Richelieu had
taken in 1637. The siege of Lérida, moreover, was proving more difficult
than anticipated. The heat, the energetic sallies by the besieged, the impenetrable rock of the citadel, and desertions of his discouraged soldiers
were even taking their toll on the impetuous Prince de Condé, and on
June 18 he decided to abandon the siege before a relieving Spanish army
could repeat its achievement of the previous year. If this were not enough,
in Germany, on that very same day, as Turenne was beginning to get his
troops across the Rhine on their way to Luxembourg, his German cavalry,

which formed the bulk of his army, first demanded their back pay, then, refusing to serve outside of Germany, mutinied and rejoined their comrades on the right bank. Four of his French regiments managed to make it up to the Low Countries, but Turenne suddenly found himself without an army and had to spend the next few months cajoling back as many as he could of his lost Germans. After twenty-nine years of fighting, nothing could have better illustrated the elusiveness, in the early seventeenth century, of either total victory or total defeat.[27]

8

Waiting for the Verdict

The reproaches of the Duke de Longueville struck Mazarin to the core, and they produced his best, his most complete, and his most eloquent self-justification to date. How could he be accused of not wanting the peace? The council had always backed him to the hilt. "There wasn't a single *mémoire* sent to you gentlemen," he remonstrated on June 22, 1647, "that wasn't read in the council in the presence of Her Majesty, His Highness, and the Prince, when they have been at court." Ignoring the three months which *preceded* the signing of the articles between the Spanish and the Dutch, he asserted that, *since* the signing, the Spanish had not been negotiating seriously. His continued insistence on the six-months truce in Portugal? "In all of the *mémoires* that you have been sent the power to give up on this point has never been taken away from you . . . . If I had wanted to impede the peace," he concluded, "I would never have reduced affairs to the state that the Spanish, by agreeing to a simple truce of six months, could conclude it in an instant." It took the news of the lifting of the siege of Lérida and the mutiny of the Weimarians to take some of the wind out of his sails. He found himself obliged to admit, in the *Mémoire du Roi* of July 6, that "fortune has not spared us in Catalonia any more than anywhere else." His tone with his plenipotentiaries also began to change from one of superiority to one of deference. He almost begged them to bail him out. And in a letter of the next day to the Prince de Condé, Mazarin, after airily inciting the prince to a whole variety of ambitious enterprises, ended up by pleading with him just to remain in Catalonia, and happily offered to submit himself to whatever his most dangerous rival would see fit to do.[1]

The war had reached a defining moment, not so much because of what had happened as because of what had not. For the last three years Mazarin had been stringing the country along on expectations that one more effort would force the enemies to make peace. The previous years had seen great financial exertions, but these years had also seen great military successes and the possibility that the great expectations would be fulfilled. Now the situation had changed. Not just one, but two successive failures before Lérida, without even considering the disappearance of an entire French army from Germany, were the last straws. It suddenly dawned upon the public—whoever the public may have been—that what loomed ahead was an endless war, fought exclusively for the personal vanity of Cardinal Mazarin and the private gain of the financiers. As if to confirm this conclusion, Particelli d'Hémery, boasting that he could fund the war for three more years, grasped this very moment to drive the old President de Bailleul from the Superintendancy of Finances. And the military stalemate showed no sign of letting up. The French Marshal Rantzau took Dixmude, the Archduke Leopold struck back by taking Landrecies, and the French Marshal Gassion took La Bassée. The Swedish general Wrangel laid siege before Egra in Bohemia, but the Emperor was assembling a large army to relieve it. Weariness with the war, moreover, was not limited to France. Popular revolts against the Spanish broke out in Sicily and Naples, the latter particularly virulent and led by the fisherman Tommaso Aniello. The Protestant princes at Osnabrück, having secured their own liberties and reasoning, just like Richelieu, the council of Spain, and Axel Oxenstierna, that what was good for their political interests was also good for their religion, were now quite prepared, if they could rid themselves of the foreign armies, to let the future spread of the Reformation fend for itself. The council of Sweden, fearing that the Duke of Bavaria would break the truce, was also feeling that if they could settle the matter of the troops, they should give up their insistence on the open practice of Protestantism in the hereditary lands, and even the insatiable Landgravin of Hesse-Cassel reduced her monetary demand.[2]

Meanwhile, Longueville, D'Avaux, and the Swedish plenipotentiaries had gotten together to work on their replies to the Imperialist peace projects. To Mazarin's encouragement to settle with the Emperor alone, Longueville and D'Avaux came out strongly in favor of doing so if they could, adding that there was little sympathy for the demand that he not help the Spanish. On July 10 the French plenipotentiaries gave the mediators a brief reply to the Imperial project, to which the Imperialists responded by holding firm to their own projects, but the news of the relief of Lérida prevented Longueville and D'Avaux from showing any signs of weakness. And for the long-suffering Peñaranda, news of the relief of Lérida changed night into day. Whereas a few days before he had been asserting that "victorious or vanquished we both need peace," a few days after he saw it as a possibility "to recoup all our losses." The French plenipotentiaries kept entreating Mazarin to get some troops back into the Empire and pay the Swedes their subsidy, as if he could have done so. On July 16 Trauttmansdorff finally executed his threat to depart, continuing the exodus from Münster and leaving the negotiations in the hands of his subordinates. On July 19 Longueville and D'Avaux gave Contarini an impressive printed project for their peace with the Emperor, to which the Imperialists also responded by holding firm. But on July 13 the Swedes had taken Egra in Bohemia, and they were preparing for more action in Westphalia. Once again, everything hung on the outcome of the campaign.[3]

Toward the end of June, the States General finally decided to respond to Servien's proposals for a treaty of guarantee. They did so, however, by trimming them down and by presenting their counterproposals as a virtual ultimatum. Nor were the Dutch willing to brook any more French "tergiversations." Either the French accepted the concessions that the Spanish had made or the republic was to proceed to an immediate signing of the peace. Even so, the province of Holland kept raising new difficulties, and the final agreement was not signed until July 29. The Dutch guaranteed most of the French conquests, including Lorraine, but they forced the French to promise to assist the Dutch in case they were attacked by the allies of France, which meant Portugal and Sweden. Moreover, at the insistence of the Dutch, there was a six-month delay before each side needed to come to the aid of its ally. The treaty sounded very much like a husband asking his unfaithful wife to repeat their marriage vows, but Servien was happy enough to have emerged with a scrap of paper that would hopefully prevent the Dutch from forming an immediate alliance with Spain. He rushed back to Münster, full of himself. His first reaction upon his return was one of horror at the manner in which his colleagues had been conducting their end of the negotiations. His second was to resume his campaign of vilification against D'Avaux. As might have been expected, the States General went on to express a full vote of confidence in their plenipotentiaries and ordered them back to Münster to put the finishing touches on their treaty with Spain.[4]

The court of France returned to Paris on August 9 with little to show for its excursion, and Mazarin was reduced, in his *Mémoire du Roi* of August 16, to following the lead of Longueville and D'Avaux by letting them concentrate on making peace with the Emperor and keeping him from assisting the Spanish. Mazarin was even prepared to leave all of the remaining modalities, even this last desideratum, to these two men and to Servien. The only exception was to hold firm on excluding Duke Charles. In a broader sense, however, Mazarin was losing his grip, not only on the country and on his plenipotentiaries, but on the future, envisaging any kind of possibility from the most catastrophic to the most sanguine. If the war went on, he was willing to continue subsidizing the Swedes—as terrified as he was, on the one hand, of their becoming dominant in the Empire or, on the contrary, of seeing the Dutch, the Brandenburgers, and the Poles rallying to the support of the Hapsburgs. But the chastened Mazarin had changed neither his spots nor his proclivity for cultivating his fantasies. One of his reasons for preferring a peace in the Empire was still that "the decision we must make must always be the opposite of what the enemies desire." And after trembling at the prospect of Swedish hegemony, he began to contemplate with a certain relish the possibility of their acquiring the other half of Pomerania if France could get the forest towns and the Breisgau. It was at this time, too, that he discovered the plots against the government, by the Duke de Vendôme, and, even more ominously, by the false Raré. A plot which questioned the legitimacy of Louis XIV was enough to make anyone wonder what God had in store for the French monarchy, but it was the revolt in Naples with which he chose to interpret the Divine Plan. It again led him to the thought about the Spanish that "God hardens their heart in order to bring about something greater than we could dare to expect."[5]

The problem, of course, was how to keep paying for such things, and the methods contrived by D'Hémery could not have been better designed to alienate every stratum in French society. One was to revive, under a different name, the tariff on products coming into Paris. Another was the creation of a second *Châtelet* (presidial court) in Paris. A third was a *taxe sur les aisés,* a forced loan upon the wealthy of every class. All these impositions seemed to presage a general and perpetual tax increase. On Thursday, August 22, the *parlement* assembled as a group, and Broussel, a judge in the *grande chambre,* declaimed against the disorders in the finances. It was decided to address remonstrances to the queen. Over the weekend Cardinal Mazarin, who generally kept above such trivia, tried to smooth over the situation. He called in the attorney general, Talon, and catalogued for his benefit all of the military reverses, which, Mazarin insisted, were beyond "reasonable prudence." He blamed the Spanish for delaying the peace and felicitated himself that while they were expecting revolts in France, revolts had broken out against them in Naples. In short, he made every effort to arouse Talon's sympathy. It did not succeed. Talon was not interested in foreign affairs. He too was angry about the administration of the finances. He emphasized the misery in the provinces and implored Mazarin not to go to the extremity of holding another *lit de justice,* but rather to seek an accommodation with the *parlement.* He succeeded. There was no *lit de justice.* The judges placed a 200,000-*livre* ceiling on the tariff and limited it to two years. The government withdrew the edict for the new *Châtelet,* and the judges reduced the *taxe sur les aisés.* Well might Mazarin encourage his plenipotentiaries to trumpet this compromise as a royal victory. He himself admitted to them that he had gotten very little. It was becoming harder and harder for him to finance the war. The Venetian ambassador observed that Mazarin was looking depressed, his complexion pale, and his hair whitening.[6]

The departure of Trauttmansdorff was followed by the disappearance of Peñaranda, whose failing health provided him with a perfect excuse to slink off to Spa and take the cure, so that the French plenipotentiaries found themselves with very little to do. On the one hand, Longueville blustered about new French war plans and made his own preparations as if to leave. On the other, he and his colleagues shuddered at the anticipated return of the Dutch, who were about to consummate their infidelity. Thus, even though Longueville and D'Avaux had previously concluded that any concessions would merely embolden their enemies, Longueville and D'Avaux, joined by Servien, caved in to the entreaties of the mediators and agreed to a softening of the new Article 3 (which still implied that French troops could assist their allies offensively) as long as it was accompanied by the mediators' separate declaration that this referred to Portugal. The concession, of course, did no good, and Peñaranda, not even deigning to return, became even more difficult, eventually demanding, through Brun, an explicit declaration from the mediators that if the French auxiliaries in Portugal intruded into Spain, this intrusion would constitute an infringement of the peace. It was the same kind of quibbling, give or take a few words, that had held up the peace three months before, except that this time it was Peñaranda who was obstructing, and by design. Meanwhile, his hand was strengthened by the return of the rest of the Dutch plenipotentiaries, eager to put the final touches on their treaty, by news of the Imperial resistance in Bohemia, and by indications that the Duke of Bavaria was about to rejoin the Emperor.[7]

By the end of August, as a result of extraordinary exertions, Mazarin claimed to have assembled 16,000 foot and 8,000 horse in Flanders with 3,000 more on the way. It was far from the 40,000 with which he had started, but he still boasted that "never in living memory has anyone seen so many elite troops together at the end of a campaign." The Spanish, according to him, had no more than 16,000 at their disposal. In spite of this disparity, however, Rantzau and Gassion did not move, and Mazarin wavered between attributing their sloth to irresponsibility or to some sort of "fatality." He was humiliated by the public spectacle of the French monarchy being fought on equal terms by the Spanish and impatiently sent direct orders to his generals to undertake some enterprise. Finally, in mid-September, they set off in the direction of Ypres, and once again they stopped in their tracks. In Italy, one of Mazarin's agents had managed to rake up an alliance against the Spanish with the Duke of Modena. The question was whether the French monarchy was still in any position to exploit it.[8]

The council of Sweden, if not its chancellor, was so eager for peace that they approved the compromise by which the Duke of Bavaria obtained the title of elector as well as the Upper Palatinate. They had good reason to be eager. On August 22 a detachment of Wrangel's army had been maneuvering in the vicinity of Treibel in Bohemia when it was met and defeated by a stronger Imperial army. He was forced to retreat and soon found himself surrounded by the Imperialists. Early in September Servien made a journey to Osnabrück in an effort to shore up the alliance, which in his mind had been imperiled principally by D'Avaux's sanctimony and threats. The Swedish plenipotentiaries were indeed suspicious that the French had purposely left them in the lurch. Servien did his best to convince them of the Mazarinian thesis that the inactivity of the Dutch and the mutiny of the Weimarians were misfortunes that "no human foresight could have foreseen." He also presented the complaints of the Catholic princes as a Jesuit plot to forestall the peace. The Swedes were particularly suspicious that the French were negotiating with the Duke of Bavaria behind their backs, and Servien only confirmed this suspicion by urging the Swedes to treat him with more regard. He left on September 7 and no sooner did he return to Münster than he turned his frustration against D'Avaux, raking up every possible rumor about his person and his entourage for transmission to Mazarin.[9]

The financial situation of the French monarchy was getting desperate, and on August 31 the government called together some of the leaders of *parlement* to the Palais Royal for a little conference. There the Duke d'Orléans, in the presence of Cardinal Mazarin, the chancellor, and the superintendant D'Hémery, informed the judges that the queen was in need of their help in order to "sustain the glory of the crown." The superintendant was the principal speaker. He described to them how the regency had begun with all of its revenues used up for years into the future, and jeered that it was easy enough to speak of disorders, but that it was impossible to reform them without betraying the very creditors who were sustaining the state. He therefore announced some new edicts, whose chance of registration one can just imagine. No wonder that in his *Mémoire du Roi* of September 13 Mazarin sounds even more subdued. All of a sudden he was terrified of the entire German nation uniting against its tormentors. All of a sudden he was aware that everyone believed that France didn't want peace. All of a sudden he dearly prized the Duke of Bavaria. All of a sudden he wanted to curry the favor of the mediators. There was no more question in his mind about the desirability of concluding the peace. Of course, by his own law of opposites, which he reiterated in this very *mémoire,* the Spanish should not have felt the same way. He was, however, unwilling to adhere to his own principles. "If the Spanish," he began to speculate, "don't have some revelations which promise them advantages by means that are incomprehensible to us, it seems as if they have never had more subject to wish for the peace than they have today." He tried to find reassurance in reviewing the state of affairs as he saw it. The Spanish were stuck in Catalonia, reduced to the defensive in the Low Countries, threatened by revolts in Italy. The conspiracies in France had come to naught, and he tried to transform his recent confrontations with the *parlement* into a vote of confidence in his government, screaming out, like a sane man in an insane world, "These are invariable truths and not illusions!" They may have been invariable truths, but they were not invariable enough to convince Mazarin himself. A week later, moreover, the Duke of Bavaria, claiming that he had only agreed to the Treaty of Ulm as a first step to a general peace and bitterly complaining that the Swedes were merely exploiting it in order to take over the Holy Roman Empire, issued a manifesto announcing that he was breaking his truce with them. The defection of Bavaria was the last straw. Mazarin ordered Turenne back to Germany, but torn between the need to support the Swedes and Turenne's patent inability to execute the order, Mazarin transferred the final responsibility on whether to break with Bavaria immediately up to his plenipotentiaries. He suggested that they write a manifesto in conjunction with the Swedes, "explaining that the crowns were being reasonable."[10]

Since the Imperialists now had all the more reason not to budge from their previous offers, the French plenipotentiaries agreed to continue working through the mediators on the first twenty articles of the peace project with the Spanish, which, with the addition of the new Article 3, now amounted to twenty-one. None of the French plenipotentiaries were optimistic, but, under Servien's influence, they kept humoring Mazarin and reassured him in their *mémoire* of September 9 that "the defection of the Dutch and the Weimarians were beyond human foresight." It was a hard line to maintain with a straight face, and the following week, while reflecting on the firmness of the Spanish, the plenipotentiaries came out with their own more sincere evaluation of what lay in store: "If only the French nation were capable of maintaining a similar conduct," they sighed. Peñaranda, though continuing to moan about his health and reiterating his request to be recalled, echoed the same prophetic sentiment when he wrote on September 19 that "as bad off as we are at present, if the French suffer the least domestic disturbance, we might be a lot better off than they." Sensing a chance to play his enemies off against each other, he was no less stalwart with the Dutch in resisting their new demands. He finally dragged himself back to Münster on September 20, and a week later the secretaries of the French and Spanish embassies signed twenty of the first twenty-one articles of their treaty, but this progress was completely illusory. Even if the semantic issue of the declaration on Portugal could be overcome, the ethical issue of the Duke of Lorraine loomed as an insuperable stumbling block. On October 9, the Spanish craftily offered to place a number of the issues in dispute with the French to the arbitration of the Dutch, and the French could not even trust the Dutch enough to accept. As for the Swedes, if they conquered Bohemia, they would become a menace; if they were defeated, they would become a burden. The French plenipotentiaries summed up the situation in their *mémoire* of September 30: "we have everything to fear." The following week they again implored Mazarin to send a French army into Germany as soon as possible. One more week and they gave him the bad news that the Swedes had no intention of joining the French in a manifesto and came up with the desperate suggestion that Mazarin corrupt the Duke of Lorraine by inviting him to conquer Naples.[11]

Toward the end of September, the army of Flanders moved again. The grumpy Gassion attempted the siege of Lens, and in the process got himself killed, although his troops finally took the city of October 2. Mazarin did not regret his passing, Lionne informing Servien that "Gassion could be said to be a good commander of six hundred horse, but he was a terrible general . . . . indecisive and careless with his victuals and with his troops." Mazarin was hoping that this would be the end of the campaign, but no sooner had the French taken Lens than the Archduke Leopold laid siege before Dixmude. Rantzau failed to relieve it and it fell on October 13. In Catalonia the Prince de Condé took Ager. Thus the grim game of tit-for-tat continued, and it was even worse on other fronts of the war. In the early days of October, Wrangel, fearful of the Bavarian army that was marching to the relief of the Imperialists, withdrew his armies from Bohemia, leaving only isolated garrisons to assert the Swedish presence. Little by little he withrew into Brandenburg, with the Imperialists and the Bavarians not far behind. Meanwhile, a second Bavarian army laid siege to the stronghold of Memmingen, which had been occupied by the Swedes since the Treaty of Ulm. The theater of war now moved from the hereditary lands to northern Germany, just where the Bavarians and Imperialists could live off the country to their hearts' content.[12]

Moreover, the situation in the Dutch Republic was going from bad to worse. The new Prince of Orange, in whom the French had placed some hope, was emerging as a nonentity, given to his pleasures and resigned to the irresistible public sentiment for peace. The net result was that will of the province of Holland went virtually unopposed, and La Thuillerie, running out of options, went to the extreme measure of suggesting that the French should try to corrupt, of all people, Adriaan Pauw. Out of the depths of this frustration, the essence of Mazarin's feelings emerged in its purest form. "We are so badly treated by the Dutch," Lionne wrote to Servien, "that His Eminence commands me to inform you that this alone would be capable of tempting us to make peace with our enemies in order to go to war against our friends." Alas, if only they could have done it! From Münster, Pauw, Knuyt, and Clant returned to The Hague for further instructions, while Gendt and Ripperda returned to their provinces, leaving only Matenesse, Nederhorst, and Donia behind. Pauw and Knuyt made the report to the States General, and in a session of October 22, at the instigation of Holland and in the presence of the Prince of Orange, the assembly voted for the acceptance of the Spanish terms, pending only the approval of the other provinces in eight days' time. The Dutch were all set to abandon the French, and Mazarin could neither make peace with his enemies nor make war against his friends.[13]

He was struggling oh so vainly to find a way out! At the end of July an assassination attempt against John de Braganza had been discovered in Lisbon. Visibly shaken, the king began thinking of abandoning the throne and sent an offer to France to transfer it to the Duke d'Orléans, the Prince de Condé, or the Duke de Longueville, accompanied by the marriage of Monsieur's or the Duke de Longueville's daughter to the King of Portugal's son. Mazarin's first reaction to this news appears to have been to write to Longueville on October 9; then, thinking further, Mazarin came up with the following bizarre plan, which required the collaboration of the Pope, of the Duke of Lorraine, and of the duke's estranged first wife in solving the problems of the French monarchy. Mazarin wrote in his *Carnet:*

> If the war continues . . . deal with the Duke of Lorraine, annulling his marriage to the present duchess who is in France to whom all sorts of advantages could be given, the said duke giving up Lorraine in return for which the present king appoints him and the people acclaim him as King of Portugal on condition that the kingdom would revert to his son, who could be married to the daughter of the said duke, who would then become legitimate through the dissolution of his marriage.

How exactly Mazarin thought that he could get a pope whom he had affronted, a duke who was owned by the house of Austria, and a duchess who would be spurned, to go along with this harebrained scheme must rank right up there in the annals of wishful thinking. And in a *Mémoire du Roi* of October 25, he went straight from this fantasy to embracing all the other desperate ideas that were being proposed to him for bringing the war to an end, such as La Thuillerie's suggestion of bribing Pauw or the plenipotentiaries' suggestion of offering the Duke of Lorraine the Kingdom of Naples. He was so desperate that in this same *mémoire* he contemplated calling an assembly of notables to advise the king on whether to pull out of the peace conferences. He was under the impression that he could still prove to the world that the enemies were at fault, and he tried to take some comfort in the assurance that God was on his side. But he was not even so sure about that any more. "Heaven," he concluded, "interferes in certain events for which there is no known cause, but prudence does not permit one to give up nor to rely on anything but on secondary causes."[14]

Heaven was certainly doing its bit in Naples, where the situation was reaching a climax. The viceroy repealed all the unpopular taxes but managed to contrive Aniello's assassination. The rebels replaced him with a duplicitous nobleman, Prince Massa, then lynched him and went back to one of their own, Gennaro Annese, a gunsmith. There was growing distrust by the rebels of the nobility, and the revolt was spreading into the countryside. Only the forts within the city, a couple of strongholds throughout the kingdom, and a few nobles holed up in their *castelli* held out for the Spanish. The Neapolitans, for their part, decided to look to the French. They sent a deputy to seek the assistance of Fontenay-Mareuil, the French ambassador in Rome. Even before he could get to the ambassador, however, the envoy was intercepted by the Duke de Guise, a swashbuckling French nobleman residing at the embassy who was eager to present himself both to the people of Naples and to the French court as the Neapolitan counterpart of the Dutch princes of Orange. Fontenay-Mareuil and his advisors did not quite know what to do with the duke, but in the midst of these negotiations, a Spanish armada of forty-two ships and twenty-one galleys, commanded by Philip IV's half-brother, Don Juan of Austria, appeared in the Bay of Naples. He acted at first as a friend, offering to confirm all the concessions made by the viceroy if only the Neapolitans would put down their arms, but they refused to do so, and on October 5 he attempted take the city by force. After four days of bloody street fighting, however, he was forced back to the fortresses and his fleet had to withdraw from the city. The infuriated Neapolitans proclaimed a republic, and on October 24 they formally invited the Duke de Guise to become their general.[15]

In Westphalia, the Swedes were wavering, the Protestant princes were pressing for peace, and the Hapsburgs, in spite of their precarious position, simply would not cooperate. The French plenipotentiaries, hoping against hope that something good would happen for their cause, pushed ahead by discussing Articles 22 to 48 of their treaty with Spain with mediators. Under the circumstances, the Spanish created difficulties. There now emerged a problem with the renumbered 22 defining the conquests; the renumbered 26 on whether the French could construct fortifications in Catalonia during the truce; the renumbered 35 on the cession of the three posts in the Liègeois (which the French were quite prepared to concede); the renumbered 36 on Casale; and, of course, the infuriating issue of the Duke of Lorraine. Everyone, the French insisted, was convinced that they wanted peace and that it was the Spanish who were stalling, which was undoubtedly true. But that was just the problem. After years of laying down the law, the French now found themselves in the predicament of having to plead with the mediators for conditions that they had previously imposed and, by blustering about future campaigns, begging the question of why they had been unable to accomplish anything in this one.[16]

The Spanish had been so successful in separating the Dutch from the French that they now tried their hand at doing the same thing with the Swedes. Their trump card in this effort was the correspondence of Longueville, which they had been collecting since the beginning of the year. On October 28 Peñaranda sent the mischief-making Brun to Osnabrück carrying, among other things, a *Mémoire du Roi* of the previous January 25 in which Mazarin had been critical of Chancellor Oxenstierna and his son, and Longueville's answer of February 4, which implied that the French had been plotting against Sweden. The French knew of Brun's trip, but they did not have the slightest idea about its purpose. He does not seem to have found a very welcome audience, Johan Oxenstierna writing to his court a few days later expressing considerable skepticism about the overture. Apparently the Spanish also showed their intercepted correspondence to the Dutch. Spanish diplomacy was functioning flawlessly, even surviving the illness and death of their third plenipotentiary, the Archbishop of Cambrai.[17]

Just about this same time, amazingly, Mazarin discovered that the Spanish had been intercepting his correspondence. His information was that they had copies of all the letters that his plenipotentiaries had written since March. For a man who was now desperate not to alienate his Swedish allies, this discovery was devastating, and we can just imagine him and Lionne asking themselves what else may have been intercepted, rummaging through their files in search of sentiments which they now regretted. Mazarin immediately wrote Longueville a letter which he asked him to decipher personally, asking him to investigate.[18]

The news of the break between the Neapolitans and Don Juan of Austria gave Mazarin something of a lift. On November 3 he sent orders to the Duke de Richelieu, commanding the naval armada in Toulon, to set sail with his fleet for Naples. Mazarin gave him powers to treat with the Neapolitans but no detailed instructions. We know, however, that Mazarin wanted the people to elect a king. He did not think much of Guise and did not yet know that the Neapolitans had offered him their generalship. Mazarin's ideal solution was to secure the throne for the Prince de Condé, who would thereby conveniently find himself both out of Mazarin's way and dependent on his support. But he had no confidence in popular revolts, and most of all, he did not want to make any commitments that would complicate the negotiations for the peace. In the end, he issued vague orders and hoped for the best, which was a recipe for disaster. In his *Mémoire du Roi* of November 8, which describes his whole predicament to his plenipotentiaries in Münster, he merely ends up with the old line about Providence setting up the Spanish for a bigger fall.[19]

From the moment of his return from The Hague, Servien had been building up his case against D'Avaux, and on November 5 he struck again: "D'Avaux," said Servien, "would be delighted at a change in which he imagines that all affairs would fall into his hands, even though, in fact, he is the feeblest of men and least suitable for great things." Servien suggested that Mazarin ask just about everyone who had ever come into contact with D'Avaux to reveal whether D'Avaux had ever stated that France did not want peace, and that, if D'Avaux were to deny these accusations, this would prove that he was a liar. Servien also claimed that Longueville was disgusted with D'Avaux, in this case because he had *prevented* the peace. This was of course classic Servien and music to Mazarin's ears, but the problem now more than ever was that D'Avaux had credibility and that, if he were recalled, he would be infinitely more troublesome sitting in the council than running around in Münster. Mazarin had enough troubles of his own, to which was added the illness of Louis XIV, who had come down with smallpox.[20]

The Imperialists, in an effort to frighten the Swedes, now decided to renew their negotiation with the French, going along with the confirmation of their agreement as it had been signed in September of the previous year. The French plenipotentiaries, trying to get the best of both worlds, borrowed money on their own credit in Amsterdam in order to advance money to the Swedes and to the Landgravin of Hesse-Cassel. The French plenipotentiaries also pushed ahead on their treaty with the Spanish, signing Articles 23 to 48 on November 16, but since they omitted all the articles in contention and the treaty with the Emperor was contingent upon the signing of the treaty with the Spanish, this progress meant absolutely nothing. Probably the most significant event of the month in Westphalia was that the first deputies of the Catholic princes— Bavaria, Würtzburg, and Bamberg—were beginning to appear at Osnabrück, apparently more reconciled to the concessions that Trauttmansdorff had made to the Protestants. A recently elected Elector of Mainz also loomed as an advocate of compromise between the religions. If the united Protestant and Catholic princes of the Empire succeeded in making peace with each other, D'Avaux's early warning might well come to pass. The Germans, like the Italians of yore, would suddenly combine to make the French superfluous.[21]

The intrepid Guise had meanwhile boarded a swift ship and managed to make his way to Naples, where he arrived on November 15, to the acclamations of the populace. He was immediately invited to dine with Gennaro Annese, whom Guise depicts in his *Mémoires* as the classic embodiment of the brutish and unrestrained canaille. Since Annese was illiterate, we do not have his side of the story, but, aristocratic snobbishness notwithstanding, Guise found the situation in Naples appalling: barely 400 foot and 300 horse, no supplies, no money, mob rule, the nobility alienated and rallying to the Spanish. He did his best to remedy the situation, levying troops, skirmishing against the Spanish, and trying to entice the nobility into the rebellion. He won a pitched battle against them in the vicinity of Aversa, which helped his reputation, but the Spanish still occupied the major fortresses in the city, and Guise needed the help of the French armada.[22]

It had been a difficult year, and Mazarin needed a lift. He looked for it, as he often did in such circumstances, in dictating a long *mémoire* in which he could reconstruct the world according to his own requirements. On this occasion it was a *Mémoire du Roi* to Fontenay-Mareuil, the French ambassador in Rome, and its purpose was to instruct him and his collaborators on how to deal with the Neapolitans. It turned out to be the longest and most systematic confession of political faith that Mazarin had ever written, and it is almost completely unknown, a casualty to the incapacity of historians to recognize the *Mémoires du Roi* as his own compositions. This one began by reaffirming his own contempt for the "fickleness" of the Neapolitan people. In spite of their unreliability, however, Mazarin thought it "imprudent" to neglect them, not because he had logic on his side, which by his own admission he did not, but because, by virtue of the purity of his queen's intentions (and contrary to his own previous misgivings) "we have cause to hope to be favored by the benedictions of heaven." One result of this divine intervention became immediately apparent when it miraculously extinguished all of Mazarin's doubts. If the Neapolitans were properly handled, he now went so far as to assert, "it is certain that we will accomplish more in three months with a few troops than we could in three years with large armies." This could be done principally by humoring the Neapolitans in their desire to establish a republic—which Mazarin in a long pseudo-Machiavellian disquisition thought was completely beyond their capacity—and then, when they would come around to Louis XIV, Fontenay-Mareuil (there was no mention of Guise) should adroitly bring them to a member of the French royal family. This would be much more convenient, Mazarin calculated, because if Louis XIV accepted the throne, it would complicate the peace negotiations at Münster, whereas a member of the French royal family (Mazarin still had Condé in mind) could enjoy French support, but still independently defend his throne without alarming the other princes of Europe. Why the Spanish or the other princes would be taken in by this ruse, Mazarin did not consider, but, the Neapolitans being so vain, he had no doubt that if one simply flattered or corrupted them sufficiently, they would accept anything. Indeed, becoming cockier as he went along, Mazarin even ordered his ambassador to hold out on signing a treaty until the Neapolitans accepted a king, before graciously leaving this gambit up to Fontenay-Mareuil. It didn't matter. If Mazarin could exploit the revolution of Naples in order to terrorize the Spanish into making peace, he was prepared to leave the Neapolitans to their fate, just as, if the Spanish had been willing to give him their Low Countries, he would have abandoned the Catalonians and the Portuguese to theirs.[23]

One thing Mazarin need not have worried about was the loyalty of the Swedes. Bluster and threaten as they might that they could go at it alone in Germany, it was the overwhelming sentiment of their chancellor, Oxenstierna, that they could not. Nothing better illustrates this point than the incident of the intercepted letters. The moment they reached Stockholm, they were referred to the chancellor, who quickly discounted them as efforts by the Spanish to break the alliance. "We hold it necessary and advisable," Christina replied to the chancellor's son, "that, just as you yourself have suggested, you not let yourself be influenced by them, so that this does not cause any suspicions with our allies." Indeed, she went on to order him not to have any further communication with the Spanish plenipotentiaries. We come up here against a powerful conjunction of interests between the Swedes and the French, which, notwithstanding all personal and religious animosities, continued to function throughout the war and in the end permitted the French monarchy to salvage the acquisition of Alsace from the Peace of Westphalia.[24]

By the end of 1647, the crisis in the finances of the French monarchy was at a point that the government had still pledged every penny that would be coming for the next two years, which suggests that it had been functioning since the beginning of the regency almost exclusively on the financial edicts that it could maneuver through *parlement* and, even more, one suspects, on extraordinary loans. In order to finance the next year's campaign, therefore, it was absolutely imperative not only to get more advances from the financiers, but also to impose some additional edicts so as to build up a new stock of collateral. The mood in Paris, however, was now so surly that Mazarin and D'Hémery could no longer hope to get these registered without resorting to a *lit de justice*. Finally, Mazarin began to give serious attention to the finances, and he devoted a good deal of time during December to considering ever more inventive ways to amass money, even going to the extent of having the king permit the holders of benefices to nominate their own successors in return for a year's income from the benefices and other advantages. But the incident of the intercepted letters was also preying on his mind, and it was one more misfortune that he found it easy to chalk up to the household, if not the person, of the unfortunate D'Avaux. The incident, as he put it in his *Mémoire du Roi* of December 20, equaled the loss of a battle, and it led Mazarin to do something else which he had long been reluctant to do—namely, to order Turenne to make a formal break with Bavaria. It also led Mazarin, in his panic, to start making concessions on a grand scale, and in his *Mémoire du Roi* of December 24, he announced that the queen, in secret consultation with the Duke d'Orléans and the recently returned Prince de Condé, had agreed to submit all of the remaining points in contention with the Spanish, with the exception of the restitution of Lorraine, to the arbitration of the Dutch Republic or to the Prince of Orange. Not that Mazarin expected anything to come of it, except possibly to gain some sympathy from the Dutch and Germans. Still, this meant that by the end of the year he had placed himself in the hands of his treacherous friends and had given up on all the demands, except for one, over which he had been holding up the negotiations with the Spanish since its beginning.[25]

Then there was the revolt in Naples. It was not until December 18 that the French armada, consisting of twenty-six ships and no galleys, anchored in the picturesque bay. Fortunately for the French, the Spanish were dispersed in various harbors and ill-prepared to defend themselves. No sooner did the French lay anchor, however, than they found themselves having to cope with the demands of the Duke de Guise. He was upset that they had not attacked the Spanish forthwith, and even more upset when he discovered that they had instructions to deal with Gennaro Annese. Guise therefore hastened to get the populace to acclaim him Duke of the Republic, while relegating the gunsmith to a subordinate status. But this move only increased the tension between Guise and the French, to say nothing of the tension between Guise and the people. He did not venture to go on board the French armada for fear of being arrested, and none of its commanders ventured to come on shore for fear of being kidnapped. The French armada finally got the better of the Spanish in a couple of naval engagements, but it did not coordinate its operations with the rebels and it was rapidly running out of supplies. Thus the Neapolitan revolt, caught between the vague orders of the court, the ambitions of Guise, and the tensions between himself and the popular party, was quickly turning upon itself.[26]

In Münster the Spanish and the Dutch settled their final differences, and the Dutch decided to make one last effort to get the French to soften their demands, or at the very least to excuse their own defection. On December 28 the Dutch collectively visited the French plenipotentiaries, begging them to facilitate the peace. The same day, Knuyt came to visit D'Avaux while Nederhorst visted Servien, but it was Knuyt who got down to brass tacks..He expostulated, one by one, on the insignificance of the remaining issues between France and Spain and the bad impression that French intransigence was making. He proposed a reduction in the time of the garrisoning of Casale, proposed a compromise on the fortifications of Catalonia, expressed the willingness of the Dutch to arbitrate the remaining differences over the conquests, and recommended the dropping of the certificate regarding Portugal. His most radical proposal, however, was in regard to Lorraine—namely, that the Spanish be allowed to aid its duke if he could not come to an understanding with the French within a year, or that the French immediately restore to him that portion of his duchy that was not feudatory to France. These offers, made unofficially without any assurance that the Spanish would accept them, had all the earmarks of an exercise in hypocrisy. Yet they were sufficient to wreak havoc upon the French delegation. Longueville and D'Avaux were in favor of accepting them, if only to delay the signing of the separate peace. Servien absolutely balked at making any concessions on Lorraine, which he believed would be completely wasted. He may well have been correct, but the greater significance of the debate was that for the first time since all three of the French plenipotentiaries had been at Münster, Longueville and D'Avaux had united to speak up.[27]

9

The Coming of the Fronde

Mazarin was in a corner. He was desperate to achieve a peace for which he needed one more exertion, yet he felt the ground in France slipping out from under him. And in the midst of his insecurity, on January 8, 1648, arrived the *mémoire* from his plenipotentiaries supporting the impertinent Dutch suggestion that France should restore the old Duchy of Lorraine. What was he to do? An acquisition which he had considered to be at his disposal was now being put into question. It was a measure of his debility that he did not fly into a rage. Instead he called a council, once again starring the queen, the Duke d'Orléans, and the Prince de Condé, which considered and reconsidered the matter at length. The traces of the consideration, which took place over the course of several sittings, are evident in a *Mémoire du Roi,* which is as remarkable in its form as it is surprising in its conclusions. It began with a rebuttal of all the arguments that Longueville and D'Avaux had advanced for accepting the Dutch offer. The Dutch, the *mémoire* retorted, could not be trusted. The situation in Germany was not so bad. Things were bound to get better in Flanders, Catalonia, and especially Italy. Indeed it maintained that "prudence requires taking a chance," and that by putting themselves in the hands of "fortune," the French could "assure the peace of Christendom by weakening of our enemies so that they can never again dream of disturbing it." By all this logic, nothing would be so absurd as to play along with the Dutch, whose suggestion, even if it were accepted by the Spanish, would merely furnish them with a congenital ally against the French monarchy. It is true, the *mémoire* admitted, that "the events of war are in the hands of God, but judging by ordinary ways, no one can condemn us of presumption if we expect success." Yet, in spite of this accommodating if implausible consensus between prudence, fortune, and reason, the *mémoire* went on to announce that the king and his mother had decided to offer the restitution of the *old* Duchy of Lorraine. Why? Not because of the external situation, but because of the increasing shortage of money in France so that "the ordinary ways will always meet greater obstacles."[1]

It is hard to imagine a more bizarrely constructed instruction. Why did Mazarin go to such lengths to counter the arguments of Longueville and D'Avaux, only to come to their same conclusion? The answer lies in the explanation that Lionne furnished to Servien, who undoubtedly would have asked himself the same question: "He does not want to bear the hatred for not having made peace when he had the chance." The answer, in other words, lies in Mazarin's assumption that the concession would not work and that he had to make it in order to regain some desperately needed favor with domestic opinion. But if one reads between the lines, there is a lot more to it. The Mazarin of 1648 was less confident about the outcome of the war than he was fearful of revolution at home. He had an inkling that domestic trouble was brewing, and the detailed explanation of his great prospects for victory was just in case a popular revolt should intervene to deprive him of it. He was preparing his legacy, for the benefit of all posterity, that on the verge of victory, requiring just one more exertion from the inconstant French nation, he had been stabbed in the back![2]

It did not take long for this very scenario to unfold. The confrontation between Louis XIV and his *parlement,* barely eluded the year before, took place on January 15. Accompanied by Anne of Austria, the Duke d'Orléans, the Prince de Condé, and the high officers of the crown, with troops lining the streets, the nine-year-old king rode in military procession from the Palais Royal to the Palais de Justice, where from his *lit de justice* in the *grande chambre* he tearfully (since he could not remember his speech) ordered his chancellor to read seven fiscal edicts. Just as the edicts of the year before, they could not have been better devised to infuriate every stratum of society: creation of new officials for the city of Paris, extortions from non-noble holders of feudal lands, creation of twelve new masters of requests, new bureaucrats for the royal council, and forced loans upon the users of the royal domains. The *parlement* did not appreciate either the intimidation or the edicts, and this time Attorney General Talon addressed himself directly to the Mazarin thesis: "It is claimed that it is easier to force the enemies by arms than by reason. Be this true or false, victories do not diminish the misery of the people." He did his best to make the distinction, so dear to the judges, between absolutism and despotism. "You are our sovereign lord," he told Louis XIV, "but it is important that we be free," and he warned him that "the good will of the people diminishes when men are persuaded that the government brings misery upon them." The show of force thus ended as just one more embarrassment for Cardinal Mazarin. The masters of requests appealed to the *parlement* against the edict which offended them, the *parlement* proceeded to discuss all the edicts, and Talon's speech burst like a clap of thunder all over Europe.[3]

In Münster, the tragedy was turning into a farce. The French were trying desperately to stop the signing of the separate peace between the Spanish and the Dutch, and D'Avaux, in particular, was building up expectations for the restitution of Lorraine. The Dutch plenipotentiaries found themselves betwixt and between, anxious to sign with the Spanish but not wanting, if at all possible, to alienate the French. Peñaranda, though he may have been willing to make peace if he could obtain the restitution, was certain that the French were merely waiting for some good news from Naples. The farce thus played itself out. As soon as they received permission to submit the remaining points, minus Lorraine, to arbitration, the French plenipotentiaries presented it to the Dutch and tried to enlist the mediators in the effort. This was not enough to satisfy the Dutch, who insisted on something more positive, and the French then begged for fifteen more days in which to obtain it. Indeed, they were so desperate that they went beyond their powers and offered to submit the Lorraine question to be settled separately by commissioners and, if necessary, by arbiters over the course of the following year. At the last moment the French obtained their fifteen days, but these were more like a stay of execution, and Servien, who had been dragged along by his colleagues, was inveighing publicly against them and privately picturing D'Avaux's efforts as a deliberate plot to give away the store. Seeing no alternative but a continuation of a war with Spain, and with Longueville about to depart, Servien now set his sights on his one remaining objective, the recall of D'Avaux. Servien was right in one respect. The last-ditch efforts to prevent the signing of the Spanish-Dutch treaty were fruitless. It was signed on January 30, with only one of the Dutch plenipotentiaries, Nederhorst, refusing to go along with his colleagues, after which all but Donia made a quick departure from Münster.[4]

No sooner did Mazarin receive the first indications of how the Spanish were behaving than, as much as he had anticipated their responses in making his concession, he began to regret it. He assembled a public council in which he, the queen, Monsieur, and the Prince de Condé listened patiently to the appeals of the nuncio and the Venetian ambassador before refusing to make any further concessions. Not that he summoned up the courage to take it out against Longueville, nor to recall D'Avaux, nor even to revoke the concession, which he ordered La Thuillerie to confirm at The Hague. Thus, even though Mazarin agreed wholeheartedly with Servien and held D'Avaux personally responsible for instigating the Dutch offer, Lionne confided to Servien: "we couldn't push him at this juncture without his partisans being able to convince everybody that he is being persecuted because he wanted to make peace." The most that Mazarin could do was to dictate another interminable *Mémoire du Roi,* bemoaning the horrible predicament in which the French now found themselves and blaming anonymous culprits for having put them into it. Fortunately for him, Anne, the Duke d'Orléans, and the Prince de Condé were still on his side—the queen because Mazarin was the only man she could trust, Monsieur in spite of being the brother-in-law of Charles IV, and the prince because he had everything to gain from a continuation of the war. But, with the exception of the queen who loved him, each of these supporters had his price and fully intended to exact it.[5]

Mazarin may have been able to hold on to the royal family, but the *parlement* was a different matter. On February 3 Jacques Le Coigneux, one of the two presiding judges in the second chamber of requests, went so far as to maintain in the *grande chambre* that the king of France had given his judicial officials the right to consent to taxation, that they acted as the intermediaries between the king and the poor, and that this responsibility was not superseded by the king's absolute power except in the most extreme of circumstances. On this audacious principle, they went on grudgingly to approve the edict on the domain and, for the moment at least, the great absolutist flinched. "The *parlement,*" Mazarin dictated for the plenipotentiaries in Münster, "has *satisfied,*" and then had Lionne cross it out and replace it by "has *begun* to satisfy His Majesty on the edicts." The queen eventually ordered the *parlement* to rescind its claims to legislative power, but it ignored her while continuing its discussions as before. The first President Molé and D'Avaux's brother, the President de Mesmes, did their best to promote the fiction that the debate was taking place "at the king's good pleasure" . . . and failed! The reappearance of Longueville in Paris on February 26 helped a bit. On the advice of his brother-in-law, Condé the duke restrained himself and adopted the official government line that it was the Spanish who were preventing the peace. By the middle of March the queen had managed to browbeat the *parlement* into admitting that it was deliberating "at the king's good pleasure," and by February 23 Mazarin had even regained enough confidence to recall D'Avaux, coldly and summarily. Thus, at the very moment when he needed to rally every moderate in the *parlement* to his cause, Mazarin went out of his way to remove the remaining symbol of moderation from the French delegation.[6]

During the entire previous year, the council in Madrid had been much more of an observer than a participant in the negotiations at Münster, content to issue encouragements and allow Peñaranda to feel his way, but in a *consulta* on February 25 they decided to take stock of the situation. The Count de Monterrey led off by arguing that, given the infirmities of the Spanish monarchy, if Peñaranda could conclude the peace with the Dutch it was still in the interest of Philip IV to make peace with France as well. Monterrey, however, showed less concern than delight over the fact that Peñaranda had left a number of issues open—notably the issue of the Duke of Lorraine—maintaining that Philip IV was in no position to abandon Charles IV. The Marquis de Leganés agreed wholeheartedly, but the perpetually feisty Count de Castrillo went even further. He complained that Peñaranda had exceeded his orders by allowing the third article on assisting one's allies and insisted that he should now ask the Dutch for assurances that the French could not assist Portugal. The recently returned Marquis de Castel Rodrigo then took a middle path, retorting that asking the Dutch for more assurances at this point would jeopardize the separate treaty, although once it was signed the Spanish would be at greater liberty to demand "emendations" in their negotiations with France. The opinions may thus have varied slightly, but clearly a fresh wind was blowing in the council of Spain. As this meeting was going on, the news arrived of the signing of the Spanish-Dutch treaty. Philip IV decided to wait before making a final decision on the *consulta*. He too was sniffing new opportunities in the continuation of the war against France alone, and he was excited by the scent.[7]

The last great hope for a breakthrough at Münster, the revolution in Naples, also vanished. Short of supplies and unable to brave the season, the French naval armada withdrew at the beginning of the year, leaving the Duke de Guise to his own devices. He achieved some military successes; his companion, the Count de Modène, even took Aversa, but Guise himself treated the popular leaders with disdain, increasing their suspicion that he was conspiring with the nobility. Alternately brutal, fearless, and indulgent, he strove to become the embodiment of the chivalric double standard by claiming to be conquering the kingdom for the favor of a young lady in Paris. His attack on February 12 against the Spanish posts in the city failed, and the new Spanish Viceroy, the Count de Oñate, who arrived on March 2 to join Don Juan, cultivated the fears of the popular leaders. There were several attempts on Guise's life, which he barely escaped. Early in April, in anticipation of the return of the French armada, he decided that he needed the tiny island of Nisida, which could provide an anchorage for their galleys. It was only some five miles from the center of the city, and on April 5 he marched up to it with his most reliable troops. But no sooner had he begun his siege than the Spanish in the city came out of their posts and, claiming that he had abandoned Naples to its fate, quickly reoccupied it. He tried to make his way out of the kingdom with a small band of followers, but was ultimately captured in the vicinity of Capua, at which time he began jauntily offering the Spanish his services to promote a revolution in France.[8]

In Münster, even the last of the Dutch plenipotentiaries eventually returned home as the negotiation between the French and the Spanish came to a complete standstill. Servien thus took the occasion to go up to Osnabrück in order to evaluate the situation there. He found the Swedes in no hurry to conclude, but fearful that their demands for the reimbursement of their troops would be undercut by the eagerness of their own Protestant allies to come to an accommodation as quickly as possible with the increasing number of Catholics who were in the city. Servien took heart from the isolation of the Swedes. It boded well for their continuing loyalty to the French alliance. His primary fear, however, was that the German princes, once they resolved their own differences, would not sign on to all the concessions which the Emperor had made to the French, not to speak of the three undecided points: the status of the Circle of Burgundy, the right of the Emperor to aid the King of Spain, and the exclusion of the Duke of Lorraine. Servien returned to Münster hoping for the best, but, as it turned out, the Swedes went on to confirm their own arrangements with the Imperialists, with the eager if grudging concurrence of the German princes. Only the payment of the Swedish troops and the reinstatement of the exiles from Bohemia remained to be settled. Thus it seemed as if the peace with Spain was as dubious as the peace in the Empire was in the offing. The most symbolic event, which seemed to destroy the last glimmer of hope for a peace with Spain, was the departure of D'Avaux, which he made as dramatic as possible by insisting until the last moment that he could have pulled it off.[9]

How Mazarin could have believed that he had any credibility left either in Europe or in France; how he could have believed that in a world of corruptible and rapacious humanity anyone who was not his creature should have the remotest interest in supporting the righteousness of his cause; how he could have believed that notwithstanding his own law of opposites, the Spanish should now be just as desperate as he was to end the troubles of Christendom may be a bit difficult to fathom, but this is what he believed, for he expressed these feelings in the *Mémoires du Roi* which he could now address exclusively to the one man with whom he had no reason to dissimulate. In the first of these *mémoires,* he insists that "only the most crude can misunderstand the passion of Their Majesties for peace." In the second he could pursue his rewriting of history by maintaining that "it is almost two years that it is France which has made all the steps toward peace." And in return for Servien's appreciation of such confidences, the queen, on April 23, promoted him to the rank of minister of state, with the right, on his return, to take a seat in the *conseil d'en haut.* But perhaps the best indication of Mazarin's complete inability to see himself in perspective is when he rails, in the third of these *mémoires,* against the maliciousness of Pauw for having roused such fears over the marriage of the king with the Infanta of Spain, something which, Mazarin now proclaimed, had been "so unlikely."[10]

On April 28 the Duke d'Orléans descended upon the *Chambre des Comptes* and Condé's brother, the Prince de Conti, unto the *Cour des Aides* to enforce the registration of the same edicts which had been brought before *parlement* in January, along with a host of others.

D'Hémery was meanwhile working feverishly to obtain advances from the financiers into the revenues of the years 1650 and 1651, and, the *paulette* having expired, it was also rumored that he intended to divide the companies by extending the privilege at no cost to the *parlement,* while extorting four years of wages out of the other sovereign courts in Paris, namely, the *Chambre des Comptes,* the *Cour des Aides,* and the *Grand Conseil.* Alarmed, the judges of the *Cour des Aides* began to call for a union with the *parlement,* and when, on April 30, the government issued its declaration on the *paulette,* it was indeed discriminatory and confirmed the judges' worst fears. The situation in Paris was reaching crisis proportions, but Mazarin still seemed to be doing his best to ignore it. He wrote Servien that Peñaranda's predictions of a revolt in France were "ridiculous," while insisting upon the inability of the Spanish to understand their own interests.[11]

Meanwhile, one of the Dutch plenipotentiaries, Gendt, had returned to Münster to prepare for the exchange of ratifications with the Spanish, while doing what he could to promote a final peace for the French as well. He suggested, among other things, an immediate suspension of arms between France and Spain, which Servien summarily rejected, playing right into the hands of Peñaranda, who let it be known that he was still prepared to make peace but intended to withdraw all his previous concessions once the campaign began. Even more alarming for Servien was the situation in Osnabrück, where the princes of the Empire were pressing both the Swedes and the Imperialists to settle their remaining disputes. As all of the Dutch plenipotentiaries were assembling in Münster for the great event, he once more hurried to Osnabrück in a attempt to obtain confirmation of the French satisfactions and to get the negotiations transferred back to Münster, but he was no longer in a position to bully and had to content himself with cordial assurances of support from his sympathizers. On May 15 came his final humiliation, when in an atmosphere of public rejoicing, the historic ratification took place in the Münster city hall of the separate peace between Peñaranda, Brun, and the entire Dutch delegation with the exception of Nederhorst, immortalized in the famous painting by Gerald Terborsch.[12]

As much as Mazarin might attempt to dismiss the troubles brewing within France itself, they insisted on getting in his way. On May 11 Broussel, who was emerging as a leader of the activists in the *parlement,* called for a meeting by the representatives of the four sovereign courts of Paris to discuss their common grievances. Such a meeting, in defiance of the government, was unprecedented; yet two days later the *parlement* passed its *arrêt d'union* by acclamation. Still, Mazarin refused to take the judges seriously. The Prince de Condé had just laid siege before Ypres and the government felt strong enough to retaliate against the *parlement* by revoking the *paulette*. But the government simply could not accumulate enough successes to rebuild its shattered image. As Condé was besieging Ypres, the Spanish retook Courtrai, a town which the Duke d'Orléans had conquered in 1646, more than offsetting the capitulation of Ypres that followed. Moreover, when on May 23 D'Avaux reappeared in Paris, this symbol of moderation was not even permitted to see the queen. The ultimate embarrassment occurred when the Duke de Beaufort, imprisoned since 1643, managed to escape from Vincennes. It seemed as if the Importants were coming out of the woodwork and the cabal of 1643 was reconstituting itself. The queen kept calling the *gens du roi* to the Palais Royal, ordering the *parlement* to stop its assemblies, and her council quashed the *arrêt d'union*, all in vain. Finally, around the middle of June, Mazarin addressed himself to the crisis. He decided that if the government caved in to the *parlement,* this would take the wind out of its sails until the next military victory could permit the government to reassert its power. So on June 21 the Duke d'Orléans called in some of the leading judges and in the presence of Cardinal Mazarin offered to intercede with the queen on practically all the issues in contention. She began by consenting to the *arrêt d'union*, and on June 30 thirty-two delegates from the four sovereign courts began meeting in the Chamber of Saint Louis. Rather than concentrating on their particular grievances, however, they went on a rampage, proceeding to a thoroughgoing reform of the state: revocation of intendants, reductions of the *taille* by one quarter, establishment of a chamber of justice to prosecute speculators, no new taxes unless verified by sovereign courts, no reduction in wages of officers, even the right of *habeas corpus*. They seemed to work on the assumption that all the evils of government were due to the financiers and that merely getting them to disgorge would solve all the financial worries—this while the government continued its headlong retreat. The queen reinstated the masters of requests, and on July 9 she dismissed the discredited D'Hémery, replacing him by the inexperienced Marshal de La Meilleraye. Though Mazarin was burning up inside, he wrote in the king's name to Servien: "Far from the enemies deriving any joy from this, it may have happened for the best by giving the king the means of establishing a secure fund with the consent of the sovereign companies." Indeed, in order to head off more recommendations (which the *parlement* was implementing with its own *arrêts*) and get the chamber to disband, on July 31 the king held another *lit de justice,* and this time the government used it to institute, under its own authority and in more moderate form, many of the reforms recommended by the Chamber of Saint Louis as well as to restore the *paulette* for good measure.[13]

The pendulum in Germany, on the other hand, was swinging back in the direction of the crowns. Early in March Turenne's painfully reconstituted army of 8,000 to 9,000 troops had effected a junction with the Swedes under Wrangel for a common invasion of Bavaria, and on May 17 the allied armies surprised the Imperialists and Bavarians at Zusmarshausen while they were in the process of crossing the Lech. In a desperate rearguard action the Imperial general Melander met his death while saving the bulk of his army, but his subordinates retreated across Bavaria in disarray, abandoning the countryside to the ravages of the enemy while barely able to hold on to the great cities. Heartened by this offensive, Servien decided to go to Osnabrück to put some pressure on the Swedes and on the German princes to return to Münster and address themselves to the French satisfactions. Arriving at Osnabrück on June 15, he immediately discovered that he had to wait his turn. The Swedes were anxious to conclude their treaty and the princes of the empire were anxious to see the last of them. The princes begged Servien to remain and to allow them to get around to the French satisfactions in Osnabrück, but the Imperialists seemed undaunted by their defeats, and on June 17 Volmar threatened to leave the conference if it took up the French satisfactions in Osnabrück and specified that the Emperor would never make peace unless he had the liberty to assist the Duke of Lorraine and the King of Spain. The next day, two of the Dutch plenipotentiaries arrived in Osnabrück with the last word from Peñaranda. Even at this late point, with goodwill on both sides, there may have been a possibility of pulling a general peace out of the hat, but that is precisely what was lacking. On June 29 Peñaranda left the conference, entertaining the vision that his departure would fan the flames of revolt in France, and Servien returned from Osnabrück with much the same thought: "If the gentlemen of the sovereign courts of Paris," he wrote to his court on June 30, "knew how much their resistance to the orders of the queen had augmented the audacity of the enemies, I have no doubt that such persons would abstain from producing such bad effects." Servien made still another trip to Osnabrück, only to see the Swedes come to terms on the payment of their troops and give up entirely on the reinstatement of the Protestant exiles from Bohemia. Would the French once more be left in the lurch?[14]

Turenne was now the junior partner in a war in which the Swedes were taking the initiative. By the beginning of June, the French and Swedish armies had reached the Inn, but they were blocked from crossing it by its high waters as well as by a motley Imperial-Bavarian army hastily reconstructed under its new commander, Piccolomini. While all the attention of Europe was focused upon this impasse, however, a small detachment of the Swedish, led by General Königsmarck, made a quick march from the Upper Palatinate into Bohemia and at dawn on July 26 seized the portion of the city of Prague on the left bank of the river Moldau. The inhabitants rushed to defend the remaining two-thirds of the city, and with most of the Imperial-Bavarian army now facing the enemy across the Iser, the position of the Emperor looked grim indeed. But for all their successes, the French and the Swedes limited themselves to foraging around Bavaria, the Swedish besiegers of Prague made no further progress, and, given the experience of the last thirty years, it was anybody's guess as to whether the campaign would confirm the peace in the Empire or merely reignite the war.[15]

Mazarin could not go on this way for long. Deprived of the capacity to borrow at huge rates of interest, he was simply incapable of carrying on either an effective war or an effective diplomacy, and he has left us a precious section of his *Carnets* where he was weighing his options at this difficult moment. None of them were very palatable: arresting the troublemakers and suspending the most troublesome chambers of the *parlement* risked a general strike by the judiciary. He thought of one more effort to convince the *parlement* that without money "armies will disintegrate and deprive us of years of victories." He thought of leaving secretly for Compiègne to confer with the Prince de Condé. He thought of getting the queen (and presumably the king) out of Paris. He felt the hot breath of men who had long been waiting in the shadows, like Chavigny and Châteauneuf, and whom he suspected of conspiring to replace him, but nothing expresses his anguish quite so poignantly as the *mémoire* that he composed on August 14 in order to obtain some solace from his like-minded friend Servien:

> At the same time that the exterior looks promising the interior is wasted . . . by a deplorable twist of fate we are in the process of causing ourselves the harm that our enemies have not been able . . . I kill myself day and night for the greatness of this crown and for the happiness of the French . . . I have no posts, no governorships, no duchies . . . they claim that I have amassed treasures . . . and attack me as a foreigner . . . the state is endangered by the French themselves while God continues to shower us with prosperities.

Whatever else Mazarin may have accomplished during his ministry, he had succeeded in constructing an impenetrable wall around himself. By the summer of 1648, all the building blocks of the Mazarinian self-justification were in place—the impending military triumph, the fortuitous stab in the back, the steadfastness of the tragic hero, the malice of his enemies—all leading up to a bizarre contradiction between the perversity of a blind fate and the sympathy of an omnipotent God. Mazarin did not notice it. He went on to recommend to Servien some further concessions. The underlying sentiment in the *mémoire,* however, was a thirst for revenge. "Maybe I will be obliged," he inserted at the bottom of a page in the copy sent, "and you would be the first to advise me . . . not to be so moderate." He had, on top of all his other virtues, been much too nice![16]

Not that the exterior looked that promising. On August 9 the Spanish had taken Furnes, and their main army was maneuvering menacingly in Picardy and Artois. It was no longer the 25,000 veterans of Rocroi, but it had managed to muster 18,000 replacements and survivors and was reinvigorated by a confident Archduke Leopold, who had a successful campaign behind him. While Condé was in the vicinity of La Bassée attempting to cope with their movements, the archduke skillfully placed his army some seven miles to the south in a favorable position on the outskirts of Lens, as if to dare the prince to displace him. The French were proportionately even more exhausted by the financial impotence of the crown. Instead of the 23,000 they had collected on the field at Rocroi, they could now only afford to muster 15,000 to 16,000 and their commander Condé had demonstrated the year before that he could be embarrassed. He had not, however, lost any of his self-confidence.

Bringing his army to the very face of his enemy on August 20, he began by attempting to draw them out of their positions by a feigned retreat. The stratagem worked. As the Spanish advanced, the French suddenly turned around and advanced as well. It was a furious battle, in which the French line came close to breaking, but it held, charged, and routed the enemy. By the end of the day, 3,000 Spanish troops had perished on the field and 5,000 were prisoners. A stunning victory, a stunning vindication for the Prince de Condé—but was it stunning enough to overawe the *parlement*?[17]

Mazarin believed it was. On August 26, after the predictable *Te Deum* in the Cathedral of Notre Dame, the Count de Comminges, lieutenant of the queen's guards, burst into Broussel's house on the Rue Saint-Landry and hustled him out in his slippers and overcoat. The operation was bungled from the start. The carriage carrying Broussel broke down: Comminges had to commandeer another in order to get his prisoner out of Paris and two more in an effort, which did not succeed, to get his prisoner to Sedan. Du Bois, exempt of the queen's guards, arrested another judge, Blancmensil, and managed to take him to Vincennes, but two other troublemakers escaped. Moreover, the bourgeois of Paris refused to be intimidated, either by the victory at Lens or by the officers of the queen's guards. The following day, with amazing spontaneity, they set up barricades across the approaches to the Palais de Justice, and Chancellor Séguier, attempting to get there in order to prohibit the *parlement* from assembling, was stopped by the obstructions and the mob. Forced to take refuge in the Hôtel de Luynes, he was only extricated by the Marshal de La Meilleraye and a detachment of light cavalry. This, the first explosion of the Fronde produced about twenty fatalities on both sides and made it possible for the *parlement,* led by the first president Molé, to march in procession to the Palais Royal in order to plead for a release of its members. The President de Mesmes warned the queen that she was in grave peril, but she was not disposed to listen, and the judges withdrew. The enraged mob, however, would not let them off so easily. It forced Molé and his colleagues to retrace their steps and to remake their appeal more emphatically. This time, in return for some vague promises of good behavior, Anne relented, and the next morning Broussel reappeared in triumph. It was as if London and Naples had come to Paris, and Mazarin knew it full well, but he tried to put the best complexion on it. He played down the concession by the queen and claimed that "since noon, there is no longer any shop closed, nor barricade, nor chain stretched out, and all things are in exactly the same condition as they were prior to the commotions."[18]

In order to assess the depth of Mazarin's humiliation, we have but to remember his pride at the beginning of the regency at how Cardinal Richelieu had single-handedly transformed France from a virtual republic into an absolute monarchy. Now, under his hand-picked successor, as if in a nightmare, it was turning into a republic once again. How could it have happened, how could the *parlement* and the scum of Paris have succeeded in outwitting the only man who, by his own estimation, possessed the requisite qualifications for guiding the country? The only explanation that he could find for this unnatural state of affairs was, as we have seen, that he had been too indulgent, and he reminded himself of this unpleasant verity lest he ever forget it. "It is necessary either to resume authority at any price," he noted in his *Carnet*, "and to raise it higher than ever, or to let all the affairs perish." What, however, could he do? Well, his first alternative having failed, he fell back upon his second, which was to get the king out of Paris. Thus he announced insouciantly that since the Palais Royal needed to be cleaned, the king was planning to go to Rueil, some nine miles west of the capital. He then spirited the young Louis XIV out of town on September 13, with the queen and the rest of the court leaving the following day. It was also imperative, with the same urgency, to get rid of the competition. Thus on September 18 Chavigny was arrested and on the same day Châteauneuf was banished to his most distant estates. All these measures, of course, cleared up any doubt as to Mazarin's intentions, and they prompted the *parlement* to respond in kind. It met on September 22 and decided to send a delegation to Rueil to plead with the queen for the return of the king. But the most striking event of this eventful meeting was the speech of President Viole, in which, for the first time, a member of the *parlement* took aim directly at Cardinal Mazarin. Viole depicted Mazarin as "more black than the devil" and demanded the implementation of an *arrêt* of 1617—issued on the occasion of the fall of the Concinis—which prohibited foreigners from participating in the *conseil d'en haut*. In the face of this escalation, the Duke d'Orléans and the returned, triumphant Prince de Condé attempted to restore a little harmony. They asked *parlement* for a conference, to which it agreed, but only on the condition that it meet only with the duke and with the prince. It was the first-time-ever vote of no confidence in a French prime minister.[19]

It was the midst of this deteriorating situation that the negotiation in Westphalia, or at least what was left of it, was winding to a conclusion. The Protestant princes of Germany had gotten satisfaction for almost all their *gravamina*, the Duke of Bavaria had secured his electoral title and the Upper Palatinate, and both Protestants and Catholics were reconciled to freezing the Reformation and desperate to rid themselves of the armies which had been ravaging their country over the last thirty years. The Swedes were not only satiated, but they feared that they could not push their demands much further without alienating most of their Protestant constituency. Thus the confirmation and elaboration of the French satisfaction were the only issues holding up the peace, and by the second half of the month of August, the deputies of the German states who were assembled in Osnabrück finally got around to them. At first things did not go smoothly. Some of the princes, and notably the Imperial city of Strasbourg, began to question the contradictory clauses in the cession of Alsace, fearing—all too prophetically—that these would eventually be interpreted to the advantage of the French monarchy. Servien insisted that he had no authority to make any changes, unless it was for the king to acquire Alsace as a fief of the Empire, which he knew the Imperialists would absolutely reject. His obstinacy worked, and the Germans, in their desire for peace, resorted to the futile gesture of circulating a writing interpreting the cession in their own way. This crisis overcome, the Germans addressed themselves to the three undecided points. Once more, in their desire for peace, and this time with the collaboration of Salvius, they composed a formula which, in this particular case, coincided with both their own interests and those of the French. The Circle of Burgundy would not now be defended by the Empire, neither the Emperor nor the Empire were to meddle in the continuing Franco-Spanish War, and the fate of the Duke of Lorraine was left for the French and the Spanish to settle among themselves. The exact wording was a little vague, but it was still a great achievement for Servien, who had managed, in spite of France's domestic straits, to make common cause with the princes of Germany. There was only one problem left—namely, to bring the Emperor into camp. The entire assembly now went back to Münster to see what the Emperor would do.[20]

Ideally the Emperor would have wanted to make peace with the Swedes so as to be free to join with the Spanish in concentrating on the French. At the very least he wanted to make a peace in the Empire which would allow him to aid the Spanish. Yet, with the Swedes besieging Prague, he and his council decided that, all things considered, they were coming out of the war very well indeed. The Hapsburgs had failed in their attempt to dominate the Empire and roll back the Protestant religion, but the hereditary lands were more secure than ever and the Emperor was more than ever the master of the religion of his own subjects. The concessions to the Swedes—Lower Pomerania, the Archbishopric of Bremen, and the Bishopric of Verden; the compensations for the Elector of Brandenburg—the Bishoprics of Halberstadt, Magdeburg, and Minden; and the compensation for the house of Brunswick-Luneburg—alternative possession between a Catholic and a Protestant for the Bishopric of Osnabrück, were all at the expense of others. The Protestants may have consolidated their gains, but, on the other hand, the Reformation too was over. Maximilian of Bavaria was one more Catholic elector, and the son of Frederick V had paid a heavy price for his father's usurpation. As to the concessions to the French, they were extremely enigmatic and just as profitable. Thus on September 16 his orders went out to his plenipotentiaries at the peace conference. They were to seek a delay of twenty days, while they could send a courier to the Imperial court and obtain its final decision on the three undecided French demands, and try their best in the intervening period to effectuate a peace between France and Spain, but if this was impossible, they were not to allow the negotiation to break down and were to subscribe to the terms of the treaty as the deputies of the German princes and states had finalized it.[21]

In France, as the blemished figure of Cardinal Mazarin was fading into the shadows, the Duke d'Orléans and the Prince de Condé emerged as the official spokesmen for the queen. In a series of conferences held between them and the representatives of the *parlement* at Saint Germain-en-Laye beginning on September 25 and extending through the month of October, it was the princes of the blood who listened while the judges imposed their vision of how the government should function. They demanded first of all the return of the king to Paris, the liberty of Chavigny and others, and, in a slight diminution of the largesse exhibited by the Chamber of Saint Louis, the lowering of the *taille* by a mere 20 percent. In the subsequent meetings the representatives of the *parlement* continued to parallel the demands of the reforming chamber, elaborating on some, moderating others, but always adhering to its original spirit, which was to impose upon the queen a series of reforms which she had no alternative but to approve. She did so in a notable declaration of October 22, 1648. It seemed as if the *parlement* of Paris had succeeded in getting the best of Cardinal Mazarin and turning France, if not into a republic, at least into a limited monarchy.[22]

It also seemed as if the war in Germany just would not end. When, on the last day of September, the Emperor's grudging submission to the desires of the German princes reached Münster, his plenipotentiaries discovered that it was in a cipher that they could not read. They had some ideas of what it said, as suggested by the fact that they asked for a telltale twenty days in which to send another courier to Vienna, but this appeal aroused so much derision that, after fishing through their files, the Imperial plenipotentiaries managed to come up with a cipher that worked and expressed their readiness to sign their treaty both with Sweden and with France. It was now Servien and Salvius who would have preferred a little procrastination, since they wanted to assure the sojourn of the French and Swedish armies in Germany throughout the winter and possibly give the Spanish one last chance to come to terms. But on October 13 Oxenstierna appeared in Münster, and, after a bit of posturing, the Swedes agreed that they too would sign their treaty in that city. The most spectacular event of the century occurred on October 24, 1648. Servien and the Swedish plenipotentiaries went to the residences of the Imperialists and signed the copies of the treaties that were to be sent back to the courts of Paris and Stockholm, after which the Imperialists visited the French and the Swedes to sign the copies that were to be sent back to the Emperor. The deputies of the electors, princes, and cities of the Holy Roman Empire also proceeded to sign in similar fashion. The bourgeois militia, as usual in arms, the usual discharges of muskets and cannons, the usual free wine for the citizens, and the Thirty Years War was over.[23]

The news of the signing was a breath of fresh air, and perhaps we can sympathize with Mazarin if he took a moment to exult. He again shared his innermost sentiments with Servien, writing to him on October 30:

You must admit that having served with as much dedication and zeal as I have, and, as the whole world has seen, having pleased God to bless my labors with success, it is most disturbing to be exposed to the malice of individuals who have spread such malicious rumors about me that there isn't a sensible man who does not detest them, and you must admit that it takes a lot of character and extraordinary zeal to re-double my efforts for the service of the public.

Still, whatever momentary sympathy we may experience for the embat-tled Mazarin, it is even more compelling to ponder the rigidity of his naked mind. Not a hint of self-doubt, not a touch of regret, God had done all right by him after all! Anyone but a scoundrel could see it, couldn't they? Gone was the memory of the fateful year when he had gambled everything on the acquisition of the Spanish Low Countries! Gone was recollection of the subsequent year when he had stubbornly held up the peace over the very demands which he had ended up abandoning! And for the moment at least, gone was the thought that he still had one old enemy to defeat and that his hands were now tied by a court full of judges backed by the court of public opinion! He looked to the future with the same arrogance with which he remembered the past, and the immediate future, at least, had revolt and exile in store for him.[24]

From the perspective of many of his contemporaries, Mazarin had accomplished very little. He was obliged to liberate Chavigny and Châteauneuf, and on December 17, in a full session of the *parlement* with the Duke d'Orléans in attendance, Aubry, a counselor in the first chamber of requests, stated that "it was difficult to believe that, after so many victories, the enemies were the principal obstacles to the peace." He did not know the half of it, but he had hit the nail right on the head, for indeed, as we have seen, Mazarin's aspirations aimed at a crushing victory which would have taken overwhelming power to achieve. Nor was the criticism of Mazarin limited to the impressions of outside ob-servers. As the revolt of the Fronde spread, it was Fouquet-Croissy, that old collaborator of d'Avaux in Transylvania and at Ulm, who became the author of one of the most poignant and wittiest of the anti-Mazarin pamphlets, the *Courrier du Temps,* which criticized the "resolutions which Cardinal Mazarin had taken to render the war interminable." And then there was the ambitious Chavigny who, after five years of twiddling his thumbs in the *conseil d'en haut,* eventually came out with his opinion on whether Mazarin had ever wanted to make peace. "I shall only say," wrote Chavigny, "that if he didn't want to make it, he had the misfortune of not understanding that it alone could have confirmed his position in the state. If he did want to make it, can it be denied that he is the most presumptuous and incompetent of men, considering the means he has used?" And Chavigny specified: "The error of having received the States as mediators of our treaty with the Spanish cannot be excused."[25]

Mazarin may well have been right in maintaining that he was on the verge of victory when the *parlement* had betrayed him, but whether he was right or wrong is beside the point. The French people and their self-appointed spokesmen had simply run out of patience, and his past behavior gave them little reason to expect that even if they gave him another chance, he would not have squandered it. The tremendous gulf between history as it is experienced and history as it is viewed through the prism of unintended consequences is one of the greatest barriers that separates us from our past. Mazarin has done well with the nationalists of the nineteenth century and of our own time. From the perspective of a patriotic Frenchman in particular, Mazarin's acquisition of Alsace and his ultimate triumph over the Fronde trumped all existential reality and, indeed, constituted more than sufficient reason to ignore it. But even if our contemporaries insist on celebrating their own vanities of the specious present, one wonders how long it will be before the political possession of Alsace, or Pomerania, or the Palatinate will be no more capable of inflaming their passions than their choice of an airline or of an ethnic restaurant.

It should come as no surprise, therefore, that I have opted in this book for the existential approach. But even if we eliminate the methodological and philosophical considerations that I advanced in the introduction, I would suggest that this approach is the key to an elementary point of seventeenth-century diplomatic history that all previous historians, in their obsession with the destiny of nations, seem to have overlooked. It is the striking differences between Richelieu and Mazarin and the striking similarities between Mazarin and Louis XIV. Richelieu, for all of his conceits, did not believe that he was the only man who could save his country, or at least, he did not have the chutzpah to put it into writing. Richelieu, for all of his hostility toward the Hapsburgs, did not believe that it was impossible to reach some sort of compromise with them. For all his trepidation at the proximity of the Spanish armies, Richelieu was certain that the annexation of the Spanish Low Countries would embroil France in a perpetual struggle against the rest of Europe. Mazarin was of a different stripe. He believed he was the only man who could save the state. He believed in the law of opposites, by which there could never be peace and harmony between France and Spain. He believed that he could annex the Spanish Low Countries, and when he discovered that he could not, he promptly began to develop lapses in his memory and search for scapegoats. This is the exact portrait of Louis XIV. The principal purpose of his *Mémoires pour l'instruction du Dauphin* was to prove to his son how a king ruling for himself was the only person fit to run the state. The principal piece of advice on foreign policy which he gave to his son in this same work was to apprise him of the permanent enmity between France and Spain. And if we move on to Louis's later literary efforts, his little-appreciated *Mémoires pour l'histoire de la guerre de Hollande* and his so-called *Réfléxions sur le métier de Roi,* we see the same passion for the acquisition of the Spanish Low Countries, the same presumption that he could pull it off, the same lapses of memory, and the same search for scapegoats. Cardinal Mazarin, therefore, not only holds the key to himself. He, much more distinctly than Cardinal Richelieu, holds the key to the character and policies of Louis XIV.[26]

Abbreviations

AAE	France, Archives du Ministère des Affaires Etrangéres
CP	Correspondance Politique
MD	Mémoires et Documents
AC	France, Archives Condé
AG	France, Archives de la Guerre
AGS	Spain, Archivo General de Simancas
E	*Estado*
AHN	Spain, Archivo Histórico Nacional
E	*Estado*
SNDF	*Sección Nobleza, Ducado de Frìas*
Aitzema VNVH	Aitzema, *Verhael van de Nederlandsche Vreede–Handeling*
AN	France, Archives Nationales
ANTT	Portugal, Arquivo Nacional da Torre do Tombo
APW	*Acta Pacis Westphalicae,* ed. Konrad Repgen
AR	France, Bibliothèque Nationale, *Catalogue général des livres imprimés: Actes royaux*
Ass. Nat.	France, Bibliothèque de l'Assemblée Nationale
AST	Italy, Archivio di Stato di Torino
MPLM	Materie Politiche, Lettere Ministri
ASVat	Vatican, Archivio Segreto
ASVen	Italy, Archivio di Stato di Venezia
AV	Österreichisches Staatsarchiv, Allgemeines Verwaltungsarchiv
HKA RA	Hofskammerarchiv *Reichsakten*
TA	Fürstlich Trauttmansdorffsches Zentral-Familienarchiv
BI	France, Bibliothèque de l'Institut
BM	France, Bibliothèque Municipale
BMaz	France, Bibliothèque Mazarine
BNE	Spain, Biblioteca Naçional

BNF	France, Bibliothèque Nationale
Ms. Baluze	*Manuscrit Baluze*
Ms. Cangé	*Manuscrit Cangé*
Ms. CCC	*Manuscrit Cinq Cents Colbert*
Ms. Clair.	*Manuscrit Clairambault*
Ms. Dupuy	*Manuscrit Dupuy*
Ms. Fr.	*Manuscrit Français*
Ms. It.	*Manuscrit Italien*
Brienne	*Mémoires du Comte de Brienne*
BVat *CCL*	Vatican, Biblioteca Apostolica Vaticana, *Codex Chisianus Latinus*
CDI	*Coleccion de documentos inéditos*
DPP	Le Boindre, *Débats du parlement de Paris pendant la minorité de Louis XIV*
Dubuisson	Dubuisson-Aubenay, *Journal des guerres civiles*
Dumont	*Corps universel du droit des gens,* ed. Dumont
Gärtner	Gärtner, *Westphälische Friedens-Cantzley*
Gazette	*Gazette de France*
Giessen	Germany, Giessen, Universitätsbibliothek
Guise	*Mémoires du Duc de Guise*
GvP	Groen van Prinsterer, *Archives . . . de la maison d'Orange-Nassau*
Hanotaux	Hanotaux, *Histoire du Cardinal Richelieu*
Haussonville	Haussonville, *Histoire de la réunion de la Lorraine à la France*
HHSA	Austria, Österreichisches Staatsarchiv, Haus-, Hof- und Staatsarchiv
GSR	Geheime Staatsregistratur
MEA *FrA*	Mainzer Erzkanzlerarchiv, *Friedensakten*
OAT	Österreichische Akten, Tyrol
Rep.	*Repertorium*
RK *FrA*	Reichskanzlei *Friedensakten*
SK *FrA*	Staatskanzlei *Friedensakten*
HSAM	Germany, Hessisches Staatsarchiv, Marburg
Isambert	*Recueil général des anciennes lois françaises,* ed. Isambert
Jacob	Jacob, *Die Erwerbung des Elsaß durch Frankreich im Westfälishen Frieden*
JOURNAL	*Journal contenant tout ce qui s'est fait et passé en la Cour du Parlöement de Paris*
K & IDR	*Nunziatura di Fabio Chigi,* ed. Kybal and Incisa della Rocchetta
KHA N	The Hague, Koninklijk Huisarchief, *Nassau Papers*

Knuttel	Netherlands, Koninklijke (Nationaal) Bibliotheek *Catalogus van de pamfletten-verzameling*, ed. Knuttel
Konv.	Konvolut (bundle)
L&BdP	Loiseleur and Baguenault de Puchesse, *L'expédition du Duc de Guise à Naples*
La Châtre	*Mémoires du Comte de la Châtre*
La Court	La Court, *Mémoires de Monsieur D. . . .*
LM	*Lettres du Cardinal Mazarin pendant son ministère*, ed. Chéruel and D'Avenel
Londorp	Londorp, *Der Römischen Kayserlichen Majestät und des Heiligen Römischen Reichs . . . Acta publica*
LR	*Lettres, instructions diplomatiques, et papiers d'état du Cardinal de Richelieu*, ed. D'Avenel
LT	*Collection des lettres et mémoires . . . du Maréchal de Turenne*, ed. Grimoard
M&N	*Mémoires et négociations secrètes de la cour de France touchant la paix de Munster*
M&P	Michaud and Poujoulat
Meiern	*Acta pacis Westphalicae publica*, ed. Meiern
Mercure	*Mercure François*
Mignet	Mignet, *Négociations relatives à la succession d'Espagne*
Modène	*Mémoires du Comte de Modène*
Montglat	*Mémoires du Marquis de Montglat*
Moreau	*Bibliographie des Mazarinades*, ed. Moreau
Motteville	*Mémoires de Madame de Motteville*
Ms.(s)	*Manuscrit(s)*
MT	Médiathèque
NNA	Netherlands, Nationaal Archief
SG	Staten Generaal
R	*Resolutiën*
VL	*Vervolg Loketkast (1576–1796)*
SH	Staten van Holland
NOUVEAU J.	*Nouveau Journal contenant tout ce qui s'est fait et passé aux Assemblées des Compagnies Souveraines du Parlement de Paris*
NS	Le Clerc, *Négociations secrètes touchant la paix de Munster et d'Osnabrug*
Ormesson	Ormesson, *Journal*, ed. Chéruel
P&M	Petitot and Monmerqué
Pastoret	Pastoret, *Le Duc de Guise à Naples*
PPI	*Praeliminaria Pacis Imperii*

Repgen
    EA   Die kaiserlich Elsaß-Angebote
    KFS   Die kaiserlich-französischen Satisfaktionartikel
Richelieu
    M   *Mémoires du Cardinal de Richelieu*
    PR   *Papiers de Richelieu*
       spe   *section politique extèrieure,* ed. Wild
       spi   *section politique intèrieure,* ed. Grillon
    TP   *Testament Politique du Cardinal de Richelieu*
SHF   Société de l'Histoire de France
Siri   Siri, *Il Mercurio*
SRA   Sweden, Riksarkivet
    AOS   *Axel Oxenstiernas Samling*
    DG   *Diplomatica Germanica*
    JOS   *Johan Oxenstiernas Samling*
    KK   *Kungliga Koncepter*
    OT   *Originaltraktater*
    RR   *Riksregistsraturet*
SRP   *Svenska Riksrådets Protokoll*
ST   *Sverges traktater med främmande magter,* ed. Rydberg and Hallendorf
Talon   Talon, *Mémoires*
TPMS   *Traités publics de la royale maison de Savoye*
Turenne   Turenne, *Mémoires,* ed. SHF
U&A   *Urkunden und Actenstücke zur Geschichte des Kurfürsten Friedrich Wilhelm von Brandenburg*
Waddington Waddington, *La République des Provinces-Unies: La France et les Pays-Bas Espagnols*

Notes

Introduction

1. Lieuwe van Aitzema, *Verhael van de Nederlandsche Vrede-Handeling* (The Hague, 1650) 2 vols.; Michael Caspar Londorp, *Der Römischen Kayserlichen Majestät und des Heiligen Römischen Reichs Geist-und Weltlicher Stände Chur- und Fürsten, Grafen, Herren und Strändte Acta publica und schrifliche Handlungen* (Frankfurt am Main, 1668) 6 vols.; Vittorio Siri, *Il Mercurio, o vero Historia de' correnti tempi: 1635–1655* (Casale, Lyon, Paris, Florence, 1644–1682) 15 vols. Volumes IV–XIII, dealing with the period of the negotiations, were published between 1655 and 1674.

2. *Mémoires et négociations secrètes de la cour de France touchant la paix de Munster* (Amsterdam, 1710) 3 vols.; *Négociations secrètes touchant la paix de Munster et d'Osnabrug ou recueil général des préliminaries, instructions, lettres, mémoires etc. concernant ces négociations depuis leur commencement en 1642, jusqu'à leur conclusion en 1648, Avec les Depêches de Mr. de Vautorte, et autres Pièces au sujet du même Traité jusqu'en 1654 inclusivement,* ed. Jean Le Clerc (The Hague, 1725–1726) 4 vols. There are tables of contents of similar compendiums in Mss. *Godefroy* 85–86, as well as actual compendiums in BNF Mss. *Fr.* 23565–23573; Mss. *Clair.* 600–611; Mss. *Fr.* 20984–20989, 15850–15864, and 17911–17918; BMaz Mss. 2219–2229, 2233–2234, and 2235–2236; AAE MD *France* 1416–1424; BNF Mss. *Fr.* 10644–10646; and NNA SG 8449/8450, 8451/8452, and 8453. The sequence of publications continued with *Westphälische Friedens-Cantzley, Darinnen die von Anno 1643 biß Anno 1648 bey denen Münster-und Osnabrückischen Friedens-Tractaten Geführte geheime Correspondence, ertheilte Instructiones, erstattete Relationes, und andere besondere Nachrichten enthalten,* ed. Carl Wilhelm Gärtner (Leipzig, 1731–1738) 9 vols. and *Acta pacis Westphalicae publica oder Westphälische Friedens-Handlungen und Geschichte in eimem mit richtigen Urkunden bestärkten historischen Zusammenhang verfasser un beschrieben,* ed. Johann Gottfried von Meiern (Hannover, 1734–1736) 6 vols.

3. Guillaume-Hyacinthe Bougeant, *Histoire des guerres et des négociations qui précéderent le Traité de Westphalie sous le règne de Louis XIII et le Ministère du Cardinal de Richelieu, et du Cardinal Mazarin Composée sur les Mémoires du Comte d'Avaux, Ambassadeur du Roi Très-Chrétien dans les Cours du Nord, en Allemagne & en Hollande, & Plénipotentiaire au Traité de Munster* (vol. I) and *Histoire du traité de Westphalie ou des négotiations qui se firent à Munster et à Osnabrug pour établir la paix entre toutes les puissances de l'Europe Composée principalement sur les Mémoires de la Cour et des Plénipotentiaires de France* (vols. II and III) (Paris, 1727–1744) 3 vols. See esp. III, 62–63. For Voltaire's judgment on the Peace of Westphalia, see his *Siècle de Louis XIV* (Geneva, 1768 and all subsequent editions) Ch. IV.

4. Leopold von Ranke, "Die grossen Mächte," *Historische-politische Zeitschrift* II (1833–1836) 1–51; *Französische Geschichte* (Stuttgart and Tübingen, 1852–1855) III, Bk. 1, Chs. II–III.

5. Pierre-Adolphe Chéruel, *Histoire de France pendant la minorité de Louis XIV* (Paris, 1879–1880) 4 vols. Preface, see esp. I, viii–x and III, Bk. 8, Ch. V, 116–117; *Lettres du Cardinal Mazarin pendant son ministère,* ed. Adolphe Chéruel and Georges d'Avenel (Paris, 1872–1906) 9 vols.; *Coleccion de documentos inéditos para la Historia de España,* ed. Feliciano de la Fuensanta del Valle *et al.* (Madrid, 1884–1885) vols. LXXXII–LXXXIV.

6. Robert R. Palmer and Joel Colton, *A History of the Modern World,* 3rd ed. (New York, 1965) 130–131.

7. For the *Annales* school, see Fernand Braudel, "Histoire et sciences sociales: la longue durée," *Annales E.S.C.* XIII n° 4 (October–December, 1958) 725–753. For a critique of rational choice theories from within the political science community itself, see Donald P. Green and Ian Shapiro, *Pathologies of Rational Choice Theory: A Critique of Applications in Political Science* (New Haven, Conn., and London, 1994). Derek Croxton, with whose *Peacemaking in Early Modern Europe: Cardinal Mazarin and the Congress of Westphalia: 1643–1648* (Selingsgrove and London, 1999) I largely disagree, has attempted to question the orthodoxy on sovereignty in his "The Peace of Westphalia of 1648 and the Origins of Sovereignty," *International History Review* XXI (1999) 569–591. For my critique of the *nouvelle histoire,* please see my "Young Person's Guide to Postmodernism," *Praesidium* 4.2 (Spring, 2004) 22–32. For my critique of the "rise of the state" thesis, please see my "What Kind of Idea Is the Idea of Balance of Power?" in *The Transformation of European Politics 1763–1848: Episode or Model in European History?* ed. Peter Krüger and Paul W. Schröder (Münster, 2002) 63–76.

8. Victor Cousin, "Des Carnets autographes du Cardinal Mazarin conservés à la Bibliothèque impériale," *Journal des Savants* (August, 1854) 457–470, (September, 1854) 521–547, (October, 1854) 600–626, (November, 1854)

687–719, (December, 1854) 753–773, (January, 1855) 19–42, (February, 1855) 84–103, (March, 1855) 161–184, (April, 1855) 217–242, (May, 1855) 304–324, (July, 1855) 430–447, (September, 1855) 525–545, (October, 1855) 622–637, (November, 1855) 703–719, (January, 1856) 48–60, (February, 1856) 105–119. Cousin also published more excerpts in his *Madame de Chevreuse et Madame de Hautefort* (Paris, 1856) 358–389 and in his *Madame de Chevreuse, Nouvelles études sur les femmes illustres et la société du xviiᵉ siècle* (Paris, 1876). Alphonse Chéruel, "Les Carnets de Mazarin pendant la Fronde," *Revue historique* IV (May–August, 1877) 403–438 and vol. 3 of his above-cited *Histoire,* 389–412. More fragments can also be found in the *Oeuvres du Cardinal de Retz* (Paris, 1870–1896) II, 648–655.

9. *Recueil des Instructions données aux ambassadeurs et ministres de France depuis les Traités de Westphalie jusqu'à la Révolution française* (Paris, 1884–); *Acta Pacis Westphalicae,* ed. Konrad Repgen, Ser. II B, *Die französischen Korrespondenzen* (Münster 1979–).

10. *Ibid.*

11. *Acta Pacis Westphalicae,* ed. Konrad Repgen, Ser. II A, *Die kaiserlischen Korrespondenzen* (Münster, 1969–); *Acta Pacis Westphalicae,* ed. Konrad Repgen, Ser. II C, *Die schwedischen Korrespondenzen* (Münster, 1965–1994); Vlastimil Kybal and Giovanni Incisa della Rocchetta, *La nunziatura di Fabio Chigi: 1640–1651* (Rome, 1943–1946) 1 vol. in two parts. Miscellanea della Reale deputazione Romana di storia patria, vols. XIV and XVI.

12. *Mémoires de Monsieur D. . . . touchant les négociations du Traité de Paix fait à Munster en l'année mil six cens quarante-huit* (Cologne, 1674). It was not until 1999 that Anuschka Tischer, in the *Anhang* of her carefully researched *Französische Diplomatie und Diplomaten auf dem Westfälischen Friedenskongreß: Außenpolitik unter Richelieu und Mazarin* (Münster, 1999), first suggested that D'Avaux was not the author.

1. The Legacies

1. David Buisseret, *Henry IV* (London, 1984).

2. AAE CP *Allemagne* 5, fols. 253–268, *Instruction de Monsieur de Schombert, Conᵉʳ du Roy en Son Conseil d'Estat Lieutenant General de Sa Maiesté en pays de Limosin haute et basse Marche pour son voyage d'Allemagne* [1617] (copies in BNF *Ms. CCC* 2, fols. 23–40 [1617], and *CCC* 101, fols. 124–159 [1617]); *Ms. Dupuy* 121, fols. 280–288 [1617], "signé Richelieu"; *Ms. Fr.* 10205, fols. 140–146, which bears the inscription "fait a Paris le Vingt neufiesme Jour de decembre mil Six cens Seize, Signé de Richelieu" [pub. in Antoine Aubery, *Mémoires pour l'histoire du Cardinal Duc de Richelieu* (Paris, 1660) I, 9–19 [1617,

Richelieu M P&M XI, 224–243, *PR spe* I, 208–235]. See also Hanotaux I, Bk. 1 and II, Bk. 1.

3. Cecilie V. Wedgwood, *The Thirty Years War* (London, 1938) Chs. I–IV.

4. See AAE CP *Hollande* 8, fols. 339–354, *Traicté de Compiegne entre le Roy de france tres chrestien, et messieurs les Estats Generaux des Provinces Unies du pays bas . . . 10 Juin 1624* (copies on fols. 317–326, 270–280, 281–288, 289–304, 305–316, 327–330, and 331–338) [pub. in the *Mercure* IX (1624), 492–495, dated June 20 and Dumont V, pt. 2, 461–463]. For more on the anti-Hapsburg offensive, see AAE CP *Danemark* 1, fols. 19–24, *Instruction baillée a M. Deshayes s'en allant en Dannemark et Suede,* September 12, 1624; *Sardaigne* 4, fols. 152–161, *Instruction baillée a M. de Bullion allant vers M. le Connestable et de la en Savoie,* September 11–12, 1624; *Venise* 43, fols. 84–99, *Instruction baillée au S^r haligre allant Amb^{eur} ord^{re} a Venise du xxviie Septemb^e 1624; Bavière* 1, fols. 10–15, *Memoire pour servir d'Instruction au Sr Fancan,* December 22, 1624. For the treaty with the Huguenots, see AAE MD *France* 782, fols. 48–50, *Articles de la Paix donnez Par Sa Maiesté a Ses Subiectz de la Religion pretendue Reformée . . . Paris le cinquiesme Febvrier 1626* with the *Acceptations Et soubmissions De la Paix des Deputez De la Religion pretendue Reformée,* same date [pub. in the *Mercure* XI (1626) 119–122]. For the treaty with Spain withdrawing French troops from the Val Telline, see AAE CP *Espagne* 14, fols. 335–354, *Traitté de Monson fait entre les Roys de france et d'espagne pour l'accomodement des Grisons* and *Articles Secrets du Traicté de Monson . . . 5 mars 1626* (copies on fols. 381–390 and 357–371, the last including an extra copy of the secret articles; there are also copies in Spanish on fols. 416–421 and 431–440, the last including the secret articles) [pub. in the *Mercure* XI (1626) 1–8 of appendix and Dumont V, pt. 2, 477–478]. See also Richelieu, *Histoire* alias *Mémoires* for 1624 to 1626, P&M XXII–XXIII, M&P XIX, or SHF, IV–V, and Hanotaux II, Bks. 2–4, III, Bk. 1, Ch. I.

5. Hanotaux III, Bk. 1, Ch. II, Bk. 2.

6. AAE CP *Mantoue* 2, fols. 288–289, *Memoire* (Cherré hand) *pour le secours de Casal,* December 10, 1628; AAE MD *France* 246, fols. 223–225, and *France* 787, fols. 159–180, *Advis* (Le Masle minute with corrections by Richelieu and Charpentier) *donné au Roy Apres La prise de La Rochelle pour Le bien de Ses affaires,* January 13, 1629 [pub. in *LR* III, 179–213, and *PR spi* IV, 24–27]; *Diaire* (Père Ange hand) *du voyage du Roy en Italie 1629 pour secourir Casal* [pub. with Richelieu *Histoire* alias *Mémoires* SHF IX, 327–356]. See also Hanotaux III, Bk. 3, Ch. I.

7. See AAE CP *Allemagne* 7, fols. 329–333, *Traitté de Paix Sur les troubles d'Italie fait a Ratisbonne 13 oct. 1630* (copies on fols. 329–333, 405–410, 411–416, and 417–423, and still more copies on fols. 262–267, 268–279, 296–305, 280–295, 387–404, 306–328, 342–359, and 360–377) [pub. in Dumont V, pt. 2,

615–618]. On Gustavus Adolphus's ambitions, see his letter to Oxenstierna of October 8, 1630 in *Rikskansleren Axel Oxenstiernas skrifter och brefvexling, Utgifna af Kongl. vitterhets-historie-och antiquitets-akademien* (Stockholm, 1888–1930) ser. 2, I, 653–657. See also Michael Roberts's excellent *Gustavus Adolphus: A History of Sweden: 1611–1632* (London, New York, and Toronto, 1958) 2 vols., and esp. II, 780. For the Treaty of Barwalde with Gustavus Adolphus, see AAE CP *Suède* 2, fols. 15–19, *Traicté de Bervald entre le Roy de France et de Suede . . . 13 janv~ 1631* text in Latin (copy on fols. 112–115) as well as SRA *OT Frankrike* n° 2A [pub. in Dumont VI, pt. 1, 1–2, and *ST* V, pt. 2, 12–16]. For the two secret treaties with the Duke of Savoy, see the copies in AAE CP *Sardaigne* 16, fols. 73–79 or AST *Trattati* 10, n°s 4 and 5, both dated March 31, 1631 [pub. in *TPMS* I, 374–389]. For the treaty with the Emperor, annotated by the French, see two copies in *Sardaigne* 16, fols. 47–57 and 64–72, or in *Trattati* 10, n°s 6 and 7, all dated April 6, 1631 [pub. in Dumont VI, pt. 1, 9–13 and *TPMS* I, 390–403]. See also Hanotaux III, Bk. 3, Chs. II–IV.

8. See AAE CP *Lorraine* 9, fols. 180–184, copy of the *Traictez faict entre le Roy et Monsr le Duc de Lorraine a Vic le 6 Jan. 1632,* including secret articles (draft with secret articles on fols. 121–133, other copy without secret articles on fols. 185–187), a treaty that obliged Charles, among other things, to cede the fortress of Marsal to France [pub. in Dumont VI, pt. 1, 39–40, without secret articles]. See also Haussonville I, Chs. IV–XII and Hanotaux V, Bk. 1, Ch. I.

9. For Richelieu's reluctance to partition the Spanish Low Countries, see AAE CP *Hollande* 16, fols. 464–468, his *Avis au Roy* [pub. in Mignet I, 174–176]. For the desperate *mémoire* after Nördlingen, see AAE CP *Suède* 3, fols. 265–266 [calendared in *LR* VIII, 273]. For the treaty with the Dutch, see AAE CP *Hollande* 17 n°s 2, 3, 5 (entire treaty), 10 (secret article), 11 (entire treaty), 12–13 (secret article), 14–15 (entire treaty), 16 (extract), February 8, 1635 (copy in NNA SG *R* 4853) [pub. in Dumont VI, pt. 1, 80–85]. For the Treaty of Rivoli with the Duke of Savoy, to which other princes were invited to adhere, see AAE CP *Sardaigne* 23, fols. 113–118, *Traitté de Ligue Conclu avec M^r le Duc de Savoie* (copies on fols. 119–129, 130–132, and 141–145, plus fols. 133 and 147, two copies of the *Article Secret*). See a beautiful original of the treaty in BNF *Ms. Fr.* 15914, fols. 121–126, including the secret article, AST *Trattati* 10, n° 19 [pub. in Dumont VI, pt. 1, 109], all of July 11, 1635. For the adherence of Parma, see AAE CP *Parme* 1, fol. 127, Duke of Parma (own hand letter sent) to Richelieu, August 6, 1635. For the treaty with Duke Bernard, see AAE CP *Allemagne* 11, fols. 290 and 290 bis. (fragment), October 27, 1635 [full treaty pub. in Dumont VI, pt. 1, 118–119]. See also Haussonville II, Chs. XIII–XV and Hanotaux V, Bk. 1, Ch. II.

10. See Louis Dedouvres, *Le Père Joseph polémiste: ses premiers écrits: 1623–1626* (Paris, 1895), who, however, attributes many works to Father

Joseph without sufficient evidence. For the gestation of the *Histoire* alias *Mémoires*, see Louis Delavaud, "Quelques collaborateurs de Richelieu," and Robert Lavollée, "Les différentes étapes de la redaction des Mémoires," in *Rapports et notices sur l'édition des Mémoires du Cardinal de Richelieu* (Paris, 1905–1922) II, pt. 2, 162–170 and 309–350, SHF.

11. See a wonderful example of the "who started it" argument in the anonymous "Discours sur l'occurrence des affaires presentes fait en Janvier 1625 par un Gentilhomme François," *Mercure* XI (1625) 56–94.

12. The classic exposition of Richelieu propaganda, encapsulating virtually all the key points, is Jérémie Ferrier's *Le Catholique d'Estat ou Discours politique des alliances du Roy Très Chrestien contre les calumnies des ennemis de son Estat* (Paris, 1625; Rouen, 1625; Paris, 1626), which Dedouvres attributed to Father Joseph. This work was also inserted by Paul Hay du Chastelet in his *Recueil de diverses pièces pour servir à l'histoire* (Paris, 1635). See Richelieu's project for the alliance with Gustavus Adolphus in AAE CP *Hambourg* 1, fol. 157, undated, with all of the precautions that were integrated in the Treaty of Barwalde, cited in note 7 above. For the idea of turning against Gustavus Adolphus, see *Allemagne* 7, fols. 522–530, *Instruction pour le Sr Baron de Charnacé con^r du Roy en Son conseil d estat et Son ambassadeur envoie par Sa Ma^{té} sur le sujet de Ses affaires presentes d'allemagne . . . fait a Chateau Thierry le xxviie Jour d'octobre 1631* and fols. 535–536, *Addition a l'instruction de Mr de Charnacé . . . 29 oct. 1631*. See also *Suède* 2, fols. 192–197 and 206–211, two copies of the *Instruction baillée a M. le Marq. de Brezé allant amb^r x^{re} vers le Roy de Suede*; fols. 198–200 and 206–211, two copies of the *Memoire baillé a M . . . le Marq. de Brezé outre ses Instructions,* all of January 5, 1632; fols. 218–220, the *Addition a l'Instruction du Sr Marquis de Brezé,* January 7, 1632; and fol. 229, *Seconde addition,* January 6 [sic], 1632.

13. Aside from the *Catholique d'Estat,* see also Father Joseph's *Grand Mercy de la Chrestienté au Roy* (1625) and his *Introduction à la vie spirituelle par une méthode facile d'oraison* (Paris, 1626). The ideas in all of these works mesh perfectly with Richelieu's *Histoire* alias *Mémoires* for 1635, P&M XXVIII, 212–215 and 300–308, or M&P VIII, 576–578 and 603–606, and with his *TP,* pt. 1, Ch. VIII, sec. 1 of any edition, except that in the latter, he accuses the Spanish of misusing the doctrine of directing the intention. See also William F. Church's classic *Richelieu and Reason of State* (Princeton, N.J., 1972).

14. For Servien's career, see BNF *Ms. Dupuy* 672, fols. 128–135, *Arrêt du Conseil d'Etat portant cassasion de trois Arrests du Parlement de Bordeaux . . .* June 29–July 4, 1628; AC *Ms.* 1086, *Relation d'Abel Servien deputé en Italie pour l'exécution de la convention de Bussoleno (10 mai 1629) sur les différends des ducs de Savoie et de Mantoue . . . Turin, 9 janvier 1630.* For Mazarin's meeting with Richelieu, see the *Mercure* XVI (1630) 20 and AAE CP *Sardaigne* 13,

fols. 352–353, *Propositions apportées par M' Masarini Avec les reponces qui ont esté resolues et données aud~ Masarini le 2 Sep'° 1630.* The account of Mazarin's appearance before the armies kept getting better with the passage of time. Compare the first account in the *Mercure* XVI (1630) 724, with the more florid description in Valeriano Castiglione's *Alla Maestà Christianissima di LUIGI XIII IL GIUSTO Rè di Francia, e di Navarra Per la Prosperità delle sue Armi* (n.d.) 21–22, with the most florid relation in the anonymous life of Mazarin published by Luigi Chiala in the *Rivista Contemporanea* IV (September–November, 1855) 552–553, which has him racing across the battle line waving a crucifix and yelling, "Pace, Pace!"

15. For Mazarin's double-dealing at Cherasco, see AAE CP *Sardaigne* 16, fols. 147–148 and 149–150, Mazarin (own hand two letters sent) to Richelieu, April, 26, 1631; fols. 220–221, Mazarin (own hand letter sent) to Richelieu, June 3, 1631; and *Sardaigne* 18, fols. 560–561, Mazarin (own hand letter sent) to Richelieu, December 20, 1631. On the other hand, Mazarin told Vittorio Siri, *Memorie recondite dall'anno 1601 sino al 1640* (Ronco, 1677–1679) VII, 416, that the Pope was in on it, and the story is repeated by Elpidio Benedetti in his *Raccolta di diverse memorie per scrivere la vita del Cardinale Giulio Mazarini Romano* (Lyon, n.d.) 36–44. But the evidence seems to support the excellent arguments of Auguste Leman, *Urbain VIII et la rivalité de la France et de la maison d'Autriche* (Lille and Paris, 1920).

16. For D'Avaux's mission to Venice, see AAE CP *Venise* 46–51 and BNF *Ms. Baluze* 163. For his first association with Father Joseph, see ASVen *Francia* 81, n° 409, Contarini (letter sent) to Senate, December 10, 1631 (transcript in BNF *Ms. It.* 1802, fols. 264–271). For the mission to Denmark, Sweden, and Poland, see AAE CP *Danemark* 1, fols. 281–287, *Instruction au S' d avaux Con°' du Roy en Son con' d'estat s'en allant Ambassadeur Extraord'° en Dannemark, Suede, et Pologne au mois de may* [sic] 1634; *Suède* 3, fols. 235–242, *Instruction au S' d'avaux Con°' du Roy en Son Conseil d'estat S'en allant amb°'' Extraord'° de Sa Ma'° en Suede* (copy on fols. 243–248); *Pologne* 2, fols. 179–183, *Instruction* (minute with corrections) *au S' Davaux s'en allant ambassad'. extraord'° en Pologne* (copy for D'Avaux in *Suède* 3, fols. 249–254), all dated June 23, 1635. For the incident in Stockholm, see François Ogier, *Panégyrique du Comte d'Avaux* (Paris, 1650) 11. For the Truce of Stormsdorf on September 12, 1635, see AAE CP *Suède* 3, fols. 435–440, D'Avaugour (letter sent) to Chavingy, September 25, 1635 [pub. in part in *Correspondance inédite du Comte d'Avaux*, ed. Auguste Boppe (Paris, 1887), 279–285, which claims incorrectly that it was addressed to Richelieu]. For the text of the truce, see *Suède* 3, fols. 396–408 [pub. in Dumont VI, pt. 1, 115–116]. For Father Joseph's message, see *Pologne* 2, fols. 365–366, Father Joseph (letter sent) to D'Avaux, October 9, 1635.

17. For the best expression of the *dévot* position, see Mathieu de Morgues, *Très humble, très véritable, et très importante Remonstrance au Roi* (1631), as well as the entire series of pamphlets that he published against Richelieu during the 1630s. For Olivares, see Madrid, Biblioteca de Palacio Ms. 1817, Olivares to Gondomar, July 8, 1625 [pub. in *Memoriales y Cartas del Conde Duque de Olivares,* ed. John H. Elliot and José F. de la Peña (Madrid, 1979) I, 139–140]; Cornelius Jansenius, *Alexander Patricii Armacani, theologi Mars gallicus, seu de justicia armorum et foederum regis galiae libri duo* (1635, 1637, 1639) or *Le Mars François ou la guerre de France, en laquelle sont examinées les raisons de la justice prétendue des armes et des alliances du Roy de France, mises au jour par Alexandre Patricius Armacanus, théologien, et traudites de la troisième édition par C.H.D.P.D.E.T.B* (1637) Bk. 2, Ch. XVI.

18. Consider Herbert H. Rowen's stimulating *The King's State: Proprietary Dynasticism in Early Modern Europe* (New Brunswick, N.J., 1980) as well as Nicolas Henshall's extremely sensible, *The Myth of Absolutism: Change and Continuity in Early Modern European Monarchy* (London and New York, 1992).

19. For French army size, see Richelieu's own estimate in his *TP,* pt. 1, *Succincte narration,* any edition. For Servien's disgrace, see the documents in BNF *Ms. Cangé* 60. For the Treaty of Wismar with Sweden, see AAE CP *Suède* 4, fols. 90–94, *Traite* (rough draft) *de Wismar fait par M^r de St Chamond et le Chan^{er} Oxenstiern* [text in Latin] xx Martii Anno 1636; fols. 95–102, cleaner copy with added secret articles, date obscured; fols. 145–152, other copy with secret articles, dated "Avril, 1636"; fols. 292–294, copy of ratified treaty as delivered by D'Avaux; fols. 284–291, other copy of ratified treaty, both without secret articles and both dated August 1, 1636; as well as SRA *OT Frankrike* n° 6A in Latin [pub. in French in Dumont VI, pt. 1, 123, and in Latin in *ST* V, pt. 2, 366–372]. For the Treaty of Emden with Hesse-Cassel, see AAE CP *Hesse-Cassel* 1, fols. 76–77, *Traité fait a Embden avec le Sr Landgrave de hesse 18 juin 1636* text in French [pub. in Dumont VI, pt. 1, 128–129]. For the Spanish acceptance of Cologne, see AAE CP *Rome* 58, fol. 114, Richelieu (Cherré minute) to Louis XIII, July 29, 1636 [pub. in *LR* V, 521–522]. Fall of Corbie (August 15, 1636): *Gazette* n° 126, August 23, 1636. D'Avaux's return: *Gazette* n° 130, August 30, 1636. Greffiership: AAE MD *France* 822, fol. 87, Richelieu (secretary's hand) to Bullion, August 24, 1636 [pub. in *LR* V, 632]. Retaking of Corbie (November 11, 1636): *Gazette* n° 177, November 17, 1636. There are two drafts of the instruction: The first (Text A) is in BNF *Ms. Fr* 10212, fols. 55–71, *Instruction pour M^{rs} les Ambassadeurs de France envoyés a Cologne pour le Traitté de la Paix Generale,* which implies that

Corbie is in French hands and that the Archduke Ferdinand had not yet been elected King of the Romans (December 22, 1636). Thus we have a dating between November 11 and late December 1636. The second (Text B) is in AAE CP *Allemagne* 15, fols. 55–71, bearing the same title, and indicates that Ferdinand had been elected King of the Romans, so it is probably of early 1637 [pub. in integrated form in *APW* I 1, 38–55]. See also Hanotaux V, Bk. 2, Ch. II.

20. For the defection of the Duke of Parma, see AAE CP *Parme* 1, fol. 258, Duke of Parma (own hand letter sent) to Louis XIII, February 4, 1637. For D'Avaux's mission to Germany, see *Allemagne* 14, fols. 258–274, *Memoires et Instruction au S^r D'Avaux Con^er du Roy en ses conseils s'en allant Ambassad^r extraord^re en Allemagne,* April 10, 1637. His activities in Hamburg are scattered in *Allemagne* 14, 15, and 16, *Suède* 3 and 4, *Hesse-Cassel* 1, and BNF *Ms. Baluze* 167–172. Capitulation of Landrecies (July 23, 1637): *Gazette* n° 109, July 30, 1637. Death of Charles de Gonzague (September 22, 1637): *Gazette* n° 155, October 3, 1637. Death of Victor Amadeus (October 7, 1637): *Gazette* n° 164, October 17, 1643. For the *dévot* offensive, see BNF *Ms. Baluze* 147, fols. 26–28, *Journal du R.P. Caussin commence le quinziesme juillet mil six cent trente sept* and *Suitte des affaires du Père Caussin et de la cabale qui luy estoit joincte* [pub. in *LR* V, 805–821]. For the Treaty of Hamburg with Sweden: AAE CP *Suède* 5, fols. 44–49, *Coppie du Mesme traitté de Hambourg Signé par l'Ambassad^r de Suede appostilé par M^r d'Avaux,* March 6, 1638, text in Latin (copies without annotations on fols. 31–34, 35–38, 25–30, 71–76, and 6–10) as well as SRA *OT Frankrike* n° 8A [pub. in French in Dumont VI, pt. 1, 161–162, and in Latin in *ST* V, pt. 2, 424–429]. AAE CP *Allemagne* 15, fols. 24–26, D'Avaux (own hand letter sent) to Richelieu, March 15, 1638. Disaster before Fontarabia (September 7, 1638): *Gazette* n° 137, September 30, 1638. Capitulation of Breisach (December 17, 1638): *Gazette* n° 180, December 29, 1638. Death of Father Joseph (December 18, 1638): *Gazette* n° 179 (December 24, 1638). Nomination of Mazarin: AAE CP *Rome* 64, fols. 243–244, Louis XIII (minute) to Urban VIII, December 18, 1638 (copy in BNF *Ms. Baluze* 147, fol. 13). See also Hanotaux V, Bks. 3–4, VI, Bk. 4, Chs. I–V.

21. BNF *Ms. Baluze* 169, fols. 32–35, 11–12, D'Avaux to Claude Bouthillier, May 30, 1639.

22. For the treaty, see AAE CP *Hesse-Cassel,* fols. 208–212, 217, 223–224, *Traité de Dorsten avec Mad. la Landgrave, 22/12 Aoust* (actually August 29) *1639* (copies on fols. 218–222, 233–245, 246–254, 258–260, 279–284, plus declarations on fols. 257, 307–310, 311–312, and 313–314); HSAM 4f *Frankreich* n° 1316, between fols. 38–39, two copies plus declarations [pub. in Dumont VI, pt. 1, 178–180, with declaration]. For the state of the finances in 1640,

see Richelieu's *TP,* pt. 2, Ch. IX, sec. 7, of any edition. Victory at Casale: *Gazette* n° 60, May 15, 1640. Taking of Arras: *Gazette* n° 105, August 17, 1640. Relief of Turin: *Gazette* n° 127, October 4, 1640. See also Hanotaux VI, Bk. 4, Chs. VI–X.

23. On the *Testament politique,* please see my "Dating of Richelieu's *Testament politique,*" *French History* XIX.2 (June, 2005) 262–272. Also see esp. Richelieu's *TP Au Roy,* pt. 1, *Succincte narration,* Ch. III, sec. 1, Ch. V, sec. 3, pt. 2, Ch. IX, sec. 7, of any edition.

24. Kathrin Bierther, *Der Regensburger Reichstag von 1640–1641* (Kallmünz/Opf., 1971). For the Treaty of Paris with the Duke of Lorraine, see AAE CP *Lorraine* 32, fols. 98–106, *Traitté fait entre Le Cardinal Duc de Richelieu pour le Roy et Le Duc Charles de Lorraine Avec Les Articles Secrets passez entre eux et la Ratification faite dudit Traitté,* March 29, 1641, with ratifications of April 2 and April 29 (copies without ratifications on fols. 61–68, 69–77, 82–86 plus fols. 95–97, and more copies of secret articles on fols. 91–92, 93–94, 95–97, and 108–110) [pub. in German in Londorp V, 739–741, and in French in Dumont VI pt. 1, 211–212 both with secret articles]. For the change of venue, see *Allemagne* 16, fols. 204–209, *Memoire* (minute) *au Sr Davaux Con^{er} du Roy en Ses Con^{ils} et son Ambassadeur extror^{re} en allemagne,* June 26, 1641 [calendared in *LR* VIII, 371]. See also Haussonville II, Chs. XVI–XVIII and Hanotaux VI, Bk. 4, Ch. XI.

25. There are three drafts of this instruction. The first (Text A) is in AAE CP *Allemagne* 15, fols. 423–457, *Instruction donnée aux Srs Mazarin et Comte D'Avaux choisis par sa Ma^{té} pour estre Ses Ambassad^{rs} plenipotentiaires en la Negotiation de la Paix.* The body of the text is in the hands of Cherré and Charpentier, but many corrections are in Richelieu's own hand. With its emphasis on retaining Lorraine, it follows the reoccupation in August 1641, with the campaign still hopeful and with Mazarin not yet a cardinal (Urban VIII promoted him on December 16, 1641, and the news was published in Paris in the extraordinary *Gazette* n° 4 of January 8, 1642). I would place the composition of this text in late November and early December of 1641, almost contemporaneous with the end of the sequel of the *Succincte narration* with which it dovetails. The corrections on the instruction, however, are clearly following the recovery of Aire by the Spanish and probably following the news of Mazarin's cardinalate, and therefore of February or March 1642. It should be noted, however, that a number of corrections and considerations relating to alternative terms were not reproduced in subsequent texts of the instruction but were expanded by the secretaries into an accompanying *mémoire,* the first text of which (Text A) is in *Allemagne* 15, fols. 411–418, and is probably also of early 1642. It is in the hand of Charpentier. The second draft of the instruction (Text B) is

on fols. 461–502, *Instruction donée aux Srs Mazarin et Comte D'Avaux choisis par sa Majesté pour estre Ses Ambassadeurs plenipotentiaries en la negocation* [sic] *de la paix.* It is in the hand of Cherré and, in spite of not correcting Mazarin's title, executes the revisions on the previous draft. I would date this text too for February or March 1642. Finally we have a very clean version of the instruction (Text C) adding a whole section on commerce in BNF *Ms. Fr.* 5202, fols. 1–12 and 25–69, made for the benefit of Mazarin and referring to him as cardinal. It is followed on fols. 95–108 by the accompanying *mémoire.* Since the texts of the instruction mention the problem of Marie de Medici, they and the accompanying *mémoire* must precede her death in June, 1642. There is also a later copy in *Allemagne* 23, fols. 304–325, with the accompanying *mémoire* on fols. 334–338 [pub. in integrated form in *APW* I 1, 58–123, 128–135, and 151–158]. For Mazarin's participation, see his letter to the French plenipotentiaries at Münster of February 16, 1646, cited in Chapter 4, note 13, to the effect that Richelieu "conferoit avec moy des orders qu'on avoit a me donner pour l'assemblée de Munster." For the preliminary treaty between France and the Holy Roman Emperor, see the printed version in Latin in AAE CP *Allemagne* 16, fols. 407–411, dated December 25, 1641 (manuscript copies on fols. 392–396, 401–403, and 404–405) [pub. in German in Londorp V, 759–761, in Latin in Dumont VI, pt. 1, 231–232, and Meiern I, 8–10]. For the treaty between the Holy Roman Emperor and the Queen of Sweden, see the printed version in Latin on AAE CP *Allemagne* 16, fols. 412–441, dated December 15/25, 1641 (copies on fols. 397–400) [pub. in Dumont VI, pt. 1, 232–233].

26. SRA *RR* 1636–1641, *Instruction* (copy) *för commisarierne till fredztractaten. Item bijmemorialet,* October 5/15, 1641 (copy of Arts, 1–27 in SRA *KK,* dated October 2/12) [pub. in *APW* I 1, 231–255]; SRA *RR* 1636–1641, *Bijmemorial* (copy) October 5/15, 1641 [pub. in *APW* I 1, 256–257]; SRA *RR* 1636–1641 *Secretre bijnstruction* (copy) October 5/15, 1641 [pub. in *APW* I 1, 258–261]; SRA *RR* 1636–1641, *Bijmemorial* (copy) October 5/15, 1641 [pub. in *APW* I 1, 261–266].

27. See the *Declaration . . . sur la régence de la Reyne. Verifiée au Parlement le 21 avril 1643* (Paris, 1643), pub. in Italian in Siri III, 616–621, in French in Isambert XVI, 550–556. For the appointment of Le Tellier, see AAE MD *France* 846, fols. 119–120, Louis XIII to Le Tellier and Mazarin to Le Tellier, April 11, 1643, and fols. 127–128, *Commission pour exercer la charge de sec-retaire d'Estat a M. le Tellier après la retraite de M. de Noyers,* April 13, 1643; Hanotaux VI, Bk. 4, Ch. XII. For the deathbed sentiments, see Antoine, *Journal de la maladie et mort de Louis XIII,* ed. Alfred Cramail (Fontainebleau, 1880) 21, 25.

2. The Queen's Beloved

1 For this sequence of events, see Motteville P&M XXXVII, pt. 2, 5–13, or M&P, ser. 2, X, 46–49; Brienne P&M XXXVI, pt. 2, 84–86, or M&P, ser. 3, III, 78; La Châtre P&M LI, 206–209, or M&P, ser. 3, III, 281–283; La Rochefoucauld P&M LI, pt. 1, 376–377, or M&P, ser. 3, V, pt. 1, 393–394. See also BM Rouen, Ms. 3268 (Coll. Leber 5775), *Observations de Monsieur le Comte de Brienne Ministre et Secretaire d'Etat, Sur les memoires de Monsieur de la Chastre,* first published in *Recueil de diverses pièces curieuses pour servir à l'histoire* (1664).

2. Ormesson I, 48–54; ASVen *Francia* 99, n° 329 I, Girolamo Giustiniani (letter sent) to Senate May 19, 1643 (transcript in BNF *Ms. It.* 1820, fols. 88–90).

3. BNF *Ms. Baluze* 174 (*Carnet* 1) pp. 86–89: "Non corra nelle gratie . . . Non p~metter niente di più alla deleg^ne de gli Ugonotti, ma parla sempre di loro in termini di stima et afetto . . . sopraintendente a lei . . . il Rosso [Condé] aspira a disporre di tutto . . . Avverta di non dar autorita in q^i principii al parlamento . . . le cose grande che si proponessero senza che io l'havessi informata avverta di non risolvere. . . . Si mantenghi con Monsieur . . . Publicam^te parli a mio vantaggio, dicendo che vuol sostenermi. . . . conservar il titolo di Madre del Re p~che non si parli mai di quello di sorella del Re di Spagna."

4. BNF *Ms. Baluze* 174 (*Carnet* 1) pp. 92, 96: "20 Maggio 1643 . . . S.M. habbi cura nell'elettione di Ministri darmi qualche amico . . . Servien voler impiegarlo qui o per la pace"; Ormesson I, 57; BNF *Ms. Baluze* 174 (*Carnet* 1) p. 99: "22 Maggio . . . Il Rosso [Condé] a me che M. Bove [the Bishop of Beauvais] essendo Card^le e posto nel consiglio, io sarro rimandato a Roma," and p. 107: "23 Maggio . . . Vendome il Prè imbroglia tutta la Corte et egli con tutta la casa non travaglia che all'unione con il P^ce." Battle of Rocroi (May 19, 1643): *Gazette* n° 65, May 27, 1643. See also Motteville P&M XXXVII, 14–22, or M&P, ser. 2, X, 49–52; and La Châtre P&M LI, 211–227, or M&P, ser. 3, III, 281–288.

5. BNF *Ms. Baluze* 174 (*Carnet* 2) p. 1: "considerato il credito che ne risultera a Anghien ma il ben dello stato deve andar avanti." See also the *Considerations sur l'entreprise de Thionivillei,* published in *LM* I, li–lvi. For the ministerial changes and other intrigues, see Ormesson I, 64–69; ASVen *Francia* 99, n°s 344 I and 347 III, Girolamo Giustiniani (letters sent) to Senate, June 9 and 16, 1643 (transcripts in BNF *Ms. It.* 1828, fols. 121–123 and 128–129); AST MPLM *Francia* 44, 22/4, Scaglia (letter sent) to Christine June 15, 1643, and 24/2, Scaglia (own hand letter sent) to Christine, June 16, 1643, 89/6, Mondino (own hand letter sent) to Christine, June 16, 1643; BNF *Ms. Baluze* 174 (*Carnet* 2) p. 24: "il Rosso [Condé] che L'assemblea di Munster servira d apparenza ma che in particolare si farra la Pace con Spagna," and p. 27: "discorso di Chattonef a M^r D'Avo intorno la Pace dicendo che bisogna farla parti-

colare"; AAE MD *France* 846, fols. 210–211, *Provisions de Secretaire d'Estat en faveur de Mgr Le Comte de Brienne le Pere,* June 22, 1643, and *France* 847 fols. 63–64, Coppie des lettres de Ministre d'Estat donnees a M. le Comte D'Avaux du xviii 7bre 1643. See also Brienne P&M XXXVI, pt. 2, 86–94, or M&P, ser. 3, III, 78–81.

6. BNF *Ms. Baluze* 174 (*Carnet* 2) pp. 43–45. For the intrigues leading to the switch in appointments, see AST MPLM *Francia* 44, 90/2 and 93/3, Mondino (own hand letters sent) to Christine, June 19, 1643, and to Prince Maurizio, June 20, 1643; and ASVen *Francia* 99, n° 352 IV and 355 III, Girolamo Giustiniani (letters sent) to Senate June 23 and 26, 1643 (transcripts in BNF *Ms. It.* 1820, fols. 137–138 and 143–144).

7. BNF *Ms. Baluze* 174 (*Carnet* 2) pp. 51–52: "S.M. dicendomi se ci sarebbe qualche modo di farmi esser contento quando sono appresso di lei gl ho risposto che come li miei dispiaceri et afflittioni non procedono da altro che dal non vederla servita come vorrei e dalla male piega che prenderanno gl'affari se non vi si rimedia, quando sono appreso di S. M. mi affliggo d'avantaggio p~che conosco piu da vicino il suo gran merito le mie obligationi e l ingratitudine di quelli che non fanno il loro dovere verso di lei—gli ho detto nel fervore del discorso che se S. M. vedesse il molto che desidero servirla e l estrema passione che ho p~ la sua grandezza si dolerebbe del poco che faccio ancorche testifichi gradirlo e li paia che complisco al mio debito—§." See also the excellent analysis of the relationship in Motteville P&M XXXVII, pt. 2, 22–23, or M&P, ser. 2, X, 52.

8. Diego de Saavedra Fajardo had already published his *Idea de un Principe poltico cristiano respresentada en cien empresas* (Munich, 1640). See his particular instructions in AGS E 2250, dated June 5, 1643. See the general instructions in AHN E 2880, probably issued on June 25, 1643. The origin and development of these instructions is admirably described in Michael Rohrschneider's *Der gescheiterte Frieden von Münster: Spaniens Ringen mit Frankreich auf dem Westfälischen Friedenskongress: 1643–1649* (Münster, 2007) 76–79. For Saavedra's passage through Paris, see BNF *Ms. Baluze* 174 (*Carnet* 2) p. 97: "Scriver in Olanda il passaggio di Saiavedra e quello si fa da questa parte p~ eludere L'artificio di Spagnuoli"; ASVen *Francia* 99, n°s 321 II and 364 III, Nani (letters sent) to Senate, July 28, and August 4, 1643 (copies in BNF *Ms. It.* 1820, fols. 176 and 181–182); AST MPLM *Francia* 44, 41/2, Scaglia (letter sent) to Christine, July 10, 1643, and 104/2, Mondini (own hand letter sent) to Prince Maurizio, July 12, 1643. Saavedra left on July 28, according to 56/2, Scaglia (letter sent) to Carron di San Tommaso of that same date.

9. HHSA RK *FrA* 52d, fols. 1–9, 20–25, Instruction (secretary's minute with corrections) for Count Ludwig von Nassau and Dr. Johann Krane in Münster, Vienna, July 15, 1643, improved minute w/Ostermay corrections in *FrA* 47b,

fols. 6–21, numerous other copies in RK *FrA,* SK *FrA,* and MEA *FrA,* final
form in RK *FrA,* 92 I, fols. 93–101 [pub. in Gärtner I, 415–430; Meiern I,
22–27; and *APW* I 1, 397–406]; HHSA RK *FrA* 46i, fols. 24–30, 35; Insruction
(Kornald Zellfe minute) for Johann Weikhart, Graf von Auersperg, and Dr.
Isaak Volmar for Osnabrück, Vienna, July 15, 1643 (copy on fols. 38–41, numerous other copies in RK *FrA,* SK *FrA,* and MEA *FrA*) [pub. in Gärtner I,
431–441; Meiern I, 28–31; and *APW* I 1, 407–413].

10. BNF *Ms. Baluze* 174 (*Carnet* 2) pp. 58–61: "Il Rosso [Condé . . .] dice que
    el Sr de Vandoma es el maior enemigo que yo tengo . . . dijo que su negotio
    de Bertagna non aila succeder porque yo a parte habia acconsejado la Reina
    de no azerloa . . . ablo tambien de la position que tengo de los parientes del
    Sr Cardinal . . . da muchas otras partes me confirma lo mismo . . . es infal-
    lible que todas las caballas de Paris son fomentadas del dicho y sus Ichos";
    p. 62: "dicono che Bove (Beauvais) habbi fatto parlare M^a di seneze
    (Senecé) Sopra la galanteria"; p. 65: "M^a chev (Chevreuse) le anima todo";
    and p. 71: "La Dame (Chevreuse) me ha decho che no cree que yo tengo La
    amistad por la Reyna al punto que ella entiende y . . . que se ne apreceviera
    luego"; Motteville P&M XXXVII, 23–32, or M&P, ser. 2, X, 52–55. For the
    encumbrances at the beginning of the regency, see D'Hémery's recollection,
    cited in Chapter 8, note 10

11. BNF *Ms. Baluze* 174 (*Carnet* 2) p. 30: "Cattive Raggioni di Avo (Avaux)," and
    p. 86: "Riconosco che Avo non mi vuol bene." See also BMaz *Ms.* 2217, fols.
    181–183, Mazarin (register copy) to Bichi, June 30, 1643: "Dal dispaccio del
    Sig Conte di Brienne intenterà [*sic*] V Em^{za} perche le [*sic*] spedisco questo
    Corriero e quello Si crede [*sic*] debba fare," and fols. 188–195, Mazarin (reg-
    ister copy) to Bichi, August 24, 1643: "quanto al negotio mi rimetto al dis-
    paccio di Monsieur di Brienne, à cui ho dato le memorie di quanto doveva
    Scriverle, doppo haverne [*sic*] La M^{ta} della Regina dichiarati li Suoi Senti-
    menti nel Consiglio" [pub. in *LM* I, 216–221 and 307–322].

12. AAE CP *Hollande* 24, fols. 339–348, *Memoire* (Chavigny's clerk's hand) *aux
    S^{rss} d'Avaux et de Chavigny Ambassadeurs extrord^{res} et Plenipotentiaires du Roy.*
    Obviously written between June 18, 1643, the date of Chavigny's appoint-
    ment as D'Avaux's colleague, and September 11, 1643, the appointment of
    Servien, this also suggests that the copy in BNF *Ms. Fr.* 15870, dated July
    24, 1643, reveals the date of the original.

13. BNF *Ms. Baluze* 174 (*Carnet* 3) pp. 4, 8–13, 17–36, and 43–63; Motteville,
    P&M XXXVII, 32–45, or M&P, ser. 2, X, 55–58; La Châtre P&M LI,
    237–238, or M&P, ser. 3, III, 290–291; La Rochefoucauld P&M LI, pt. 1,
    377–387, or M&P, ser. 3, V, pt; 1, 394–397.

14. For the siege of Thionville, see the *Gazettes* n°s 83, 87, 90, 91, 94, 98, and
    101, July 2, 11, 18, 23, 29, August 6 and 13, 1643. For the pressures for an

armistice, see BNF *Ms. Baluze* 174 (*Carnet* 2) p. 71: "Il Nuntio che inten-
dendo che van male le cose a Thionville propone di nuovo la sospensione,"
and p. 104: "Sospensione in Thionvilla come si fece a Casale e Torino
p~mezzo mio l'Internontio al N° dicendo che la francia ne ha bisogno come
loro." For Mazarin's pride, see BNF *Ms. Baluze* (*Carnet* 3) p. 51: "S. M. avia
servido de resolverla persuadida de my solo consejo que preferia al de todos
los de mas que eran contrarios y porque Turena sospecho que le Principe de
Conde era contrario, no quiso ablar a La Reyna antes de saber La intention
del Principe, y beendo que venia en ello ablo despues a S. M.," and his letter
to Bichi of August 24, cited in note 11 above. For the great plan, see BNF
Ms. CCC 103, fols. 26–31, *Instruction* (copy) *a M. le Duc d'Anguyen allant
vers la Sarre le xxv^e Septem~ 1643* (other copy in AG *A*¹ 89, fols. 18–22).

15. BMaz *Ms.* 2214, fol. 87rv [sic], Mazarin (register copy) to Châteauneuf, August 13, 1643 [pub. in *LM,* I, 277]; ASVen *Francia* 99 n°s. 393 III, 394 IV
and 398 IV, Girolamo Giustiniani (letters sent) to Senate, two of September
8 and one of September 15, 1643 (transcripts in BNF *Ms. It.* 1820, fols.
221–222, 223–225, and 232–233); Motteville P&M XXVII, 45–57, or M&P,
ser. 2, X, 59–63; La Châtre P&M LI, 238–241, or M&P, ser. 3, III, 290–292;
La Rochefoucauld P&M LI, pt. 1, 387–391, or M&P, ser. 3, V, pt. 1,
397–398.

16. Claude Dulong, "Du Nouveau sur le Palais Mazarin: L'achat de l'hôtel
Tubeuf par le Cardinal," *Bibliothèque de l'Ecole des Chartes* (CLIII, 1, 1995)
131–155; Ormesson I, 112, 116; *Gazette* n° 129, October 10, 1643. For the
appointment of Servien, see BNF *Ms. Baluze* 174 (*Carnet* 3) p. 72: "mandar
Servien e far restar Schavigni." The collaboration between Mazarin and
Chavingy continued, but Lionne clearly took over the bulk of Mazarin's
correspondence, beginning with AAE MD *France* 847, fol. 79, Mazarin (Lionne minute) to Lantucci, October 26, 1643, followed by two other letters
AAE CP *Hollande* 24, fols. 373 and 385, Mazarin (Lionne minutes) to La
Thuillerie, November 20, and to plenipotentiaries, November 28, 1643. For
the appointment of Longueville, see the titles of the instructions cited in
the next note.

17. We have numerous texts of the instructions, all from late September, which
I would arrange in roughly the following order. AAE CP *Allemagne* 17, fols.
194–258, *Instruction donnée a Messieurs le Duc de Longueville, Henry d'Orleans Prince et Comte Souverain de Neufchastel Comte de Dunois et de Tancar-
ville, Connestable hereditaire de Normandie Gouverneur et lieutenant general
du Roy aud~ pais Chevallier de Ses orders et Cappitaine de cent hommes
d'armes de ses ordonnances, le Comte d'Avasux Claude de Mesmes Comman-
deur des orders de Sa Ma^té Surjntendant des Finances de France et l'un des Ministres d'Estat, Et le Comte de la Roche des aubiers Abbel Servien Con^er de Sa*

Ma^{té} en tous ses conseils Tous trois envoyez de la part de leurs Majestés en Alle-magne en qualité d'Ambassadeurs extraordinaires Plenipotentiaires pour la Paix generale qui Se doit traiter a Munster . . . d^{er} Sep^{re} 1643; Allemagne 17, fols. 166–184, *Instruction donnée a Messieurs le Duc de Longueville, Henry d'Orleans &c. le comte d'Avaux, Claude de Mesmes, &c, et le Comte de la Roche des Aubiers, Abel Servien &c, tous trois envoiés de la part de leus Majestés en Allemagne, en qualité d Ambassadeurs extraordinaires, Plenipotentiaires pour la Paix generale qui doit se traitter a Munster . . . fait a Paris le dernier Jour de Septembre 1643; Allemagne* 17, fols. 259–265, *Memoire aux S^{rs} d'Avaux et de* ~~Chavigny~~ (crossed out and replaced by *Servien*) *Ambassadeurs ext^{res} et Plenipotentiaires du Roy* [for Holland] *fait a Paris le dernier jour de septembre 1643, Hollande* 24, fols. 197–200, *Memoire Servant d'Instruction que le Roi a commande estre baille au Sieur Claude de Mesmes Comte d'Avaux, Comman-deur de Ses ordres, Surintendant des finances de France et l'un des ministres d'Estat, et au Sieur Abel Servien comte de la Roche des Aubiers Conseiller de S. M. en tous ses conseils, estant deux des trois Plenipotentiaires nommés par S.M. pour traiter de la Paix generale Conjointement avec Ses Alliés, et envoiés Ses Ambassadeurs extraordinaires en Hollande . . . faict a Paris le dernier jour de Septemb. 1643. Allemagne* 18 contains a beautiful final copy of the instruc-tion for Münster, signed by Louis XIV and Brienne; BNF *Ms. Fr.* 4414, fols. 1–44, contains a beautiful final copy of both instructions. AAE CP *Alle-magne* 21, fols. 5–40, contains what appears to be a working copy of the in-struction for Münster, and *Allemagne* 56, fols. 284–289, contains a working copy of the instruction for Holland. The text in *Hollande* 24, fols. 197–200, was first published in Waddington II, 377–383, and all of these instructions are published in integrated form in *APW* I 1, 24–149, but it will be observed from my remarks in note 12 above and from the order of citation in the present note that I have adopted a slightly different sequence, and I do not see any evidence that the *mémoire* on alternative terms accompanying the 1642 instruction (see Chapter 1, note 25) was added to this one.

18. HHSA RK *FrA* 46k, Konv. a, fols. 85–113, Instruction (Konrad Zelffe minute) for Münster and Osnabrück, Kaiser-Ebersdorf, September 23, 1643 (clean copy with corrections in Johann Söldner's and one more hand, pos-sibly Kurz's, on fols. 35–79, other copies, in fols. 136–172; RK *FrA* 47b, fols. 35–58 and 60–105; RK *FrA* 92 I, fols. 234–261; and SK *FrA* 1, n° VIII, fols. 77–105) [pub. in *APW* I 1, 413–440].

19. For the departures, see AST MPLM *Francia* 44, 112/2, Scaglia (letter sent) to Christine, October 9, 1644. For the voyage, compare AAE CP *Hollande* 24, fols. 353–360, the *Relation* (Servien's secretary's minute) *faite par M. Servien du voyage de M^{rs} les Plenipotentiaires de Paris a la haye*, which Servien apparently composed in the expectation that he would be writing

their common letters to the court with the letter that D'Avaux apparently composed, fols. 260–263, D'Avaux and Servien (duplicate for Mazarin) to Anne, November 16, 1643. This comparison provides an interesting contrast between their writing styles. See also *Hollande* 24, fols. 361–364, what would seem to be Godefroy's *Commencement du Journal de ce qui s'est passé a la Conférence pour la Paix Entre les Ambassadeurs de Louis XIV Roy de France et ceux de l'Empereur Ferdinand III et Philippes IV Roy d'Espagne A Munster en Westphalie* ~~l'an 1644~~ (crossed out).

20. See the *Journal* cited in the previous note, AAE CP *Allemagne* 21, fols. 141–149, D'Avaux, Servien, and La Thuillerie (letter sent) to Anne, December 23, 1643 (duplicate sent in *Hollande* 24, fols. 298–309). For the first French project, see *Hollande* 27, fols. 117–119 [probably of December 27, 1643] (copy sent in *Allemagne* 21, fols. 227–229). See it also in NNA SG R 4853.

21. We do not have Servien's letter of complaint, nor do we have D'Avaux's letter to Anne, but he mentions his offer in AAE CP *Hollande* 24, fols. 292–293, D'Avaux (secretary's hand letter sent) to Mazarin, December 19, 1643. For D'Avaux's account of the squabble, see AAE CP *Hollande* 24, fols. 322–327, D'Avaux (secretary's hand letter sent) to Mazarin, December 26, 1643. See Servien taking over the pen in *Hollande* 27, fols. 110–116, D'Avaux, Servien, and La Thuillerie (Servien secretary's minute) to Brienne, January 4, 1644 (letter sent in *Allemagne* 21, fols. 170–178, duplicate sent in *Hollande* 30, fols. 15–24). For further proof, see AAE CP *Hollande* 30, fols. 11–14, D'Avaux (secretary's hand letter sent) to Brienne, same date.

22. For the Swedish decision, see *SRP* X, 161–163 and 181–183, May 4/14, and June 6/16, 1643. For the short memorials, see SRA *RR* 1643–1645 Memorial (copy) for Rosenhane June 10/20, 1643 [pub. in *APW* II C 2, 1–3]; and SRA *KK* Memorial (copy) for Oxenstierna, Bielke, Salvius, August [ ] 1643 [pub. in *APW* II C 1, 7–10]. For the orders to wait in Minden, see SRA *RR* 1643–1645, Christina (copy) to Oxenstierna and Salvius, Stockholm, August 5/15, 1643 [pub. in *APW* II C 1, 10–12]. See the Swedish Manifesto in German in Londorp V, 846–859, dated January 16, 1644. For East Frisia, see BMaz *Ms.* 2214, fol. 133, Mazarin (register copy) to La Thuillerie, October 30, 1643 [pub. in *LM* I, 438–439].

23. For Anne's revenge, see BMaz *Ms.* 2214, fol. 146, Mazarin (register copy) to Roqueservières, December 20, 1643 [pub. in *LM* I, 513–514]. For the rejection of D'Avaux's offer, see BMaz *Ms.* 2214, fols. 152–153, Mazarin (register copy) to D'Avaux, January 16, 1643 [pub. in *LM,* I, 546–548]. For the 2 million *livres*, see AAE CP *Hollande* 30, fols. 190–191, Mazarin (Silhon minute) to D'Avaux, February 13, 1644 (register copy in BMaz *Ms.* 2214, fols. 160–161) [pub. in *LM* I, 584–586]. For Mazarin's ideas on the truce,

see AAE CP *Hollande* 30, fols. 5–8, *Mem^re* (Lionne minute) *Sur Lequel M. le Comte de Brienne a dressé l'Instruction du Roy a M^rs les plenipot^res du 12e Jan^er 1644* which, however, developed into Lionne's minute in Ass. Nat. *Ms.* 272, fols. 55–58, and then into the *mémoire* in *Hollande* 30, fols. 83–84, Anne (clean copy) to D'Avaux, Servien, and La Thuillerie, January 23, 1643 (copy sent in *Hollande* 29, fols. 100–104, other copies in *Hollande* 27, fols. 204–206, and *Allemagne* 21, fols. 282–283) [pub. in *APW* II B 1, 844–846]. For the reflections on the Swedish invasion, see AAE CP *Hollande* 30, fols. 34–38, Mazarin (Lionne minute) to D'Avaux, Servien, and La Thuillerie, January 15, 1643 (copy in *Hollande* 27, fols. 174–179).

24. For the French articles (now numbered) with the Dutch responses, see AAE CP *Hollande* 27, fols. 137–142 (copy sent in *Allemagne* 21, fols. 209–213, and other copies in *Hollande* 25, fols. 88–94, and NNA SG *R* 4853) [pub. in *APW* II B 1, xlii–xlviii]. For a description of the negotiation, see AAE CP *Hollande* 27, fols. 145–157, D'Avaux, Servien, and La Thuillerie (secretary's minute with Servien corrections) to Brienne, January 12, 1644 (letter sent in *Allemagne* 21, fols. 191–202, with the articles and responses attached).

25. The party was on February 8, 1644, the Monday of Carnival. D'Avaux claimed Servien told him he would regret it. See D'Avaux's writing of September 3, cited in Chapter 3, note 7. AAE CP *Hollande* 27, fol. 272–277, Servien (own hand minute) to Brienne, which I would date around February 23, 1644, along with fol. 278, Servien (own hand minute), *Articles sur lesquels le Sr Servien Suplie M. le Comte de brienne de ~~Scavoir les~~* (crossed out) *fasse [sic] regler M. d'avaux et luy contre les contestations qui pourroient [ ] entre eux.*

26. For copies of the Dutch writing, which the French were careful to procure, see AAE CP *Hollande* 27, fols. 311–312, and *Hollande* 30, fols. 296–297, 500, 287–291, and 312–315. For the treaty with the comments of the French negotiators, see *Hollande* 27, fols. 363–369, March 1, 1643 (copy to Mazarin in *Hollande* 30, fols. 370–374; copy to Brienne in *Allemagne* 32, fols. 20–24). For copies of the treaty of alliance pure and simple, see *Hollande* 30, fols. 333–338, *Traicte de holande Signé A La haye le Premier mars 1644* (copies on fols. 339–345 and 346–351) [pub. in Italian in Siri IV, pt. 1, 98–104]. However, the text in NNA SG *R* 4853 and the published versions in Aitzema *VNVH* I, 470–477; Dumont VI, pt. 1, 293–295; and Gärtner II, 499–507, all have the treaty followed by the Dutch writing. For an overall description of the negotiation, see AAE CP *Hollande* 27, fols. 336–339, D'Avaux, Servien, and La Thuillerie (secretary's minute, with Servien marginal corrections) to Brienne, March 1, 1643 (letter sent in *Allemagne* 32, fols. 9–13; duplicate sent in *Hollande* 30, fols. 366–369, without the final paragraph; copy of the

entire letter in *Hollande* 26, fols. 437–442) [pub. in Waddington II, 390–392]. See also *Hollande* 30, fols. 405–413, D'Avaux and Servien (duplicate sent) to Brienne, The Hague, March 6, 1644.

27. There are various versions of this speech. See AAE CP *Hollande* 30, fols. 331–332, dated March, 1644, the printed versions in Knuttel in French, 5105, and in Dutch, 5106–5109, all dated March 3; in Latin in Londorp V, 902–903, undated; and in French in *NS* I, 193, dated March 5. D'Avaux actually gave the speech on March 3. The sense of the cited passage is in all of them.

3. Dissensions in Westphalia

1. See the campaign plan in AAE CP *Hollande* 30, fols. 323–328, the minute in Lionne's hand . . . *du ix^e Mars 1644 A Mr de la Tuillerie et en Son absence a M. Brasset.*

2. For the entry of D'Avaux, see AAE CP *Allemagne* 26, fols. 109–111, D'Avaux (own hand letter sent) to Anne, March 18, 1644 (copy on fols. 120–123; copy sent *Allemagne* 32, fols. 45–48) [pub. in *NS* II, 1, 3–4; Gärtner II, 549–555; and *APW* II B 1, 1–5]. For the entries of D'Avaux and Chigi, see ASVen *Munster* 1, fols. 369–373 and 374–379, two letters of Contarini (copy to Senate) to Girolamo Giustiniani, both of March 25, 1644. For the entry of Chigi, see also BVat CCL A I 22, fol. 81, Chigi (register) to Albizzi, March 25, 1644 [pub. in K & IDR I, pt. 1, 380]. For the preparation of the circular letter, see AAE CP *Allemagne* 26, fols. 218–219, D'Avaux (own hand minute) to Anne, March 25, 1644 (copy sent on fols. 212–213) [pub. in *NS* II, 5–6; Gärtner II, 598–601; and *APW* II B 1, 26–28]. For the dispute over "*Sacra Rega M.*," see AAE CP *Allemagne* 29, fols. 265–266, Servien (own hand minute) to Lionne [July 11(?), 1644]. For the circular letter itself, see *Allemagne* 26, fols. 341–343, 345–349 (copy to Brienne in *Allemagne* 32, fols. 150–154; copy to Mazarin in *Allemagne* 37, fols. 30–35; in Italian in ASVen *Munster* 1, fols. 515–519) [pub. in Italian in Siri V, pt. 2, 391–395; in German in Londorp V, 903–905; and in Latin and French in *NS* I, 247–250]. For the entry of Servien, see AAE CP *Allemagne* 32, fols. 96–99 and 100–102, two letters sent of Servien to Brienne, April 9, 1644 (copy of the first in *Allemagne* 26, fols. 359–363; copies of the second in *Allemagne* 29, fols. 198–200, and *Allemagne* 37, fols. 40–41) [pub. in *APW* II B 1, 68–73], ASVen *Münster* 1, fols. 393–395 and 396–399, Contarini (copies to Senate) to Girolamo Giustiniani, both of April 8, 1644. Death of Zapata (April 3, 1644), see AGS E 2345, Saavedra Fajardo (copy) to Philip IV, April 4, 1644 [pub. in *CDI* LXXXII, 23–24].

3. For the responses of Frederick Henry, see AAE CP *Hollande* 30, fols. 475–480, La Thuillerie (copy) to Brienne, March 24, 1644. For the exchange of powers,

see BVat CCL A I 8 (7), fols. 48–49 (Chigi Diary), April 7, 9, 13, 14 and 16, 1644 [pub. in *APW* III C 1/1, 210–212]; BVat CCL A I 42, fols. 2–4 (Chigi Short Diary), same dates [pub. in K & IDR I, pt. 1, 98–101]. For the French complaints, see AAE CP *Allemagne* 26, fols. 407–413, D'Avaux and Servien (Servien secretary's minute) to Brienne, April 16, 1644 (other minutes on fols. 407–413 and 401–406, copy sent in *Allemagne* 32, fols. 112–119, and copy for Mazarin in *Allemagne* 37, fols. 48–54). BVat CCL A I 42, fol. 4 (Chigi Short Diary), April 19 and 25, 1644 [pub. in K & IDR I, pt. 1, 193–105]; ASVen *Munster* 1, fols. 436–443, Contarini (copy to Senate) to Girolamo Giustiniani, April 22, 1644. For Oxenstierna's arrival, see SRA *JOS* A I, Johan Oxenstierna (own hand minute) to Christina, March 29/April 8, 1644 (copy sent in SRA *DG* 2, fols. 227–228; duplicate on fols. 229–239) [pub. in *APW* II C 1, 202–203]. For the French complaints against the powers of the Emperor and the Spanish, see AAE CP *Hollande* 25, fols. 132–140, with powers on the other side. See also ASVen *Munster* 1, fols. 436–443, Contarini (copy to Senate) to Girolamo Giustiniani, April 22, 1644. For the military events, see the *Gazettes* n[os] 60–87, June 3 to July 23, 1644.

4. For the insulting exchange, see AAE CP *Allemagne* 29, fols. 273–275, Servien (own hand minute) to D'Avaux, June 27, 1644, plus fol. 276, a fragment of the original letter signed by Servien (copy on fols. 253–256, dated July 21; what may be the copy sent in *Allemagne* 27, fols. 252–255; copy later sent by D'Avaux to Brienne in *Allemagne* 33, fols. 106–108; and copy sent to Lionne for Mazarin in *Allemagne* 37, fols. 229–231), *Allemagne* 29, fols. 300–316, D'Avaux, what may be a copy sent to Servien, July 6, 1644 (copy sent to Brienne in *Allemagne* 33, fols. 110–123, and what may be a copy sent to Mazarin in *Allemagne* 37, fols. 269–277). For further proof that these letters were communicated to the court, see *Allemagne* 29, fols. 375–377, Lionne (letter sent) to Servien, July 23 1644 [pub. in *APW* II B 1, 387–390]. For the 196-page letter, see AAE CP *Allemagne* 30, fols. 42–120, Servien (copyist hand) to D'Avaux, August 6, 1644. This exchange produced a large number of copies. It was first published in *Lettres de messieurs d'Avaux et Servien, ambassadeurs pour le Roy de France en Allemagne concernant leurs differents et leurs responses de part & d'autre en l'année 1644,* [MDCL], later in *NS* I, 75–76, 77–82, 83–107, and 205–215, and partially in *APW* II B 1, 295–298 and 317–328. D'Avaux responded by addressing himself directly to the court. See AAE CP *Allemagne* 33, fols. 281–286, D'Avaux to Anne, August 18, 1644 (copies for Mazarin in *Allemagne* 38, fols. 81–86; other copies in *Allemagne* 30, fols. 214–220, and *Allemagne* 24, fols. 82–85, and *Allemagne* 38, fols. 37–55) [pub. in *NS* I, 107–109].

5. Capitulation of Gravelines: *Gazettes* n°s 90 and 91, August 1 and 5, 1644. Capitulation of Lérida: *Gazette* n° 95, August 13, 1644. For the King's circular

letter, see AAE CP *Allemagne* 28, fols. 6–13, dated August 20, 1644 [pub. in *NS* I, 288–289, and Meiern I, 272–273]. For Mazarin's reactions to the dissensions, see AAE CP *Allemagne* 38, fols. 108–109, Mazarin (Chavigny minute) to D'Avaux and Servien, September 3, 1644 (copy sent in *Allemagne* 28, fols. 98–100; Servien's copy in *Allemagne* 30, fols. 248–249) [pub. in *NS* II, pt. 1, 131–132; Gärtner III, 417–421; and calendared in *APW* II B 1, 481–482]. See also AAE CP *Allemagne* 33, fol. 319, Brienne (secretary's hand minute) to D'Avaux, September 3, 1644 (copy sent in *Allemagne* 28, fols. 101–103), and *Allemagne* 30, fols. 252–253, Lionne (secretary's hand copy sent) to Servien, September 3, 1644 [pub. in *APW* II B 1, 483–486].

6. Capitulation of Speyer (August 29, 1644): *Gazette* n° 111, September 14, 1644. Siege of Phillipsburg (August 25–September 9, 1644): *Gazettes* n°s 107 and 111, September 7 and 14, 1644. Capitulation of the Sas (September 6, 1644): *Gazette* n° 112, September 16, 1644. Swedish movements: *Gazette* n° 113, September 17, 1644. Capitulation of Phillipsburg (September 9, 1644): *Gazette* n° 115, September 20, 1644. Surrender of Worms (September 13, 1644): *Gazette* n° 118, September 24, 1644; and Mainz (September 17, 1644): *Gazette* n° 120, September 29, 1644. More Swedish movements: *Gazette* n° 121, October 1, 1644. Election of Innocent X (September 15, 1644): *Gazette* n° 128, October 25, 1644.

7. See AAE CP *Allemagne* 38, fols. 105–106, D'Avaux (letter sent) to Mazarin, September 3, 1644 (copies in *Allemagne* 30, fols. 261–262, and *Allemagne* 24, fols. 170–171), which enclosed *Allemagne* 38, fols. 37–53, a lengthy and documented writing by D'Avaux against Servien, a copy of which was apparently published by D'Avaux's supporters in Paris, according to Servien's *Diverses entreprises,* cited in the following note [also pub. in *NS* I, 205–215]. See also AAE CP *Allemagne* 33, fols. 345–358, copy of the Instruction for Fouquet-Croissy, September 15, 1644 (other copy in *Hollande* 25, fols. 230–244). For the second circular letter, see *Allemagne* 33, fols. 375–378, September 4, 1644, which is a copy sent to Brienne [pub. in *NS* I, 289–293; and Meiern I, 269–272]. For the haggling over the powers, see AAE CP *Allemagne* 31, fols. 31–32 (Servien secretary's and Servien's own hand minute) *de M^{rs} les Plenip^{res} touchant la reformation des pouvoirs,* October 2, 1644, and *Allemagne* 34, fols. 23–26, *Remarques contre la validité des Pouvoirs données par l'empereur et le Roy Catholique a Messrs les Plenipotentiaires*; fols. 29–30, *Quo desiderantur a Plenipotentiarijs Gallicis & repraesentatur Ex parte Regis Hispaniarum* (copy in *Hollande* 25, fols. 258–260; HHSA RK FrA 47a, Konv. b, fols. 329–331). AAE CP *Allemagne* 34, fols. 27–28, *Pro parte sacrae Caesareae Majestatis postulatur* (copy in *Hollande* 25, fols. 256–258). See also HHSA RK FrA 92 III, n° 398, fols. 355–358, Nassau and Volmar (minute) to Ferdinand III of September 23, 1644 (copy sent in *FrA* 47a, Konv. b, fols. 315–318) [pub. in *APW* II A 1,

648–651]; ASVen *Munster* 2, fols. 267–272 and 275–281, Contarini (copies to Senate) to Nani and to Giovanni Giustiniani, September 23 and 30, 1644; AAE CP *Allemagne* 31, fols. 27–30, D'Avaux and Servien (Servien secretary's minute) to Brienne, October 1, 1644 (D'Avaux secretary's clean minute) in *Allemagne* 24, fols. 358–363, copy sent in *Allemagne* 34, fols. 9–14, and duplicate for Mazarin in *Allemagne* 38, fols. 161–166) [pub. in *NS* II, 144–146; Gärtner III, 486–495; and *APW* II B 1, 533–537]. AAE CP *Hollande* 25, fols. 254–256, Servien (copy) to Brienne, October 1, 1644; HHSA RK *FrA* 92 III, n° 410, fols. 396–404, Nassau and Volmar to Ferdinand, October 6, 1644 (copy in KHA *N A* IV 1628/13, copy sent in HHSA RK *FrA* 47a, Konv. b, fols. 321–327 and 332) [pub. in *APW* II A 2, 6–13]; AAE CP *Allemagne* 24, fols. 478–485, D'Avaux and Servien (D'Avaux's own hand minute) to Brienne, October 22, 1644 (Servien secretary's clean minute in *Allemagne* 31, fols. 92–103; copy sent in *Allemagne* 34, fols. 56–64; and duplicate for Mazarin in *Allemagne* 38, fols. 196–203) [pub. in *NS* II, 157–160; Gärtner III, 553–567; and *APW* II B 1, 570–577]. For the agreement, see ASVen *Munster* 2, fols. 367–370 and 365, Contarini (copy to Senate) to Nani, November 4, 1644. For the agreement on the agreement, see numerous copies of numerous texts in ASVat *Paci* 15, fol. 99; ASVen *Munster* 2, fols. 424 and 438–439; AAE CP *Allemagne* 34, fols. 223, 230–235; *Hollande* 25, fols. 312–313; *Allemagne* 38, fols. 244–245 and 258–260; HHSA RK *FrA* 46g, fol. 61, and *FrA* 92 III, fol. 560; SRA *DG* 2, fol. 797 [pub. in *NS* I, 289; and Meiern I, 281]; BVat CCL A I 1, fols. 37–39, Chigi (register) to Innocent X, two letters of November 18, 1644 (letters sent in ASVat *Paci* 15, fols. 97–98, and *Paci* 18, fol. 18), and CCL A I, 1, 24, fols. 10–12, Chigi (register) to Bagni, three letters of November 19, 1644 [all letters pub. in K & IDR, 550–561]; ASVen *Munster* 2, fols. 447–453 and 431–437, Contarini (copies to Senate) to Nani, November 19 and 21, 1644; AAE CP *Allemagne* 31, fols. 234–242, D'Avaux and Servien (secretary's and Servien's own hand minute) to Brienne, probably written on November 20, but dated November 25, which D'Avaux refused to sign (copy in *Allemagne* 34, fols. 151–157); *Allemagne* 34, fols. 138–149 and 158–163, D'Avaux (secretary's hand letters sent) to Brienne, November 23 and 24, 1644 (copies of the second in *Allemagne* 25, fols. 122–128, and *Hollande* 25, fols. 280–284) [pub. in *APW* II B 1, 643–647]. The letter that D'Avaux refused to sign ultimately became AAE CP *Allemagne* 34, fols. 173–183, Servien (letter sent) to Brienne, November 25, 1644 (copy to Mazarin in *Allemagne* 38, fols. 251–257) [pub. in *APW* II B 1, 651–662]. See also AAE CP *Allemagne* 34, fols. 195–204, Servien (copy) to Mazarin November 25, 1644 (other copy in *Hollande* 25, fols. 289–297); *Allemagne* 31, fol. 233, Servien (own hand minute) to Anne, November 25, 1644 (letter sent in *Allemagne* 34, fols. 169–172; copy in *Hollande* 25, fols. 288–289), *Allemagne* 31, fols. 267–268, Servien (secretary's and own hand minute) to Lionne, November 26, 1644, with attachments in *Allemagne* 38, fols. 245 and 258–260; HHSA RK *FrA* 92 III n° 459, fols. 578–584, Nassau and Volmar (minute) to Ferdinand III (copy in KHA *N* A IV 1628/15, and copy sent in HHSA RK *FrA* 47a, Konv. b, fols. 385–391 and 394–396) [pub. in *APW* II A 3, 68–72]. For the in-fighting, see AAE CP *Allemagne* 34, fols. 185–188 and fols. 311–316, copies of Servien to Saint-Romain, November 25 and 27, 1644 (other copies in *Hollande* 25, fols. 297–299, and fols. 315–323). For the correspondence between the secretaries, see the copies in AAE CP *Allemagne* 34, fols. 245–259, November 29–December 3, 1644, and *Allemagne* 34, fols. 282–293, November 29–December 1, 1644, forwarded in D'Avaux's and Servien's letters to Brienne of December 3, cited in the next note (copies of some of the copies in *Hollande* 25, fols. 327–334) plus *Allemagne* 38, fols. 282–284, of December 3, forwarded in Servien to Mazarin of December 3, cited in the next note. For the exchange of powers between the Imperialists and the Swedes, see HHSA RK *FrA* 92 III, n° 468, fols. 618–622, Protocol of November 28, 29, 30, 1644 (copy in KHA *N* A IV 1628/16) [pub. in *APW* II A 2, 77–78].

8. For the feuding vs. the proposals, see AAE CP *Allemagne* 34, fols. 260–264, D'Avaux (letter sent) to Brienne, December 2, 1644 (copy in *Hollande* 25, fols. 335–339) [pub. in *APW* II B 1, 696–701]; AAE CP *Allemagne* 31, fols. 274–280, Servien (Servien's secretary's minute) to Brienne, December 3, 1644 (copy sent in *Allemagne* 34, fols. 274–280, and copy for Mazarin in *Allemagne* 38, fols. 265–272) [pub. in *APW* II B 1, 701–705]. AAE CP *Allemagne* 31, fols. 287–290, Servien (minute) to Mazarin, December 3, 1644 (copy sent in *Allemagne* 38, fols. 274–280) [pub. in *APW* II B 1, 707–710]; AAE CP *Allemagne* 25, fols. 268–270, Saint-Romain (copy for Chavigny) to Brienne, December 3, 1644 [pub. in *APW* II B 1, 711–716], plus *Allemagne* 34, fols. 297–303, Servien's *Diverses entreprises de M. D'Avaux au preiudice des Commandemens de la Reyne et de l honneur du S*^r *Servien desquelles se demande tres hublement Justice et reparation a Sa Ma*^{té} (copy in *Hollande* 25, fols. 339–346, gives the date of December 4, 1644). For the French proposals, see AAE CP *Allemagne* 34, fols. 346–347 and 370–372 (copy in SRA *DG* 2, fol. 800, Italian translation in ASVen *Munster* 2, fols. 468–469) [pub. in Italian in Siri V, pt. 2, 498–499; in German in Londorp V, 919–920; and in the original French in *NS* I, 318, and Meiern I, 320–321]. Swedish proposal: SRA *DG* 2, fol. 803 (copy in HHSA RK *FrA* 48a, fols. 101–104, dated November 26/December 5); AAE CP *Allemagne* 34, fols. 372–373 [pub. in French in the *Gazette* n° 14, Feb, 3, 1645; in Latin and Italian in Siri V, pt. 2, 500–502; in German in Londorp V, 919, dated November 27; in Latin and French in *NS* I, 303–304; and in the original Latin in Gärtner III, 688–690, and Meiern I, 313–314]. Spanish proposal: AAE CP *Allemagne* 34,

fols. 348–349; SRA *DG* 2, fol. 842; in Latin on fol. 843; in Italian in ASVen *Munster* 2, fols. 463–465 [pub. in Spanish and Italian in Siri V, pt. 2, 495–498; in French summary in *NS* I, 318–320; and in Spanish and Latin in Meiern I, 318–320]. Imperial proposal to the French: HHSA RK *FrA* 92 III, fols. 624 and 627 (copies KHA *N* A IV 1628/16; and AAE CP *Allemagne* 34, fols. 344–345 and 368–369) [pub. in Latin and Italian in Siri V, pt. 2, 492–495; in Latin and French in *NS* I, 321; and in Latin in Meiern I, 317–318]. Imperial proposal to the Swedes: HHSA RK *FrA* 48a, Konv. c, fol. 99 (copy on fol. 121, other copy in SRA *DG* 2, in Latin on fol. 841, and in German on fol. 864) [pub. in Gärtner III, 753–754]. See also AAE CP *Allemagne* 31, fols. 337–346, Servien (secretary's minute) to Brienne 337–346, December 10, 1644 (copy sent in *Allemagne* 34, fols. 355–367; duplicate for Mazarin in *Allemagne* 38, fols. 306–313) [pub. in *APW* II B 1, 740–747] and ASVen *Munster* 2, fols. 480–491 and 476–478, Contarini to Nani and to Giovanni Giustiniani, December 9, 1644, as well as the relation in *NS* I, 309–320. For the marriage proposal, see Saavedra to Rojas, December 10, 1644, reported in AGS *E* 2346, the *consulta* of February 21, 1645.

9. AAE CP *Allemagne* 43, fols. 25–26, contains Mazarin's partial minute, dated January 2, 1645, followed by fols. 13–20, 21–24, and 501–506, *Memoire* (three minutes, the last two in Lionne's hand) *du Roy a Messrs les Plenipot^res*, January 1, 1645 (Brienne copy in Ass. Nat. *Ms.* 274, fols. 7–16; other copy in *Allemagne* 50, fols. 18–26, both dated January 1, 1645) [pub. in *NS* II, pt. 2, 3–6; Gärtner IV, 6–26; and *APW* II B 2, 1–12]. See also AAE CP *Allemagne* 43, fols. 32–34, minute with Lionne corrections of the expanded propositions, dated January 4, 1645, and the copies in fols. 400–402 (for Spain) and 507–508 (for Emperor). [The proposal for the Emperor is pub. in Italian in Siri V, pt. 2, 609–612.] For the cave-in to the Dutch, see Ass. Nat. *Ms.* 274, fol. 44, Louis XIV (Brienne minute) to D'Avaux and Servien, January 11, 1645 (copy sent in AAE CP *Allemagne* 54, fol. 26; other copy in *Allemagne* 50, fols. 58–59) [pub. in *NS* II, pt. 2, 15; Gärtner IV, 93–94; and *APW* II B 2, 35–36].

10. For the plenipotentiaries' quandary, see BNF *Ms. Fr.* 17897, fols. 2–17, D'Avaux and Servien (Brasset register copy) to Brienne, January 31, 1645 (copy sent in Ass. Nat. *Ms.* 274, fols. 92–113; duplicate for Mazarin in AAE CP *Allemagne* 43, fols. 66–84, dated January 20; other copy in *Allemagne* 50, fols. 144–153). For D'Avaux's trip, see *Allemagne* 50, fols. 191–193, D'Avaux (letter sent) to Servien, February 7, 1645 (copies sent to Brienne with Servien comments in margin in Ass. Nat. *Ms.* 274, fols. 136–138 and 280–289, the latter dated February 8; duplicate for Mazarin in AAE CP *Allemagne* 43, fols. 127–129) [pub. in *APW* II B 2, 123–126], as well as SRA *JOS* A I, Johan Oxenstierna and Salvius (Mylonius minute) to Christina, February 12/22, 1645 (copies sent in *DG* 3, fols. 124–132 and 324–329). See also the discussion of

this trip in Servien's and D'Avaux's letter to Brienne of March 3, cited in this note below. For the French proposals, see copies sent to Brienne in Ass. Nat. *Ms.* 274, fols. 149–151 (for the Emperor) and fols. 153–155 (for the Spanish); AAE CP *Allemagne* 54, fols. 12–15 and 90–92, copies of the proposal to the Emperor; ASVen *Munster* 3, fols. 17–19, copy of proposal to Emperor; BNF *Ms. Fr.* 10649, fols. 42–46 and 204–205 (draft in Doulceur's hand with Gode-froy corrections and clean copy in Doulceur's hand of the proposal to the Spanish); other copies in AAE CP *Allemagne* 46, fols. 81–82 and 121–126 (to the Spanish), and 83–58 and 127–128 (to the Emperor); AAE MD *Allemagne* 9, fols. 186–187 (to the Emperor); AGS E 2346, *Copia de la propositcion de los Fran^s para la paz con El Emp^{or} dada en Munster a 24 de feb^{ro} 1645* in French and Spanish, and E 2063, *Escritura dada de los franceses a los Plenipotentiarios del Enp^{or} en Munster* same thing in French only. The version published in *NS* I, 328–30, as *SECONDE PROPOSITION Des Plénipotentiaires de France pour parvenir à une Paix en Allemagne, comme aussi en Italie, A Munster le 24. Fevrier 1645 & délivrée le 1 Avril* is very misleading. It is actually the Imperial one with the last sentence of the Spanish one attached. The ones published in Gärtner IV, 423–428, and Meiern I, 358–360, are more accurate versions of the proposition to the Emperor. For their transmission, see BVat CCL A I 45, fols. 123–125 and 126–127, Chigi (register) to Pamfili, two letters of February 24, 1645 (copies sent in ASVat *Paci* 17, fols. 78–80, and *Paci* 18, fols. 97–99) [pub. in K & IDR I, pt. 2, 854–861]; and ASVen *Münster* 2, fols. 678–685, Contarini (copy to Senate) to Nani, February 24, 1645; BVat CCL A I 24, fols. 31–32, Chigi to Bagni, February 25, 1645 [pub. in K & IDR I, pt. 2, 864–866]; ASVen *Münster* 3, fol. 3, Contarini (copy to Senate) to Nani, February 25, 1645; and AAE CP *Allemagne* 46, fols. 136–168, Servien and D'Avaux (minute) to Brienne, March 4, 1645 (Brasset register copy in BNF *Ms. Fr.* 17897, fols. 18–49, dated March 3; copy sent in Ass. Nat. *Ms.* 274, fols. 192–239; duplicate for Mazarin in AAE CP *Allemagne* 43, fols. 174–318, and copy in *Allemagne* 50, fols. 295–311) [pub. in *NS* II, pt. 2, 43–56, dated February 30; Gärtner IV, 437–496, dated February 28; and APW II B 2, 150–166, the last with omissions]. For D'Avaux's request for his recall, see AAE CP *Allemagne* 46, fol. 135, D'Avaux (minute) to Brienne, March 3, 1645 (copy sent in Ass. Nat. *Ms.* 274, fol. 252).

11. See Peñaranda's instructions in AHN E 2880, dated February 25, 1645. See the powers for Peñaranda, Brun, and Saavedra, dated January 5, 1645 in AAE CP *Allemagne* 55, fols. 308–310 [pub. in Spanish and Italian in Siri V, pt. 2, 404–408; and in Spanish and French in *NS* I, 323–324]. For the Battle of Jankau, see the *Gazette,* n° 32, March 24 and n° 35, March 30, 1645.

12. For the campaign plans, see especially AAE CP *Hollande* 33, fols. 84–89, Mazarin (Chavigny's minute) to D'Estrades, February 10, 1645; and BNF

Ms. Baluze 174 (*Carnet* 6), p. 61: "Saper dal P^e d Oranges se sarra possibile far qualcosa contra Mardic con li Vascielli andando tirar & abbaterlo." For the campaign treaty with the Dutch, see AAE CP *Hollande* 33, fols. 182–192, April 10 and 20, 1645. On D'Avaux's return, see Ass. Nat. *Ms.* 274, fol. 248, Louis XIV (minute) to D'Avaux, April 6, 1645 (copy sent in AAE CP *Allemagne* 54, fol. 151) [pub. in NS II, pt. 2, 77; and Gärtner IV, 716–717, dated April 5]. For the interesting views of a Hessian minister on the possible loss of D'Avaux, see HSAM 4h 1694, fols. 21–23, Krosieg (letter sent) to Scheffer, April 22/May 2, 1645. See also AAE CP *Allemagne* 51, fols. 100–102, Lionne (letter sent) to Servien, April 7, 1645 [extract pub. in APW II B 2, 243–246], and AAE CP *Allemagne* 54, fols. 162–163, Mazarin (copy sent) to D'Avaux, April 15, 1645.

13. For a Spanish copy of the French proposals of February 14, 1645, see AGS E 2346. For the transmission of the French proposals, see BVat CCL A I 25, fols. 137–138, Chigi (register) to Rospigliosi, April 8, 1645 [pub. in K & IDR I, pt. 2, 977–979]. For the arrival of Oxenstierna and the outbreak of violence between Servien and D'Avaux, see ASVen *Munster* 3, fols. 97–107, Contarini (copy to Senate) to Nani, April 7, 1645. See the Spanish reply in Ass. Nat. *Ms.* 274, fols. 482–486, dated April 18, 1645 [pub. in Italian in Siri V, pt. 2, 665–673; in German in Londorp V, 935–937; and in Spanish and Italian in NS I, 347–352]. For the transmission of the Spanish reply and Contarini's conversation with D'Avaux, see ASVen *Munster* 3, fols. 135–142, Contarini (copy to Senate) to Nani, April 21, 1645. For the fateful overture on the marriages, see Servien's letter to Lionne of June 19, 1645, cited in note 17 below.

14. For Servien's preparatory documents, see AAE CP *Allemagne* 51, fol. 215 (Servien's own hand minute of the preamble of the French project); *Allemagne* 51, fols. 235–239, 290–292, and 245–249 (three minutes of French project); and *Allemagne* 51, fols. 293–298 (Servien's own hand minute of his comments on the French project, with copy on fols. 299–309). For the discussions over the projects, see *Allemagne* 51, fols. 310–323 and 332, Servien (own hand minute) and D'Avaux to Brienne, May 13, 1645 (clean minute on fols. 270–289; copy sent in Ass. Nat. *Ms.* 272, fols. 532–563; copy for Mazarin in *Allemagne* 43, fols. 403–431; copy in *Allemagne* 46, fols. 446–464; and Brasset register in BNF *Ms. Fr.* 17897, fols. 92–105) [pub. in NS II, pt. 2, 251–261; Gärtner V, 64–103; and with omissions in APW II B 2, 325–343], as well as SRA *JOS* A I, Johan Oxenstierna and Salvius (Mylonius minute) to Christina, May 2/12, 1645 (copy sent in DG 3, fols. 425–430) [pub. in APW II C 1, 581–588]. See also Ass. Nat. *Ms.* 274, fols. 566–568 (copy of amended French project for Brienne), fols. 520–521 (copy of Servien's comments for Brienne), fols. 570–571 (copy of Swedish

project for Brienne); AAE CP *Allemagne* 43, fols. 434–436 (copy of French project for Mazarin), fols. 438–445 (copy of Servien's comments for Mazarin), and fols. 432–433 (copy of Swedish project for Mazarin); *Allemagne* 46, fols. 440–441 and fol. 443 (copies of French project and Swedish projects); SRA *DG* 3, fols. 455 and 454 (copies of Swedish and French projects for Christina); SRA *JOS* A I, Johan Oxenstierna and Salvius (Mylonius minute) to Christina, May 2/12, 1645 (copy sent in *DG* 3, fols. 425–430) [pub. in *APW* II C 1, 581–588]. For the Swedish proposition at this point, see *DG* 3, fol. 454; for the the French, see *DG* 3, fols. 455–456 [pub. in Gärtner IV, 424–428]. For the defeat at Megentheim, see the *Gazette* n° 60, May 26, 1645.

15. Ass. Nat. *Ms.* 272, fols. 276–285, *Mémoire* (minute) *du Roy,* May 30, 1645 (copies in AAE CP *Allemagne* 54, fols. 239–256 and 258–259, and *Allemagne* 51, fols. 395–400) [pub. in *APW* II B 2, 384–393]. See also Ass. Nat. *Ms.* 272, fols. 286–288, *Remarques* (minute) *faites par le conseil du Roy* (copies in AAE CP *Allemagne* 54, fols. 213–218, and *Allemagne* 51, fols. 401–402) [pub. in *APW* II B 2, 393–394].

16. For the Servien–D'Avaux debate, see AAE CP *Allemagne* 47, fols. 135–138, *Relation du voyage de monsieur de Saint Romain a Osnabruck vers Messieurs les ambassadeurs de Suede,* June, 17, 1645 (other copies on fols. 139–140 and in *Allemagne* 51, fols. 505–506; copy sent to Brienne in *Allemagne* 55, fols. 91–92) [pub. in *APW* II B 2, 436–439]. See also SRA *JOS* A I, Johan Oxenstierna and Salvius (Mylonius minute) to Christina, June 6/16, 1645 (copy sent in *DG* 3, fols. 743–750, and duplicate on fols. 801–809) [pub. in *APW* II C 1, 637–648]; BNF *Ms. Fr.* 17897, fols. 105–115, Servien and D'Avaux (Brasset register) to Brienne, June 20, 1645 (letter sent in AAE CP *Allemagne* 55, fols. 52–71; duplicate for Mazarin in *Allemagne* 44, fols. 75–96; Servien's copy in *Allemagne* 51, fols. 534–543) [pub. in *APW* II B 2, 451–463], as well as ASVen *Munster* 3, fols. 232–238 and 246–250, Contarini (copy to Senate) to Nani and Giovanni Giustiniani, June 16 and 17, 1645. For the propositions, see the final French proposition in AAE CP *Allemagne* 47, fols. 62–67; *Allemagne* 44, fols. 47–51; BNF *Ms. Fr.* 10649, fols. 238–243; AAE MD *Allemagne* 9, fols. 192–195, all of June 11, 1645, with addition of June 14; SRA *DG* 3, 767–770, 782–786, and 864–866 [pub. in *NS* I, pt. 2, 372–374, with addition; Gärtner V, 246–252; and Meiern I, 443–445, and in Latin on 445–448, without addition]; in Italian in ASVen *Munster* 3, fols. 240–242, without addition; and the final Swedish proposition in SRA *DG* 3, fols. 751–753, 753–759, and 776–780; AAE CP *Allemagne* 55, fols. 78–84; copy for Mazarin in *Allemagne* 44, fols. 78–84; and AV TA 108, n° 22 [pub. in *NS* I, 428–439, with French translation; and in Meiern I, 435–437, with German translation on 439–442]. For D'Avaux's

decision to stay, see AAE CP *Allemagne* 43, fols. 518–519, D'Avaux (letter sent) to Mazarin, May 31, 1645 (copy in *Allemagne* 51, fols. 417–418).

17. AAE CP *Allemagne* 51, fols. 519–523, Servien (own hand minute) to Lionne, June 19, 1645 [pub. in *APW* II B 2, 446–450]. Capitulation of Rosas: *Gazette* n° 66, June 8, 1645. Fall of Mardick: Gazette n° 88, July 14, 1645. Entry of Duke de Longueville (June 30, 1645): *Gazette* n° 92 July 19, 1645, or *NS* I, 374–375. Entry of Peñaranda: *NS* I, 376–377. Outbreak of war between the Ottoman Empire and Venice: *Gazette* n° 95, July 22, 1645. Battle of Nördlingen: *Gazette* n° 109, August 21, 1643. For Contarini's second overture, see AAE CP *Allemagne* 55, fols. 263–285, Longueville, D'Avaux, and Servien (copy sent) to Brienne, August 12, 1645 (duplicate for Mazarin in *Allemagne* 48, fols. 77–83) [pub. in *NS* II, pt. 2, 114–119; Gärtner V, 702–726; and *APW* II B 2, 582–592]. AAE CP *Allemagne* 52, fols. 462–467, Servien (clean minute) to Lionne, September 9, 1645 [pub. in *APW* II B 1, 668–673].

18. For the fears of the Turks, see AAE CP *Turquie* 5, fols. 262–265, La Haye (duplicate) for D'Avaux and Servien, July 22, 1645. See also Joseph von Hammer-Purgstall, *Geschichte des osmanischen Reiches* (Pest, 1827–1835) V, 393–394. For the peace with Rakocsy (August 24, 1645), see the copies in BI *Ms. Godefroy* 90, fols. 6—7, 8–15, and 16–21). The first treaty was published in German in Londorp V, 1044–1045, and both were published in *NS* I, 389–399. Military operations in Bohemia: *Gazettes* n°s 122, 128, 131, and 134, September 16, 30, October 7, and 14, 1645. For the Imperial replies, see HHSA RK *FrA* 92 VI, fols. 149–152 (minute), and *FrA* 48a, Konv. c, fols. 67–70, *Proposition der kaiserlichen Gesandten in Osnabrück an die Reichstande*, Osnabrück, September 25, 1645 (copies in RK *FrA*, fols. 131–134; SK *FrA* 7, 165–171; KHA *N* A IV 1628/18; and Giessen 204, 952–962) [pub. in Gärtner VI, 266–273, and Meiern I, 615–617]. HHSA RK *FrA* 48a, Konv. c, fols. 71–77, *Responsio ad propositionem Sueciam*, October 16, 1645, actually delivered on September 25, 1645, at Osnabrück (copies in AV TA 108 n° 23; KHA *N* A IV 1628/18; Giessen 204, 1132–1150; SRA *DG* 4, fols. 945–948; and AAE CP *Allemagne* 56, fols. 87–93, dated Osnabrück, September 25) [pub. in Italian in Siri V, pt. 2, 797–815; in Latin and French in *NS* I, 428–441; Gärtner VI, 136–148; and Meiern I, 618–623, and in German on 623–628]. See also SRA *JOS* A 1, Johan Oxenstierna (his and Mylonius minute) to Christina, September 19/29, 1645 (copy sent in *DG* 4, fols. 142–148, duplicate on fols. 183–190) [pub. in *APW* II C 1, 758–767]. HHSA RK *FrA* 48a, Konv. c, fols. 79–84, *Responsio ad propositionem Gallicam,* undated, delivered on September 25 at Münster (copies in KHA *N* A IV, 1628/18; Giessen 204, 962–977; and AAE CP *Allemagne* 56, fols. 95–105) [pub. in Gärtner VI 119–126; *NS* I, 400–403; and in Latin and

French, Meiern I, 628]. For the distribution of the offers, see HHSA RK *FrA* 48a, Konv. c, fols. 61–66, Lamberg and Krane to Ferdinand III, September 28, 1645 (copies in KHA *N A IV* 1628/18; and Giessen 206, 433–450) [pub. in Gärtner VI, 280–290; and *APW* II A 2, 488–493]; ASVen *Munster* 3, fols. 448–451 and 456–462, Contarini (copies to Senate) to Nani, September 29, and October 6, 1645, and fols. 481–488, *Risposta dell Imp^{re} alla Popositione de Svedesi . . . Li 24 Sett^{re} 1645 (Tradotta dal Latino)* and 474–479 *Risposta dell Imp^{re} alle Propositioni de Francesi . . . 25 Sett^{re} 1645 (Tradotta dal Latino).* For the Treaty of Brömsebro, see SRA *OT Danmark* n° 13A in Danish, August 13 o.s., 1645 (copy in Latin in AAE CP *Suède* 8, fols. 317–335) [pub. in Latin and Italian in Siri V, pt. 2, 56–121; in German in Londorp V, 937–948; in Latin in Dumont VI, pt. 1, 314–321; and in Danish in *ST* V, pt. 2, 595–626].

19. For the *lit de justice,* see AN *U* 137, 384–419; Ormesson I, 309–310; ASVen *Francia* 102, n°s 212 III and 215 III, Nani (letters sent) to Senate, September 5 and 12, 1645 (transcripts in BNF *Ms. It.* 1825, fols. 795–801 and 823–830). The summary of the edicts is also in the *Gazette* n° 120, September 13, 1645. Capitulation of Armentières: *Gazette* n° 121, September 15, 1645. For Mazarin's first reactions to the marriage proposal, see AAE CP *Allemagne* 44, fols. 402–404, *Mémoire* (Lionne minute) *du Roy pour M^{rs} les Plenipotentiaries,* September 30, 1645 (Brienne minute in Ass. Nat. *Ms.* 272, fols. 424–426, and copy in AAE CP *Allemagne* 52, fols. 524–525) [pub. in *NS* II, pt. 2, 160–161; Gärtner VI, 330–335; and *APW* II B 2, 722–724].

20. We know of the *consulta* from AHN *SNDF* 27/1, fols. 154–160, Philip IV to Castel Rodrigo, September 26, 1645 (deciphered copy on fols. 162–167), which Castel Rodrigo then forwarded to Peñarnda. See also AGS *E* 2255, Peñaranda to Castel Rodrigo, February 19, 1646. For the first intimations, coming from the mouth of Castel Rodrigo, that the peace would be put into the hands of Anne of Austria (that is, Mazarin), see AAE CP *Allemagne* 45, fols. 343–345, Mazarin (Lionne minute) to Longueville, December 23, 1645 (copy in *Allemagne* 53, fols. 434–459) [pub. in *LM* II, 271–272] and *Allemagne* 45, fols. 331–332, Mazarin (Silhon minute) to D'Avaux, December 23, 1645 (copy sent in *Allemagne* 54, fols. 325–326; other copy in *Allemagne* 53, fols. 460–462) [calendared in *LM* II, 702].

21. HHSA SK *FrA* 1, fols. 210–217 (Ferdinand's own hand), Linz, October 16, 1645 [pub. in *APW* I 1, 440–452].

22. NNA SG R 4854, *Instructie van de hoog ende Mogen heren Staten der Vereenichde Nederlanden voor de Edele Gestrenge Hoochgeleerde Wijse Voorsichige Heere. . . .* October 28, 1645 [pub. in Aitzema *VNVH* I, 570–607; in Latin in Londorp V, 1032–1041]. See also Waddington II, 162–165. For the hints that Frederick Henry was supportive of the peace efforts, see AV TA

124, fols. 39–41, Trauttmansdorff (minute) to Ferdinand III, January 7, 1646 (letter sent in HHSA RK *FrA* 50b, fol. 5, other copy on fols. 6–7).

23. For the Swedish instructions, see *SRP* XI, 224–227, October 18/28, 1645; SRA *AOS* A II, vol. 3, Christina (Axel Oxenstierna own hand) to Johan Oxenstierna and Salvius, November 10/20, 1645 (copy in *RR* 1643–1645) [pub. in *APW* II C 1, 843–851]. For the *gravamina,* see HHSA RK *FrA* 48a, Konv. c, fols. 212–230 [pub. in German in Londorp V, 1046–1056; in Latin and French in *NS* I, 443–454; in German in Gärtner VII, 75–119; and in Meiern I, 740–765].

24. For the visit of Saavedra, see AAE *CP Allemagne* 53, fols. 194–198, Longueville, D'Avaux, and Servien (minute) to Brienne November 8, 1645 (copy sent in *Allemagne* 56, fols. 209–214; duplicate for Mazarin in *Allemagne* 45, fols. 121–125, and other copy in *Allemagne* 49, fols. 26–29) [pub. in *NS* II, pt. 1, 197–199; Gärtner VI, 651–660; and *APW* II B 2, 821–825]. For Peñaranda's anger at Volmar, see Peñaranda to Philip IV of October 28, 1645, which we know only though the *consulta* of December 22, cited in note 20 above. For Peñaranda's request for further instructions, see his letter to Philip IV, December 1, 1645, which we know only through the *consulta* of January 8, 1646, cited in Chapter 4, note 6. We can presume the request for the recall of Saavedra from its approval in the same *consulta* of January 8.

25. BNF *Ms. Baluze* 174 (*Carnet* 7), fols. 16 and 37. For Bagni's letter to Ropigliosi, his fellow nuncio in Spain, November 15, 1645, see the published excerpt in Siri VI, 1134–1135. We have the overtures of Roncalli in a letter of Castel Rodrigo to his court of December 11, 1645, referred to in his subsequent letter of December 30, summarized in AGS *E* 2348, the *consulta* of March 5, 1646, which also contains the correspondence of Castel Rodrigo with the nuncio in Paris. We know of the remarkable discussion with Mattei through letters of Castel Rodrigo of February 10 and 29, 1646, transmitted *verbatim* in ASVen *Munster* 4, Contarini (copy to Senate) to Nani, March 30, 1646, *"essersi trattati piu di una volta col Solo Card.¹ Mazarino, che parlò in primo luogo del matrimonio con la dote di tutti li paesi Bassi. . . . che Mazarini.havesse mandato dietro al Marchese Mattei il regalo di una gioia per animarlo a conduir questa pratica."* For the additional instructions, see AAE *CP Allemagne* 45, fols. 168–184, *Addition* (minute with Lionne corrections) *a l'instruction de messieurs les plenipotentiaires contenant les intentions du Roy sur la negotiation de Munster dans l'estat present des affaires . . . 23 novembre* 1645 (Brienne minute in *Allemagne* 56, fols. 290–309; copies in *Allemagne* 49, fols. 122–134, dated November 22, and 135–145; and *Allemagne* 53, fols. 276–284) [pub. in *APW* II B 2, 872–890].

26. For the passage of the Queen of Poland in Brussels between December 12 and 17, 1645, see the *Gazette* n° 2, January 11, 1646. For the enticements

by the Marquis de Castel Rodrigo, see the letters of Mazarin of December 23, cited in note 20 above. For Castel Rodrigo's other doings, see AGS E 2255, *Papel que dio Mons' de Noermont sobre quatro puntos tocantes al Principe de Orange,* undated, but sent to the court with letters of February 3, 1646. For Trauttmansdorff's initial offers through the mediators, see ASVen *Munster* 3, fols. 668–672 and 678–679, Contarini (copy to Senate) to Nani, December 15, 1645, which the French reported in AAE CP *Allemagne* 78, fols. 603–609, a partial secretarial minute with Servien's corrections; and more fully in *Allemagne* 56, fols. 367–385, *Response (copy sent) des Plenipotentiaires de France au Memoire de la Cour du 23 Novemb~ 1645,* December 22, 1643 (duplicate for Mazarin in *Allemagne* 45, fols. 282–292, and copy in *Allemagne* 53, fols. 468–488) [pub. in APW II B 3/1, 121–133]. For Trauttmansdorff's trip to Osnabrück, see HHSA RK *FrA* 50a, fols. 29–37, Trauttmansdorff (own hand letters sent) to Ferdinand III, December 18, 25, and 28, 1645; as well as SRA *JOS* A I, Johan Oxenstierna and Salvius (minutes) to Christina, December 8/18, and 15–25, 1645 (letters sent in *DG* 4, fols. 799–801 and 815–817) [pub. in APW II C 2, 21–31]. For the discussions between the French and Swedes, compare SRA *JOS* A I, Johan Oxenstierna (minute) to Christina, December 29, 1645/January 8, 1646 (copy sent in *DG* 4, fols. 903–913) [pub. in APW II C 2, 39–52] with the recollections of this discussion in the letter of the plenipotentiaries of January 18, 1646, cited in Chapter 4, note 2.

27. For the rescinding of the instructions, see AHN *SNDF* 27/1, fol. 21, Philip IV (letter sent) to Peñaranda, December 30, 1645 (deciphered copy on fol. 23). See AGS E 2063, the *consulta* of January 1, 1646, over the letter from Bagni to Rospigliosi, cited in note 25 above, to which the council and Philip IV responded favorably. We learn that Philip sent the offer of mediation on January 2 from ASVat *Paci* 19, fol. 69, Rospigliosi (copy to Pamfili) to Chigi, January 2, 1646.

4. The French Show Their Hand

1. For the troublesome Prince de Condé, see the *mémoire* of Mazarin to the plenipotentiaries of January 20, 1646, the last of the three, cited in note 10 below, and the short letter of Mazarin to the plenipotentiaries of the same date, cited in the same note.

2. For the reply as drawn up by the French plenipotentiaries, see AAE CP *Allemagne* 76, fols. 601–603, *Notes ou observations pour dresser la Replique de Messeigneurs les Plenipotentiaires de France a la response des Imp^{aux}, incorrectly dated June 15, 1646.* For the reply as jotted down by Contarini in Italian and corrected by the French, see ASVen *Munster* 3, fols. 733–736, titled *Replica de'*

Francesi and dated January 7, 1646. There are slightly more ample and better-organized Latin versions in AAE CP *Allemagne* 59, fols. 41–45, *Summa capita eorum qua' loco Replicae ad Responsa Caesareanorum Gallici Plenipotentiarji die 7° Ianuarij 1646 apud Mediatores oretenus Jusius exposuerunt ab Jisdem Mediatoribus excerpta primum Italico idiomate in Latinum versa*, in ASVat *Paci* 19, fols. 24–27, HHSA RK *FrA* 52a, fols. 17–18, and *FrA* 92 VII, fols. 227–246; Giessen 210, n° 4; AV TA 108; KHA N A IV, 1628/56 and 1628/57; and in both Latin and Spanish in AGS *E* 2348) [pub. in German in Londorp V, 1074–1075; in French in *NS* III, 394–396; and in Latin in Gärtner VII, 374–380, and Meiern II, 200–203]. See also BVat *CCL* A I 14, fols. 10–14, 14–17, 17–19, 19–20, and 20–21, Chigi (register) to Pamfili (letters sent of the first, second, and last are in ASVat *Paci* 19, fols. 14–19, 20–23, and 28–29); ASVen *Munster* 3, fols. 737–741, Contarini (copy to Senate) to Nani, January 12, 1646; AAE CP *Allemagne* 59, fols. 73–75, plenipotentiaries (duplicate for Mazarin) to Brienne, January 18, 1646 (copies in *Allemagne* 63, fols. 168–169, and *Allemagne* 75, fols. 110–111) [pub. in *M&N* I, 8–14; *NS* III, 16–18; and Gärtner VII, 540–546, without p.s. and dated January 14; and *APW* II B 3/1, 252–256]. For the transmission of these demands to the Imperialists, which did not take place until January 18, see ASVen *Munster* 3, fols. 749–754, Contarini (copy to Senate) to Nani, January 19, 1646.

3. See the Imperial protocol of the Swedish verbal demands in HHSA AV TA 109 (copies in RK *FrA* 50b, fols. 22–37 and 54–74; *FrA* 91 II, fols. 1–22; *FrA* 92 VII, fols. 227–246, 249–259, and 261–273; Giessen 210, 21–64 and 206–236; KHA N A IV, 1628/56 and 1628/57; OAT 20d, 149–172; ASVat *Paci* 19, fols. 48–53; and in both Latin and Spanish in AGS *E* 2347 and in Spanish in *E* 2348) [pub. in German in Londorp V, 1076–1079; Gärtner VII, 380–411; and Meiern II, 183–190. There is Swedish protocol published in German in Meiern II, 190–203.] See also SRA *DG* 7, fol. 925, *Contenta Replicae Suedicaae ad Resolutionem Caesaream oretenus propositae* [pub. in Meiern II, 203–204]. See also AV TA 111, Trauttmansdorff (minute) to Ferdinand III, January 8, 1646 (letter sent in HHSA RK *FrA* 52b, fols. 12–20) [pub. in *APW* II A 3, 113–120] and SRA *JOS* A I, Johan Oxenstierna and Salvius (minute) to Christina, December 31/January 10, 1645–1646 (letter sent in SRA *DG* 7, fols. 914–934) [pub. in *APW* II C 2, 56–71].

4. See the letter of the plenipotentiaries to Brienne, cited in note 2 above. For the comments of Axel Oxenstierna, see AAE CP *Suède* 9, fols. 23–26, Chanut (copy to Mazarin) to plenipotentiaries, February 24, 1646.

5. See AAE MD *France* 260, fols. 15–21, Mazarin (register) to Grimaldi, January 12, 1646 [calendared in *LM* II, 707]. See also AAE CP *Allemagne* 59, fols. 172–176, *Mem^re* (Lionne minute) *du Roy a Ms^rs les Plenipot~*, February 3, 1646 (corrected minute in Ass. Nat. *Ms*. 272, fols. 99–103; copies in AAE

CP *Allemagne* 63, fols. 285–290, and *Allemagne* 75, fols. 173–174) [pub. in *M&N* I, 169–177; *NS* III, 41–43; Gärtner VIII, 28–36; and APW II B 3/1, 333–335], as well as AAE CP *Allemagne* 59, fols. 177–182, *Mem^re* (Lionne minute) *du Card^l Mazarin a M^rs les Plenipot^res* of same date (copies in *Allemagne* 63, fols. 291–297, and *Allemagne* 75, fols. 175–178) [pub. in *M&N* I, 178–189; *NS* III, 43–46; and Gärtner VIII, 36–38; calendared in *LM* II, 716; also pub. in *APW* II B 3/1, 335–341]. For Cardinal Antonio's arrival in Paris, see Ormesson I, 343.

6. The numerous texts of this *consulta* attest to its importance. See AGS E 2255 for a rough draft of the opinions of Monterrey (with numerous additions), Santa Cruz, and Chinchon, as well as a cleaner copy of Monterrey's, not dated, but with a separate sheet dating them for January 9, 1646. Then in E 2348, there is a complete text, summarizing the letters received, and containing all of the above opinions, plus that of Castrillo and the handwritten decision of Philip IV, dated Madrid, January 8, 1646, which seems the more reliable date [pub. in *CDI* LXXXII, 244–269]. It is not clear how the recommendation for giving up some portions of the Low Countries became specifically translated into the four strongholds which the Spanish plenipotentiaries offered on March 21 (see note 25, below) or the entire counties which they offered on April 24 (see Chapter 5, note 6) or how the decision was reached to allow Peñaranda, in consultation with Castel Rodrigo, to exceed his orders, but this whole package must have been sent in letters January 13 (or 15) which are lost, since Peñaranda in a letter of May 14 to Coloma (AGS E 2347) refers to having received no orders since that difficult-to-read date. See also in E 2348, the *consulta* of February 2, 1646, which confirms and amplifies the discretionary order, although Peñaranda had not received this confirmation by May 14.

7. For D'Avaux's opinion, see AAE CP *Allemagne* 59, fols. 58–60, D'Avaux (letter sent) to Mazarin, January 13, 1646 (copy in *Allemagne* 75, fols. 83–87) [pub. in *APW* II B 3/1, 232–234]. For Servien's view, see AAE CP *Allemagne* 75, fols. 88–94, 95–97, and 99, Servien (own hand minute) to Lionne, January 13–16, 1646, and fol. 98 (own hand minute), *Differences entre la satisfaction de la France et celle de la Suede.* For Longueville's opinon, see *Allemagne* 59, fols. 68–70, Longueville (letter sent) to Mazarin, January 16, 1646 (copy in *Allemagne* 75, fols. 101–104) [pub. in *APW* II B 3/1, 249–251].

8. NNA SG VL 12588.37 III, Dutch plenipotentiaries (letters sent) to States General, January 14 and 17, 1646 (copies in SG R 4854). See also the letter of the French plenipotentiaries to Brienne and those of Contarini to Nani, cited in note 2 above, as well as one of two letters of Peñaranda to Philip IV of February 3, 1646, cited in note 11 below.

9. Contarini's letters to Nani, cited in note 2 above.

10. For the two *mémoires*, see AAE CP *Allemagne* 59, fols. 82–87, *Memoire* (Lionne minute) *de Son Em^ce a M^rs les Plenipotentiaires* (copies in *Allemagne* 63, fols. 180–188, and *Allemagne* 75, fols. 112–116) [pub. in M&N I, 101–115; NS III, 20–24; Gärtner VII, 585–588; big excerpt pub. in Italian in Siri VI, 820–828; Mignet I, 177–182; calendared in *LM* II, 710–711, and pub. in its entirety in APW II B 3/1, 266–273] and AAE CP *Allemagne* 59, fols. 88–90. *Raisons* (Lionne minute) ~~desquelles~~ (crossed out) *qui Semblent devoir persuader aux Esp^ols le parti* ~~proposé~~ (crossed out) *dont est question* (copies in *Allemagne* 63, fols. 189–192, and *Allemagne* 75, fols. 117–119). The *mémoires* appear to have been written between January 19 and 20. The first was initially undated and bears the date "20 Jan. 1646" in a secretarial hand. The second was initially dated "du 19e Janvier 1646" by Lionne, who then changed the date to "20e" [pub. in M&N I, 115–121; NS III, 24–25; Gärtner VII, 590–560; big excerpt in Siri VI, 829–833; calendared in *LM* II, 711; and entirely pub. in APW II B 3/1, 274–276]. See also AAE CP *Allemagne* 59, fols. 94–97, *Memoire* (Lionne minute) *du Card^l Mazarin a M^rs les Plenipot^res* (copies in *Allemagne* 63, fols. 176–179, and *Allemagne* 75, fols. 120–122) [pub. in M&N I, 121–127; NS III, 25–27; Gärtner VII, 603–610; calendared in *LM* II, 710; and pub. in its entirety in APW II B 3/1, 262–266], all of January 20, 1646. See also AAE CP *Allemagne* 59, fol. 81, his short letter to the plenipotentiaries of January 20, 1646 (copy in *Allemagne* 75, fols. 123–124). For the reply to D'Avaux, see AAE CP *Allemagne* 59, fols. 169–171, Mazarin (Silhon minute) to D'Avaux, February 3, 1646 (letter sent in *Allemagne* 79, fols. 6–8, and copy in *Allemagne* 75, fols. 183–186) [pub. in *LM* II, 281–284; and APW II B 3/1, 344–347].

11. BNE *Ms.* 2377, *Proposicion a los deputados de Holanda . . . en Munster a 28 de Enero de 1646* [pub. in French in Aitzema *VNVH* II, 14–15; in Italian in Siri VI, 844–845; and in the original Spanish in *CDI* LXXXII, 271] (copies in French in NNA SG *VL* 12588.37 III and SG *R* 4854, which also contain a letter from the Dutch plenipotentiaries to the States General of January 30, 1646). See also AGS *E* 2255, Peñaranda (deciphered copy) to Terranova, February 2, 1646; ASVen *Munster* 3, fols. 770–776, Contarini (copy to Senate) to Nani, February 2, 1646, AGS *E* 2255, Peñaranda (two deciphered copies) to Philip IV and (copy) to Castel-Rodrigo, three letters of February 3, 1646. There are more copies of the Spanish proposal in Ass. Nat. *Ms.* 275, fol. 64, and AAE CP *Allemagne* 59, fol. 115. For the exchange discussions, see ASVen *Munster* 3, fols. 760–763, Contarini (copy to Senate) to Nani, January 26, 1646, and Contarini's letter of February 2, cited above. AAE CP *Allemagne* 59, fols. 122–126, *Response* (letter sent) *des Plenipotentiaires de france aux Memoires de Son Eminence du xii et xiii janvier 1646,* January 27, 1646 (copy in *Allemagne* 75, fols. 148–149) [pub. in APW

II B 3/1, 300–302] and one of the two letters of Peñaranda to Philip IV of February 3, 1646, cited above.

12. For D'Avaux in Osnabrück, compare AAE CP *Allemagne* 63, fols. 415–421 and 441–447, D'Avaux (minutes) to Longueville and Servien, February 16 and 27, 1646 (copies in *Allemagne* 75, fols. 233–237 and 341–344, duplicate of the first for Brienne in Ass. Nat. *Ms.* 275, fols. 117–122 and 109–114; duplicate of both for Mazarin in AAE CP *Allemagne* 59, fols. 229–236 and 397–404) [pub. in *M&N* I, 298–328, and *NS* III, 84–91, all dated February 24; and in *APW* II B 3/1, 407–416 and 488–500] with SRA *DG* 7, fols. 203–211, Johan Oxenstierna and Salvius (letter sent) to Christina, February 9/19, 1646 [pub. in *APW* II C 2, 141–150]. For the warnings about the marriage and exchange proposal, see AAE CP *Allemagne* 59, fols. 237–244, *Response* (letter sent by Longueville and Servien) *des Plenipotentiaires de France au Memoire de Son Eminence du 3 febvr~ 1646*, February 17, 1646 (copies in *Allemagne* 63, fols. 375–377, and *Allemagne* 75, fols. 256–258) [pub. in *M&N* I, 224–232; *NS* III, 70–72; Gärtner VIII, 61–70, all dated February 3; and *APW* II B 3/1, 433–437].

13. For the D'Estrades's instruction, see BNF *Ms. Clair.* 574, pp. 7–10, *Pour M. d'Estrades allant en holande* undated [pub. in Italian in Siri VI, 987–990, and in the original French in Waddington II, 402–405], as well as the details about the mission in AAE CP *Allemagne* 59, fols. 214–226, *Replique* (Lionne minute) *du Card^l Mazarin au mem^re de m^rs les plenipot^res du 20^e Janvier 1646*, February 16, 1646 (copies in *Allemagne* 63, fols. 349–370, and *Allemagne* 75, fols. 238–245) [pub. in *M&N* I, 253–283, and *NS* III, 49–56, both dated 6th; calendared in *LM* II, 718–721; and pub. in its entirety in *APW* II B 3/1, 386–402], to which he added AAE CP *Allemagne* 59, fol. 227, *Raisons* (secretary's hand with Lionne corrections) *que doibvent porter Messrs les Estats a* ~~consenter a~~ (crossed out) *desirer L'eschange de la catalogne et mesme du Roussillon avec la Flandre et le comté de Bourgogne entre la France & l'Espagne* (copies in *Allemagne* 63, fols. 371–372, and *Allemagne* 75, fol. 246) [pub. in Italian in Siri VI, 833–835, and in the original French in *M&N* I, 283–286; *NS* III, 56; and *APW* II B 3/1, 402–403].

14. AGS E 2255, Peñaranda (deciphered copy) to Castel Rodrigo, February 18, 1646. ASVen *Munster* 3, fol. 183, Contarini (copy to Senate) to Nani, February 23, 1646, and *Munster* 4, Contarini (copy to Senate) to Nani, Ferbruary 24, 1646; BVat *CCL* A I 14, fols. 47–51, Chigi (register) to Pamfili, February 23, 1646 (letter sent in ASVat *Paci* 19, fols. 84–90). See also Ass. Nat. *Ms.* 275, fols. 97–105, plenipotentiares (letter sent) to Anne (duplicate for Mazarin in AAE CP *Allemagne* 59, fols. 288–292; copies in *Allemagne* 63, fols. 429–433, and *Allemagne* 75, fols. 293–295) [pub. in *M&N* I, 288–296; *NS* III, 82–84; Gärtner VIII, 326–335; and *APW* II B 3/1, 466–470]. AAE CP *Allemagne* 63,

fols. 434–437, D'Avaux to Mazarin (letter sent with p.s.) in *Allemagne* 59, fols. 278–283, and copy in *Allemagne* 75, fols. 302–310) [pub. in *APW* II B 3/1, 473–478], *Allemagne* 59, fols. 284–287, Longueville (letter sent) to Mazarin (copy in *Allemagne* 75, fols. 297–301) [pub. in *APW* II B 3/1, 470–473], all of February 24, 1646, as well as *Allemagne* 75, fols. 311–318, Servien (minute) to Mazarin, February 25, 1646 (other partial minute in *Allemagne* 63, fols. 439–440) [pub. in *APW* II B 3/1, 479–486].

15. See AAE CP *Allemagne* 59, fols. 295–302, *Memoire* (Lionne minute) *de S. E. a M^rs les Plenip^res*, March 3, 1646 (copies in *Allemagne* 64, fols. 9–19, and *Allemagne* 75, fols. 321–325A) [pub. in *M&N* I, 414–435; *NS* III, 99–104; Gärtner VIII, 381–402; calendared in *LM* II, 725–726; and pub. in its entirety in *APW* II B 3/1, 500–510]. For more on the campaign, see AAE CP *Allemagne* 59, fol. 359, Mazarin (Lionne minute) to Longueville, March 8, 1646 (copy in *Allemagne* 75, fols. 368–369) [calendared in *LM* II, 728, and pub. in its entirety in *APW* II B 3/1, 557–558].

16. See Mazarin to the plenipotentiaries of March 3, cited in the previous note. For Brienne's presence at the council, see Mazarin's letter to Longueville of April 7, 1646, cited in Chapter 5, note 1.

17. See AAE CP *Allemagne* 59, fols. 343–346, Anne (Lionne minute) to plenipotentiaries, March 7, 1646 (Brienne minute in Ass. Nat. *Ms.* 272, fols. 147–172; copies in AAE CP *Allemagne* 64, fols. 50–53, and *Allemagne* 75, fols. 363–365, all dated March 8) [pub. in *M&N* II, 22–29; *NS* III, 109–111; Gärtner, VIII, 443–451; and *APW* II B 3/1, 548–552] and *Allemagne* 59, fol. 342, Anne (Lionne minute) to plenipotentiaries, March 7, 1646 (Brienne minute in Ass. Nat. *Ms.* 272, fol. 145; copies in AAE CP *Allemagne* 64, fol. 55, and *Allemagne* 75, fol. 266, all dated March 8) [pub. in Italian in Siri VI, 1037–1038, dated March 6; and in the original French in *M&N* II, 30–31; *NS* III, 111; Gärtner VIII, 451–453; and *APW* II B 3/1, 552–553]. AAE CP *Allemagne* 59, fol. 329, Duke d'Orléans (secretary's minute with Lionne corrections) to Longueville, March 7, 1646 (copies in *Allemagne* 64, fol. 33, and *Allemagne* 75, fol. 356) [pub. in *M&N* II, 16–17; *NS* III, 107; Gärtner VIII, 427–428; and *APW* II B 3/1, 545]. AAE CP *Allemagne* 64, fol. 56, Condé (D'Avaux copy) to plenipotentiaries, March 8, 1646 [pub. in *M&S* II, 32–33; *NS* III, 112; Gärtner VIII, 453–454; and *APW* II B 3/1, 557], all letters for potential public display, in contrast to *Allemagne* 59, fols. 331–336, *Memoire* (secretary's minute with Lionne additions) *du Roy a Messrs les Plenipo^res*, March 7, 1646 (Brienne minute in Ass. Nat. *Ms.* 275, fols. 155–162, dated March 8, 1646; copies in AAE CP *Allemagne* 64, fols. 36–40 and 41–47, and *Allemagne* 75, fols. 352–355 [pub. in *M&N* II, 3–15; *NS* III, 104–107; Gärtner VIII, 414–427; and *APW* II B 3/1, 535–541] and AAE CP *Allemagne* 59, fols. 347–349, Mazarin (Lionne's minute) to

Longueville, March 7, 1646 (copy in *Allemagne* 75, fols. 358–362) [pub. in *LM* II, 285–299, dated February 7; and in *APW* II B 3/1, 542–545].

18. NNA SG R 4855, *Provinciael advis van Hollandt ingebracht den 24ᵈᵉ February 1646* (in French in AAE CP *Hollande* 36, fols. 65–66); and also in SG R 4855, the resolution of February 25, 1646. See also *Hollande* 36, fol. 78 (copy of news letter of February 27, 1646, received by Brasset); BNF *Ms. Fr.* 17898, fols. 168–170, Brasset (register) to plenipotentiaries, same date (copy for Mazarin in AAE CP *Hollande* 36, fols. 79–82). For D'Estrades's first letter, see AAE CP *Hollande* 36, fol. 69–71, D'Estrades (own hand letter sent) to Mazarin, February 26, 1646 [pub. in *APW* II B 3/1, 555–556]. For his second, see AAE CP *Hollande* 36, fol. 75, D'Estrades (own hand letter sent) to Mazarin, February 27, 1646 (copy in *Allemagne* 59, fol. 354) [pub. in *APW* II B 3/1, 556].

19. AAE CP *Allemagne* 59, fols. 355–356, Memʳᵉ (Lionne minute) *du Cardˡ Mazarin a Mʳˢ les Plenipotʳᵉˢ*, March 8, 1646 (copies in *Allemagne* 64, fols. 57–58, and *Allemagne* 75, fol. 367) [pub. in *M&N* II, 33–36; *NS* III, 112–113; Gärtner VII, 454–457; calendared in *LM* II 727–728; and pub. in its entirety in *APW* II B 3/1, 553–555]. For the remarkable accusation, see AAE CP *Allemagne* 75, fol. 374, Lionne (letter sent) to Servien, March 8, 1646 [pub. in *APW* II B 3/1, 559–560]. For Mazarin's orders to pursue the matter with Contarini, see AAE CP *Allemagne* 59, fols. 372–373, *Memoire* (Lionne minute) *du Cardˡ Mazarin a Mʳˢ les Plenipotʳᵉˢ*, March 10, 1646 (copies in *Allemagne* 79, fols. 17–18, and *Allemagne* 75, fols. 375–378, without a p.s. [calendared in *LM* II, 728, and pub. in its entirety in *APW* II B 3/1, 562–564].

20. AAE CP *Hollande* 36, fol. 78, copy of newsletter of March 2, 1646, received by Brasset, BNF *Ms. Fr.* 17898, fol. 171, Brasset (register) to Servien, March 2, 1646 (letter sent in AAE CP *Hollande* 36, fols. 89–90); AAE CP *Hollande* 36, fol. 91, D'Estrades (copy to Mazarin) to plenipotentiaries, March 2, 1646, fol. 98, D'Estrades (own hand letter sent) to Mazarin, March 5, 1646. BNF *Ms. Fr.* 17898, fols. 193–195, Brasset (register) to plenipotentiaries, March 9, 1646 (copy to Mazarin in AAE CP *Hollande* 36, fols. 104–105); Aitzema *VNVH* II, 19–21.

21. For this extremely important collection of *Gutachten* and the instructions that they produced, see, on the *gravamina,* HHSA RK FrA 52d, fols. 1–66, *Votum ad Imperatorem über der Kayserl: Gesandte eingeschickte unterschiedliche Relationes der franzosen und Schweden Replicas betreffendt d.d. 10 febr 1646,* transmitted through FrA 51b, fols. 65–159, Ferdinand III (minute) to Trauttmansdorff, Nassau, Lamberg, Krane, and Volmar, February 27, 1646 (copies in HHSA GSR, Rep. N 96/68, unpartitioned n° 15 and N 96/68, pt. 5, n° 9) [pub. in *APW* II A 3, 279–311]. On the Swedish

and French satisfactions: HHSA RK *FrA* 52d, fols. 1–93, *Votum ad Imperatorem in Satisfactionis Coronarum d.d. 22 febr. 1646,* transmitted through *FrA* 51b, fols. 2–88, Ferdinand III (minute) to Trauttmannssdorff, Nassau, Lamberg, Krane, and Volmar, March 5, 1646 (copy in GSR Rep N 96, 68, pt. 16) [pub. in *APW* II A 3, 341–380] as well as *FrA* 49b, Konv. a, fols. 257–281, *Gutachten der geheimen Räte Februar 25, 26, and 28 Conclusum des Kaisers, Linz, March 1, 1646,* transmitted as *Gradus observandi in tractatibus cum Gallis ratione Alsatiae, item conditiones, sine quibus non,* of which the original in code is missing, but copies of which are in RK *FrA* 50c, fols. 86–87, March 2, 1646 [pub. in *APW* II A 3, 335–337]; and OAT 20e, fols. 150–151 [pub. in Jacob, 316–318] and RK *FrA* 49b Konvolut f, fols. 29–31, March 2, 1646; AV HKA RA 157, fols. 151 and 154–156. See also HHSA RK *FrA* 50c, fols. 62–63, Ferdinand III (own hand minute) to Trauttmansdorff, March 2, 1646 [pub. in Jacob, 315–316, and *APW* II A 3, 334–335]. On extending the amnesty to the crowns, see RK *FrA* 52d, fols. 1–102, *Votum ad Imperatorem in Puncto Amnistia d.d. 27 febr. 1646,* transmitted in part through GSR Rep N 96, pt. 5, n° 7, Ferdinand III (minute) to Trauttmansdorff, Nassau, Lamberg, Krane, and Volmar, March 12, 1646 (copy in GSR Rep N 96, 68, pt. 5) [pub. in *APW* II A 3, 311–326].

22. Ass. Nat. *Ms.* 275, fols. 151–162, plenipotentiaries (letter sent) to Brienne, March 17, 1646 (duplicate for Mazarin in *Allemagne* 59, fols. 405–410; copies in *Allemagne* 64, fols. 106–110, and *Allemagne* 75, fols. 431–435, and 426–430) [pub. in *M&N* II, 40–51; *NS* III, 118–121; Gärtner VIII, 542–554; and *APW* II B 3/1, 611—617]. AAE CP *Allemagne* 64, fols. 111–112, D'Avaux (own hand minute) to Mazarin, March 17, 1646 (letter sent in *Allemagne* 59, fols. 414–415; copy in *Allemagne* 75, fols. 424–425) [pub. in *APW* II B 3/1, 620]. AAE CP *Allemagne* 75, fols. 436–437, Servien to Lionne, March 17, 1646 [pub. in *APW* II B 3/1, 621–622]. AAE CP *Allemagne* 59, fols. 416–417, Longueville (letter sent) to Mazarin, March 17, 1646 (copy in *Allemagne* 75, fols. 422–423) [pub. in *APW* II B 3/1, 618–619]. For a wonderful analysis of Longueville's disaffection, written by Servien, see AAE CP *Allemagne* 75, fols. 458–466, Servien (own hand minute) to Lionne, March 24, 1646 [pub. in *APW* II B 3/1, 648–656].

23. *Fin de la Guerre des Pays Bas aux Provinces qui sont encor sous l'obeissance d'Espagne, item La DESCOUVERTE des Profondeurs d'Espagne CACHEES Sous ceste Proposition de Donner au ROY de FRANCE en mariage l'INFANTE D'ESPAGNE avec Les dixsept Provinces des Pays-Bas en constitution de dot . . . En l'An de nostre Seigneur 1645* [found in Knuttel: 5185; in Dutch in Knuttel: 5314–5315; in German in Knuttel: 5316; and pub. in French in *NS* III, 479–484]. *MUNSTERS PRAETIE Deliberant Dum fingere nesciunt* Gedruct int Iaer ons Heeren 1646 [six printings found in Knuttel: 5290–5295]. *Antwoordt*

Op 't: Munsters Praetie, Anniantur Sed cave te ipsum (Dortrecht, 1646) [found in Knuttel: 5296, 5296a, 5297a–b], *FRANSCH PRAETIE Sic vos non vobis* (Münster, 1646) [found in Knuttel: 5297–5299]. AAE CP *Hollande* 36, fol. 110, Frederick Henry (copy to Mazarin) to D'Estrades, March 20, 1646 (copy in *Allemagne* 76, fol. 52) [pub. in Italian in Siri VI, 1060, and in the original French in *APW* II B 3/2, 693]. For a wonderful analysis of Frederick Henry's behavior, written by Servien, see Servien's letter to Lionne of March 24, 1646, cited in the previous note.

24. For Mazarin's self-delusion, see AAE CP *Allemagne* 59, fols. 386–389, *Mem^{re}* (Lionne minute) *du Card^l Mazarin a M^{rs} les Plenipot^{res}*, March 16, 1646 (copies in *Allemagne* 64, fols. 96–100, and *Allemagne* 75, fols. 408–411, both dated March 17, 1646) [pub. in *M&N* II, 95–106; *NS* III, 127–130; Gärtner VIII, 577–589; *LM* II, 730; and *APW* II B 3/1, 597–604]. For evidence that Mazarin was still intent on the exchange, see AAE CP *Hollande* 36, fol. 100, Mazarin (Lionne minute) to Brasset, March 17, 1646. For the interview, see ASVen *Francia* 104, n° 311, Nani (letter sent) to Doge, March 20, 1646 (transcript in BNF *Ms. It.* 1827, fols. 27–30) and ASVat *Francia* 94, fols. 82–84, Bagni to Pamfili, March 23, 1646.

25. AHN E 967, fol. 529, *Sustancia de lo que se propuso a Françeses por mano de los medianeros*. BVat *CCL* A I 14, fols. 72–75, 75–77, 77–78, and 78–79, Chigi (register) to Pamfili, March 23, 1646 (letter sent of the first and last in ASVat *Paci* 19, fols. 127–132 and fol. 125). ASVen *Munster* 4, Contarini (copy to Senate) to Nani, March 23, 1646; AAE CP *Allemagne* 60, fols. 25–28, plenipotentiaries (letter sent) to Mazarin, March 24, 1646 (copies in *Allemagne* 64, fols. 173–175, and *Allemagne* 75, fols. 446–447) [pub. in *M&N* II, 54–60; *NS* III, 122–123; Gärtner VIII, 556–563, all dated March 17; and *APW* II B 3/1, 644–646]. Ass. Nat. *Ms.* 275, fols. 167–174, plenipotentiaries (letter sent) to Brienne, March 14, 1646 (duplicate for Mazarin in AAE CP *Allemagne* 60, fols. 12–16; copies in *Allemagne* 64, fols. 176–179, and *Allemagne* 75, fols. 456–457) [published without p.s. in *M&N* II, 60–68; *NS* III, 132–134; Gärtner VIII, 626–628; and *APW* II B 3/1, 639–643]. See also AAE CP *Allemagne* 64, fols. 180–181, D'Avaux (own hand minute) to Mazarin, March 24, 1646 (letter sent in *Allemagne* 60, fols. 17–19; copy in *Allemagne* 75, fols. 452–455) [pub. in *APW* II B 3/1, 647–648]. AAE CP *Allemagne* 75, fols. 458–466, Servien (own hand minute) to Lionne, March 24, 1646 [pub. in *APW* II B 3/1, 648–656]. It is interesting to note that there is no letter from Longueville to Mazarin of this date. See also BVat *CCL* A I 14, fols. 79–81, Chigi (register) to Pamfili, March 30, 1646 (letter sent in ASVat *Paci* 19, fols. 142–145; ASVen *Munster* 4, Contarini (copy to Senate) to Nani, March 30, 1646, where we also find that the French made a more ample verbal reply on March 26.

26. HHSA RK *FrA* 92 VIII, fols. 97–98, *Memoriale* (Volmar minute) *pro dominis mediatoribus* [March 28, 1646] (copies in *FrA* 52a, fols. 204–205, and OAT 20d, 763–765) [pub. in Italian in ASVen *Munster* 4 and in part in the original Latin in Repgen EA, 95–96]. See also ASVat *CCL* A I 14, fols. 84–88, Chigi (register) to Pamfili (letter sent in ASVat *Paci* 19, fols. 150–153); ASVen *Munster* 4, Contarini (copy to Senate) to Nani; AAE CP *Allemagne* 64, fols. 202–205, D'Avaux (own hand minute) to Mazarin (letter sent in *Allemagne* 60, fols. 61–64, and copy in *Allemagne* 76, fols. 44–48) [pub. in *APW* II B 3/2, 680–683]; AAE CP *Allemagne* 60, fols. 56–60, Longueville (letter sent) to Mazarin (copy in *Allemagne* 76, fols. 38–43) [pub. in *APW* II B 3/2, 677–680] all of April 6, 1646.

27. AAE CP *Allemagne* 60, fols. 40–41, *Mem^{re}* (Lionne minute) *du Roy a M^{rs} les Plenipot^{res}*, March 31, 1646 (Brienne copy in Ass. Nat. *Ms.* 272, fols. 189–191; copies in *Allemagne* 64, fols. 188–191, and *Allemagne* 75, fols. 475–476) [pub. in *M&N* II, 138–142; *NS* III, 140–141; Gärtner VIII, 682–688; and *APW* II B 3/1, 671–673]. AAE CP *Allemagne* 60, fols. 49–55, *Lettre d'un Gentilhoè Venetien escrite de Munster le 2e Avril 1646 a un de Ses amys a lion . . . a Turin traduite de l'Italien* which appeared in many forms. See BNF *Ms. Fr.* 15884, fols. 418–437, the *Gazette* n° 53, May 25, 1646; Knuttel: 5300–5302; and *NS* III, 410–414. See also AAE CP *Allemagne* 75, Lionne (letter sent) to Servien, fol. 483, March 31, 1646 [pub. in *APW* II B 3/1, 675–676].

5. The Emperor Gives Way

1. AAE CP *Allemagne* 60, fol. 65, Mazarin (Lionne minute) to Longueville, April 7, 1646 (copy in *Allemagne* 76, fols. 51–52) [calendared in *LM* II, 736–737; and pub. in its entirety in *APW* II B 3/2, 692–693]. AAE CP *Allemagne* 60 (fols. 66–67), Mazarin (Silhon minute) to D'Avaux, April 7, 1646 (letter sent in *Allemagne* 79, fols. 34–35, and copy in *Allemagne* 76, fols. 53–55) [calendared in *LM* II, 737, and pub. in its entirety in *APW* II B 3/2, 693–694].

2. For D'Avaux's expectations, see AAE CP *Allemagne* 64, fols. 202–205, D'Avaux (own hand minute) to Mazarin, April 6, 1646 (letter sent in *Allemagne* 60, fols. 61–64) [pub. in *APW* II B 3/2, 680–683]. For the interview with Trauttmansdorff, see AAE CP *Allemagne* 64, fols. 249–255, D'Avaux (own hand minute) to Mazarin, April 18, 1646 (letter sent in *Allemagne* 60, fols. 127–134, and copy in *Allemagne* 76, fols. 139–149, dated April 14) [pub. in *APW* II B 3/2, 764–770]. For the beginning of D'Avaux's "hallucination," see his letter to Mazarin on the Duke of Lorraine of October 8, 1646, cited in Chapter 6, note 3, in which D'Avaux says that "cette pensée m'est venue dans l'esprit il y a six mois."

3. See HHSA RK *FrA* 92 VIII, fols. 262–267, Volmar's own hand minute of three drafts of the Imperial memorial of April 14, 1646, one beginning "Regis Christianissimi plenipotentiarii," the other two beginning "Ad Praetensam Satisfactones" (copy in ASVat *Paci* 19, fols. 193–194, in Italian in BVat Q III 71, fols. 82–84, and ASVen *Munster* 4: *"Ristretto delle ultime offerte d'Imp^li date in scritto piu amplio alli Mediatori e da questi comunicate ai francesi il medesimo giorno 14 Aprile)."* See two versions of the *revised* memorial in AAE CP *Allemagne* 60, fols. 151–155 and 156–157, one misleadingly titled *Premier escrit des Imperiaux,* with comments of the French plenipotentiaries dated Münster, April 19, 1646, another titled *Second Ecrit des Imperiaux du 19 avr 1646* beginning with the words "Ad praetensam satisfactionem." See two Spanish translations of this last version in AGS E 2347. [Both versions are combined in French in *NS* III, 420–421, while the first version is published in Latin in Gärtner IX, 102–107, dated April 13, 1646; and the *revised* version is published incompletely in German in Londorp VI, 27–28, and in its entirety in Latin in Meiern III, 6–7]. See also ASVen *Münster* 4, Contarini (copy to Senate) to Nani, April 17, 1646; AAE CP *Allemagne* 76, fols. 150–155, and p.s. in fol. 162, plenipotentiaries (secretary's and Servien's minute) to court, April 14–19, 1646 (copy in fols. 158–161 without p.s., letter sent in Ass. Nat. *Ms.* 275, fols. 223–240; with p.s. and duplicate for Mazarin in AAE CP *Allemagne* 60, fols. 138–146, also with p.s.) [pub. *APW* II B 3/2, 774–781]. BVat *CCL* A I 14, fols. 95–100, Chigi (register) to Pamfili, April 20, 1646 (letter sent in ASVat *Paci* 19, fols. 187–192). For Servien's mission, see Ass. Nat. *Ms.* 275, fols. 313–327, *Relation* (copy sent to Brienne) *de ce qui S'est passé au voyage d'Osnabrug,* May 7, 1646 (duplicate for Mazarin in *Allemagne* 60, fols. 240–250, copies in *Allemagne* 65, fols. 33–41, and *Allemagne* 76, fols. 327–332) [pub. in *M&N* II, 249–265, *NS* III, 172–176, and Gärtner IX, 617–634].

4. For the campaign in Flanders, compare Ronette's report cited in the following note with the *mémoire* on the campaign, cited in note 10 below. For the visit of Prince Thomas, compare AAE CP *Sardaigne* 40, fol. 59, Plessis Praslin (letter sent) to Mazarin, April 15, 1646, announcing Prince Thomas's departure on that date, with the *mémoire* on the campaign, cited in note 10 below and with *Sardaigne* 40, fols. 76–77, Le Tellier (letter sent) to Servien (the French ambassador in Turin) May 7, 1646, indicating that Prince Thomas had recently left. For Mazarin's qualms about the siege of Lérida, see his recollections in *Espagne* 25, fol. 347, Mazarin (secretary's minute with Lionne corrections) to Harcourt, August 23, 1646. For the campaign in Germany, see the *mémoire* on the campaign, cited in note 10 below. For the voyage of the court, see *Allemagne* 60, fol. 229, Mazarin (Lionne minute) to Longueville, May 5, 1646 (copy in *Allemagne* 76, fols. 308–309) [calendared in *LM* II, 749; and pub. in its entirety in *APW* II B 3/2, 885–887] and Ass.

Nat. *Ms.* 272, fols. 236–237, Brienne (minute) to plenipotentiaries, May 5, 1646 (copies in AAE CP *Allemagne* 65, fols. 19–20, and *Allemagne* 76, fol. 310) [pub. in *M&N* II, 277–279; *NS* III, 168; Gärtner IX, 594–596; and *APW* II B 3/2, 884–885].

5. AAE CP *Pays Bas Espagnols* 21, fols. 104–107, *Memoire de ce qui S'est passé de plus important en ma negociaòn de holande* [avril et may 1646 Mr de Ronette]; *Hollande* 39, fols. 24–25, Brasset (letter sent) to Brienne, April 23, 1646; *Hollande* 38, fols. 7–10, La Thuillerie (letter sent) to Mazarin, April 24, 1646.

6. For Peñaranda's preparations, see AGS E 2347, Peñaranda (copy) to Terranova, April 19, 1646. For the exchange of proposals, compare ASVen *Münster* 4, *Repliche et offerte de Spag^li con le Dupliche risposte de' Francesi,* April 20–24, 1646 (copy in HHSA RK *FrA* 52a, pt. 2, fols. 70–71) with Ass. Nat. *Ms.* 275, fols. 282–287, *Memoire* (sent to Brienne) *des Plenipotentiaires* (Longueville and D'Avaux) *de France, fait a Munster xxvii Avril 1646* with AAE CP *Allemagne* 60, fols. 208–210, *Proposition* (sent to Mazarin) *des Espagnols pour la paix 27 avril 1646,* noting that the Italian version includes a specific French demand for Rosas, whereas the French versions do not. The French sent them to their court on April 27. The Dutch have a French version in NNA SG *R* 4855. Peñaranda's letter to Philip IV of April 26, 1646, is lost, but it is summarized in the *consulta* of June 1–3, cited in note 13 below. See also BVat *CCL* A I 14, fols. 106–112 and fols. 113–115, Chigi (register) to Pamfili, two letters dated April 27, 1646 (first of these letters sent in ASVat *Paci* 19, fols. 201–208), ASVen *Munster* 4, Contarini (copy to Senate) to Nani, April 27, 1646, Ass. Nat. *Ms.* 275, fols. 258–280, *Memoire* (copy sent) *des Plenipotentiaires* (Longueville and D'Avaux) *de France,* April 27, 1646 (copy to Mazarin in AAE CP *Allemagne* 60, fols. 192–207, and other copy in *Allemagne* 76, fols. 262–269) [pub. in *APW* II B 3/2, 851–862]. See also AAE CP *Allemagne* 64, fols. 256–257, D'Avaux (own hand minute) to Mazarin, April 20–27, 1646 (copy sent in *Allemagne* 60, fols. 212–124, and other copy in *Allemagne* 76, fols. 256–258, both dated April 27, 1646) [pub. in *APW* II B 3/2, 867–869].

7. For the pressure from both Protestants and Catholics, see HHSA RK *FrA* 90 II (Volmar Diary) April 4, 1646 [pub. in *APW* III C 2/1, 582–588]. We know of Ferdinand's own hand letter only through Volmar's entry in this same diary of May 6, 1646 [pub. in *APW* III C 2/1, 619–620]. See also HHSA RK *FrA* 51a, pt. 5, fols. 2–15, *Duplica d. Kays. Gesandten Zu Osnabrug 1 maij 1646* (copy in SRA *DG* 7, fols. 722–731) [pub. in in Londorp V, 1079–1083; Meiern III, 54–62; and Gärtner IX, 536–558]. See a French translation in *NS* III, 421–426, and a Spanish translation in AGS E 2349. See also HHSA RK *FrA* 51a, pt. 5, fols. 16–20, *Punctis Satisfactionis* [pub. in Meiern III, 62–66]. See the first draft of the Imperial response to the French in HHSA

RK *FrA* 92 VIII, fols. 441–452 (copy in ASVat *Paci* 19, fols. 237–244). For the response to the French as revised, see HHSA RK *FrA* 92 VIII, 470–479 (copies sent in Ass. Nat. *Ms.* 275, fols. 328–338), *Duplica Ceasareanorum* (French translation on fols. 339–344, copy titled *Duplicata Caesareanorum ad Sensum mediatorum abbreviata iisdemque exhibita Sabatho 5 Maii 1646* in AAE CP *Allemagne* 65, fols. 9–16) [printed version in *Allemagne* 65, fols. 5–8; pub. in French in *NS* III, 426–429; and in the original Latin in Meiern III, 13–17]. *Instrumentum Pacis* for the French: HHSA RK *FrA* 54c (last part), fols. 173–189. *Instrumentum Pacis* for the Swedes: HHSA RK *FrA* 51a, pt. 5, fols. 38–50 (two copies in longer and shorter versions in both Latin and French in AAE CP *Allemagne* 65, fols. 61–78, 79–84, 91–106, 85–90, and other copy in Latin in ASVat *Paci* 19, fols. 320–321) [pub. in Meiern III, 66–73; and Gärtner IX, 24–44 and 642–661]. For the various reports of the proceedings, see BVat *CCL* A I 14, fols. 116–119, Chigi (register), to Pamfili, May 4, 1646 (letter sent in ASVat *Paci* 19, fols. 229–232); ASVen *Munster* 4, Contarini (copies to Senate) to Nani, May 4, 5, and 8, 1646; Ass. Nat. *Ms.* 275, fols. 301–312, *Memoire* (sent) *des Plenipotentiaires de france,* May 7, 1646 (duplicate for Mazarin in AAE CP *Allemagne* 60, fols. 233–237; other copies in *Allemagne* 65, fols. 26–29, and *Allemagne* 76, fols. 324–326) [pub. in *M&N* II, 235–243; *NS* III, 168–170; Gärtner IX, 603–611; and *APW* II B 3/2, 891–895], Ass. Nat. *Ms.* 275, fols. 295–300, plenipotentiaries (letter sent) to Brienne, May 7, 1646 (duplicate for Mazarin in AAE CP *Allemagne* 60, fols. 230–232; other copies in *Allemagne* 76, fols. 322–323, and *Allemagne* 65, fols. 30–32) [pub. in *M&N* II, 244–248; *NS* III, 171–172; *Gärtner* IX, 612–617; and *APW* II B 3/2, 888–890], AAE CP *Allemagne* 60, fols. 251–252, Longueville (letter sent) to Mazarin, May 7, 1646 (copy in *Allemagne* 76, fols. 312–314) [pub. in *APW* II B 3/2, 904–905], AAE CP *Allemagne* 65, fols. 45–49, D'Avaux (own hand minute) to Mazarin, May 7, 1646 (copy sent in *Allemagne* 60, fols. 253–258, and other copy in *Allemagne* 76, fols. 315–371), *Allemagne* 76, fols. 288–303, Servien (secretary's minute with own hand corrections) to Lionne, probably also of May 7, 1646 [pub. in part in *APW* II B 3/2, 910–915], SRA *DG* 7, fols. 719–721, Johan Oxenstierna and Salvius (letter sent) to Christina, April 27/May 7, 1646 [pub. in *APW* II C 2, 259–262]; HHSA RK *FrA* 51a, pt. 5, fols. 23–25, Trauttmansdorff, Lamberg, and Krane (letter sent) to Ferdinand III, May 7, 1646 (copy in Giessen 207, 191–296) [pub. in Gärtner IX, 597–600; and *APW* II A 4, 143–144], and *FrA* 50a, Konvolut a, fols. 98–99, Trauttmansdorff (own hand letter sent) to Ferdinand III, May 8, 1646 [pub. in *APW* II A 4, 147–148].

8. AAE CP *Allemagne* 65, fols. 147–153, D'Avaux (own hand minute) to Mazarin, May 14, 1646 (letter sent in *Allemagne* 60, fols. 276–283, other copy

in *Allemagne* 76, fols. 345–355) [pub. in *APW* II B 3/2, 930–935]. There is no mention of the conversation with D'Avaux, however, in NNA SG VL 12588 37 III, Dutch plenipotentiaries (letter sent) to States General, May 18, 1646 (copy in SG R 4855). D'Avaux became explicit in his distrust of both Pauw and Knuyt in his letter to Mazarin of June 4, cited in notes 11 and 12 below, and repeated his position on both the Swedes and the Dutch in AAE CP *Allemagne* 66, fols. 69–72, D'Avaux (own hand minute) to Mazarin, June 18, 1646 (copy sent in *Allemagne* 61, fols. 42–46, and other copy in *Allemagne* 76, fols. 608–613) [pub. in *APW* II B 4, 63–67].

9. See AGS E 2347 for the Spanish offer of May 13, 1646, and NNA SG R 4855 for the Dutch offer of May 13, 1646 [pub. in Latin in Londorp VI, 5–6]. See also AGS E 2347 for three translations of the Dutch offer, one from Flemish to Spanish, one apparently from Flemish to French, and the third from French to Spanish, as well as Peñaranda (deciphered copy) to Philip IV and Peñaranda (copy) to Castel Rodrigo, all forwarding the offer, as well as two other copies of letters to Philip IV and one to Pedro Coloma all of May 14, 1646. The articles are published in Dutch in Aitzema *VNVH* II, 54–78, and in Latin in Londorp VI, 6–11, but in both incorrectly dated for May 17. See in the same AGS E 2347, Peñaranda to Philip IV, May 17, 1646, for Peñaranda's reaction to the Dutch offer, as well as three copies of the Spanish answer of May 17 to the Dutch, two in Spanish and the one in French, expressing some minor cavils. The French version is also in NNA SG R 4855, which also contains an *Escript delivré aux Espagnols le 18* [sic] *May 1646*. See AGS E 2347 and 2348 for two translations from French to Spanish of this answer. The letters are published in *CDI* LXXXII, 302–322. The Spanish answer is pub. in French in Aitzema *VNVH* II, 73–82, in Latin in Londorp VI, 11–13, and in Spanish in *CDI* LXXXII, 322–326. For Servien's panicky letter, see AAE CP *Allemagne* 76, fols. 373–376, Servien (own hand minute) to Lionne, May 17, 1646 [pub. in *APW* II B 3/2, 943–947].

10. For the court at Compiègne, see the *Gazettes* n°s 52 and 56, May 19 and 26, 1646. For the military and diplomatic planning, see AAE CP *Allemagne* 60, fols. 293–298, *Estat* (secretary's hand with Lionne's corrections and additions) *general des forces du Roy au Commencem[t] de l'a Camp[ne] de l'année 1646 avec les proiects des desseins ausquels on peust les occuper . . . envoyé a Munster 19 may 1646* (copy in AAE MD *France* 856, fols. 189–191). For the orders to Turenne, see AAE CP *Allemagne* 65, fols. 157–160, Mazarin (Silhon minute) to Turenne, May 18, 1646 [pub. in Turenne I, 256–264]. See also *Allemagne* 60, fols. 299–305, *Memoire* (Lionne minute) *du Roy a Messieurs les plenipotentiaires sur les affaires de l'Empire, Compiegne le 19 may 1646* (copies in Ass. Nat. *Ms.* 272, fols. 253–256; AAE CP *Allemagne* 76, fols. 389–395, and *Allemagne* 65, fols. 165–171) [pub. in *M&N* II, 320–324; *NS*

III, 189–192; Gärtner IX, 900–914; and *APW* II B 3/2, 962–970], AAE CP *Allemagne* 60, fols. 286–292, *Memoire* (Lionne minute) *du Roy a Messieurs les Plenipotentiaires sur les affaires d'Espagne . . . du 19 may 1646* (copies in Ass. Nat. *Ms.* 272, fols. 257–260; AAE CP *Allemagne* 76, fols. 396–406; and *Allemagne* 65, fols. 176–182) [pub. in *M&N* II, 303–320; *NS* III, 182–186; Gärtner IX, 827–844; and *APW* II B 3/2, 952–961].

11. ASVen *Munster* 4, Contarini (copy to Senate) to Nani, May 22, 1646, Contarini (copy to Senate) to Nani, May 29 and June 5, 1646; BVat *CCL* A I 14, fols. 145–150 and 152–160, Chigi (register) to Pamfili, May 25 and June 1, 1646 (letters sent in ASVat *Paci* 19, fols. 312–319 and 326–335). HHSA RK *FrA* 50a, Konv. a, fols. 112–127, Trauttmansdorff (own hand letters sent) to Ferdinand III, May 22, 25, 27, 29, June 1, 4, and 5, 1646 [pub. in *APW* II A 4, 209, 219, 239–240, 253–254, 265–266, 270, and 276–277]. For the French report, see Servien's partial minute in AAE CP *Allemagne* 76, fols. 478–484, probably of May 27, 1646 (copy sent in Ass. Nat. *Ms.* 275, fols. 375–393, dated May 29, 1646; duplicate for Mazarin in AAE CP *Allemagne* 60, fols. 340–350; and other copy without p.s. in *Allemagne* 76, fols. 485–491) [pub. in *APW* II B 3/2, 1011–1019]; and AAE CP *Allemagne* 65, fols. 270–274, D'Avaux (own hand minute) to Mazarin, May 29, 1646 (letter sent in *Allemagne* 60, fols. 352–357). See also Ass. Nat. *Ms.* 275, fols. 400–409, *Memoire des Plenipo^{res} de France,* June 4, 1646 (duplicate for Mazarin in AAE CP *Allemagne* 60, fols. 415–419, dated June 5; other copies in *Allemagne* 66, fols. 10–13, and *Allemagne* 76, fols. 538–540) [pub. in *M&N* II, 405–412; *NS* III, 214–216; and *APW* II B 3/2 1068–1072]; AAE CP *Allemagne* 66, fols. 16–17, D'Avaux (own hand minute) to Mazarin, June 4, 1646 (copy sent in *Allemagne* 60, fols. 408–409, and other copy in *Allemagne* 76, fols. 529–530) [pub. in *APW* II B 3/2, 1073–1074]; AAE CP *Allemagne* 60, fol. 407, Longueville (letter sent) to Mazarin, June 4, 1646 (copy in *Allemagne* 76, fols. 526–527) [pub. in *APW* II B 3/2, 1072–1073]; and AAE CP *Allemagne* 76, fols. 542–547, Servien (own hand minute) to Lionne, June 5, 1646 [pub. in *APW* II B 3/2, 1074–1080]. For the Imperial memo, see HHSA RK *FrA* 52a, pt. 2, fols. 177–182, *Postrema Caesaranorum in Puncto Satisfact^{is} Gallicae declaratio,* of May 29, 1646; copies in ASVat *Paci* 19, fols. 336–339; Ass. Nat. *Ms.* 275, fols. 410–415; and in Spanish in AGS E 2348) [pub. in German in Londorp VI, 28–30; in Latin and in French in *NS* III, 429–434; and in Latin in Meiern III, 31–35]. For the French reply, see AAE CP *Allemagne* 65, fols. 249–250, *Projet de reponse a la proposition donnee par les Imperiaux, Allemagne* 76, fols. 458–465, minute of the *Reponse des Plenipo^{res} de France a la proposition donnée par M^{rs} les med^{eurs} le 29 may de la part de M. Les Plenip^{res} de l Emp^{r}* (copy sent in Ass. Nat. *Ms.* 275, fols. 416–421; other copies in AAE CP *Allemagne* 65, fols. 231–238,

239–247, and 251–253; and HHSA RK *FrA* 52a, pt. 2, fols. 193–196) [pub. in inaccurate French and Latin in Meiern III, 37–45].

12. For the negotiation, see also NNA SG R 4855, *Escript delivré aux Espagnols le 24 May 1646,* and AGS E 2347, two copies, one in French and one in Spanish, titled *Resp^{ta} de Los Olandeses al Papel que Los S^{res} Plenipotenciarios de Su Ma^d Les dieren en 17 de Mayo En Munster a 24 de Mayo 1646.* There is another Spanish translation in AGS E 2348. A French version is published in Aitzema *VNVH* II, 84–86, and a Latin one in Londorp VI, 13. See also AGS E 2348, *Resp^{ta} de los SS. Plenip^{os} de Su Mag^d en 27 de Mayo 1646 al papel q~ Holandeses dieron en 24 del dhò,* which makes the concession on 's Hertogenbosch. See NNA SG R 4855 for a French copy of this titled *"Escript des Espagnols delivré le 28 May* [pub. in Aitzema *VNVH* II, 86–88, and in Latin in Londorp VI, 14–15, both dated May 27]. See also AGS E 2348 for the copy of Peñaranda's *mémoire* "Desde que . . ." of May 28, 1646, explaining his concessions and copies of his two letters to Castel Rodrigo of the same date in which he describes the growing Dutch interest in involving themselves in the negotiations with France [letters pub. in *CDI* LXXXII, 348–349 and 338–341]. See also in E 2348, *R^{on} de lo que paso con Quenuilt diputado de Celanda a los SS^{res} Arcobpò de Cambray y Consejero Brun en 31 de Mayo 1646.* See also NNA SG R 4855, the Dutch writing beginning with *"Sur le dernier escript,"* dated May 31, 1646, which in AGS E 2348 becomes the *Respuesta de Olandeses al papel q~ se les dio en 27 de Mayo 1646, Munster a 30 de Mayo 1646* [pub. in Aitzema *VNVH* II, 88–89; and Londorp VI, 15] as well as in AGS E 2348, Peñaranda (deciphered copies) to Castel-Rodrigo, May 31, June 4, and June 7, 1646 [pub. in *CDI* LXXXII, 342–346], where one can follow both the progress of the negotiation and the skillful way in which the Spanish plenipotentiaries draw the Dutch into involving themselves into the negotiations with France. There is still no mention of this matter, however, in NNA SG *VL* 12588.37 IV, Dutch plenipotentiaries (letters sent) to the States General, June 1 and 12, 1646 (copies in NNA SG R 4855). For the French plenipotentiaries' knowledge of the Spanish-Dutch negotiations, see their report of May 29, cited in note 11 above. For their reaction, or lack of reaction, to the Dutch offers to involve themselves, compare D'Avaux's letter of June 4, with Longueville's letter of the same date, and Servien's letter of June 5, cited in note 11 above. However, in AAE CP *Allemagne* 61, fols. 18–33, plenipotentiaries (letter sent) to Mazarin, June 14, 1646 (copy in *Allemagne* 76, fols. 570–578) [pub. in *APW* II B 4, 37–43] there is the implication that a Dutch mediation would be undesirable. Peñaranda explains his motives for encouraging it in AGS E 2347, Peñaranda (deciphered copy) to Philip IV, September 27, 1646 [pub. in *CDI* LXXXII, 415–416]; and in BVat *CCL*

A I 14, fols. 340–342, Chigi (register) to Pamfili, November 23, 1646 (letter sent in ASVat *Paci* 20, fols. 353–357).

13. For the most important *consulta*, see AGS E 2347 (Pedro Coloma's minute with marginal corrections) dated Madrid, June 1, 1646, E 2065 (clean copy in large secretarial hand) dated Zaragoza, June 3, 1646. It refers to a *consulta* of June 2, 1646, regarding the Prince of Orange and also contains Philip IV's long and reasoned approval. For the revised plenipotentia, see NNA SG VL 12588.37 IV, a copy and a translation into Dutch, both dated June 7, 1646, including the words *"provincias libres"* and *"vrije verenigde provintien."* There are references in E 2347 to other *consultas* of June 1, 1646, that were removed from this volume and some references to their content, including possibly the reinstitution of the marriage and exchange proposal, in the *consulta* of October 13, 1646, cited in Chapter 6, note 9.

14. For the movements of the court, see the *Gazette* n°s 59, 63, and 67, June 2, 9, and 16, 1646. For the decision on Courtrai, compare AAE CP *Pays Bas Espagnols* 19, fols. 199–200, Mazarin (secretary's and Lionne's minute) to La Rivière June 5, 1646: "Je ne scais pas les resolutions qu'on prendra" (copy in *Pays Bas Espagnols* 18, fols. 268–269) with *Pays Bas Espagnols* 19, fol. 201, Mazarin (secretary's minute) to Rantzau, June 7, 1646: "Les intentions de S.A.R. vont a Courtray." For the siege itself, see the *Gazette* n° 73, June 26, 1646.

15. AAE CP *Allemagne* 61, fols. 48–59, *Mémoire* (Lionne minute) *du Roy a M^rs les Plenipot^res*, June 22, 1646 (Brienne minute in Ass. Nat. Ms. 272, fols. 310–321; copies in *Allemagne* 76, fols. 626–633, and *Allemagne* 66, fols. 87–97) [pub. in M&N III, 61–86; NS III, 227–232; and APW II B 4, 77–90]. See also *Allemagne* 61, fols. 60–61, Mazarin (Lionne minute) to Longueville, same date (copy in *Allemagne* 76, fols. 634–636) [pub. in APW II B 4, 91–92]. For the change of mind about the junction, see AAE CP *Allemagne* 66, fols. 83–85, Mazarin (Silhon minute) to Turenne, June 22, 1646 [pub. in Turenne I, 271–274]. For the ambiguous but harder line on Portugal, see AAE CP *Allemagne* 61, fols. 91–94, *Memoire* (Lionne minute) *du Roy a M^rs les plenipot^res*, June 30, 1646 (Brienne minute in Ass. Nat. Ms. 272, fols. 333–337; copies in AAE CP *Allemagne* 76, fols. 685–688, and *Allemagne* 66, fols. 132–136) [pub. in M&N III, 96–106; NS III, 238–240; and APW II B 4, 133–138]. Mazarin later used this *mémoire* along with others to claim that he had permitted his plenipotentiaries to give in completely on the interests of the Portuguese. See Chapter 8, note 1.

16. For the death of Brezé, see the *Gazette* n° 74, June 29, 1646. For the affair of the admiralty, see AC M 33, fols. 85 and 86, Condé (two own hand copies of the same letter sent) to Enghien, July 24, 1646, AAE MD *France* 856, fol. 4, Mazarin (secretary's minute) to Condé, August 2, 1646 (copy sent in AC M

33, fols. 175–176); AC M 33, fols. 173–174, Mazarin (secretary's hand letter sent) to Enghien, August 2, 1646; AC M 33, fols. 182–185. Condé (*mémoire* in secretary's hand) to Mazarin, August 3, 1646 (two copies on fols. 186–189 and 191–194); AAE MD *France* 856, fol. 7, Mazarin (secretary's minute) to Condé, August 5, 1646, and fol. 18, Mazarin (Lionne minute) to Condé, August 10, 1646. For the alienation of Chavigny, see BNF *Ms. Baluze* 174 (*Carnet* 8), pp. 37, 41–42, and 44; and AAE MD *France* 856, fols. 4–6, Gaudin (own hand letter sent) to Servien, July 3, 1646. For the military operations in Flanders and in Italy, see the *Gazettes* n°s 77, 80, 90, 92 93, and 100, July 5, 9, August 3, 4, 6, and 18, 1646. For Mazarin's dissatisfaction with his commanders, see BNF *Ms. Baluze* 174 (*Carnet* 8), p. 48.

17. For the Spanish-Dutch negotiations, see NNA SG *R* 4855, the revised powers in Spanish dated July 3, 1646, which seems to have been the date of transmission [pub. in Spanish and French in *NS* III, 442–443, also dated July 3, 1646], as well as SG *R* 4855, *Articulen provisionelick verdragen tusschen de Ambassad[en] extraordinaris & plenipotentiarisen van den Coninck van Spaegnen ter eene & d'Ambasad[en] extraordinaris ende plenipotentiarisen van Staten Generael der Vereenigde Nederlanden ter ander syde, omne geinserert te vorden in het Tractaet t'vreede gemaeckt zal werden tot Munster* in seventy articles, a copy, indicating that it had been signed by the Spanish plenipotentiaries, made by the secretary of the Dutch embassy on July 15, 1646, and AGS *E* 2348, *Articulos provisionales Entre los Embaxadores Extraordinarios y Plenipotenciarios del Rey de España de una parte y los Embaxadores extraaordinarios y Plemipot. de los Estados generales de las Provincias Unidas de Los Paises bajos de la otra parte, que se han de poner en el tratado que se hara a Munster* (two copies . . . *firmado de parte y otra* now reduced to seventy articles, but containing no signatures sent "*c[n] carta de 8 de Julio 646*" [pub. in *CDI* LXXXII, 382–399; and in French in *NS* III, 435–441]. See also in AGS *E* 2348, Peñaranda (deciphered copy) to Philip IV, July 8, 1646, which refers to the instrument as "ajustado firmado," but not specifying by whom [pub. in *CDI* LXXXII, 380–381]. However, in his complaint to the States-General cited in note 21 below, Brasset claims to have received word of the signing in a letter of July 10 and in his letter to Brienne of July 23. The same note tells of learning from Nederhorst that Gendt, Knuyt, and Pauw had signed, while Nederhorst and Ripperda had refused, and Chigi, in BVat *CCL* A 1 14, fols. 215–217, his letter to Pamfili, August 10, 1646 (copy sent in ASVat *Paci* 19, fols. 501–503), also identifies the Dutch deputies who signed as those of Gelderland (Gendt), Holland (Knuyt) and Zeeland (Pauw). For the French reactions, see Ass. Nat. *Ms.* 275, fols. 489–510, *Memoire des Plenipo[res] de France,* July 9, 1646, with an addition on fols. 511–513 (duplicate for Mazarin in AAE CP *Allemagne* 61, fols. 110–122,

without addition, and other copy in *Allemagne* 77, fols. 67–72, without addition) [pub. in *M&N* III, 114–132, with partial addition on 106–111; *NS* III, 247–251, with addition on 244–245; and *APW* II B 4, 178–189, with addition]. For French copies of the provisional articles, see Ass. Nat. *Ms.* 276, fols. 56–69; and AAE CP *Allemagne* 65, fols. 317–346, 347–359, and 360–385. There is also a copy in French in ASVat *Paci* 19, fols. 683–690. For the explicit Dutch offers of interposition, see NNA SG *VL* 12588.37 IV, Gendt, Pauw, Knuyt, Reede, and Ripperda (letter sent) to States General, July 13, 1646 (copy in NNA SG *R* 4855); and AAE CP *Allemagne* 77, fols. 94–95, plenipotentiaries (Servien largely own hand minute) to Mazarin, July 9 [10], 1646 (letter sent in *Allemagne* 61, fols. 123–125) [pub. in *M&N* III, 111–114; *NS* III, 246–250; and *APW* II B 4, 190–191]. See also *Allemagne* 61, fols. 128–130, Longueville (letter sent) to Mazarin, July 9, 1646 (copy in *Allemagne* 77, fols. 74–77); *Allemagne* 66, fols. 168–173, D'Avaux (own hand minute) to Mazarin, July 9, 1646 (letter sent in *Allemagne* 61, fols. 132–135, and copy in *Allemagne* 77, fols. 78–80); and *Allemagne* 77, fols. 84–89 and 93, Servien (own hand minute) to Lionne, July 9 [10], 1646 [all pub. in *APW* II B 4, 194–196]. Later, in their letter of September 28, 1646, to the States General cited in note 26 below, Pauw, Donia, and Clant claimed that Contarini had incited them to intervene, but Contarini makes no such statement in his correspondence.

18. HHSA RK *FrA* 90 II (Volmar Diary), July 12 and 13, 1646 [pub. in *APW* III C 2/1, 533]; HHSA RK FrA 51a, pt. 5, fols. 156–166, *Weitere und Entliche Compositions Vorschläge in p^{to} gravamimum,* undated (copy in SRA *DG* 7, fols. 1324–1337, dated July 12, 1646 [pub. in Meiern III, 193–199], the *Memoire des Plenipo^{res} de France,* cited in the previous note; AAE CP *Allemagne* 77, fols. 101–102, the French *Resultat de la conference tenue le Jeudi 12 Juillet 1646* (which also includes a conference with Johan Oxenstierna of July 14, 1646); and SRA *DG* 7, fols. 1311–1323, Johan Oxenstierna (letter sent) to Christina, July 13/23, 1646 [pub. in *APW* II C 2, 370–381].

19. AAE CP *Allemagne* 61, fols. 174–177, *Memoire* (Lionne minute) *du Roy a M^{rs} les plenipot^{res},* July 20, 1646 (Brienne minute in Ass. Nat. *Ms.* 275, fols. 540–542 and 545, and copy in AAE CP *Allemagne* 77, fols. 127–133) [pub. in *NS* III, 306–308, and *APW* II B 4, 234–237]. AAE CP *Allemagne* 61, fols. 178–182, Mazarin (Silhon minute) to D'Avaux, July 20, 1646 (letter sent in *Allemagne* 79, fols. 66–70, and copy in *Allemagne* 77, fols. 134–136) [pub. in *APW* II B 4, 239–243], views confirmed in Mazarin's letter to D'Avaux of November 9, 1646, cited in Chapter 6, note 5. AAE CP *Allemagne* 77, fol. 145, Lionne (letter sent) to Servien, June 20, 1646 [pub. in *APW* II B 4, 244].

20. AAE CP *Allemagne* 66, fols. 205–212, D'Avaux (own hand minute) to Mazarin, July 30, 1646 (letter sent in *Allemagne* 61, fols. 198–204, and copy

in *Allemagne* 77, fols. 175–184) [pub. in *APW* II B 4, 277–282]. See also ASVat *Paci* 19, fol. 522, *Conversatis a Trautmanstorff habita cum Com: d'Avaux 29 Julij 1646* given by Trauttmansdorff to the mediators. Curiously, Trauttmansdoff makes no mention of this conversation in HHSA RK ГіА 50a, Konv. a, fols. 156–157, his own hand letter sent to Ferdinand III, July 31, 1646 [pub. in *APW* II A 4, 480–481].

21. For the Prince of Orange, see AAE CP *Hollande* 37, fols. 62–63 and 58–59, D'Estrades (own hand letters sent) to Mazarin and to Brienne, July 24, 1646. For the return of the Dutch plenipotentiaries, see *Hollande* 39, fols. 56–59 and 52–54, Brasset (letters sent) to Mazarin and to Brienne, July 23, 1646, and *Hollande* 37, fols. 56–57, Brasset (copy to Mazarin) to plenipotentiaries, July 24, 1646. For their report, see NNA SG R 4855, July 26, 1646. For Brasset's complaints, see the same SG R 4855, dated July 27, 1646, and AAE CP *Hollande* 37, fols. 67–68, July 17, 1646 (copies in NNA SG VL 12588.37 IV, and ASVat *Paci* 19, fols. 513–514) [pub. form in Aitzema *VNVH* II, 104–106] and AAE CP *Hollande* 37, fol. 69, Brasset (copy to Mazarin) to plenipotentiaries, July 27, 1646. For La Thuillerie's complaint, see NNA SG R 4855, August 8, 1645; AAE CP *Hollande* 38, fols. 59–62 (copies in NNA SG VL 12588.37 IV; AAE CP *Hollande* 37, fols. 116–118 and 119–122; and ASVat *Paci* 19, fols. 555–557) [pub. in Aitzema *VNVH* II, 106–110]. For the resolution, see NNA SH 1374, August 10, 1646. For the beginning of considerations of making a peace instead of a truce, see the Le Roy diatribe, cited in Chapter 6, note 26.

22. Compare the detailed and sanguine report in Ass. Nat. *Ms.* 276, fols. 45–55, *Memoire des Plenipotentiaires de France,* August 13, 1646 (duplicate for Mazarin in AAE CP *Allemagne* 61, fols. 261–268; other copies in *Allemagne* 77, fols. 249–252, and *Allemagne* 66, fols. 239–244) [pub. in *M&N* III, 184–195; *NS* III, 270–273; and *APW* II B 4, 331–336], with the general and negative reports in ASVen *Munster* 4, Contarini (copy to Senate) to Nani, August 14, 1646, and BVat *CCL* A I 14, fols. 220–222, Chigi (register) to Pamfili, August 17, 1646. For the Prince of Orange's pitiful campaign, see AAE CP *Hollande* 37, fols. 134–135 and 132–133, D'Estrades (own hand letters sent) to Mazarin and to Brienne, August 14, 1646. For the declaration of the States-General, see NNA SG R 4855, Resolution of August 21, 1646: *"Sur la proposition . . .* (copies in AAE CP *Hollande* 38, fols. 69–70; *Hollande* 37, fols. 150–151 and 157–158; and ASVat *Paci* 19, fols. 617–618) [pub. in Aitzema *VNVH* II, 119–121]. There is also a longer version drawn up by one of Godefroy's assistants in AAE CP *Hollande* 37, fols. 152–156. Fall of Mardick: *Gazette* n° 105, August 31, 1646. Fall of Furnes (September 7, 1646): *Gazette* n° 112, September 14, 1646.

23. Compare the observations on D'Hémery and on the *parlement* in Ormesson I, 354–356, with the extremely interesting section of the *Mémoire du Roi* of September 28, cited in Chapter 6, note 1, in which Mazarin informs his plenipotentiaries that "leurs M^tés^ pourvoyent avec grande application pour Soutenir la guerre s'il est besoin l'année prochaine et q une aff^re^ Seule extra-ord^re^ dont on a traité fournira vingt quatre millions de livres" and then crosses it out! See also BNF *Ms. Baluze* 174 (*Carnet* 8), pp. 63–64.

24. For the compromise offer by the Protestants, see *Der Evangelischen Schluß zu Langerich, oder Gegen-Erklärung in puncto Gravaminum* [pub. in Meiern III, 330–340]. We can follow the Imperial-French negotiations, largely in Latin, in the following order: HHSA RK *FrA* 92 X, n° 1404, fols. 203–209, The Imperial *Ultima generalis declaratio,* August 31, 1646 with corrections on fol. 205, copy in *FrA* 92 X, n° 1409, fols. 219–226, with corrections on fol. 221, and in KHA *N A* IV, 1628/40, without corrections) [pub. in Meiern III, 712–718, with corrections]; BVat *CCL* Q III 58, fols. 284–292; and ASVat *Paci* 19, fols. 585–590, Chigi's copies of this writing; BVat *CCL* Q III 58, fols. 292–297, Chigi's copy of *Caput* 3 and 4 of this writing; Q III 58, fols. 303–306, a heavily corrected version of this writing, revised in conferences with the French on September 1 and 2; ASVen *Munster* 5, Contarini (copy to Senate) to Nani, September 4, 1646; ASVat *Paci* 19, fols. 591–594, corrected Imperial writing on *Caput* 3 and 4, transmitted September 4, 1646; BVat *CCL* Q III 58, fols. 298–299; and ASVat *Paci* 19, fols. 595–596, the short Imperial explanation of September 4, 1646. ASVat *Paci* 19, fols. 597–598, BVat *CCL* Q III 58, fols. 319–324, Imperial writing of September 4, 1646, revised in conferences with the French on September 5, 1646; BVat *CCL* Q III 58, fols. 308–309, Chigi's notes of September 5, 1646; ASVat *Paci* 19, fol. 599, fragment of French corrections to an Imperial writing, September 5–6, 1646. BVat *CCL* Q III 58, fol. 302, the first page of a French reply of September 6, 1646. See also BVat *CCL* A I 14, fols. 241–246, Chigi (register) to Pamfili, September 7, 1646; Ass. Nat. *Ms.* 276, fols. 136–141, Longueville, D'Avaux, and Servien (letter sent) to Brienne, September 10, 1646 (duplicate for Mazarin in AAE CP *Allemagne* 61, fols. 338–342; copies in *Allemagne* 66, fols. 384–386; and *Allemagne* 77, fols. 351–352) [pub. in *M&N* III, 296–297; and *NS* III, 296–297]; HHSA *FrA* 92 X, fols. 282–283, Trauttmansdorff, Nassau, and Volmar (minute) to Ferdinand III, September 11, 1646 (copy sent in *FrA* 52a, pt. 3, fols. 124 and 134; other copies in KHA *N A* IV, 1628/41; and Giessen 207, 1057–1062) [pub. in *APW* II A 4, 579–581]; ASVen *Munster* 5, Contarini (copy to Senate) to Nani, September 11, 1646; BVat *CCL* Q III 58, fols. 301–314, Imperial writing of September 11, 1646, which contains the approval of the contradictory article; BVat *CCL* Q III 58, fol. 316, last-minute French concessions, September 12–13,

1646 (copy on fol. 317); BVat *CCL* A I 14, fols. 251–253, Chigi (register) to Pamfili, September 14, 1646 (letter sent with an added paragraph in ASVat *Paci* 19, fols. 605–607. Final agreement: Ass. Nat. *Ms.* 276, fols. 154–162, September 13, 1646, with marginal comments in French by the French plenipotentiaries (copy for Mazarin with marginal comments in *Allemagne* 61, fols. 350–356; copy in *Allemagne* 66, fols. 405–410; and extract in French in Ass. Nat. *Ms.* 276, fols. 192–193), HHSA RK *FrA* 92 X, n° 1428, fols. 308–312 and 315 (copies in *FrA* 52a, pt. 3, fols. 150–154; *FrA* 52c, pt. 2, fols. 12–15 and 27–23; AV TA 109, n°s 40–44, fols. 423–427; OAT 20f, 2332–2341; Giessen 200, 105–109; BVat *CCL* Q III 58, fols. 325–335; and ASVat *Paci* 19, fols. 609–614, September 13, 1646; in Italian in ASVen *Munster* 5; and in the original Latin in NNA SG 8413, fols. 81–85) [pub. in Latin and French in *NS* III, 450–456; in Latin in Meiern III, 723–727, dated September 7, 1646; and in Repgen KFS, 204–213, dated September 13]. See also HHSA RK *FrA* 92 X, n° 1427, fols. 301–305, Trauttmansdorff, Nassau, and Volmar to Ferdinand III, September 14, 1646 (copy sent in *FrA* 52a, pt. 3, fols. 135, 147, and 136–138; other copies in KHA N A IV, 1628/41, and OAT 20f, 2318–2326) [pub. in *APW* II A 4, 584–589]. Ass. Nat. *Ms.* 276, fols. 149–151, Longueville, D'Avaux, and Servien (letter sent) to Anne, September 17, 1646 (copy to Mazarin in AAE CP *Allemagne* 61, fols. 362–364; other copies in *Allemagne* 66, fols. 439–440; and *Allemagne* 77, fols. 377–378) [pub. in *M&N* III, 242–245; *NS* III, 299–300; and *APW* II B 4, 449–452]; ASVen *Munster* 5, Contarini (copy to Senate) to Nani, September 18, 1646.

25. For the French promise, see ASVen *Munster* 5, *Punti sopra i quali si sono obligati francesi in voce di trattar con li Svezzesi e Protestani.* For the secret article, see Ass. Nat. *Ms.* 276, fol. 152, and HHSA RK *FrA* 92 X, n° 1438, fol. 313 (copies in *FrA* 52a, pt. 3, fol. 148; *FrA* 52c, pt. 2, fol. 16; AV TA 109, fol. 428; OAT 20f, 2344, and Giessen 200, 109) [pub. in Repgen KFS, 214].

26. For the military movements, see the *Gazette* n° 116, September 28, 1646. For the Spanish-Dutch conferences, see NNA SG 8413, fols. 37–38, *Premiere ouverture faicte par le Espagnols le 18ᵉ Septembre à Munster, sur quoy on a commence de parler avec les Plenipotʳᵉˢ de France à Osnabrugge le 20ᵉ Jour de Septembre et suivants* and SG VL 12588.37 IV, Pauw, Donia, and Clant (letters sent) to States General, September 18 and 28, 1646 (copy of the second in French in AAE CP *Allemagne* 61, fols. 393–396. See also the Spanish response of December 23, cited in Chapter 6, note 21, and Le Roy's *Relation,* cited in Chapter 6, note 26. For the French-Swedish conferences, see Ass. Nat. *Ms.* 276, fols. 209–215, *Memoire* (sent) *des Plenipoʳᵉˢ de France,* October 1, 1646 (copy to Mazarin in AAE CP *Allemagne* 62, fols. 16–22) [pub. in *M&N* III, 255–263; *NS* III, 337–338; and *APW* II B 4, 499–503]; *DG* 8,

fols. 187–195 and 418–422, Johan Oxenstierna and Salvius (letters sent) to
Christina, September 14/24, and September 21/October 1, 1646 [pub. in
APW II C 2, 455–465 and 477–483]. For the visit of the Dutch, see the
Memoire of October 1, just cited, and AAE CP *Allemagne* 77, fols. 387–389,
Servien's copy of the *Points plus importants desquels M^{rs} les Plenipotentiaires
de france et d'Espagne doivent concerter avant toutes choses,* dated September
23, 1646 (copy in Ass. Nat. *Ms.* 276, fols. 188–189, dated September 22,
1646) [pub. in Italian in Siri VIII, 885–887]. Servien's copy includes a note
at the end: "faut mettre icy celuy de Portugal." The Ass. Nat. copy states explicitly: "Le Roy de Portugal Sera compris dans la paix ou dans la Treve aux
conditions qui Seront convenues." The Dutch copy of this document in
NNA SG 8413, fols. 38–39, however, merely states: "Messrs les Ambass^{rs} ont
esté prié de bouche de parler de L'affaire de Portugal." The Dutch account
of this visit in Pauw, Donia, and Clant to the States General of September
28, just cited, is very general but the Brun relation of September 26, cited in
Chapter 6, note 2, which recapitulates the French terms as given to him by
the Dutch, makes absolutely no mention of Portugal at all. Thus the French
plenipotentiaries gave an inaccurate report to their own court, and the
Dutch compounded the obfuscation in their report to the Spanish. For the
cave-in by Innocent X, see AAE CP *Rome* 94, fols. 293–303, Saint-Nicolas
(copy) to Brienne, September 18, 1646.

27. For the continued French refusal to accept Article 9, see Ass. Nat *Ms.* 276,
fols. 110–112, *Reponse aux Plenipotentiaires de Messieurs les Estatz,* sent
with fols. 122–131, Longueville, D'Avaux, and Servien (letter sent) to Brienne, September 3, 1646. There is also a copy in NNA SG R 4855. For the
States General, see NNA SG R 4855 and 4856, the Resolution of September
18 and October 27, 1646, which was held up by Zeeland and reached its
final form in R 4856, *Resolutien genoomen in haer Ho. Mo. Vergaderinge de
17, 19, 20, 21 novemb~ 1646.* [in Spanish in AGS E 2350, including November 22]. See also the description of these pivotal deliberations in
Aitzema *VNVH* II, 143–165.

6. The Defection of the Dutch

1. For the arrival of De La Gardie, see the *Gazette* n° 114, September 15, 1646.
For his interviews with Mazarin, compare SRA *JOS* B II, De La Gardie
(letter sent) to Johan Oxenstierna and Salvius, September 18/28, 1646
[pub. in *APW* II C 2, 467–469], which only reports the assurances; with
AAE CP *Allemagne* 61, fols. 398–416, September 28, 1646, *Mem^{re} du Roy a
M^{rs} les plenipot^{re},* September 28, 1646 (Brienne minute in Ass. Nat. *Ms.* 276,
fols. 170–187, copies in AAE CP *Allemagne* 67, fols. 44–57, and *Allemagne*

78, fols. 61–74) [pub. in *NS* III, 326–336, dated September 28; and *APW* II B 4, 513–535, dated October 4], which only reports the warnings.

2. For two of the four conferences between the Spanish and the Dutch plenipotentiaries, see AGS E 2347, *Punctos que el Consejero Brum tomo por escrito de los Plenipotençiarios de Olanda en Munster a 26 de S^e 1646 con la respuesta de los ministros de su Maj^d al pie de cada uno; R^{on} de lo que paso al Sr de Brum con los Pleniponençiarios en Munster a 27 de 7t^{bre} 1646,* and Peñaranda (deciphered copy) to Philip IV, September 27, 1646 [pub. in *CDI* LXXXII, 415–416]. See also the letter of Pau, Donia, and Clant to the States General and of the French plenipotentiaries to Brienne, both cited in Chapter 5, note 26, as well as NNA SG *VL* 12588.37 IV, Pauw, Donia, Ripperda, and Clant (letter sent) to States General, October 3, 1646 (copy in SG *R* 4855, in French in AAE CP *Allemagne* 67, fols. 33–36). For a number of French copies of the Spanish response, see *Allemagne* 78, fols. 56–57 and 54–55; *Allemagne* 62, fols. 45–46; and Ass. Nat. *Ms.* 276, fols. 226–227, all dated October 1, 1646 [pub. in *APW* II B 4, 620–630, in the notes]. For the French response, see AAE CP *Allemagne* 67, fols. 24–26 and 27–30; *Allemagne* 78, fols. 58–60; *Allemagne* 62, fols. 47–50; and Ass. Nat. *Ms.* 276, fols. 228–233, all dated October 3, 1646; as well as NNA SG 8413, fols. 42–44, dated October 2, 1646 [also pub. in *APW* II B 4, 620–630, in the notes].

3. For the consultation with Salvius, see the recollection in the letter of D'Avaux to Mazarin of December 31, 1646, cited in note 25 below. See also AAE CP *Allemagne* 67, fols. 2–7, plenipotentiaries (secretary's hand) to Christina, October 1, 1646 (copy to Mazarin in *Allemagne* 62, fols. 10–15, titled *Projet de letter pour envoyer a la Reyne de Suede dressee par M. D'Avaux, n'a esté envoyée M. Servien ne l'ayant voulu signer* [pub. in *APW* II B 4, 506–508]. For the dissension between D'Avaux and Servien, see AAE CP *Allemagne* 67, fols. 61–66, D'Avaux (own hand minute) to Mazarin, October 8, 1646 (letter sent in *Allemagne* 62, fols. 56–61, and copy in *Allemagne* 78, fols. 89–97) [pub. in *APW* II B 4, 551–556]. For D'Avaux's proposal on Lorraine, see AAE CP *Allemagne* 67, fols. 71–74, D'Avaux (own hand minute) to Mazarin, October 8, 1646 (letter sent in *Allemagne* 62, fols. 51–55, and copy in *Allemagne* 78, fols. 98–103) [pub. in *APW* II B 4, 548–551]. D'Avaux persists in this idea, in AAE CP *Allemagne* 67, fols. 102–104, D'Avaux (own hand minute) to Mazarin, October 15, 1646 (letter sent in *Allemagne* 62, fols. 103–105, and copy in *Allemagne* 78, fols. 156–159) [pub. in *APW* II B 4, 604–606]. In this letter, D'Avaux also claims that the Dutch plenipotentiaries have made a similar suggestion, and he himself goes so far as to suggest giving Alsace and Breisach back to the house of Austria in return for their giving the Duke of Lorraine a portion of Silesia!

4. For the Spanish reply, through the Dutch, to the French, see AAE CP *Allemagne* 67, fols. 79–80; *Allemagne* 78, fols. 129–131; *Allemagne* 62, fols.

67–68; or Ass. Nat. *Ms.* 276, fols. 234–235 [pub. in Italian in Siri VIII, 895–897]. Capitulation of Dunkirk: *Gazette* n° 125, October, 17, 1646.

5. AAE CP *Allemagne* 62, fols. 77–85, *Memoire* (Lionne hand and heavily revised) *du Roy a M^{rs} les Plenipot^{res},* October 14, 1646 (Brienne minute in Ass. Nat. *Ms.* 272, fols. 466–474, and copy in AAE CP *Allemagne* 78, fols. 137–143) [pub. for the first time in *APW* II B 4, 574–584]. For the Duke of Lorraine, see Ass. Nat. *Ms.* 272, fols. 475–477, *Memoire a Mrs les Plenipotentiaires sur l'affaire du duc charles.* For Mazarin's dismissal of D'Avaux's proposal, see AAE CP *Allemagne* 62, fols. 163–164, Mazarin (Lionne minute) to D'Avaux, October 26, 1646 (copies in *Allemagne* 78, fols. 240–241, and *Allemagne* 79, fols. 100–101) [pub. in *APW* II B 4, 675–676] and AAE CP *Allemagne* 79, Mazarin (copy) to D'Avaux, November 9, 1646 [pub. in *APW* II B 4, 781–785]. For proof that Mazarin did not seriously expect this offer to be accepted, see the *Mémoire du Roi* of January 17, 1648, cited in Chapter 9, note 1.

6. For the French response, see AAE CP *Allemagne* 67, fols. 93–94, dated October 14, 1646, *Allemagne* 78, fols. 134–135, dated October 14, *Allemagne* 62, fols. 71–74, dated October 13, or Ass. Nat. *Ms.* 276, fols. 236–238, dated October 14. See also NNA SG 8413, fols. 45–48, *Escrit des Plenip^{res+} de France du 14e d'Octobre dont la substance a esté dicté à Monsr de Brun le 15e dudit mois.* For the immediate Spanish reaction see AGS E 2348, Peñaranda (deciphered copy) to Castel Rodrigo, October 15, 1646. For the advice of the Archbishop of Cambrai and of Brun, we must rely on its recapitulation in E 2347, the *consulta* of November 24, 1646.

7. *SRP* XI, 450–456, September 13/23 and 17/27, 1646; and SRA *KK*, Christina (minute) to Johan Oxenstierna and Salvius, September 19/29, 1646 (copy in *RR* 1645–1646 Svensk) [pub. in *APW* II C 2, 470–476].

8. HSAM 4h, n° 2121, fols. 412, 448, and 453–454, Amalia Elizabeth (secretary's minute) to Vultejus, Krosieg, and Müldener, October 5/15, 20/30 and 22/November 1, 1646. See also the Hesse-Cassel demands, cited in note 15 below.

9. On the character and hopes for Balthazar Carlos, see Matias Novoa, *Historia de Felipe IV, Rey de España,* published in *CDI* LXXXVI, 260–261. For his death, see Philip IV to Leganés, October 9, 1646 [reproduced in the *Gazette* n° 145, November 22, 1646]. For the *consulta,* see AGS E 2427, two drafts of the *consulta* of October 13, 1646, the second with Philip IV's comments in the margin.

10. AAE CP *Allemagne* 62, fols. 117–123, *Observations* (Lionne hand) *sur la response des Espagnols,* October 19, 1646 (Brienne minute in Ass. Nat. *Ms.* 272, fols. 484–489, and copy in AAE CP *Allemagne* 78, fols. 185–189) [pub. in Italian in Siri VIII, 910–919; and in the original French in *APW* II B 4,

620–630]. See also *Allemagne* 78, fols. 183–184, Lionne (letter sent) to Servien, October 19, 1646 [pub. in *APW* II B 4, 631–633].

11. See a copy of the Spanish reply in AGS E 2348, *Respuesta de los Plenipot^{os} de su M^d a los puntos q~ el Consejero Brun tomo de Holandeses en 15 de 8bre*, Munster 18 de 8bre (other copies in AHN SNDF 33/1, fols. 180–181 and BNE *Ms.* 18200, fols. 60–61). See also AGS E 2348, Peñaranda (deciphered copy) to Castel Rodrigo, October 18, 1646 [pub. in *CDI* LXXXII, 434–435]. For the French versions, see AAE CP *Allemagne* 78, fols. 200–201; *Allemagne* 67, fols. 127–128; or *Allemagne* 62, fols. 122–125, all dated October 22, 1646 [pub. in Italian in Siri VIII, 919–921]. For Contarini's knowledge of the Dutch interposition, see ASVen *Munster* 4, Contarini (copy to Senate) to Nani, October 23, 1646. For Chigi's knowledge, see BVat *CCL* A I 14, fols. 291–293, Chigi (register) to Pamfili, October 26, 1646 (copy sent in ASVat *Paci* 19, fols. 679–681). For D'Avaux's internal feeling, see his remarkable statement about following the orders of the court in AAE CP *Allemagne* 87, D'Avaux (own hand minute) to Mazarin, January 14, 1647 (letter sent in *Allemagne* 80, fols 244–246, copy in *Allemagne* 98, fols. 99–103) [pub. in *NS* IV, 3–4 and *APW* II B 5/1, 294–297] and D'Avaux's support for the French terms in his letter of March 11, 1647, cited in Chapter 7, note 13. For French cockiness, see Ass. Nat. *Ms.* 276, fols. 257–277, *Response des Penipo^{res} de France au Memoire du Roy du iiii [sic] Octobre 1646 apporté par le Courrier Clinchamp*, October 24, 1646 (duplicate for Mazarin in AAE CP *Allemagne* 62, fols. 134–154; copies in *Allemagne* 67, fols. 142–151, and *Allemagne* 78, fols. 212–222) [pub. in *M&N* III, 281–301; *NS* III, 347–352; and *APW* II B 4, 649–659]. For the French response adding Cadaqués, see AAE CP *Allemagne* 67, fols. 156 and 157–158; Ass. Nat. *Ms.* 276, fols. 281–282; or AAE CP *Allemagne* 62, fols. 155–156, all dated October 25; NNA SG 8413, fols. 48–49, *Escrit des Plenipot^{res} de France delivré le 25e d'Octobre*, and the Spanish translation, slightly different, in AGS E 2348, dated October 27, 1646 [pub. in Italian in Siri VIII, 921–923, dated October 25].

12. AAE CP *Allemagne* 78, fols. 256–269, Servien (own and secretary's hand) to Lionne, October 30, 1646. After writing "qu'on est oblige de f ~ quand il est possible," Servien, feeling that he had been a little too blunt, crossed it out and put in the margin "qu on ne doit pas se priver Volontairem^t quand ilz se presentent" [pub. in *APW* II B 4, 690–704].

13. We have four versions of this draft article: AAE CP *Allemagne* 78, fols. 323–325, dated November 6, 1646, with Servien's own hand remarks on the margin; Ass. Nat. *Ms.* 276, fols. 310–313, is a copy sent to Brienne, dated November 3; AAE CP *Allemagne* 62, fols. 219–222, contains a copy sent to Mazarin, including, in a secretarial hand, Servien's remarks in the margin, dated November 5; and on fols. 188–191, another copy, apparently sent to

Mazarin, without marginal remarks, dated November 3. See also NNA SG 8413, fols. 49–52, *Projet d'Article touchant Casal, delivré par les francois le 3ᵉ de Novembre*. The Dutch gave it to the Spanish on November 5, according to Brun's *mémoire* of November 8, cited in note 15 below. In Spanish tin AGS E 2348, AHN *SNDF* 33/1, fols. 174–176, and BNE *Ms*. 18200, fols. 73–74 [pub. in Italian with Servien's remarks in Siri VIII, 1010–1017].

14. Combine AAE CP *Allemagne* 62, fols. 236–243, *Memoire* (Lionne hand) *du Roy a Mʳˢ les plenipotʳᵉˢ* begun November 2, 1646, but dated November 6 (Brienne minute in Ass. Nat. *Ms*. 272, fols. 534–543, copy in *Allemagne* 78, fols. 299–305) [pub. in *APW* II B 4, 740–749], and AAE CP *Allemagne* 62, fols. 192–200, *Memʳᵉ* (Lionne's hand) *du Roy a Mʳˢ les plenipotʳᵉˢ* begun November 4, 1646, and dated November 5; and fols. 201–202, *Addition* (Lionne's hand) also dated November 5, which contains the cited passage (Brienne minute in Ass. Nat. *Ms*. 272, fols. 523–533; copies in *Allemagne* 78, fols. 274–281, 282–284, and 304–305) [pub. in *APW* II B 4, 707–719]; with AAE CP *Allemagne* 62, fols. 283–290, *Replique* (Lionne minute) *du Roy a la response de Mʳˢ les plenipʳᵉˢ aus observations du 19 octobre,* November 16, 1646 (Brienne minute in Ass. Nat. *Ms*. 272, fols. 561–567; copies in *Allemagne* 67, fols. 296–306, and *Allemagne* 78, fols. 108–111) [pub. in Italian in Siri VIII, 1121–1130, and in the original French in *APW* II B 4, 808–816]. For the capitulations of Piombino and Porto Longone, see the *Gazettes* nᵒˢ 129 and 140, October 23 and November 13.

15. For Peñaranda's hopes and fears, see AGS E 2348, Peñaranda (deciphered copies) to Philip IV, three of November 7 and one of November 8, 1646 [pub in *CDI* LXXXII, 424–433]. For the Spanish reply, see AGS E 2348, *Respuesta de los Sʳᵉˢ Plenipotentʳᵒˢ de Su Mᵈ a los dos papeles de puntos que le Consejero Brun tomo dé Holandeses an 27 de 8ᵇʳᵉ y 5 de 9ᵇʳᵉ Munster a 7 de 9ᵇʳᵉ* (other copies in AHN *SNDF* 33/1 and BNE *Ms*. 18200, fols. 90–92) and NNA SG 8413, fols. 53–55, *Raisons pour Justifier la derniere resolution des Espagnols delivré le 9ᵉ Novembre 1646*. The Dutch turned it into SG 8413, fols. 56–57, *Escrit delivré aux Plenipotʳᵉˢ de France pour server à l'accommodement des differences qui restent à vuider entre les deux Couronnes le 11ᵉ de Novembre*. See it also in AAE CP *Allemagne* 78, fols. 349–351; *Allemagne* 67, fols. 284–285; Ass. Nat. *Ms*. 272, fols. 314–315; and in AAE CP *Allemagne* 62, fols. 252–253. For the French answer, see *Allemagne* 78, fols. 373–374; *Allemagne* 67, fols. 310–311; Ass. Nat. *Ms*. 276, fols. 363–364; and AAE CP *Allemagne* 62, fols. 227–228. For the Swedish and Hessian replies, see SRA *DG* 8, fols. 858–859, *Postulata in puncto satisfactionis Sveciae,* November 7/17, 1646 (copy in HHSA RK *FrA* 52a, pt. 4, fols. 119–120; *FrA* 92 XI, nᵒ 1523, fols. 65–55; *FrA* 96 V; AV TA 109, fols. 446–447; OAT 20f, 2685–2687; Giessen 200, 329–330; AAE CP Allemagne 67, fols. 314–315 and 316; Ass. Nat. *Ms*.

276, fols. 358–359; and in Spanish in AGS E 2350) [pub. in Italian. in Siri VIII, 1083–1085, dated November 28, and in the original Latin in Meiern III, 754 755] and HSAM 4h, n° 2137, fols. 29–30, *Praetensio Satisfactionis Serenissima Domus Hasso-Castellanae*, November 7/17, 1646 (copy on fols. 201–212; SRA DG 8, fols. 860–861; HHSA RK FrA 52a, pt. 4, fols. 107–108; FrA 92 XI, n° 1524, fols. 67–68; FrA 96 V; AV TA 109 fol. 448; OAT 20f, 2689–2691; AN K 1335, n°s 99 and 98; and in Spanish in AGS E 2350) [pub. in the original Latin in Meiern III, 755–756]. See also SRA DG 8, fols. 856–857, Johan Oxenstierna and Salvius (letter sent) to Christina, November 9/19, 1646 [pub. in APW II C 3, 52–54]. For the new Swedish instructions, see SRP XI, 501–504, November 6/16, 1646, and SRA RR 1645–1646 Svensk, Christina (minute) to Johan Oxenstierna and Salvius, November 7/17, 1646 [pub. in APW II C 3, 44–49]. For the impasse in the Empire, see Turenne I, 85–101.

16. AAE CP *Allemagne* 78, fols. 419–424, Servien (secretary's and own hand minute) to Mazarin, November 24, 1646 [pub. in APW II B 5/1, 25–33]. For Servien's announcement of his trip to The Hague, see his letter to Lionne of December 15, cited in the following note.

17. Ass. Nat. Ms. 276, fols. 380–388, *Memoire des Plenipotentiaires de France*, December 3, 1646 (duplicate for Mazarin in AAE CP *Allemagne* 80, fols. 15–20, and copy in *Allemagne* 78, fols. 459–467) [pub. in M&N IV, 3–12; NS III, 380–382; and APW II B 5/1, 66–74]. See also AAE CP *Allemagne* 78, fols. 476–481, Servien (own hand minute) to Lionne, December 4, 1646 [pub. in APW II B 5/1, 79–85]. For the return of the Dutch and the Servien-Brun encounter, see AGS E 2350, Peñaranda (deciphered copy to court) to Castel Rodrigo, December 10, 1646, and his second letter (deciphered copy) to Philip IV, December 17, 1646; as well as AAE CP *Allemagne* 78, fols. 518–534, Servien (own hand minute) to Lionne, December 11, 1646 [pub. in APW II B 5/1, 108–130]. For more abuse on D'Avaux, see AAE CP *Allemagne* 80, fols. 550–551 and 548–549, Servien (own hand minute) to Lionne, December 15, 1646, which also announces his trip to The Hague [pub. in APW II B 5/1, 143–146]. See *Allemagne* 80, fols. 56–57 for two articles of the treaty composed by Servien [the second pub. in Italian in Siri VIII, 1168]. For the Spanish response, see NNA SG 8413, fols. 60–61, *Moyens d'accommodement entre la France et l'Espagne comm ilz sont proposez et delivrez par escrit à Messrs les Plenipot^res de France le 9e et aussi envoyez à ceux d'Espagne le 10e Decembre 1646* (copies in AAE CP *Allemagne* 68, fols. 6–7, and 10–11; *Allemagne* 78, fols. 498–499; Ass. Nat. Ms. 276, fols. 390–391; and AAE CP *Allemagne* 80, fols. 41–42, all dated December 9, 1646; and *Allemagne* 89, fols. 473–474, undated) [pub. in Italian in Siri VIII, 1169–1171]. For the French reply, see AAE CP *Allemagne* 68, fols. 8–9

and 12–13; *Allemagne* 78, fols. 500–501; Ass. Nat. *Ms.* 276, fols. 392–393; and AAE CP *Allemagne* 80, fols. 67–68, also dated December 9, 1646; as well as NNA SG 8413, fols. 61–62, dated December 19 [pub. in Italian in Siri VIII, 1171–1172, dated December 25]. For the logic behind the inclusion of Charlemont, see Ass. Nat. *Ms.* 276, fols. 447–449, *Memoire* (fragment of letter sent) *des Plenipotentiaires de France,* December 31, 1646 (complete copy in AAE CP *Allemagne* 68, fols. 162–166; complete duplicate for Servien in *Allemagne* 78, fols. 658–665; other complete copy on fols. 555–570) [pub. in *M&N* IV, 40–49; *NS* III, 391–393; and *APW* II B 5/1, 203–211]. For Servien's role in the additional demand, see his letter to Mazarin of February 12, 1647, cited in Chapter 7, note 8.

18. AAE CP *Espagne* 26, fols. 361–362, *Relacion Verdadera del infelis sucesso de Lerida,* dated November 27, 1646. *Gazette* n° 155, December 13, 1646.

19. AAE CP *Allemagne* 80, fols. 36–38, *Mem^re* (Lionne minute) *du Roy a M^rs les Plenipot^res,* December 9 1646 (Brienne minute in Ass. Nat. *Ms.* 272, fols. 606–609; copy in AAE CP *Allemagne* 78, fols. 515–517, dated December 11, 1646 [pub. in *APW* II B 5/1, 95–98]. See also *Allemagne* 80, fol. 53, Mazarin (secretary's hand minute) *Addition a la lre de M. de Longueville du 10^e De^bre 1646* (copy in *Allemagne* 78, fols. 485–486) [extract pub. in *LM* II, 340–341, and in its entirety in *APW* II B 5/1, 94–95].

20. On the first reactions of the plenipotentiaries, see Ass. Nat. *Ms.* 276, fols. 399–407, *Memoire des Plenip^res de France en response aux Memoires du 29 et 30 No^bre et 7 Decemb~,* December 17, 1646 (duplicate for Mazarin in AAE CP *Allemagne* 80, fols. 81–88; copies in *Allemagne* 68, fols. 128–132, and *Allemagne* 78, fols. 556–559) [pub. in *M&N* IV, 20–29; *NS* III, 386–388; and *APW* II B 5/1, 148–155]. See copies of of the "article de la retention des conquestes" in Ass. Nat. *Ms.* 276, fols. 416–419, and AAE CP *Allemagne* 80, fols. 126–128, dated December 20, 1646 as well as the copy in NNA SG 8413, fols. 62–65, *"delivrée par Les Ambass^rs de France le 19 Decembre 1646,"* in Spanish in AHN *SNDF* 33/1, fols. 41–44 and BNE *Ms.* 18200, fols 147–149, [pub. in Italian in Siri VIII, 1241–1244, dated December 24]. See also Ass. Nat. *Ms.* 276, fols. 409–413, *Memoire des Plenipo^res de France qui respond aux Mem^res du Roy des ix et xiii Decemb~,* December 24, 1646 (duplicate for Mazarin in AAE CP *Allemagne* 80, fols. 120–123; copies in *Allemagne* 68, fols. 149–152, and *Allemagne* 78, fols. 612–616) [pub. in *M&N* IV, 32–37; *NS* III, 389–390; and *APW* II B 5/1, 179–183]. See also BNE *Ms.* 18200, fols. 145–146. Peñaranda to Philip IV, December 20, 1646, which enclosed the new French demands in a state of shock and asked what to do about Porto Longone and Piombino. For the new Swedish pressures, see the letter of Salvius to D'Avaux of December 16/26, 1646, published in Meiern IV, 239, and *APW* II C 3, 153–154.

21. For the new Dutch demands, see AGS E 2350, *Proposiciones nuevas q~ Los Plenipot^os de Olanda presentaron a los de Su Ma^d a 13 de x^e demas de otros articulos que este dia tambien dieron pretendiendo mudar y agregarlos en el tratado principal de paz en lugar de tregua* [pub. in *CDI* LXXXII, 448–449]. For the Spanish answer to the French, which was written in French, see NNA SG 8413, fols. 65–69, *Communiqué aux francois le 28e Decembre 1646* (copies in AAE CP *Allemagne* 78, fols. 647–654, and in Spanish in AGS E 2350. This Spanish answer was dated December 23, according to the *Reponces de l'Espagne,* cited in note 27 below.

22. AAE CP *Allemagne* 78, fols. 621–625 and 627–629, Servien (secretary's and own hand minute) to Lionne, December 24, 1646, and fols. 630–634, the *Projet d'instruction.* On fols. 626–627, crammed inside this minute, there are in Servien's hand some articles which he had drafted for the projected treaty, and, in his letter to Mazarin of January 21, 1647 cited in Chapter 7, note 3, Servien himself talks of "un projet de tout le traitté que j'avois dressé et dont nous demeurasmes d'accord a Munster avant mon depart." See also the mention of the plenipotentiaries working together on the articles in Longueville to Brienne of March 11, 1647, cited in Chapter 7, note 11, and in Longueville's *Response* of March 25, cited in Chapter 7, note 15.

23. AAE CP *Allemagne* 80, fols. 107–110, Mazarin (Lionne minute) to Servien (letter sent in *Allemagne* 78, fols. 586–589) [calendared in *LM* II, 835, and pub. in its entirety in *APW* II B 5/1, 167–172].

24. ASVen *Francia* 105, n° 439 4^a, Nani (letter sent) to Senate, January 1, 1647 (transcript in BNF *Ms. It.* 1828, fols. 177–178) as well as the *Gazettes* n°s 162 and 163, December 29 and 31, 1646.

25. See Frederick William's letter to his plenipotentiaries at Münster and his response to Georg von Plettenberg, Imperial envoy, both of December 23, 1646, published in Meiern III, 779–792 (in Spanish in E 2350). See also AAE CP *Allemagne* 68, fols. 168–170, D'Avaux (own hand minute) to Mazarin, December 31, 1646 (letter sent in *Allemagne* 80, fols. 164–167, and copy in *Allemagne* 78, fols. 678–682) [pub. in *APW* II B 5/1, 219–223].

26. See AGS E 2350, Le Roy's instructions, dated December 28, 1646, and Le Roy (deciphered copy) to Castel Rodrigo, January 1, 1647, which announces his arrival and preparations to have his writing translated from French into Flemish. For the plans to send Brun to The Hague, see in the same E 2350 *Copia de la Instruccion para el Consejero Brun,* January 6, 1647 [pub. in *CDI* LXXXII, 493–498] and Peñaranda (deciphered copy) to Castel Rodrigo, January 7, 1647 [pub. in *CDI* LXXXIII, 3–5]. For Le Roy's letter to the States General and his *Beschendelich ende vaarachtig verhael van't geene gepaseert is tot den derden dach der Maent van December too jnde handelinge van Frede tuschen de Heeren plenipot^en van Spagnen ende van Vanckryck*

namentes tzedert dat die dat die van de Heeren Staten Generael van de Vereenichde Nederlanden sich tussen beyden gebruycht hebben . . . lectum 9ᵉⁿ January 1647, see NNA SG 8413, fols. 1–37. See also AAE CP *Allemagne* 80, fols. 427–453, titled *"Pertinent et Veritable recit de ce qui s est passé iusques au troisiesme Decembre en la negotiation de la Paix entre Messieurs les Plenipotens d Espagne et ceux de france, Scavoir depuis la mediation des Plenipots de Messrs les Estats Generaux des Provinces Unies."* On the top of the page is written "Janvier 1647" and, in an other hand: "Escrit de Philippe Le Roy." On fol. 441 in Lionne's hand, we have "Ecrit de Philippe Le Roy pñté a Mrs les Estat [page cuts]. On fol. 499 we have Le Roy's dedicatory letter to the States-General, also dated "Janᵉʳ 1647." There is also a copy in AN *K* 1335, nº 3, and a Spanish translation of it in AGS *E* 2350. AAE CP *Hollande* 43, fols. 57–94, contains French and Dutch versions of Le Roy's dedication and another Dutch version of his whole writing, *Lectum 9ᵘᵐ January 1647.* There is another Dutch version in *Allemagne* 87, fols. 48–73, dated "9 Januari" [found in Knuttel: 5428 and 5429, and pub. in Aitzema *VNVH* II, 203–245. Two other French versions are published in *NS* III, 461–466, and IV, 391–401]. Brun mentions the passport in his letter to the States General of January 31. See a copy of Le Roy's letter to the States General in *Allemagne* 80, fol. 299, dated January 1647. For his account of the delivery, see AGS *E* 2350, Le Roy (deciphered copy) to Castel Rodrigo, January 8, 1647.

27. NNA SG *VL* 12588.47 I, *Memoire van't geene in verscheyden conferentien gepasseert is, tusschen de Plenipotᵉⁿ van der Coninck van Spagnien ende die van de Staten Generaal raeckende het different op het stuck van de Religie inde Meyerie van 's Hertogenbosch* (copy in SG R 4856). For Pauw's commentary and the Spanish reply, see NNA SG 8413, fols. 69–71 and 71–73, *Demandes de la France pour la paix . .* , *Communiqué aux Francois le 1ᵉʳ de Janvier apres midi, et aux Espagnols en a esté fait rapport le 1ᵉʳ de Janvier apres midi 1647* and *Reponces de l'Espagne sur les demandes de La France . . . Communiqué aux Francois le 1ᵉʳ Janvier apres midi 1647 et aux Espagnols aussi* (copies in AAE CP *Allemagne* 87, fols. 76–78 and 79–80, which state: "envoye avec depeche du 10 Janvier 1647," although they were actually sent with the letter of January 13 cited in this note; other copies in Ass. Nat. *Ms.* 277, fols. 36–39 and 40–42, and AAE CP *Allemagne* 80, fols. 228–230 and 231–233) [pub. in Italian in Siri IX, 54–58]. See also AAE CP *Allemagne* 98, fols. 34–39, Longueville and D'Avaux (letter sent) to Servien, January 4, 1647 [pub. in *APW* II B 5/1, 228–234]. See copies of the first French protest, dated January 7, 1647, in AAE CP *Allemagne* 87, fols. 17–19, 21–22, 26–29, and 33–37; Ass. Nat. *Ms.* 277, fols. 30–33; AAE CP *Allemagne* 80, fols. 178–181; BI *Ms. Godefroy* 22, fols. 266–267; AN K 1336, nº

36, NNA SG R 4856 [pub. in Aitzema *VNVH* II, 190–195, in Italian in Siri IX, 61–65, and in the original French in *APW* II B 5/1, 285–288]. See also AAE CP *Allemagne* 80, fols. 174–175, Longueville (letter sent) to Mazarin, January 7, 1647 (copy in *Allemagne* 98, fols. 44–45), Ass. Nat. *Ms.* 277, fols. 7–9, D'Avaux and Longueville (letter sent) to Brienne, January 7, 1647 (duplicate for Mazarin in AAE CP *Allemagne* 80, fols. 176–177, copy for Servien in *Allemagne* 98, fols. 46–47). See copies of the second French protest, dated January 8, 1647, in AAE CP *Allemagne* 87, fols. 23–24, 31–33, and 38–39; Ass. Nat. *Ms.* 277, fols. 28–29; AAE CP *Allemagne* 80, fols. 182–183; BI *Ms. Godefroy* 22, fol. 268; and AN K 1336, n° 36 [pub. in Aitzema *VNVH* II, 195–196; in Italian in Siri IX, 68–69; and in the original French in *APW* II B 5/1, 288–289]. See copies of the articles in French in AAE CP *Hollande* 43, fols. 10–23, 24–37, and 43–54, and in *Espagne* 28, fols. 5–14. There is a copy in AGS E 2350 in Spanish titled *Articulos concertados provisionalmente a 15 de Deciembre 1646 entre los Embax^res extraordinarios y Plenipot^rios de España de Una parte y los embajadores estra^os y Plenipot^rios de los Estados generales de las Provincias Unidas del Pays Vajo de la otra parte para inserter en el tratado q~ Se hiciere en Munster* (in 74 articles) *a 8 de henero* 1647, showing signatures by all the plenipotentiaries on both sides except for Nederhorst. Peñaranda's letters to Castel Rodrigo and Philip IV between January 7 and 9, 1647, are lost, but we have their summary in AGS E 2350, the *consulta* of Leganés, Villahermosa, and Melo of February 7, 1647. See also AAE CP *Allemagne* 98, fols. 47–50, 51–56, and 57–61, Longueville and D'Avaux (letters sent) to Servien, January 8, 9, and 10, 1647 [pub. in *APW* II B 5/1, 235–249]; NNA SG *VL* 12588.47 I, Dutch plenipotentiaries to States General, December 28, 1646, and Gendt, Matenesse, Pauw, Knuyt, Donia, Ripperda, and Clant (all but Nederhorst) to States General, January 10, 1647 (copies in SG R 4856; fragment of the second in French in AAE CP *Allemagne* 80, fol. 188, and Ass. Nat. *Ms.* 277, fol. 51). Ass. Nat. *Ms.* 277, fols. 9–27, *Mémoire des Plenipo^res* (Longueville and D'Avaux) *De France,* January 13, 1647 (duplicate for Mazarin in AAE CP *Allemagne* 80, fols. 208–225, duplicate for Servien in *Allemagne* 98, fols. 88–90, and other copy in *Allemagne* 98, fols. 82–87 [pub. in *NS* IV, 68–73, dated January 3, and in part in *APW* II B 5/1, 280–285]. AAE CP *Allemagne* 80, fols. 205–206, Longueville (letter sent) to Mazarin, January 12–13, 1647 (copy in *Allemagne* 98, fols. 91–92) [pub. in *APW* II B 5/1, 278–279]. The articles were quickly published as *Poincten der Artijckulen, Ter Vergaderighe van de . . . Staten Generael Der Vereenichde Nederlanden gearresteert, Waer na De Heeren Plenipotentiarisen, ende Extraordinarij Ambassadeurs van desen Staet In het Tractaet van Vreden tot Mvnster met die van den*

Coninck van Spanien hebben te verhandelen (Dortrecht, 1647) [found in Knuttel: 5430 and 5430a–5432. See also Knuttel: 5433–5436. They are pub. in Italian in Siri IX, 1221–1236, dated December 27].

7. Playing the Blame Game

1. AAE CP *Allemagne* 80, fols. 198–203, Mazarin (Lionne minute) to Longueville and D'Avaux, January 11, 1647 (duplicate for Servien in *Allemagne* 98, fols. 70–75, and copy in *Allemagne* 90, fols. 324–334) [pub. in LM II, 345–355, and APW II B 5/1, 260–269]. In Spanish in BNE *Ms.* 1026, fols. 38–42 [pub. in *CDI* LXXXIII, 8–16].

2. See *Mémoire des Plenipo^res de France* of January 13, 1647, cited in Chapter 6, note 27. See also Ass. Nat. *Ms.* 277, fols. 75–86, Longueville's *Response* (letter sent) *au Mem^re du Roy du xi Janvier 1647,* January 21, 1647 (duplicate for Mazarin in AAE CP *Allemagne* 80, fols. 303–311, extract to D'Avaux in *Allemagne* 87, fols. 144–149; extract to Servien in *Allemagne* 98, fols. 142–146; and full copy in *Allemagne* 98, fols. 133–138) [pub. in APW II B 5/1, 346–357]. In Spanish in BNE *Ms.* 1026, fols. 48–55 [pub. in *CDI* LXXXIII, 50–57]. For the French project of the treaty with Spain, see AN *K* 1336, n° 44, in Doulceur's hand, titled *Le Proiect pour le Traicté de Paix entre les Rois de France et d'Espagne Delivré de la part des Plenipotentiaires de France a Munster l'an 1647* ~~au Mois de Janvier~~ (crossed out) *le 21 Febvrier* (correction in Godefroy's hand) in fifty-nine articles plus two additions, NNA SG 8413, fols. 86–110, "R^a 25° Januarij 1647," SRA *DG* 10, fols. 1273–1286; BVat CCL Q III 57, fols. 29–44.and 50–60, with fifty-nine articles plus secret articles; and ASVat *Paci* 23, fols. 92–111, not numbered plus additions and secret articles. See also Ass. Nat. *Ms.* 277, fols. 124–129, Longueville's *Response* (letter sent) *au Mem^re du Roy du xv Janvier,* 1647, fols. 116–122, Longueville (letter sent) to Brienne; and AAE CP *Allemagne* 80, fol. 407, Longueville (letter sent) to Mazarin, all of January 28, 1647 (duplicate of the first and second for Mazarin in AAE CP *Allemagne* 80, fols. 383–386 and 387–391; and copies of all three for Servien in *Allemagne* 98, fols. 192–196, 197–201, and 217–218, dated January 29) [The first and the third are pub. in APW II B 5/1, 434–440.]. The first and second are in Spanish in *Ms.* 1026, fols. 97–100 and 93–96 [pub. in *CDI* LXXXIII, 96–99 and 91–94]. It would appear, however, from Ass. Nat. *Ms.* 277, fol. 173–175 (copy in AAE CP *Allemagne* 87, fols. 250–251, titled *Articles pour les part^ers donne aux Amb^rs des Estats*) and *Allemagne* 87, fols. 252–253, *Articles changez et ajoutez au projet du traité avec l'Espagne,* both sent with Longueville's letter to the court of February 5, as if at least some of the additional articles were delivered between

January 28 and February 5 [pub. in *Traicté Et Articles De Paix Entre les Couronnes de France & D'Espagne, exhibez à Munster par Monseigneur le Duc de Longueville & Messieurs les Comtes D'Avaux et Servient, Ambassadeurs & Plenipotentiaires du Roy Tres-Chrestien ès années 1646 & 1647* (Paris, 1650). Moreau: 3799, without additions, which seems, however, to precede BNF Ms. Fr. 10643, *Traité de Paix exhibé par Monsieur le Duc de Longueville pour la France,* an undated manuscript that contains the additions and refers to the published version, while Articles 41 and 42 are pub. in *NS* IV, 335–337]. See also Longueville's justifications in AAE CP *Allemagne* 80, fols. 262–263, Longueville (letter sent) to Servien, February 5, 1647 [pub. in *APW* II B 5/1, 516–519]. See NNA SG *R* 4857 for the entire treaty in French, sent in by Pauw on March 12; and AGS *E* 2429 for the first twenty articles in Spanish. For the date of transmission to the Spanish, see AGS *E* 2350; the *consulta* of May 25, 1647; and Longueville's *mémoire* to the court of February 11, cited in note 6 below.

3. For Servien's arrival, see AAE CP *Hollande* 39, fol. 269, Brasset (duplicate for Mazarin) to Brienne, January 7, 1647. For Servien's harangue see *Hollande* 40, fols. 22–32, or the copies in *Hollande* 43, fols. 95–102, 103–110, and 111–116 (answer on fols. 117–120); *Allemagne* 87, fols. 92–103; or the copy sent to Brienne in Ass. Nat. *Ms.* 277, fols. 60–70. See it also in NNA SG *R* 4856 [pub. as *Harangue de Mons. le Comte de La Roche Servient, conseill. du roi en ses conseils et son ambass. extraord. pour la paix générale, faite à La Haye en l'assemblée de MM. les Etats Généraux* (Paris, 1647), Moreau: 1556, Knuttel: 5438, 5439. See also Knuttel: 5440–5442, 5442a, and 5443–5444, and *NS* IV, 210–215]. For the proposed treaty, see AAE CP *Hollande* 40, fols. 73–77 (minute with Servien corrections) "Le Roy et la Reyne Regente. . ." (copy to Mazarin in *Allemagne* 80, fols. 287–292, copy to Brienne in Ass. Nat. *Ms.* 277, fols. 108–111, copy in Doulceur's hand with Godefroy corrections in AN *K* 1336, n° 44, and other copy in NNA SG *R* 4855) [pub. in Aitzema *VNVH* II, 249–254, and in Latin in Londorp VI, 146–148]. For Servien's developing impressions, see AAE CP *Hollande* 40, fol. 53, Servien (minute with Servien corrections) to Mazarin, January 15, 1647; and *Hollande* 40, fols. 54–57, Servien (minute with Servien corrections) to Brienne, January 15, 1647 (letter sent in Ass. Nat. *Ms.* 277, fols. 44–48; other copies in AAE CP *Hollande* 43, fols. 123–125 and 128–131) [pub. in *APW* II B 5/1, 307–311]. See also AAE CP *Allemagne* 87, fols. 128–135, Servien (copy) to Longueville and D'Avaux, January 17, 1647 (copy for Mazarin in *Allemagne* 80, fols. 259–266; copy for Brienne in Ass. Nat. *Ms.* 277 fols. 97–101) [pub. in *APW* II B 5/1, 313–322]; AAE CP *Hollande* 43, fols. 137–142, Servien (letter sent) to Longueville and D'Avaux, January 20, 1647 (duplicate for Mazarin in *Allemagne* 80, fols. 293–298;

and duplicate for Brienne in Ass. Nat. *Ms.* 277, fols. 102–107) [pub. in *APW* II B 5/1 341–346]; AAE CP *Hollande* 40, fols. 80–86, Servien (own hand minute) to Mazarin January 21, 1647 (letter sent in *Allemagne* 80, fols. 331–348, with additions) [pub. in part in *APW* II B 5/1, 375–388]; AAE CP *Hollande* 40, fols. 87–90, Servien (secretary's minute) to Brienne, January 21, 1647 (letter sent in Ass. Nat. *Ms.* 277, fols. 52–55; duplicate for Mazarin in *Allemagne* 80, fols. 320–327) [pub. in *APW* II B 5/1, 367–373].

4. AAE CP *Allemagne* 87, fols. 116–118 and 152–161, *Memore* (D'Avaux own hand minute) *de l'Amb^r de france arrivé a Osnabrug le 16 de Janvier 1647,* January 21, 1647 (letter sent in Ass. Nat. *Ms.* 277, fols. 87–94; duplicate for Mazarin in AAE CP *Allemagne* 80, fols. 252–257; and copy in *Allemagne* 98, fols. 148–160) [pub. in *NS* IV, 6–9, and *APW* II B 5/1, 357–358]. SRA *DG* 9, fols. 34–39, Johan Oxenstierna and Salvius (letter sent) to Christina, January 11/21, 1647 [pub. in *APW* II C 3, 212–219]. For the elector's latest orders, see *Electoris Brandenburgici Legatorum Replicato ad Recompesationem a Caesareanis oblatam, exib. d. 6 Febr. 1647,* February 6/16, 1647 (copy in SRA *DG* 9, fols. 188–189) [pub. in Meiern IV, 293–294] as well as the Brandenburg proposals of January [9/19] 1647 (in Spanish in AGS *E* 2350) [pub. in Meiern IV, 240–242 and 225–227], the second slightly amending the first. We get D'Avaux's threat only from the Wittgenstein-Fromhold-Wesenbeck Relation, January 13/23, 1647, published in *U&A* III, 494–510].

5. For Mazarin's mellowing, see AAE CP *Allemagne* 80, fols. 278–279 and 281–284, Mazarin (two Lionne minutes) to Servien, January 18, 1647 (Brienne minutes in Ass. Nat. *Ms.* 273, fols. 36–40, letters sent in AAE CP *Hollande* 40, fols. 59–66) [pub. in *LM* II, 359—369, and *APW* II B 5/1, 328–338]. For his change of tone, see AAE CP *Allemagne* 80, fols. 363–372, *Memoire* (Lionne minute) *du Roy a M^{rs} les Plenipot^{res},* January 25, 1647 (Brienne minute in Ass. Nat. *Ms.* 273, fols. 47–56); duplicate for Servien in AAE CP *Allemagne* 98, fols. 175–184, D'Avaux copies in *Allemagne* 87, fols. 180–191 and 193–204) [pub. in *APW* II B 5/1, 404–419]. In Spanish in BNE *Ms.* 1026, fols. 73–86 [pub. in *CDI* LXXXIII, 76–91]. See also AAE CP *Allemagne* 80, fols. 349–357, Mazarin (Lionne and other secretary's minute) to Servien, January 25, 1647 (Brienne minute in Ass. Nat. *Ms.* 273, fols. 57–64; letter sent in AAE CP *Hollande* 40, fols. 91–98) [pub. in *LM* II, 372–82, and *APW* II B 5/1, 419–431]. For his return to form, see AAE CP *Hollande* 43, fols. 156–158 and 147–150, Mazarin (Lionne minutes) to Servien, February 1, 1647 (Brienne's minute of the first in Ass. Nat. *Ms.* 273, fols. 82–84; letters sent in AAE CP *Hollande* 40, fols. 123–126 and 127–130) [pub. in *APW* II B 5/1, 474–484] as well as AAE CP *Hollande* 40, fol. 139, Lionne (letter sent) to Servien, February 1, 1647 [pub. in *APW* II B 5/1, 485–486]; and AAE CP *Allemagne* 81, fol. 20, Mazarin (Lionne

minute) to D'Avaux, February 1, 1647 [calendared in *LM* II, 852–853, and pub. in its entirety in *APW* II B 5/1, 472–474].

6. AGS E 2350, *consulta* of January 13, 1647 [pub. in *CDI* LXXXIII, 31–36]. See also E 2350, the *consulta* of Leganés, Villahermosa, and Melo of February 7, 1647 [pub.in *CDI* LXXXIII, 118–124]. Brun to the States General, January 31, 1647 [pub. in *NS* IV, 258–249]; Brun to States of Holland, February 3, 1647, copies in NNA SG R 4856; AAE CP *Hollande* 43, fols. 196–197 and 198–203, dated February 4, 1647 [pub. in Italian in Siri IX, 266–267]; Brun to States General, February 11, 1647, copies in NNA SG *VL* 12588.47 I; Ass. Nat. *Ms.* 277, fols. 352–356; AAE CP *Hollande* 43, fols. 250–255 and 256–260; Ass. Nat. *Ms.* 273, fols. 100–105; BI *Ms. Godefroy* 22, fols. 331–333 [in Dutch in Knuttel: 5448–5449, 5450, 5451, 5478 (17–20), and 5479 (82–83); in Italian in Siri IX, 267–273; and in French in *NS* IV, 222–223 and 259–261].

7. For Nederhorst's justification, see NNA SG *R* 4856, January 22, 1647. See also NNA SG *VL* 12588.47 I, the *"Sommier verhael"* signed by Gendt, Matenesse, Pauw, Knuyt, Donia, Ripperda, and Clant, dated February 3, 1647, without justificatory pieces (copy in SG *R* 4856; in French in Ass. Nat. *Ms.* 277, fols. 245–248; AAE CP *Allemagne* 81, fols. 23–30; and *Allemagne* 87, fols. 232–238; in Spanish in AGS E 2350) [pub. in Italian in Siri IX, 258–265]. Ass. Nat. *Ms.* 277, fols. 165–170 and 190–203, *Response au Memoire du Roy du xxv Janvier 1647* and *Memoire du Duc de Longueville,* February 4 and 11, 1647 (duplicates for Mazarin in AAE CP *Allemagne* 81, fols. 34–39 and 65–74; copies in *Allemagne* 98, fols. 244–247 and 288–289) [pub. in *NS* IV, 75–80, and *APW* II B 5/1, 486–490 and 539–548]. The second only is in Spanish in BNE *Ms.* 1026, fols. 121–128 [pub. in *CDI* LXXXIII, 127–135]. See also AAE CP *Allemagne* 81, fols. 75–77, *Notes sur l'escrit dellivré par messieurs les ambassadeurs des Provinces unies. . .* (copies in *Allemagne* 87, fols. 257–259, dated February 6, 1647, and in NNA SG 8413, fols. 76–77). Ass. Nat. *Ms.* 277, fols. 280–290, *Response au Memoire du Roy du xv Fevrier 1647,* February 25, 1647 (duplicate for Mazarin in AAE CP *Allemagne* 81, fols. 178–184; copies in *Allemagne* 87, fols. 444–448, and *Allemagne* 98, fols. 409–416) [pub. in *APW* II B 5/1, 692–698]; in Spanish in BNE Ms. 1026, fols. 147–153 [pub. in *CDI* LXXXIII, 151–157]. In keeping with Mazarin's project of October 14, 1646, Longueville also composed Ass. Nat. *Ms.* 277, fols. 291–292, *Article pour le duc Charles de Lorraine* (duplicate for Mazarin in AAE CP *Allemagne* 81, fols. 185–186; other copies in *Allemagne* 87, fols. 450–451 and *Allemagne* 98, fols. 416–418) although in his *Reponse,* Longueville indicates that he had not yet transmitted the article. See also ASVen *Munster* 7, Contarini (copy to Senate) to Nani, February 26, 1647; BVat CCL A I 15, fols. 92–95, Chigi (register) to Panzirolo, March 1, 1647;

and AGS *E* 2350, Peñaranda (five deciphered copies) to Philip IV, January 28, 1647. For the Spanish proposal, see NNA SG 8413, fols. 121–127 and 128–137, the first in French, the second in Spanish titled *Instrumento o modelo del Tratado de paz entre las dos Coronas de España y Francia propuesto por los Plenipotenciarios de Su Mag^d Catholica a 24 de febrero 1647* (copy in Ass. Nat. *Ms.* 277, fols. 338–344, 346, and 345, two copies in AAE CP *Allemagne* 87, fols. 408–419 and 420–423; copy in French in AAE CP *Allemagne* 81, fols. 158–166; fragments in Spanish with French marginalia in BI *Ms. Godefroy* 22, fols. 341–346, 349, and 351; AN K 1336, n° 45a in Italian, n° 45b in Spanish, and n° 45c in French, all in Doulceur's hand with Godefroy commentary; BVat CCL Q III 57, fols. 62–71 in Spanish; SRA *DG* 10, fols. 1260–1265; in Spanish, and a copy in French sent in by Pauw on March 12 in NNA SG R 4857 [pub. in Spanish and French in *NS* IV, 224–233, and in Italian in Siri IX, 315–325]. For the intercepted correspondence, see AGS E 2250, Peñaranda (copy) to Philip IV, February 10, 1647 [pub. in *CDI* LXXXIII, 127]. It is these letters which I cite in Spanish from BNE *Ms.* 1026. Finally, see Longueville's *Reponse au Memoire du Roy du 22 Fevrier 1647* and his letter to Mazarin of March 1, 1647, cited in note 11 below.

8. See NNA SG R 4856, February 13, 1647, for a description of the reading of the Dutch plenipotentiaries' report along with its justificatory documents, which I have cited in their place from NNA SG 8413. There is a copy in Spanish in AGS *E* 2350. For Servien's negotiation and reactions on the reading, see AAE CP *Allemagne* 98, fols. 214–215, Servien (secretary's and own hand minute) to Longueville and D'Avaux, January 28, 1647 (copy for Mazarin in *Allemagne* 80, fols. 395–402; copy for Brienne in Ass. Nat. *Ms.* 277, fol. 148–151; and other copy in AAE CP *Hollande* 43, fols. 179–185) [pub. in *APW* II B 5/1, 447–453] as well as AAE CP *Hollande* 40, fols. 113–119, Servien (secretary's and own hand minute) to Mazarin, January 29, 1647 (letter sent in *Allemagne* 80, fols. 414–426, and copy to Brienne in Ass. Nat. *Ms.* 277, fols. 142–147) [pub. in *APW* II B 5/1, 455–463], AAE CP *Hollande* 40, fols. 175–184, Servien (own hand minute) to Mazarin, February 12, 1647 (letter sent in *Hollande* 43, fols. 295–311 [pub. in part in *GvP* IV, 186–188, and in its entirety in *APW* II B 5/1, 560–581], AAE CP *Hollande* 43, fols. 317–318, Servien (secretary's and own hand minute) to Longueville and D'Avaux, February 14, 1647 (copy in *Hollande* 43, fols. 319–321) [pub. in *APW* II B 5/1, 582–584]; AAE CP *Hollande* 40, fols. 210–216, Servien (secretary's and own hand minute) to Mazarin, February 19, 1647 (copy in *Hollande* 43, fols. 341–353) [pub. in part in *GvP* IV, 188, and in its entirety in *APW* II B 5/1, 628–636] and AAE CP *Hollande* 40, fols. 217–224, Servien (secretary's and own hand minute) to Brienne, February 19, 1647 (letter sent in Ass. Nat. *Ms.* 277, fols. 234–244, and other copy in

AAE CP *Hollande* 43, fols. 358–370) [pub. in part in GvP IV, 188–191, and in its entirety in *APW* II B 5/1, 620—628]. For Servien's writing to the States-General, see Ass Nat. *Ms.* 277, fols. 355–373, *Response de L amb^eur de france sur quelques poinctz de la lettre escritte par M. Brun l un des Plenipo^res d Esp^ne a M^rs les Estats gñaux des provinces unies des pays bas, et sur quelques endroits de la Relation faicte par M^rs plenip^res de leurs Seig^ries* (copies in AAE CP *Hollande* 40, fols. 279–305; *Hollande* 43, fols. 435–448 and 449–478; and NNA SG VL 12588.47 I). See also AAE CP *Hollande* 40, fols. 356–364, the printed, *"ESCRIPT Donné a Messieurs les Estats Generaux des Provinces Unies des Pays Bas par Monsieur l'Ambassadeur de France Le 4 Mars 1647."* It appears, however, that Servien's secretaries inadvertently skipped a number of paragraphs thus requiring a reprinting [found in Knuttel: 5455 and 5456 in French, 5457 and 5459 in Dutch, which also divide it into numbered articles. In Italian in Siri IX, 421–443, without numbered articles and in French in *NS* IV, 261–270, with numbered articles]. There is also a copy of this speech spanning the end of NNA SG R 4856 and the beginning of 4857. This work was accompanied by AAE CP *Hollande* 40, fols. 343–352, *Lettre d'un gentilhomme français* (copy on fols. 353–364) [found in Knuttel: 5460–5461 and pub. in *NS* IV, 273–275].

9. SRA DG 9, fol. 68, *Suedica Resolutio Ultima & Peremptorialis, in puncto Satisfactionis, ratione Pomerania* (copies in HHSA RK *FrA* 53a, fols. 130–131; *FrA* 92 XI, n ° 1608, fol. 408 and fol. 409; KHA *N A* IV, 1628/56; Giessen 200, 352–353, and Giessen 208, 538–552; Ass. Nat. *Ms.* 277, fol. 134, with French commentary; AAE CP *Allemagne* 80, fol. 458, with French commentary; BNF *Ms. Dupuy* 739, fols. 108–109; and in Spanish in AGS E 2350 [pub. in German in Londorp VI, 36; in Italian in Siri IX, 189–191; in Latin in Meiern IV, 262–263; *Baltische Studien* XIV.2 (1852) 184–185; *PPI* II, 280–281; and Gustav Breucker, *Die Abtretung Vorpommerns an Schweden und die Entschädigung Kurbrandenburgs* (Halle, 1879) 85]. See also AAE CP *Allemagne* 87, fols. 211–212, D'Avaux (own hand minute) to Chanut, January 28, 1647 [pub. in *NS* IV, 11]; the Wittgenstein relation of January 18/28, 1647, published in *U&A* IV, 512–521; and SRA DG 9, fols. 57–66, Johan Oxenstierna and Salvius (letter sent) to Christina, January 25/February 4, 1647 [pub. in *APW* II C 3, 229–244]. For the Swedish-Brandenburg agreement, see SRA *DG* 9, fols. 117–118, February 1/11, 1647; AAE CP *Allemagne* 87, fols. 285–287; Ass. Nat. *Ms.* 277, fols. 274–277; AAE CP *Suède* 11, fols. 19–22, 28–31, and 108–109; BI *Ms. Godefroy* 22, fols. 321–325 and 327–328, some dated February 7; and NNA SG VL 112588.47 II [pub. in Italian in Siri IX, 215–219; in Latin and French in *NS* IV, 218–221; in Latin in Meiern IV, 309–311; in French in Dumont VI, pt. 1, 366–367; and in Latin in Julius von Bohlen, *Die Erwerbung Pommerns durch die Hohenzollern, Zur Erinnerung an die vor funfzig*

Jahren erfolgte Wiedervereinigung des ganzen Pommern unter die Herrschaft seines erlauchten Königshauses (Berlin, 1868) 115–117. There is also a final sligtly amended agreement pub. in Meiern IV, 330–335]. See also AAE CP *Allemagne* 87, fols. 245–248, D'Avaux (own hand minute) to Chanut, February 4–11, 1647, which he also used as a basis for a *Memoire de l Ambassadeur de france qui est a Osnabrug* (copy of letter to Chanut on fols. 295–297 and copy of the *Mémoire* on fols. 291–294; *Mémoire* sent to Brienne in Ass. Nat. Ms. 277, fols. 204–208; to Mazarin in AAE CP *Allemagne* 81, fols. 81–83; and a copy in *Allemagne* 98, fols. 305–310) [both pub. in *NS* IV, 19–21; *Mémoire* pub. in *APW* II B 5/1, 550–555]. For the armistice talks, see AAE CP *Bavière* 2, fol. 13, Turenne instruction for Tracy, January 22, 1647; and SRA *DG* 9, fols. 328–330, Wrangel's instruction for Mortaine, Douglas, and Snoilski, February 10/20, 1647 [pub. in *APW* II C 3, 270–271]. The instruction for Fouquet-Crossy is lacking. For D'Avaux's crisis of conscience, see AAE CP *Allemagne* 87, fols. 328–330, D'Avaux (secretary's minute with D'Avaux's corrections) to Longueville, February 15, 1647. For the Imperial-Swedish agreement, see the protocol of February 17, 1647 in HHSA *FrA* 53a, fols. 385–394; KHA *N A* VI, 1628/21; Giessen 208, 733–739; and Giessen 209, 267–279 [pub. in *APW* II A 5, 524–526], and the agreement itself in HHSA RK *FrA* 96 V; Giessen 208, 805–819, without secret articles; SK *FrA* 5, only secret articles; GSR Rep. N 95, pt. 3, n° 8, only secret articles; SRA *DG* 9, fols. 160–163. February 8/18, 1647 (copy in AAE CP *Allemagne* 87, fols. 341–346; Ass. Nat. Ms. 277, fols. 268–271; AAE CP *Allemagne* 81, fols. 151–155; and *Suède*, fols. 35–36) [pub. in Clas Odhner, *Sveriges deltagande i Westfaliska fredskongressen och grunläggningen af det Svenska väldet i Tyskland* (Stockholm, 1875) 341–353, and *ST* VI, pt. 1, 152–159]. For D'Avaux's adoption of the *dévot* position, see AAE CP *Allemagne* 87, fols. 377–391, D'Avaux (own hand minute) to Chanut and to court, February 22, 1647 (letter sent in Ass. Nat. Ms. 277, fols. 251–267; duplicate for Mazarin in AAE CP *Allemagne* 81, fols. 117–133; and copy in *Allemagne* 98, fols. 368–369) [pub. in *NS* IV, 23–29, and *APW* II B 5/1, 671–601]. The Horace quote is from *Carmina* 3:3:8.

10. See AAE CP *Allemagne* 81, fols. 143–148, *Memoire* (Lionne ninute) *du Roy a M^rs les Plenipot^res*, February 22, 1647 (Brienne minute in Ass. Nat. Ms. 273, fols. 127–134; copy sent in AAE CP *Allemagne* 87, fols. 362–369, and copy to Servien in AAE CP *Allemagne* 98, fols. 348–360) [pub. in *APW* II B 5/1, 648–657]. See also *Allemagne* 91, fols. 187–188, Mazarin (Lionne minute) to Longueville, March 1, 1647 (copy for Servien in *Allemagne* 99, fols. 89–90, dated March 8, other copy on fols. 22–25) [extract pub. in *LM* II, 387–388]; Ass. Nat. Ms. 273, fol. 118, Brienne (minute) to Longueville, March 1, 1647 (copies in AAE CP *Allemagne* 87, fols. 472–473, and *Allemagne* 99, fols. 27–28) [pub. in *APW* II B 5/1, 717–719]. In Spanish in BNE

Ms. 1026, fols. 154–156 [pub. in *CDI* LXXXIII, 157–159]. See, finally, AAE CP *Allemagne* 81, fols. 237–240, *Memoire* (Lionne's hand) *du Roy au S^r d'Avaux,* March 9, 1647 (Brienne minute in Ass. Nat. *Ms.* 273, fols. 151–156; copy sent in AAE CP *Allemagne* 79, fols. 163–171, dated March 8, and duplicate for Servien in *Allemagne* 99, fols. 80–88) [pub. in *APW* II B 5/1, 777–784], and AAE CP *Allemagne* 82, fols. 64–68, *Advis de Mgr le Card^l Sur la Conduite qu il faut tenir avec les Suedois approuvé dans le Con^il le 14e mars et envoyé par ordre de S.M^té a M^r. d'Avaux po~ regler Sa conduite. . . . du 15e Mars 1647* [pub. in *LM* II, 392–399].

11. AAE CP *Allemagne* 81, fols. 201–211, Longueville (duplicate for Mazarin), *Response au Memoire du Roy du 22 fevrier 1647,* March 4, 1647 (copies in *Allemagne* 87, fols. 487–495, and *Allemagne* 99, fols. 35–46) [pub. in *APW* II B 5/1, 732–741]. In Spanish in BNE *Ms.* 1026 fols. 157–165 [pub. in *CDI* LXXXIII, 160–169]. AAE CP *Allemagne* 81, fols. 221–223, Longueville (letter sent) to Mazarin, March 4, 1647 (copy in *Allemagne* 99, fols. 47–51); *Allemagne* 82, fols. 18–24, Longueville (duplicate for Mazarin) to Brienne, March 11, 1647 (copy in *Allemagne* 99, fols. 103–105) [pub. in *NS* IV, 99–100, misdated May 11, 1647, and *APW* II B 5/1, 790–796].

12. ANTT 1342, fols. 26–28, Sousa Coutinho (copy) to John IV, March 15, 1647 [pub. in *Correspondencia Diplomatica de Francisco de Sousa Coutinho durante a sua embaixada em Holanda* (Coimbra and Lisbon, 1920–1955) II, 58–61]; AAE CP *Hollande* 43, fols. 542–545, Servien (duplicate for Mazarin) to Longueville, March 14, 1647 [pub. in *APW* II B 5/1, 824–826]. See also AAE CP *Hollande* 40, fols. 423–427, Servien (minute with Servien corrections) *Responce au memoire du Roy du 8^e Mars 1647,* March 19, 1647 (letter sent in Ass. Nat *Ms.* 277, fols. 377–384, and duplicate for Mazarin in AAE CP *Allemagne* 82, fols. 102–111) [pub. in *APW* II B 5/2, 865–871]. See also AAE CP *Hollande* 40, fols. 419–422, Servien (own and secretary's hand minute) to Mazarin, March 18, 1647 (letter sent in *Hollande* 43, fols. 558–564, dated March 19, 1647) [pub. in part in *GvP* IV, 194–195, and in its entirety in *APW* II B 5/2, 872–883].

13. This interesting and possibly sanguine recollection of French policy in the heyday of Gustavus Adolphus is in AAE CP *Allemagne* 87, fols. 497–502, D'Avaux (secretary's minute) *Memoire de l Amb^r de France qui est a Osnabrug* to court, March 4, 1647 (copy sent to Brienne in Ass. Nat. *Ms.* 277, fols. 330–337; duplicate for Mazarin in AAE CP *Allemagne* 81, fols. 194–200; and copy in *Allemagne* 99, fols. 56–64) [pub. in *NS* IV, 34–36; and *APW* II B 5/1, 741–748]. See also AAE CP *Allemagne* 87, fols. 503–504, D'Avaux (own hand minute) to Mazarin, March 4, 1647 (letter sent in *Allemagne* 81, fols. 214–217, and copy in *Allemagne* 99, fols. 66–68) [pub. in *NS* IV, 36–37, and *APW* II B 5/1, 749–751]. For the Swedish view of the same events, see SRA

DG 9, fols. 259–263, Johan Oxenstierna and Salvius (letter sent) to Christina, February 22, March 4, 1647 [pub. in *APW* II C 3, 297–309]. See also the *Evangelorum Declaratio in puncto Gravaminum Legatis Suecicis d. 27, Febr. Anno 1647 exhibita,* February 27/March 9, 1647 (copies in SRA *DG* 9, fols. 318–320; ASVat *Paci* 23, fols. 230–240; and in German in NNA SG *VL* 12588.47 I and NNA *R* 4857) [pub. in Latin in Meiern IV, 89–99, and in German on 99–109]. For D'Avaux's further impressions, see AAE CP *Allemagne* 87, fols. 525–535, D'Avaux (own hand minute) *Memoire de l'Amb^r de France qui est a Osnabrug,* initially written for Longueville, sent in modified form to the court and shorter form to Chanut, March 11, 1647 (copy sent to the court in Ass. Nat. *Ms.* 277, fols. 389–399; its duplicate for Mazarin in AAE CP *Allemagne* 82, fols. 27–39, copies in *Allemagne* 99, fols. 107–120, and extract in 217–219) [pub. in *NS* IV, 37–41 and 42–44, as well as in *APW* II B 5/1, 801–812]. See also AAE CP *Allemagne* 87, fols. 536–547, D'Avaux (own hand minute) to Brienne, March 11, 1647 (letter sent in Ass. Nat. *Ms.* 277, fols. 405–406) [pub. in *NS* IV, 41–42, and *APW* II B 5/1, 799–800]. For the Swedish views of the same events, see SRA *DG* 9, fols. 308–310, Johan Oxenstierna and Salvius (letter sent) to Christina, March 1/11, 1647 [pub. in *APW* II C 3, 320–325]. For the Franco-Bavarian truce at Ulm, see AAE CP *Bavière* 2, in French on fols. 73–82, 89–97, 112–119, and 83–88; BI *Ms. Godefroy* 22, in Latin on fols. 386–397, with Dulceur's marginal comments, and in French on fols. 398–401; AAE CP *Suède* 11, in Latin on fols. 58–68; and ASVat *Paci* 23, in Latin on fols. 309–314 [pub. in Italian in Siri IX, 958–967; in Latin and French in *NS* IV, 251–258; in Dumont VI, pt. 1, 377–380; and in Latin in Meiern V, 6–12, and in *ST* VI, pt. 1, 82–90]. For the Swedish-Bavarian truce, see SRA *DG* 9, fols. 516–527, in German [pub. in Londorp VI, 186–191; in Dumont VI, pt. 1, 380–384; *ST* VI, pt. 1, 58–76; and in Walter Ziegler, ed., *Altbayern von 1550–1651: Dokumente zur Geschichte von Staat und Gesellschaft in Bayern,* Abt. 1, III, pts. 1–2 (Munich, 1992) 1212–1223]. For Trauttmansdorff's major concessions, including an alternative on Minden, see HHSA RK *FrA* 53a, fols. 82–83, *Declaratio Domonorum Plenipotentiariorum Caesareanorum, exhibita Dominis Legatis Suecisis die 5. Mart. styl. vet. Anno 1647,* March 15, 1647 (copy in SK *FrA* 11, fols. 159–189) [pub. in Meiern IV, 118–128]. For more alarm about the Swedes, see Longueville and D'Avaux's letter to the court of March 25, cited in note 15 below.

14. AAE CP *Allemagne* 82, fols. 118–123, Mazarin (Lionne minute) to Longueville (duplicate for Servien in *Allemagne* 99, fols. 210–214) [pub. in LM II, 402–412].

15. NNA SG 8413, fols. 110–115 and 115–121, *Declaracion o Replica de parte de España sobre los articulos contenidos en el Instrumento para la Paz presentado*

de parte de francia and *Declaration ou replique de la part d'Espagne sur les articles contenus en l'Iinstrument pour la paix presenté par la France* (copies in French in SG R 4857; AAE CP *Allemagne* 87, fols. 596–603; for Mazarin in *Allemagne* 82, fols. 95–99; more copies in French in AN K 1336, n°s 47a and 47b; and partial copies in BI *Ms. Godefroy* 22, fol. 410, and in BNF *Ms. Dupuy* 738, fol. 95) [pub. in Italian in Siri IX, 397–406]. Longueville reply in AAE CP *Allemagne* 87, fols. 604–608, *Pour mettre sur les articles du projet de Messieurs les Plenipotentiaires d'Esp[ne]* (copy for Mazarin in *Allemagne* 82, fols. 134–138; copy in *Allemagne* 99, fols. 233–239, and Trauttmansdorff copy in AV TA 114 n° 78) [pub. In Italian in Siri IX, 388–394]. NNA SG VL 12588.47 I, Pauw (letters sent) to States General, March 19 and 26, 1647 (copies in SG R 4857; copy in French of the first in AAE CP *Allemagne* 82, fols. 100–101, and of the summary in *Munster* 1, fol. 28) [in Italian in Siri IX, 460–462 and 466–467]. ASVen *Munster* 6, Contarini (copy to Senate) to Nani, March 19 and 26, and April 2, 1647; BVat CCL A I 15, fols. 105–108, Chigi (register) to Panzirolo, March 15, 1647 (copy in ASVat *Paci* 23, fols. 202–205), BVat CCL A I 15, fols. 112–119 and 121–123, Chigi (register) to Panzirolo, March 22, 1647 (deciphered copy of the second in ASVat *Paci* 21, fols. 147–151) and BVat CCL A I 15, fols. 124–130, Chigi (register) to Panzirolo, March 29, 1647. AAE CP *Allemagne* 82, fols. 141–157, Longueville's *Response* (duplicate for Mazarin) *au Memoire du Roy du 15 Mars 1647*, March 25, 1647 (copy in *Allemagne* 99, fols. 223–231) [pub. in APW II B 5/2, 912–926]. In Spanish in BNE *Ms.* 1026, fols. 176–186 [pub. in CDI LXXXIII, 177–189]. AAE CP *Allemagne* 82, fols. 214–217, Longueville (duplicate for Mazarin) to Brienne, April 8, 1647 (copy in *Allemagne* 99, fols. 309–311) [pub. in NS IV, 83–85 and APW II B 5/2, 999–1002]. In Spanish in BNE *Ms.* 1026, fols. 216–220 [pub. in CDI LXXXIII, 213–217]. ASVen *Munster* 6, Contarini (copy to Senate) to Nani, April 9, 1647, BVat CCL A I 15, fols. 147–155, 156–157, and 157–159 plus 161–164, three letters of Chigi (register) to Panzirolo, April 12, 1647 (deciphered copies of the second and third in ASVat *Paci* 21, fols. 181–183, 185–187 plus 175–179) and BVat CCL A I 15, fols. 164–169 and 170–172, two letters of Chigi (register) to Panzirolo, April 19, 1647 (deciphered copy of the second in ASVat *Paci* 21, fols. 170–172). AAE CP *Allemagne* 82, fols. 265–273, Longueville *Response* (duplicate for Mazarin) *au Memoire du Roy du 5[me] Avril 1647*, April 15, 1647 (copies in *Allemagne* 88, fols. 98–101 and *Allemagne* 99, fols. 323–348 and 360–366) [pub. in APW II B 5/2, 1057–1063]. In Spanish in BNE *Ms.* 1026, fols. 228–234 [pub. in CDI LXXXIII, 220–221]. See also one copy of the twenty-point project with Longueville's marginal remarks in *Allemagne* 88, fols. 64–71, another for Servien on fols. 72–81, or a third partial copy in BI *Ms. Godefroy* 22, fols. 424–425.

16. NNA SG R 4857 March 21, 1647, *Provinciael advis van Hare Ed. Groot Mo: opt Stuck van Guarantie met Vranckryck* [pub. in Aitzema *VNVH* II, 313–314, in Italian in Siri IX, 465, dated March 30, and in German in Londorp VI, 167], AAE CP *Hollande* 43, fols. 584–589, Servien (duplicate for Mazarin) to Longueville, March 25, 1647 [pub. in *APW* II B 5/2, 927–933], AAE CP *Hollande* 40, fols. 439–445, Servien (secretary's minute) to Brienne, March 26, 1647 (duplicate for Mazarin in *Hollande* 43, fols. 599–612) [pub. in part in GvP IV, 199–202, and in its entirety in *APW* II B 5/2, 933–940].

17. AAE CP *Allemagne* 88, fols. 29–35, D'Avaux *Memoire* (secretary's minute) *de l'Amb^r de france qui est a Osnaburg,* April 8, 1647 (duplicate for Mazarin in *Allemagne* 82, fols. 219–227 and duplicate for Servien in *Allemagne* 99, fols. 298–306) [pub. in *NS* IV, 54–57 and *APW* II B 5/2, 1003–1010]. SRA *DG* 9, fols. 506–508, Johan Oxenstierna and Salvius (letter sent) to Christina, March 29/April 8, 1647 [pub. in *APW* II C 3, fols. 368–372]. AAE CP *Allemagne* 88, fols. 104–107. D'Avaux (secretary's minute) to Chanut, April 15, 1647, which was the basis of the more extensive *Allemagne* 82, fols. 254–261, *Memoire* (sent) *de l ambassadeur de france qui est a Osnabrug,* of the same date (duplicate for Servien in *Allemagne* 99, fols. 349–356) [letter pub. in *NS* IV, 61–63; *Memoire* in *APW* II B 5/2, 1065–1072]. SRA *DG* 9, fols. 574–576, Johan Oxenstierna and Salvius (letter sent) to Christina, April 5/15, 1647 [pub. in *APW* II C 3, 376–379]. AAE CP *Allemagne* 88, fols. 148–151, D'Avaux (own hand minute) to Chanut, April 22, 1647 [pub. in *NS* IV, 65–66]. AAE CP *Allemagne* fols. 144–147, D'Avaux, *Memoire* (own hand minute) *de l'Amb^r de france qui est a Osnaburg,* April 22, 1647 (*Memoire* sent in *Allemagne* 88, fols. 36–39, and duplicate for Servien in *Allemagne* 99, fols. 388–391) [pub. in *NS* IV, 63–65, and *APW* II B 5/2, 1113–1119]. The cited passage appears in both letters of April 22. SRA *DG* 9 fols. 620–623, Johan Oxenstierna and Salvius (letter sent) to Christina, April 12/22, 1647 [pub. in *APW* II C 3, 387–391]. For the demands of the Landgravin, see HSAM 4h, n° 2137, fols. 69–70, April 14/24, 1647. See also D'Avaux's remarkable letter to Mazarin of April 29, cited in note 20 below.

18. Victor Cousin, *Madame de Chevreuse, Nouvelles études sur les femmes illustres et la société du xviie siècle* (Paris, 1876), Ch. VII and its notes. For the plots, see the *mémoires* and letters cited in Chapter 8, note 5.

19. AAE CP *Allemagne* 82, fols. 198–202, Mem^re (Lionne minute) *du Roy a M^rs les plenipot^res en response de leur depesche du 25e Mars,* April 5, 1647 (Brienne minute in Ass. Nat. Ms. 273, fols. 203–207; duplicate for Servien in AAE CP *Allemagne* 99, fols. 280–287; copy in *Allemagne* 88, fols. 2–8) [pub. in *APW* II 5/2, 979–986], AAE CP *Allemagne* 82, fols. 207–208, Mem^re (Lionne minute) *du Roy a M^rs les plenipot^res,* April 7, 1647 (clearer minute with

Lionne corrections on fols. 203–205; Brienne minute in Ass. Nat. *Ms.* 273, fols. 208–210; letter sent in AAE CP *Allemagne* 88, fols. 15–17; and duplicate for Servien in *Allemagne* 99, fols. 291–295, all dated April 6) [pub. in *APW* II B 5/2, 996–999]. AAE CP *Allemagne* 82, fols. 240–244, Mem*re* (Lionne minute) *du Roy a M*rs *les plenipot*res, April 12, 1647; Brienne minute in Ass. Nat. *Ms.* 273, fols. 217–225; duplicate for Servien in AAE CP *Allemagne* 99, fols. 315–329; and copy in *Allemagne* 88, fols. 80–89) [pub. in *APW* II B 5/2, 1022–1033]; AAE CP *Allemagne* 82, fols. 275–279, Mem*re* (Lionne minute) *du Roy a M*rs *les Plenipot*res, April 19, 1647 (Brienne minute in Ass. Nat. *Ms.* 273, fols. 235–239; letter sent in AAE CP *Allemagne* 88, fols. 46–52, and duplicate for Servien in *Allemagne* 99, fols. 369–377) [pub. in *APW* II B 5/2, 1097–1103], AAE CP *Allemagne* 83, fols. 63–73, *Memoire* (Lionne minute) *du Roy a M*rs *les plenipot*res *en response de leur depesche du 15*e, April 26, 1647 (Brienne minute in Ass. Nat. *Ms.* 273, fols. 248–259, and duplicate for Servien in AAE CP *Allemagne* 99, fols. 401–422) [pub. in *APW* II B 5/2, 1143–1157]. For the rumors, see ASVen *Francia* 106, n° 508 I, Nani (letter sent) to Senate, April 2, 1647 (transcript in BNF *Ms. It.* 1829, fols. 45–49). For Mazarin's awareness of Machiavelli's maxim, see the *Mémoire du Roi* of January 17, 1648, cited in Chapter 9, note 1, and his letter to Servien of August 14, cited in Chapter 9, note 16.

20. ASVen *Munster* 6, Contarini (copy to Senate) to Nani, April 23, 1647; BVat CCL A I 15, fols. 172–176, 176–179, and 179–180, Chigi (register) to Panzirolo, April 26, 1647 (deciphered copy of second and third in ASVat *Paci* 21, fols. 198–201 and 202–203); Ass. Nat. *Ms.* 277, fols. 440–455, Longueville and D'Avaux, *Response aux Mem*res *du Roy du 6 12 et 19 Avril 1647*, April 29, 1647 (duplicate for Mazarin in AAE CP *Allemagne* 83, fols. 85–98, and duplicate for Servien in *Allemagne* 99, fols. 441–454) [pub. in *NS* IV, 89–92, and *APW* II B 5/2, 1167–1178], in Spanish in BNE *Ms.* 1026, fols. 244–254 [pub. in *CDI* LXXXIII, 231–241]. In this letter, Longueville and D'Avaux also announce that they had transmitted the famous article on Lorraine to the mediators [pub. in Italian in Siri X, 1707, dated implausibly November 7, 1647, and in *NS* IV, 375, as having been delivered to the mediators in July, which is more likely the time the Spanish received it]. For more on D'Avaux's mood after his return, see AAE CP *Allemagne* 88, fols. 168–171, his own hand minute and remarkable letter to Mazarin, April 29, 1647 (letter sent in *Allemagne* 83, fols. 79–84, and another copy in *Allemagne* 99, fols. 433–438) [pub. in *APW* II B 5/2, 1179–1183]; ASVen *Munster* 6, Contarini (copy to Senate) to Nani, April 30, 1647; and BVat CCL A I 15, fols. 181–183, 184–185, and 185–187, Chigi (register) to Panzirolo, May 3, 1647 (deciphered copies of the second and third in ASVat *Paci* 21, fols. 208–209 and 204–207). See also AGS E 2350, *Puntos & Cartas del C. de*

Peñaranda p^a Su Mg^d y el S^{rio} P^o Coloma de diferentes fechas del los meses de Abril y Mayo 1647.

21. For Servien's proposals to the States General, see AAE CP *Hollande* 44, fols. 118–119, Servien own hand minute (copy on fols. 114–116 and in *Hollande* 41, fols. 139–140; Godefroy copy in BNF *Ms. Fr.* 3784, fols. 53–56; NNA SG R 4857, April 17, 1647) [pub. in Aitzema *VNVH* II, 326–328; in Italian in Siri IX, 1251–1252; in Latin in Londorp VI, 170–171; and in the original French in *NS* IV, 303–304]. For Pauw's relation, see NNA SG R 4857, *Sommier vant geene bij den Heere van Heemstede en van de extraordinaris Ambassadeurs ende Plenipotentarisen van haer Ho. Mo. in der secrete Vergaderinge wejttloopig is gerapporteert den 17 en 18 April 1647* (copy in SG VL 12588.47 I, and in French in AAE CP *Hollande* 41, fols. 143–149, dated April 20) [pub. in part in Aitzema *VNVH* II, 328–335, dated April 20; in Italian in Siri IX, 1246–1249, dated April 17 and 18; and in Latin in Londorp VI, 170–172, dated April 20]. There are summaries in French in AAE CP *Hollande* 44, fols. 120–121 (for April 17) and *Hollande* 41, fols. 142–143, and *Hollande* 44, fols. 122–123 (for April 18), which includes additional evens of that day. See also NNA SG R 4857, the provincial advice of Holland, April 19, 1647 (summarized in French in AAE CP *Hollande* 41, fol. 160 and *Hollande* 44, fol. 140) [pub. in Latin in Londorp VI, 172–173, and summarized in French in *NS* IV, 304]. For Servien's view of the situation, see AAE CP *Allemagne* 83, fols. 22–28, Servien (duplicate for Mazarin) to Longueville and D'Avaux, April 22, 1647 (copy in *Hollande* 44, fols. 143–148) [pub. in *APW* II B 5/2, fols. 1119–1127]. For his circular letter, see *Hollande* 44, fols. 191–198; *Hollande* 41, fols. 184–187, printed; and Ass. Nat. *Ms.* 277, fols. 469–472, April 26, 1647 [Moreau: 2040, pub. in Aitzema *VNVH,* II 336–342, and in Italian in Siri IX, 1261–1267]. Pauw's response is reported by Contarini in his letter of April 30, cited in the previous note. For the refusal of the subsidy, see NNA SG R 4857, May 30, 1647.

22. *Gazette* n° 44, April 20, 1647. See also Renate Schreiber, *Erzherzog Leopold Wilhelm. Kirche, Krieg und Kunst,* Diplomarbeit (Vienna, 1998).

23. AAE CP *Hollande* 44, fols. 173–179, *Memoire* (Lionne minute) *du Roy au Sr Servien,* May 3, 1647 (Brienne minute in Ass. Nat. *Ms.* 273, fols. 267–273; letter sent in AAE CP *Hollande* 41, fols. 216–229; copy in *Hollande* 44, fols. 162–170; and fragments in *Allemagne* 80, fol. 197, and Ass. Nat. *Ms.* 278, fol. 143) [pub. on *APW* II B 5/2, 1219–1227]; AAE CP *Allemagne* 83, fols. 110–113, *Memoire* (Lionne minute) *du Roy a M^{rs} les Plenip^{res},* May 3, 1647 (Brienne minute in Ass. Nat. *Ms.* 273, fols. 262–265; duplicate for Servien in *Allemagne* 100, fols. 23–30; and copy in *Allemagne* 88, fols. 154–158) [pub. in *APW* II B 5/2, 1206–1211], AAE CP *Hollande* 44, fols. 180–182, Mazarin (Lionne minute) to Servien, May 3, 1647 [pub. in *APW* II B 5/2,

1227–1231]. For the military movements, see AAE CP *Suède* 6, fols. 104–105 and 106–108, Mazarin (copies) to La Ferté-Seneterre and to La Ferté-Imbault, May 14, 1647; and *Espagne* 27, fols. 111–116, Mazarin (Lionne minute) to Condé, May 27, 1647 (letter sent in AC P 1, 86–91, dated May 28) [pub. in Henri d'Aumale, *Histoire des Princes de Condé pendant les XVIè et XVIIè siècles* (Paris, 1863–1896) V, 525–527]. For the arrival of Condé before Lérida, see note 27 below.

24. See various copies of the offer of arbitration as taken down by the mediators in ASVat *Paci* 23, fols. 381 and 383, and ASVen *Munster* 6. See the new version of Article 3 in Ass. Nat. *Ms.* 277, fols. 17–18; AAE CP *Allemagne* 84, fol. 41; and ASVat *Paci* 23, fol. 390 [pub.in Italian in Siri X, 960–961]. See various texts of the explanatory declaration in Ass. Nat. *Ms.* 278, fols. 30–33; AAE CP *Allemagne* 84, fols. 42–44; ASVat *Paci* 23, fols. 363 and 384–385; and NNA SG 8413, fol. 185 [one such text is pub. in Italian in Siri X, 961]. Both article and declaration are in AAE CP *Allemagne* 85, fol. 150. See also Ass. Nat. *Ms.* 277, fols. 499–509, Longueville and D'Avaux *Memoire des Plenip^res de France du 13 May 1647* (duplicate for Mazarin in AAE CP *Allemagne* 83, fols. 143–153, and copy for Servien in *Allemagne* 100, fols. 89–97) [pub. in *NS* IV, 101–104 and *APW* II B 5/2, 1279–1289]. In Spanish in BNE *Ms.* 1026, fols. 274–280 [pub. in *CDI* LXXXIII, 254–261]. More on the negotiation in ASVen *Munster* 6, Contarini (copy to Senate) to Nani, May 14, 1647; BVat CCL A I 15, fols. 204–212 and 212–216, Chigi (register) to Panzirolo, May 17, 1647 (letter sent of first in ASVat *Paci* 23, fols. 373–380); Ass. Nat. *Ms.* 277, fols. 522–533, *Memoire des Plenipotentiaires de France,* May 20, 1647 (duplicate for Mazarin in AAE CP *Allemagne* 83, fols. 173–181; copies for Servien in *Allemagne* 100, fols. 119, 125–130, and 133–134, variously dated) [pub. in *APW* II B 5/2, 1314–1321]. In Spanish in BNE *Ms.* 1026, fols. 281–289, dated May 21 [pub. in *CDI* LXXXIII, 281–289]. For Longueville's desire to return, see AAE CP *Allemagne* 83, fol. 169, Longueville (letter sent) to Mazarin, May 20, 1647 (copy in *Allemagne* 100, fols. 120–121) [pub. in *APW* II B 5/2, 1321–1322]. Still more on the negotiation in ASVen *Munster* 6, Contarini (copy to Senate) to Nani, May 21, 1647, NNA SG *VL* 12588.47 I; BVat CCL A I 15, fols. 218–221 and 223–225, Chigi (register) to Panzirolo, May 24, 1647 (letter sent of the first in ASVat *Paci* 23, fols. 392–395). See also AGS E 2350, *Puntos & Cartas del C. de Peñaranda,* cited in note 20 above, and *Extracto de Carta del C. de Peñaranda para el Sr Marquis de Castel R^o en Munster a 13 de Mayo 1647.* For the agreement on the *gravamina,* see Meiern IV, 548–550, and NNA SG R 4857. For the Lutheran-Calvinist squabbling, see Meiern VI, 248–261, as well as NNA SG R 4857. For the orders on Osnabrück, see HHSA RK *FrA* 90 II (Volmar Diary), May 21, 1647 [pub. in *APW* III C 2, 843]. For Servien's proposal, see

AAE CP *Hollande* 44, fol. 365 (copies on fols. 319, 358, and 378–379; *Hollande* 41, fols. 319–320; Ass. Nat. *Ms.* 277, fol. 570; and ASVat *Paci* 23, fol. 320) [pub. in Aitzema *VHVH* II, 351, and in Italian in Siri IX, 1371–1372].

25. AAE CP *Allemagne* 83, fols. 187–192, *Mem^re* (Lionne's hand) *du Roy a M^rs les Plenipot,* May 25, 1647 (Brienne minute in Ass. Nat. *Ms.* 273, fols. 297–302, duplicate for Servien in *Allemagne* 100, fols. 142–152; copy in *Allemagne* 88, fols. 254–261) [pub. in APW II B 5/2, fols. 1342–1347]. For the progress of the siege of Lérida, see note 27 below. For the mood in Paris, see ASVen *Francia* 106, 540 III, Nani (letter sent) to Senate, May 28, 1647 (trascript in BNF *Ms. It.* 1829, fols. 141–143).

26. ASVen *Munster* 6, Contarini (copy to Senate) to Nani, May 28, 1647; BVat CCL A I 15, fols. 226–235, and 237–238, Chigi (register) to Panzirolo, May 31, 1647 (first letter sent in ASVat *Paci* 23, fols. 407–415). Ass. Nat. *Ms.* 278, fols. 8–16, Longueville and D'Avaux's *Memoire des Plenipo^res de France,* June 3, 1647 (duplicate for Mazarin in AAE CP *Allemagne* 84, fols. 33–40, duplicate for Servien in *Allemagne* 100, fols. 239–245, and other copy in *Allemagne* 100, fols. 213–222) [pub. in *NS* IV, 113–115, and APW II B 5/2, 1407–1414]. ASVen *Munster* 6, Contarini (copy to Senate) to Nani, June 4, 1647; BVat CCL A I 15, fols. 241–246 and 248–249, Chigi (register) to Panzirolo, June 7, 1647 (copy of first letter sent in ASVat *Paci* 23, fols. 431–434). Ass. Nat *Ms.* 278, fols. 38–50, *Memoire des Plenipo^res de France en Response des Mem^res du Roy du 25^e May et 1 Juin 1647,* June 10, 1647 (duplicate for Mazarin in AAE CP *Allemagne* 84, fols. 54–61, and copy in *Allemagne* 100, fols. 265–275) [pub. in *NS* IV, 116–118, and APW II B 5/2, 1455–1462]. AAE CP *Allemagne* 84, fols. 63–64, Longueville (letter sent) to Mazarin, June 10, 1647 (copy in *Allemagne* 100, fols. 276–277) [pub. in APW II B 5/2, 1463–1464]. AGS E 2350, *Puntos de Cartas del Conde de Peñaranda desde 27 de Mayo 1647 hasta 17 de Junjo . . . y otras del Consejero Ant^o Brun de 7 de Junio.* BVat CCL A I 15, fols. 250–253, Chigi (register) to Panzirolo, June 14, 1647 (copy in ASVat *Paci* 23, fols. 457–459). ASVen *Munster* 6, Contarini (copy to Senate) to Nani, June 18, 1647. For the Emperor's proposals to the Swedes, see the *Caesareanorum Instrumentum Pacis Dominis Suecicis Legatis in fine Maji exhibitum trigeimo ejusdem collatum & 3 Junii publicé dictatum per Direct. Magunt.* (copies in NNA SG VL 12588. 47 II, and SG R 4857) [pub. in Meiern, IV, 556–590]. For the shift in the Hessian demands, see HHSA RK *FrA* 94 III, n° 410; SRA *DG* 9, fols. 1002–1015; or AN *K* 1335, n° 104, dated June 20, 1647. For the Emperor's proposals though Chigi to the French, see HHSA RK *FrA* 54c, fols. 1–22 and fols. 153–170 (copy in Chigi ASVat *Paci* 23, fols. 527–538). For the Emperor's proposals through Contarini to the French, see HHSA RK *FrA* 54c, fols. 61–87, 90–124, and 127 (copies in Ass. Nat. *Ms.* 278, fols. 171–178; and in AAE CP *Allemagne* 84, fols. 217–224, titled *Projet du traitté de l'Empire*

donné a M. les Pleniponentiaires) [similar but more extensive version pub. in Meiern V, 130–140]. See also SRA *DG* 9, fols. 959–962, Johan Oxenstierna and Salvius (letter sent) to Christina, June 6/16, 1647 [pub. in *APW* II C 3, 456–460] and Ass. Nat. *Ms.* 278, fols. 95–102, *Memoire des Plenipotentiaires de France,* June 24, 1647 (duplicate for Mazarin in AAE CP *Allemagne* 84, fols. 105–110 and other copy in *Allemagne* 100, fols. 347–354) [pub. in *NS* IV, 122–124].

27. Fall of Armentières: *Gazette* n° 61, June 14, 1647. For the raising of the siege of Lérida, see AAE CP *Espagne* 26, fol. 465, Condé (own hand letter sent) to Mazarin, June 19, 1647, *Espagne* 26, fols. 466–467 and 483–484, two Spanish accounts, the last titled *Sucesos fatales contra franceses sobre Lerida en esto año de 647, Gazettes* n°⁵ 60, 63, 66, 69, 71, June 12, 15, 22, and 29, and July 6, 1647. See also the *Memoires du Maréchal de Gramont,* P&M, ser. 2, LVI, 399–404, or M&P, ser. 3, VIII, 272–273; Monglat, P&M, ser. 2, L, 79–81, or M&P, ser. 3, V, 182–183]. For the revolt of the Weimarians, see AAE CP *Allemagne* 88, fols. 375–376 and 389, Rosen (letters sent) to Turenne, June 18 and 19, 1647; fols. 397 and 398, Turenne (own hand letters sent) to Mazarin, June 20 and 22, 1647; fols. 401–402, Vautorte (letter sent) to Mazarin, June 24, 1647 [pub. in *MT* I, 314–320]; and fol. 403, Officers of the Weimar army (letter sent) to Mazarin, June 24, 1647; fol. 404 (in French) [pub. in German in Londorp VI, 250]. See also AAE CP *Allemagne* 88, fols. 555–559, *Memoire de M' de Turenne pour l'affaire de Rose, 24 juillet 1647.* It was ignored in the *Gazette* n° 68 of June 29, 1647, and glossed over in the *Gazette* n° 72 of July 11, 1647.

8. Waiting for the Verdict

1. AAE CP *Allemagne* 84, fols. 99–102, Mazarin (Lionne minute) to Longueville, June 22, 1647 (copy in *Allemagne* 100, fols. 336–343) [pub. in part in *LM* II, 440–445, and in its entirety in *APW* II B 5/2, 1538–1543]. For the impact of the reproaches, see AAE CP *Hollande* 41, fol. 434, the extract of Longueville's letter of June 10 which Mazarin forwarded to Servien at The Hague on June 22. *Allemagne* 84, fols. 146–153, *Mem*ʳᵉ (Lionne minute) *du Roy a M*ʳˢ *les Plenip*ʳᵉˢ July 6, 1647 (Brienne minute in Ass. Nat. *Ms.* 273, fols. 375–383; duplicate for Servien in AAE CP *Allemagne* 101, fols. 46–63; and other copy in *Allemagne* 88, fols. 423–431) [pub. in *APW* II B 6, 72–80]; AAE CP *Espagne* 27, fols. 142–148, Mazarin (Lionne minute) to Condé, July 7, 1647 (copy in *Espagne* 28, fols. 73–98) [Chéruel's extracts in *LM* II, 919–922, omit some of the most psychologically revealing parts].

2. For the mood change in France, see Peñaranda's letter to Castel Rodrigo cited in note 3 below, where he says, "Que mas claro puede decirnos que

este es el proprio tiempo de introducer division en Francia?" just before expressing his hopes of recouping all their losses. For the appointment of
d'Hémery, see Ormesson I, 385–387 and 389–390, July 5, 6, 10, 24, and August 3, 1647, as well as AST MPLM *Francia* 51, 115/2, Ponte to Christine,
July 12, 1647. Fall of Dixmude (July 12): *Gazette* n° 77·, July 18, 1647. Fall
of La Bassée (July 19): *Gazette* n° 81, July 22, 1647. Fall of Landrecies (July
17): Mentioned only by inference in the *Gazette* n° 82, July 27, 1647. See
also Alessandro Giraffi, *Le Revolutioni di Napoli* (Venice, 1647). For the
change in Swedish perspective, see SRA RR 1646–1647 Svensk, Christina to
Johan Oxenstierna and Salvius, July 2/13, 1647 [pub. in *APW* II C 3, 490].
For the Landgravin, see HSAM 4h, n° 2137, fols. 126–127, *Sonderveertige
Uffsat. . . . 3 July* [o.s.] *1647 Ubergebend* (copy on fols. 124–125).

3. Ass. Nat. *Ms.* 278, fols. 95–102, 114–120, 130–134, 149–160, 165–170,
    181–190, 206–212, and 233–249, *Memoires des Plenipotentiaires de France,*
    June 24, and 31 [*sic*] July 8, 15, 19, 22, and 29, and August 5, 1647 (dupli-
    cates for Mazarin in AAE CP *Allemagne* 84, fols. 105–110, 135–139 dated
    July 1, 154–157, 190–197, 226–231, 239–244, 264–269, and *Allemagne* 85,
    fols. 21–33; copies [c] or duplicates [d] in *Allemagne* 100, fols. 347–354 [c],
    Allemagne 101, fols. 22–29 [c] dated July 1, fols. 64–68 [d], 100–115 [d],
    141–147, 154–164 [c], 193–200 [c], and 212–221 [c]) [pub. in *NS* IV,
    122–124, 125–127 dated June 30, 127–128 dated July 7, 129–132, 133–134,
    136–139, and *APW* II B 5/2, 1549–1555; II B 6, 47–52, 89–93, 129–138,
    164–168, 177–186, 216–220, and 246–258]. The July 29 and August 5 *mé-
    moires* in Spanish are in BNE *Ms.* 1026, fols. 331–348 [pub. in *CDI* LXXXIII,
    362–367 and 372–383]. See also BVat *CCL* A I 15, fols. 282–288, 297–298,
    304–306, and 310–317, Chigi (register) to Panzirolo, July 12 (copy in ASVat
    Paci 23, fols. 500–506), July 19 (deciphered copy in *Paci* 21, fols. 312–315),
    July 26 (copy in *Paci* 23, fols. 523–525), and August 2, 1647 (copy in *Paci*
    23, fols. 546–551); ASVen *Munster* 6, Contarini (copy to Senate) to Nani,
    June 25, July 2, 9, 16, 23 and 30, 1647. Compare AGS *E* 2350, Peñaranda
    (deciphered copy) to Caracena, June 27, 1647, with BNE *Ms.* 8747, fols.
    12–17, Peñaranda (copy) to Castel Rodrigo, July 12, 1647 (incorrectly dated
    12 de Junio) [pub. in *CDI* LXXXIII, 312–314 and 334–340]. I cannot find
    the brief French reply, but I do find the Imperial reply to it in Ass. Nat. *Ms.*
    278, fols. 194–195, *Notationes circa Articulum Satisfactonis Gallica* (copy in
    ASVat *Paci* 23, fols. 553–554). It was communicated by the mediators on
    June 15, according to Chigi's letter of August 2, cited above. See the printed
    French instrument in Latin in AAE CP *Allemagne,* 88, fols. 569–582 (with
    handwritten marginalia noting Imperial objections); ASVen *Munster* 6; AGS
    E 2350; and HHSA MEA *FrA* 19. There is a summary in French in *NS* IV,
    344–354, and full text in Latin in Meiern V, 140–166. See the Imperial reply

in Ass. Nat. *Ms.* 278, fols. 250–251, *Notationes ad Instrumentum Gallicum* in two columns (copy in HHSA MEA *FrA* 19, dated July 22, and AAE CP *Allemagne* 88, fols. 583–586). The mediators got them on July 27 and passed them on the next day, according to Chigi's letter of August 2, cited above. Fall of Egra (July 17): *Gazette* n° 89, August 10, 1647.

4. NNA SG R 4857, June 28, and July 4, 1647, AAE CP *Hollande* 44, fols. 573–577, *Projet delivré par M. de Servien aux Comm^res de M^rs les Estats Sur celuy qui avoit esté donné de leur part* (undated). For the negotiation, see NNA SG 4857, July 8, 9, 12, 13, 15–18, 21, 23, and 26–30, 1647, and Aitzema *VNVH* II, 362–370. See the treaty in Ass. Nat. *Ms.* 278, fol. 142, and NNA SG R 4857. See also *Accord Gemaeckt ende besloten Tusschen de Croon Vranckrijck. . . . ende de Vereenighde Provintien . . . Over de Ligue Garentie, Ghedaen den 29 July 1647* [Knuttel: 5487–5488; also pub. in Aitzema *VNVH* II, 370–373; in Londorp VI, 175; in Italian in Siri X, 817–819; in French in Dumont VI, pt. 1, 396–397; and in Latin and French in *NS* IV, 372–373]. For the return of Servien, see AAE CP *Allemagne* 101, fols. 250–258, Servien (own hand minute) to Lionne, August 13, 1647 (partial clean copy on fols. 259–262, other copy in *Hollande* 45, fols. 225–228) [pub. in *APW* II B 6, 281–283]. NNA SG R 4857, August 10 and 13, 1647.

5. AAE CP *Allemagne* 85, fols. 59–70, *Mem^re* (Lionne minute) *du Roy a M^rs les Plenipot^res*, August 16, 1647 (Brienne minute in Ass. Nat. *Ms.* 273, fols. 416–427; copies in AAE CP *Allemagne* 88, fols. 603–608, and *Allemagne* 101, fols. 264–281) [pub. in *APW* II B 6, 285–302], which is the source of the quotes. See also AAE CP *Allemagne* 85, fols. 86–93, *Mem^re* (Lionne minute) *du Roy a M^rs les Plenipot^res*, August 23, 1647 (Brienne minute in Ass. Nat. *Ms.* 273, fols. 434–440, copies in AAE CP *Allemagne* 89, fols. 14–25 and *Allemagne* 101, fols. 323–329) [pub. in *APW* II B 6, 323–329]. Mazarin first mentioned the plots in the *mémoire* of August 16 and then described them in great detail in the *mémoire* of August 23. After having done this, however, he decided to cross out the details of the Raré plot and replace them by a more sanitized relation, because, ostensibly, he did not want "such diabolical things" go out in the king's name and, more plausibly, did not want to give any bright ideas to Longueville and to D'Avaux. Mazarin did permit Lionne to insert the details in his personal letter to Servien (AAE CP *Allemagne* 103, fols. 332–333) [pub. in *APW* II B 6, 329–330] of the same date, with orders to burn it. Servien did not. We can thus read the details in both places. Also, a mole in Paris communicated some of the content of the *mémoire* of August 16 to Peñaranda, according to Peñaranda's letter to Castel Rodrigo of August 29 and its extremely interesting attachment cited in note 7 below, marking the second leak in the French correspondence.

6. See, in this order, Ormesson I, 392, August 22, 1647; Talon, P&M, ser. 2, LXI, 88–91, or M&P, ser. 3, VI, 201–202; Ormesson I, 394–396, August 28, 30, and September 1, 5, 1647. For the truncation of the edicts, see AN *U* 139*, pp. 213–224, *Arrêté* of September 7, 1647. See Mazarin's interpretation in the *Mémoire du Roi* of September 13, cited in note 10 below. See also AST MPLM *Francia* 51, 153/2, Ponte to Christina, same date.

7. Ass. Nat. Ms. 278, fols. 258–263, 266–272, and 275–288, *Mémoire des Plenipotentiaires de France,* August 19, 26, and September 2, 1647 (duplicates for Mazarin in AAE CP *Allemagne* 85, fols. 72–75, 105–110, and 139–149; copies in *Allemagne* 102, fols. 24–28, and *Allemagne* 101, fols. 294–297 and 334–336) [all pub. in *NS* IV, 148–155, and in *APW* II B 6, 308–311, 332–337, and 364–372]. August 19 *mémoire* in Spanish is in BNE Ms. 1026, fols. 354–359 [pub. in *CDI* LXXXIII, 415–419]. See two drafts of the softened French article in BVat *CCL* Q III 57, fols. 120 and 125, and of the second draft in Italian in ASVen *Munster* 7 as well as copies of the declaration demanded by the French and by the Spanish in ASVat *Paci* 23, fols. 619 and 621, and in ASVen *Munster* 7, the one demanded by the French, dated August 22, and the one by the Spanish, both dated August 24, 1647, in the ASVen copies. See also BVat *CCL* A I 15, fols. 337–348 and 348–350, fols. 354–362 and 366–367, Chigi (register) to Panzirolo August 23 (two letters) August 30 and September 6, 1647 (letters sent in ASVat *Paci* 23, fols. 582–592; *Paci* 21, fols. 375–377 (deciphered copy); and *Paci* 23, fols. 606–619 and fols. 636–367). See also ASVen *Munster* 6, Contarini (copies to Senate) to Nani, August 20 and 26, and *Munster* 7, Contarini (copy to Senate) to Nani, September 3, 1647, as well as BNE Ms. 8747, fols. 70–72 and 136–140, Brun (copy) to Peñaranda and Peñaranda to Brun, August 25, 1647, Peñaranda (letters sent) to Castel Rodrigo, August 29 (with extremely interesting *Avisos de Paris*) and September 2, 1647 [pub. in *CDI* LXXXIII, 434–443].

8. AAE CP *Allemagne* 85, fols. 129–132, Mem^re (Lionne minute) *du Roy a M^rs les Plenipot^res,* August 30, 1647 (Brienne minute in Ass. Nat. Ms. 273, fols. 443–446, copies in AAE CP *Allemagne* 89, fols. 28–34, and *Allemagne* 101, fols. 356–359) [pub. in *APW* II B 6, 353–357]. For the direct orders to the generals, see the *Mémoire du Roi* of October 11, 1647, cited in note 11 below. Junction of French armies for attack on Ypres (September 22 and 25, 1647): *Gazette* n°s 107 and 112, September 17 and 30, 1647. For the "certaine fatalité," see the *Mémoire du Roi* of October 11, 1647, cited in note 11 below. For the alliance with the Duke of Modena, see AAE CP *Modène* 1, fols. 180–181, *Capitoli Segreti accordati tra l'Em Sig. Cardinal Grimaldi, come Plenipotentiario di S. M^ta xpmà in Italia e l'Illmo Marchese Mario Caleagnini Penip^o del Ser^mo Sig^r Duca di Modena, In Sampierd^a 2 7bre 1647.* The entire

treaty is published in Italian in Siri X, 648–655, and in French in Dumont VI, pt. 1, 397–399, in both with the secret articles].

9. For the Swedish acceptance of the Palatine settlement, see SRA RR, 1646–1647 Svensk, Christina to Johan Oxenstierna and Salvius, August 14/24, 1647 [pub. in *APW* II C 3, 548]. For Servien's visit, compare AAE CP *Allemagne* 102, fols. 75–80, Servien's own hand report, two copies of which are found on fols. 81–84 and 85–89 and inserted *verbatim* in the *Memoire des Plenipotentiaires* of September 9, cited in note 11 below, with SRA *DG* 10, fols. 276–282 [pub. in *APW* II C 3, 564–571]. Servien's "no human foresight could have foreseen" line comes from his report, whereas we have to rely on the Swedish report for his bad-mouthing of the Jesuits. Battle near Treibel in Bohemia (August 22, 1647): *Gazette* n°s 104 and 109, September 14 and 26, 1647, which try to downplay the Imperial victory. For the campaign against D'Avaux, see AAE CP *Allemagne* 102, fols. 93–96, Servien (own hand minute) to Lionne, September 11, 1647 (clean copy on fols. 97–100) [pub. in *APW* II B 6, 405–407].

10. For the approach to *parlement,* see AN *U* 139*, pp. 206–210, AAE CP *Allemagne* 85, fols. 177–184, Mem^{re} (Lionne minute) *du Roy a M^{rs} les Plenipot^{res},* September 13, 1647 (Brienne minute in Ass. Nat. *Ms.* 273, fols. 455–463; copies in AAE CP *Allemagne* 89, fols. 98–109, and *Allemagne* 102, fols. 101–108) [pub. in *APW* II B 6, 412–422]. For the Duke of Bavaria's manifesto, see AAE CP *Bavière* 2, fols. 267–280, *Manifestum Bavaricum Sive Rationes quae Electorem Bavariae Armistitio cum Corona Sueciae inito renunciare coegerunt,* September 14, 1647 (copy in German in SRA *DG* 10, fols. 562–570; in Spanish in BNE *Ms.* 8747, fols. 183–195) [pub. in German in Londorp VI, 213–217; in Italian in Siri X, 1091–1100; and in Spanish in *CDI* LXXXIV, 37–48]. For his letter to Mazarin, see AAE CP *Bavière* 2, fols. 279–300, Maximilian (letter sent) to Mazarin, September 18, 1647. See also *Allemagne* 85, fols. 267–274, Mem^{re} (Lionne minute) *du Roy a M^{rs} les Plenipot^{res},* October 4, 1647 (copies in *Allemagne* 89, fols. 241–253, and *Allemagne* 102, fols. 208–216) [pub. in *APW* II B 6, 520–532].

11. Ass. Nat. *Ms.* 278, fols. 293–308 and 320–326, *Memoire des Plenip^{res} de France,* September 9 and 16, 1647 (duplicates for Mazarin in AAE CP *Allemagne* 85, fols. 162–175 and 194–200, Servien's own hand partial minute of the first *mémoire* in *Allemagne* 102, fols. 75–80, partial copies on fols. 70–71, 81–84, and 85–91, and copy of the second on fols. 120–121) [pub. in *NS* IV, 156–162, and *APW* II B 6, 396–404 and 428–433], *Allemagne* 85, fols. 222–228 and 249–255, *Memoire* (duplicates for Mazarin) *des Plenipotentiaires de France,* September 23 and 30, 1647 (copies in *Allemagne* 102, fols. 147–149 and 173–176) [pub. version of the first in *NS* IV, 163–165, and of both in *APW* II B 6, 460–464 and 499–503]. AAE CP *Allemagne* 85,

fols. 281–286 and 301–315, *Memoire* (duplicates for Mazarin) *des Plenipotentiaires de France,* October 7 and 14, 1647 (copies in *Allemagne* 102, fols. 225–228 and 275–280) [pub. in *NS* IV, 166–172, and *APW* II B 6, 538–543 and 571–579]. ASVen *Munster* 7, Contarini (copy to Nani) to Senate, Septetember 10, 17, 24, and October 1, 8, and 15, 1647, BVat *CCL* A I 15, fols. 370–373, 376–380, 386–390, 397–406, and 407–408; and 410–415, Chigi (register) to Panzirolo, September 13, 20, 27, October 4 (two letters) and 11 (copies sent in ASVat *Paci* 23, fols. 643–645, 650–653, 662–667, and 674–681; deciphered copy in *Paci* 21, fols. 425–426; and copy in *Paci* 23, fols. 706–710. AGS *E* 2350, six letters of Peñaranda (deciphered copies) to Philip IV, September 11–12, 1647 [pub. in *CDI* LXXXIII, 468–476 and 479–482], BNE Ms. 8747, fols. 84–100 and 105–108, Peñaranda (letters sent and copy) to Castel Rodrigo, September 19, 23, and 27, 1647 [pub. in *CDI* LXXXIII, 492–497 and 503–506], BNE Ms. 8747, fols. 148–154, Peñaranda (copy) to Philip IV, October 6, 1647 [pub. in *CDI* LXXXIII, 554–560]. Copies of the twenty-one articles (skipping article 18) in French, AAE CP *Allemagne* 80, fols. 408–412; undated and misplaced, ASVat *Paci* 23, fols. 684–688; dated September 27, 1647, in Italian in ASVen *Munster* 7; in Spanish (skipping number 18) with twenty points in BNE Ms. 8747, fols. 108–116 [pub. in Italian skipping number 18 in Siri IX, 1211–1217]. Both the ASVat and ASVen show subscription by the French plenipotentiaries on September 26, 1647, and signing by their secretary on September 27. BNE Ms. 8747 shows subscription by the Spanish plenipotentiaries and their secretary. There is also a copy with twenty-one articles and subscriptions in NNA SG 8413, fols. 160–167. See a copy of the Spanish offer to submit to Dutch arbitration in ASVat *Paci* 23, fol. 719.

12. Fall of Lens: *Gazette* n° 116, October 8, 1647. AAE CP *Allemagne* 85, fols. 291–294, *Mem^re* (Lionne minute) *du Roy a M^rs les Plenipot^res,* October 11, 1647 (Brienne minute in Ass. Nat. Ms. 273, fols. 487–491; copies in AAE CP *Allemagne* 89, fols. 313–319; and *Allemagne* 102, fols. 257–260) [pub. in *APW* II B 6, 559–564]. AAE CP *Hollande* 45, fols. 366–367, Lionne (own hand minute) to Servien, same date (copy sent in *Allemagne* 102, fols. 270–272) [pub. in *APW* II B 6, 567–569]. Siege of Dixmude: *Gazette* n°s 119, 120, and 123, October 12, 18, and 22, 1647. Capture of Ager (October 9): Also in the *Gazette* n° 123. On the movements of Wrangel, see the *Gazette* n°s 122, 125, 129, 133, and 137, October 19, 26, November 2, 9, and 16, 1647.

13. AAE CP *Hollande* 45, fols. 243–246 and 270–273, La Thuillerie (letters sent) to Mazarin, August 29 and September 3, 1647; *Hollande* 45, fol. 387, Lionne (own hand minute) to Servien, October 18, 1647 (letter sent in *Allemagne* 102, fols. 329–332) [pub. in *APW* II B 6, 609–610]. NNA SG R 4858, October 22, 1647, which includes the *Sommier vant gene de heeren van*

heemstede en de Knuyt mede Plenipot^{en} van haer ho: mo, affgesonden van de andere herren Plenipot^{en} tot munster ter Vergaderinge van hoochgemelte haer hooch mogende hebben geraporteert den 21 October des Jaers 1647. See also the report on this meeting and its results by Contarini in ASVen *Munster* 7, Contarini (copy to Senate) to Nani, October 29, 1647, which provides much supplementary information.

14. AAE CP *Portugal* 2, fols. 461–466 and 473–478, Lanier (letters sent) to Mazarin, August 10 and 17, 1647. They do not mention the offer, however, which must have been sent *viva voce.* AAE CP *Allemagne* 85, fols. 264–266, Mazarin (Lionne minute) to Longueville, October 4, 1647 (copy in *Allemagne* 102, fols. 217–220) [extracts pub. in *LM* II, 500–502, and in its entirety in *APW* II B 6, 532–535], BNF *Ms. Baluze* 174 (*Carnet* 9), fols. 15–16. AAE CP *Allemagne* 86, fols. 13–22, Mem^{re} (Lionne minute) *du Roy a M^{rs} les plennipot^{res}* October 25, 1647 (Brienne minute in Ass. Nat. *Ms.* 273, fols. 501–512; copy in AAE CP *Allemagne* 89, fols. 388–401; and partial copy in *Allemagne* 102, fols. 378–385) [pub. in *APW* II B 6, 629–642].

15. AAE CP *Rome* 105, fols. 200–211, 212–220, 223–224, 243–251, 253–262, and 263–275, Fontenay-Mareuil (letters sent) to Mazarin, September 9, 16, and 18, October 8, 14, and 22, 1647, and fols. 141 and 192–193, Fontenay-Mareuil (duplicates for Mazarin) to plenipotentiaries, September 28 and October 12, 1647 [extract of September 28 and October 12 pub. in *LM* II, 505, note 1, and 511–512, note 2]; *Gazette* n° 132, November 8, 1647. For Guise's self-promotion, see his *Instruction pour mon frère le chevalier, sur les choses que je le prie de vouloir traiter pour moi a la cour,* Rome, September 16, 1647, and his *mémoire* for Mazarin, sent with a letter of September 18, 1647, in Guise, *P&M, LV,* 91–94 and 102–103, or *M&P,* ser. 3, VII, 26–27 and 29–30. See also *Modène* II, 122–147.

16. AAE CP *Allemagne* 85, fols. 340–352, *Memoire* (duplicate for Mazarin) *des Plenipotentiaires de France,* October 21, 1647 (copy in *Allemagne* 102, fols. 350–355) [pub. in *NS* IV, 172–175, and *APW* II B 6, 611–619] enclosing *Allemagne* 85, fols. 318–321, a slightly amended article on Casale (copy in Spanish in ASVat *Paci* 23, fol. 735). Ass. Nat. *Ms.* 278, fols. 335–343, *Memoire des Plenipo^{res} de France,* October 28, 1647 (duplicate for Mazarin in AAE CP *Allemagne* 86, fols. 51–58, and copy in *Allemagne* 102, fols. 398–401) [pub. in *NS* IV, 176–178, and *APW* II B 6, 648–653]. Ass. Nat. *Ms.* 278, fol. 343, enclosing an "Extrait" whose duplicate for Mazarin is in AAE CP *Allemagne* 86, fol. 62. BVat *CCL* A I 15, fols. 322–424 and 432–436, Chigi (register) to Panzirolo, October 18 and 25, 1647 (copies sent in ASVat *Paci* 23, fols. 715–716 and 728–731).

17. For Peñaranda's decision, see AGS *E* 2433, Peñaranda (deciphered copy) to Philip IV, November 18, 1647. See also Ass. Nat. *Ms.* 278, fols. 443–451,

Memoire des Plenipotentiaires de France, December 9, 1647 (duplicate for Mazarin in AAE CP *Allemagne* 86, fols. 306–312, and copy in *Allemagne* 103, fols. 329–338) [pub. in *NS* IV, 195–198]. We know the thrust of Oxenstierna's letter to Christina of October 22/November 1, 1647, only through the hints in her answer of December 11/21, cited in note 24 below.

18. For strong evidence that Mazarin and Lionne carefully reviewed their old correspondence, see the *Mémoire du Roi* of December 20, cited in note 25 below. See also AAE CP *Allemagne* 86, fols. 64–65, Mazarin (Lionne minute) to Longueville, November 1, 1647 (copy in *Allemagne* 103, fols. 41–43) [extract pub. in *LM* I, 519, and in its entirety in *APW* II B 6, 677–679].

19. Mazarin to Duke de Richelieu, November 3, 1647, in Modène I, 119–121 and MT Orléans *Ms.* 532 (419), fols. 188–197. Brienne (letter sent) to Fontenay-Mareuil, November 8, 1647, published in L&BdP, 148–154. AAE CP *Allemagne* 86, fols. 103–111, Mem^re (Lionne's hand) *du Roy a M^rs les plenipot^res,* November 8, 1647 (Brienne minute in Ass. Nat. *Ms.* 273, fols. 524–532, and copy in *Allemagne* 103, fols. 105–111).

20. AAE CP *Allemagne* 103, fols. 70–77, Servien (own hand minute) to Lionne, November 5, 1647 (clean copy on fols. 59 and 62–69) [pub. in *APW* II B 6, 696–703].

21. Ass. Nat. *Ms.* 278, fols. 345–349, 363–384, 386–396, 414–422, 432–441, and 443–451, *Memoire(s) des Plenipo^res de France,* November 4, 11, 18, and 25, and December 2, and 9, 1647 (duplicates for Mazarin in AAE CP *Allemagne* 86, fols. 83–88, 123–143, 160–169, 198–204, 277–284, and 306–312; copies in *Allemagne* 103, fols. 46–50, 122–126, 193–201, 232–238, 277–284, and 329–338) [pub. in *NS* IV, 178–188 and 189–191, dated November 22, 192–198, and the *mémoires* of November 4, 11, and 18; also in *APW* II B 6, 684–693, 730–742, and 775–783]. See also AAE CP *Allemagne* 86, fols. 148–149, Longueville (own hand letter sent) to Mazarin, November 12, 1647 (copy without p.s. in *Allemagne* 103, fols. 132–133) [pub. in *APW* II B 6, 744–745]. BVat *CCL* A I 15, fols. 440–441, 446–456, 474–477, 480–483, and 486–488, Chigi (register) to Panzirolo, November 1, 8, 15, 22, and 29, and December 2, 1647 (copies sent in ASVat *Paci* 23, fols. 744–745, 757–765, 785–790, 808–810, 837–840, and 860–861). For the new Franco-Imperial agreement, see Ass. Nat. *Ms.* 278, fols. 398–403, *Punctum Satisfactionis Coronae Galliae jnserendum de verbo ad verbun Tractatu universalj pacis Germanica absq~ ulla facultate addendi demendi i mutandive . . . xi Novembris Anno Dñi 1647,* signed by Joseph Boulanger (copies in AAE CP *Allemagne* 86, fols. 116–121, and HHSA RK FrA 54a, fols. 116–121). For the Franco-Spanish articles 23–48, see AAE CP *Allemagne* 86, fols. 209–218 in French and fols. 213–230 in Spanish; BI

Ms. *Godefroy* 87, fols. 305–330; AN K 1336, n°s 58 and 59, in French; ASVat *Paci* 23, fols. 821–824 in French and fols. 812–818 in Spanish, signed by the respective secretaries of the embassies on November 16, 1647. There is also a copy in French in NNA SG 8413, fols. 178–188 [pub. in Italian in Siri X, 1694–1706]. For the arrival of the first Catholics in Osnabrück, see SRA *DG* 10, fols. 969–970, Salvius (letter sent) to Christina, November 15/25, 1647 [pub. in *APW* II C 4/1, 104–106].

22. Guise, P&M, LV, 165–249, M&P, ser. 3, VII, 49–76. See also Modène II, 160–251].

23. MT Orléans Ms. 532 (419), fols. 238–279, *Memoire* (copy sent) *du Roy au Sr Marquis de Fontenay son Ambassadeur extraord^{re} prez du Pape,* November 28, 1647 [pub. in L&BdP, 196–224].

24. SRA *RR,* fols. 3189–3190, Christina (register) to Johan Oxenstierna, December 11/21, 1647 [pub. in *APW* II C 4/1, 142–143].

25. We get the precious financial recollection from AAE CP *Allemagne* 121, fols. 286–287, Lionne (letter sent) to Servien, August 6, 1648. Compare it with the effort to obtain advances, cited in Chapter 9, note 11. For Mazarin's frantic project, see AAE CP *Rome* 103, fols. 318–319, Mazarin (minute) to Fontenay-Mareuil, undated [pub. in *LM* II, 585–586]. For the suspicions of D'Avaux's household, see AAE CP *Allemagne* 103, fols. 382–383, Lionne (letter sent) to Servien, December 13, 1647. See also *Allemagne* 86, fols. 347–356, *Mem^{rw}* (Lionne minute) *du Roy a M^{rs} les plenipo^{res},* December, 20, 1647 (Brienne minute in Ass. Nat. Ms. 273, fols. 571–585, and copy in AAE CP *Allemagne* 103, fols. 414–422). Lionne's minute, which is devoted exclusively to the issue of the intercepted letters, contained orders for the plenipotentiaries to take new security measures. These orders are crossed out in Lionne's minute, restored with some changes in Brienne's minute, and do not appear in Servien's copy. However they were the subject of a separate *Memoire du Roi* of the same date, which I find only in Servien's papers in *Allemagne* 103, fol. 413. For the eruption of concessions, see *Allemagne* 86, fols. 387–395, *Mem^{re}* (Lionne minute) *du Roy a M^{rs} les plenipo^{res},* December 24, 1647 (Brienne minute in Ass. Nat. Ms. 273, fols. 593–601).

26. Guise, P&M, LV, 305–365 or M&P, ser. 3, VII, 94–116; Modène II, 251–290.

27. NNA SG VL 12588.47 II, Dutch plenipotentiaries (letter sent) to States General, December 12, 1647 (copy in NNA SG R 4858) and SG R 4858, Dutch plenipotentiaries (copy) to States General, January 3, 1648; Ass. Nat. Ms. 278, fols. 488–509, *Memoire des Plenipo^{res} de France,* December 30, 1647 (duplicate for Mazarin in AAE CP *Allemagne* 86, fols. 424–437, and copy in *Allemagne* 103, fols. 477–492) [pub. in *NS* IV, 205–207]; *Allemagne* 86, fols.

420–421, Longueville (letter sent) to Mazarin, December 30, 1647 (copy in *Allemagne* 103, fols. 493–494); *Allemagne* 90, fols. 301–308, D'Avaux (own hand minute) to Mazarin, December 30, 1647 (letter sent in *Allemagne* 85, fols. 410–419, and copy in *Allemagne* 103, fols. 490–510); *Allemagne* 103, fols. 512–521, Servien to Lionne, December 31, 1647 (clean copy on fols. 522–534).

9. The Coming of the Fronde

1. AAE CP *Allemagne* 116, fols. 68–69, Mazarin (Lionne minute) to Longueville, January 16, 1648 (copy in *Allemagne* 118, fols. 102–108) [extract pub. in *LM* III, 2–4]; *Allemagne* 116, fols. 88–109, *Memoire* (secretary's revision with Lionne corrections.) *du Roy a Mrs Les Plenipot^res,* January 17, 1648 (Brienne minute in Ass. Nat. *Ms.* 272, fols. 27–54, and copy in AAE CP *Allemagne* 118, fols. 109–158).

2. AAE CP *Allemagne* 118, fol. 63, Lionne (letter sent) to Servien, January 11, 1648, which already announces the composition of the *Mémoire du Roi* cited in the previous note.

3. See the edicts in AN *U* 28, fols. 144–147. Compare Talon's own version in P&M, ser. 2, LXI, 114–121, or M&P, ser. 3, VI, 209–212, and the versions in Knuttel: 5622 and 5623, with the excerpt in Isambert XVII, 66–67. See also Ormesson I, 420–422, 426, and 429–430; Dubuisson I, 4; and ASVen *Francia* 107, D 658 III, Nani to Senate, January 21, 1648 (transcript in BNF *Ms. It.* 1830, fols. 86–91).

4. AAE CP *Allemagne* 116, fols. 24–30, 52–61, 80–84, and 85–87, *Memoire(s) des Plenipotentiaires de France,* January 6, 13, 15, and 17, 1648 (copies in *Allemagne* 118, fols. 34–45, 64–74, 95–101, and 173–178). NNA SG VL 12588.56 II, Dutch plenipotentiaries (letters sent) to States General, January 3 and 18, 1648 (the second in French in AAE CP *Allemagne* 107, fols. 8–10). ASVen *Munster* 7, Contarini (copies to Senate) to Nani, January 7, 14, and 16, 1648. BVat *CCL* A I 16, fols. 6–13, 17–27, 27–30, and 30–31, Chigi (register) to Panzirolo, January 10 and three letters of January 17, 1648 (copies sent in ASVat *Paci* 24, fols. 33–38, and/or deciphered on fols. 58–67, and in *Paci* 22, fols. 12–14 and 15–18. For the last-minute French proposal, see AAE CP *Allemagne* 107, fols. 34–35, "*donné a M^rs les plenipot^res des provinces Unies le 10e Janvier* 1648" (partial copy on fol. 17; full copy in *Allemagne* 118, fols. 260–261; other copies in NNA SG 8413, fols. 189–190, dated January 13; and in SG R 4858 with the Spanish reply; and in ASVat *Paci* 24, fols. 68–71) [pub. in Italian in Siri XII, 6–7]. See also AAE CP *Allemagne* 116, fol. 74, *Ecrit de M. Chabo touchant M^r D avaux 16 Jan. 1648,* which seem instead to have been written by Servien and was integrated into

Allemagne 118, fols. 76–81, Servien's own hand minute on his accusations against D'Avaux, blaming him for everything from having botched the peace in 1646 to his having connived for the restitution of Lorraine, both writings of January 13, 1648. The accusations against D'Avaux seem to have influenced AST MPLM *Munster* 3, Saint Maurice (letters sent) to Christina, January 14 and 16, 1648, and AAE CP *Allemagne* 118, fol. 73, Saint Maurice's own hand minute, apparently to Mondino, for transmission to Mazarin. See an excellent account of the signing of the Spanish-Dutch treaty in AAE CP *Allemagne* 116, fols. 192–200, *Memoire des Plenipotentiaires de France,* February 3, 1648 (copy in *Allemagne* 118, fols. 285–290. For the final treaty, see NNA SG *VL* 12588.56 II and SG *R* 4858, all copies in Dutch and French, with respective powers [found in Knuttel in Dutch: 5733–5736, in French: 5737, and in Latin: 5738; published in Italian in Siri XII, 157–179; in Dutch in Aitzema *VNVH* II, 575–596; in Latin in Londorp VI, 331–338; and in French in Dumont VI, pt. 1, 429–439]. See a copy of the treaty in Latin with ratifications and inclusions in AAE CP *Allemagne* 107, fols. 109–156.

5. AAE CP *Allemagne* 116, fols. 145–164, *Memoire* (secretary's revisions with Lionne corrections) *du Roy a Messrs Les Plenip^{res}* (Brienne minute in Ass. Nat. *Ms.* 272, fols. 67–85, and copy in AAE CP *Allemagne* 118, fols. 230–245), *Allemagne* 116, fols. 127–139, Lionne (own hand minute) to Servien (letter sent in *Allemagne* 118, fols. 251–252) [extract pub. in *LM* III, 18, note 2]; AAE CP *Allemagne* 116, fols. 141–142, Mazarin (secretary's minute) to D'Avaux, (copy in *Allemagne* 118, fols. 246–250) [extract pub. in *LM* III, 16–18]; *Allemagne* 116, fols. 143–144, Mazarin (Lionne minute) to Longueville [extract pub. in *LM* III, 14–16], all of January 28, 1648. Mazarin also had the Duke d'Orléans write directly to Longueville and Condé write directly to the plenipotentiaries.

6. Coigneux speech and Edict on Domain: AN *U* 336*, pp. 26–28 [pub. in *DPP* I, 41–42], and Ormesson I, 435, 437–441. Mazarin's hedging: AAE CP *Allemagne* 116, fols. 204–208, *Mem^{re}* (Lionne minute) *du Roy a M^{rs} les plenipot^{res},* February 7, 1648 (Brienne minute in Ass. Nat. *Ms.* 278, fols. 105–108, and copy in AAE CP *Allemagne* 118, fols. 307–313). More confrontations: AN *U* 336*, pp. 38–43 [pub. in *DPP* I, 48–53]; Ormesson I, 444–451; and Talon, P&M, ser. 2, LXI, 122–143, or M&P ser. 3, VI, 212–220. Return of Longueville: Ormesson I, 452, and BNF *Ms. Fr.* 10273, pp. 19–25 [pub. in Ormesson I, 453, note 1]. See also ASVen *Francia* 107, D 678 III, Nani to Senate, March 3, 1648 (trascript in *Ms. It.* 1830, fols. 152–154). Compromise solution: AN *U* 336*, pp. 80–90 [pub. in *DPP* I, 72–77]; Ormesson I, 460–465; and Dubuisson I, 13. Recall of D'Avaux: AAE CP *Allemagne* 116, fol. 312, Louis XIV (minute) to D'Avaux, March 13,

1648 (Brienne minute in Ass. Nat. *Ms.* 272, fol. 169). See also AAE CP *Allemagne* 116, fols. 385–386, *Memoire* (Lionne minute) *du Roy au Sr Servien*, April 10, 1648 (Brienne minute in Ass. Nat. *Ms.* 272, fols. 243–247, and copy sent in AAE CP *Allemagne* 119, fols. 243–247).

7. AGS E 2353, *consulta* of February 25, 1648 [pub. in *CDI* LXXXIV, 51–67].

8. Guise, P&M, LV, 365–455, and LVI, 1–241, or M&P, ser. 3, LVI, 114—224. Modène II, 290–506. See also BNF *Ms. Dupuy* 775, fols. 167–168, Guise (letters sent) to Anne of Austria and to Mazarin on behalf of Mlle. de Pons, February 27 and 28, 1648 [pub. in Modène I, 168–171; Pastoret, 268; and Guise, P&M, LV, 44–46, or M&P, ser. 3, VII, 9–10].

9. AAE CP *Allemagne* 116, fols. 218–225, *Response* (by D'Avaux and Servien) *au Memoire du Roy du 29e Jan^{er}* February 10, 1648 (copy in *Allemagne* 118, fols. 320–323); *Allemagne* 118, fols. 379–388, Servien (own hand minutes) to Lionne, February 16, 1648. *Allemagne* 116, fols. 248–251, D'Avaux (copy for Mazarin) to Brienne, February 17, 1648 (copy in *Allemagne* 118, fols. 389–394); *Allemagne* 118, fols. 403–410, Servien (own hand minute) to Lionne, February 23, 1648 (copy on fols. 411–418), as well as fols. 419–426, Servien's (own hand minute) *Memoire public dont il faut envoyer une copie a S.E. et a M. le C. de Brienne,* same date. On the rush to conclude, see the printed *Abhandelung PVNCTI SATISFATIONIS So von den Herrn Kay: unnd Schwedischen Abgesandten zu Osnabur geschehen den 9/19 Martii 1648* (Vor den Minnenbrüder in Loret, 1648) in NNA SG VL 12588.56 II, which includes: the Abhandelung *Wegen* REFORMATION *Der Iustitz So woll am Kayserl. Cammergericht als Reichshoffraht Wie zwischen den Herrn Kays. un~ Schwedischen Abgesandeten zu Oßnabrück beygelegt und geschlossen worden den 2 Martii 1648;* CIRCA SATISFACTIONEM CORONAE SVECIAE CAUSAM PALATINAM ET *Praetensionem Hassicam* OSNABRUGI PER ACTA die 8 stilo veteri aut 18 Martii stilo novo 1648, 9 Martii stilo veteri & 19 Martii stilo novo 1648, and 8 Apr. & 19 Martii stilo novo 1648, along with a German translation of the first two [also pub. in Latin and French in NS IV, 497–501, and in Latin in Meiern V, 593–596]; *Die* AUTOTONOMIA *Oder* PVNCTVS *Von freystellung der Religion Wie derselbe zwischen den Herrn Kayserl. unnd Schwedschen Abgesandtten zu Oßnabrück ist vergleichen und abgehandelt worden . . . am 18 Maritj 1648* [also pub. in Latin in Meiern V, 538–540]; *Abhandelung PVNCTI AEQVIVALENTIAE Oder entgeltnuß So Ihrer Churfürstl. Durchleucht zu Brandenburg wegen vorgeschehener abtretung beyzulegen Wie von den Herrn Käyserl. und Schwedischen Abgesandten zu Oßnabrüg geschlossen worden den 9/19 Martij 1648* [also pub. in Latin in Meiern V, 589–592, dated March 7/17]; *Abhandelung Des Braunschweig-Lüneburgischen AEQVIVALENTIS Oder Entgeldnus So selbigen Fürstt.hause beyzulegen von den Herrn Kayserl. unnd Schwedischen Abgesandten zu*

Oßnabrüg geschlossen worden, 9/19 Martii 1648; and the CONVENTIO *super* AMNISTIA *Vniversalis* OSNABRVGIS *11/21 Aprilis 1648 transacta & subscripta.* See also. the *Punctus Gravaminum inter Sacrae Caesarae Majestatis & Coronae Sueciae Legatos Plenipotentiarios. D 24 Marti 1648 Osnabrugi conclusus* published in Meiern V, 562–576, as well as SRA *DG* 12, fols. 137–145, 196–205, 259–265, 291–298, 363–376, and 475–483; Johan Oxenstierna and Salvius (letters sent) to Christina, January 31/February 10, February 7/17, February 21/March 2, March 6/16, 13/23 and 20/30, 1648 [pub. in *APW* II C 4/1, 230–238, 244–252, 261–267, 275–283, 308–321, 325–333, and 345–352].

10. First *mémoire:* AAE CP *Allemagne* 116, fols. 385–385, *Mem^{re}* (Lionne minute) *du Roy au Sr Servien,* April 10, 1648 (Brienne minute in Ass. Nat. *Ms.* 272, fol. 201, copy sent in *Allemagne* 119, fols. 243–247). Second *mémoire:* AAE CP *Allemagne* 116, fols. 407–409, *Mem^{re}* (Lionne minute) *du Roy au Sr Servien,* April 17, 1648 (Brienne minute in Ass. Nat. *Ms.* 272, fols. 209–211, and copy sent in AAE CP *Allemagne* 119, fols. 303–307). Appointment as minister of state: *Allemagne* 119, fol. 391, Mazarin (letter sent) to Servien, April 24, 1648. Third *mémoire: Allemagne* 117, fols. 29–32, *Mem^{re}* (Lionne minute) *du Roy au Sr Servien Son plenipot^{re} a l'assemblée generale,* April 24, 1648 (Brienne minute in Ass. Nat. *Ms.* 272, fols. 220–222, copy sent in AAE CP *Allemagne* 119, fols. 385–390).

11. Ormesson I, 481–482; Dubuisson I, 18; Talon, P&M, ser. 2, LXI, 150 and (for the advances) 346, or M&P, ser. 3, VI, 222 and (for the advances) 300; BNF *Ms. Fr.* 10273 *(Remarques Journalieres)* p. 32 [pub. in Ormesson I, 482–483, note 3]. ASVen *Francia* 107, D 704 II, D 709 III, and D 712 III, Nani to Senate, April 28, May 5, and 12 1648 (transcript in BNF *Ms. It.* 1830, fols. 243–245, 263–265, and 274–277). AAE CP *Allemagne* 117, fols. 70–76, *Mémoire* (Lionne minute) *du Card^l Mazarin a M. Servien,* May 8, 1648 (copy sent in *Allemagne* 120, fols. 61–66) [extracts pub. in *LM* III, 108–111 and 112–113, as two letters].

12. NNA SG VL 12588.56 II, Gendt (letters sent) to States General, March 26, two of April 2, and one each of April 6, 8, 17, and 21 1648 (copies in NNA SG R 4858); AAE CP *Allemagne* 119, fols. 278–286, Servien (own hand minute) to king, April 13, 1648 (duplicate for Mazarin in *Allemagne* 116, fols. 392–401, and other copy in *Allemagne* 119, fols. 289–297); *Allemagne* 119, fols. 331–339, Servien (own hand minute) to king, April 20, 1648 (cleaner minute in *Allemagne* 119, fols. 364–374; duplicate for Mazarin in *Allemagne* 117, fols. 15–28; and copy in *Allemagne* 119, fols. 340–351); *Allemagne* 119, fols. 405–412, Servien (own hand minute) to king, April 28, 1648 (duplicate for Mazarin in *Allemagne* 117, fols. 44–52, and other copy in *Allemagne* 119, fols. 396–404); ASVen *Munster* 8, Contarini (copy

to Senate) to Nani, April 28, 1648; AAE CP *Allemagne* 120, fols. 31–37, Servien (own hand partial minute) to Brienne May 4, 1648 (duplicate for Mazarin in *Allemagne* 117, fols. 60–64, and other copy in *Allemagne* 120, fols. 38–47); *Allemagne* 120, fols. 48–53, Servien (copy) to Lionne, May 4, 1648; SRA *DG* 12, fols. 794–799, Johan Oxenstierna and Salvius to Christina, April 24/May 4, 1648 [pub. in APW II C 4/1, 432–437]. See copies of the exchange, one signed by each of the contracting parties, in NNA SG *VL* 12588.56 II, both dated May 15, 1648. For a description of the exchange, see NNA SG *VL* 12588.56 II, Dutch plenipotentiaries (brief letter sent) to States General, May 19, 1648 (copy in SG *R* 4858) and BNE *Ms.* 8747, fols. 327–334, the much longer *Relacion de la forma con que se han hecho las entregas & las ratificaciones de la Paz de España y los Estados Generales De las Provincias Unidas y de Su publicacion que se zelebriò en la Ciudad de Munster de Vestfalia à 15 de Mayo de este año 1648* [pub. in *CDI* LXXXIV, 210–216]. There is also a French description in AAE CP *Allemagne* 108, fols. 82–85 (copies on fols. 86–89 and 117–120).

13. Broussel and the *arrêt d'union:* AN *U* 336*, pp. 107–120 [pub. in *DPP* I, 87–94]; Ormesson I, 489–490; Talon, P&M, ser. 2, LXI, 150–151, or M&P, ser. 3, VI, 222–223; and BNF *Ms. Fr.* 10273, pp. 33–34. For the *arrêt* itself, see *U* 336*, p. 120 [pub. in *DPP* I, 93–94]; *U* 139*, pp. 393–394; BNF *Ms. Fr.* 23319, fol. 2; JOURNAL, p. 3; and NOUVEAU J., p iii. Siege before Ypres (May 12, 1648): *Gazette* n° 74, May 22, 1648. Return of D'Avaux: Ormesson I, 497. The loss of Courtray (May 19, 1648) is barely mentioned in the *Gazette* n° 79, May 30, 1648. Capitulation of Ypres (May 28, 1648): *Gazette* n° 80, June 2, 1648. Escape of Beaufort: Ormesson I, 502–503. Confrontations: Ormesson I, 496–512; and Talon, P&M, ser. 2, LXI, 153–175, or M&P, ser. 3, VI, 224–231. Orders to stop assemblies (May 22): AN *U* 139*, pp. 394–397, and *U* 336*, pp. 123–125 [pub. in *DPP* I, 95–96] and (May 24), *U* 139*, pp. 397–399 and *U* 336*, pp. 126–129 [pub. in *DPP* I 97–99]. Quashing the *arrêt* (June 10): BNF *Ms. Fr.* 23319, fol. 3; JOURNAL, p. 4; NOUVEAU J., p. iv; Ormesson I, 514–515, 517; Talon, P&M, ser. 2, LXI, 175, or M&P, ser. 3, VI, 231; and BNF *Ms. Fr.* 10273, pp. 39–40. More confrontations: AN *U* 336*, pp. 161–170 [pub. in *DPP* I, 112–121]; Ormesson I (June 16) 518–527; and Talon, P&M, ser. 2, LXI, 175–198, or M&P, ser. 3, VI, 231–239. For Mazarin's change of tactics, see AAE MD *France* 848, fol. 266–267, the anonymous *mémoire,* which sounds very much like Mazarin himself, titled "*Touchant quelq~ harangues du Parlemᵗ.*" I would date this *mémoire* for mid-June 1648. For Duke d'Orléans's overtures, see AN *U* 336*, pp. 180–208 [pub. in *DPP* I, 127–142]; and Talon, P&M, ser. 2, LXI, 198–199, or M&P, ser. 3, VI, 239. Queen's concession (June 27): BNF *Ms. Fr.* 23319, fols. 9–13; JOURNAL, p. 9; Ormesson I, 530–531; and Talon, P&M,

ser. 2, LXI, 202–203, or M&P, ser. 3, VI, 240. For the articles of the Chamber of Saint Louis, see AN *U* 336*, pp. 210–233 [pub. in *DPP* I, 143–155]; BNF *Ms. Fr.* 23319, fols. 181–200; JOURNAL, pp. 9–19; NOUVEAU J., pp. 5–12; and Talon, M&P, ser. 3, VI, 241–245, note 1, in different versions. See also Ormesson I, 531–532, and BNF *Ms. Fr.* 10273, pp. 55–56. Disgrace of Hémery: Ormesson I, 540; Talon, P&M, ser. 2, LXI, 215, or M&P, ser. 3, VI, 248; and AAE CP *Allemagne* 117, fols. 349–352, *Mem^re* (Lionne and other secretary's minute) *du Roy au Sr Servien Son plenipot^re a L'assemblee generale,* July 10, 1648 (Brienne minute in Ass. Nat. *Ms.* 272, fols. 345–348, and copy sent in AAE CP *Allemagne* 121, fols. 77–83) [extract pub. in *LM* III, 151–154]. *Lit de Justice:* AN *U* 336*, pp. 326–331 [pub. in *DPP* I, 207–210], BNF *Ms. Fr.* 23319, fols. 84–92, oddly dated August 7, 1648; JOURNAL, pp. 45–48; Ormesson I, 548–549; Talon, P&M, ser. 2, LXI, 230–237, or M&P, ser. 3, VI, 256–261; BNF *Ms. Fr.* 10273, pp. 69–70; and barely recounted in the *Gazette* n° 116, August 4, 1648. Lionne also expresses the hope that a beneficial reform of the finances was in the offing in AAE CP *Allemagne* 121, fols. 286–287, his own hand minute to Servien, August 6, 1648.

14. Turenne I, 119–127; La Court, 100–105; *Gazette* n° 81, June 4, 1648; AAE CP *Allemagne* 120, fols. 383–390, Servien (own hand minute) to king, June 15, 1648 (duplicate for Mazarin in *Allemagne* 117, fols. 233–238 and, other copy in *Allemagne* 120, fols. 391–400); HHSA RK *FrA* 90 II (Volmar Diary), June 17, 1648 [pub. in APW III C 2, 1085–1090]. For his written protest, made on June 11/21, 1648, see HHSA RK *FrA* 55b, fols. 99–103 (copy in SRA *DG* 13, fols. 204–206) [pub. in Italian in Siri XII, 551–555, dated June 11, and in German in Meiern V, 916–918, also dated June 11]. There is a French translation in AAE CP *Allemagne* 108, fols. 248–251. For the last-ditch Dutch efforts, see NNA SG *VL* 12588.56 II, *Memoire des points qui seront proposés à Osnabrug au Sieur de Servien Ambass^r de France . . . Faict à Munster le 16e Juin 1648* (copy in NNA SG 8413, fols. 230–231); AAE CP *Allemagne* 108, fols. 269–270, and *Ecrit donné par les Amb^rs de Hollande a M^r. Servien,* June 18, 1648 (copies on fols. 271–272 and 273 and AAE CP *Allemagne* 117, fol. 235) [pub. in Italian in Siri XII, 584–585]; *Allemagne* 108, fols. 275–278, *Reponse de l amb^eur de France a l escrit du 18e Juin,* June 19, 1648 (copies on fols. 284–287 and 288–290, and *Allemagne* 117, fols. 260–261; NNA SG *VL* 12588.56 II; and SG 8413, fols. 233–234) [pub. in Italian in Siri XII, 586–589]; AAE CP *Allemagne* 120, fols. 437–449, Servien (own hand minute) to king, June, 22, 1648 (duplicate for Mazarin in *Allemagne* 117, fols. 269–277, and other copy in *Allemagne* 120, fols. 450–464); *Sommaire du Memoire des Srs Plenipotentiaires d' Espagne donné le 24e Juin aux Plenipòts^s de M^rs les Estats generaux des Provinces Unies En reponse du Mem^e que Monsr le Comte de Servien Plenipòts de France a donné le 19e Juin 1648 a*

Osenbrug aux Plenipòts des^s Seigneurs Estats gener . . . delivré au Sr de Servien le 27e Juin 1648 (copies in NNA SG 8413, fols. 240–241, and AAE CP *Allemagne* 108, fols. 305–306, 307–308, 343–345; and *Allemagne* 117, fols. 278–280) [pub. in Italian in Siri XII, 594–596] and NNA SG VL 12588.56 II, Dutch plenipotentiaries (letters sent) to States-General, June 21 and 27, 1648 (summary of the last in French in AAE CP *Allemagne* 108, fol. 323), SRA *DG* 13, Johan Oxenstierna and Salvius (letters sent) to Christina, June 5/15, 12/22, and 19/29, and July 3/13, 10–20, and 17–27, 1648 [pub. in *APW* II C 4/2, 509–514, 525–536, 552–559, 576–583, 589–596, and 600–604]. Agreement by States of Empire on payment of troops: SRA *DG* 13, fols. 9–11, June 28/July 8, 1648 [pub. in *ST* VI, 1, 233–237]. There is a summary in NNA SG VL 12588.56 II. See also AAE CP *Allemagne* 120, fols. 498–506, Servien (own hand minute) to king, June 30, 1648 (copy on fols. 507–516, copy for Mazarin in *Allemagne* 117, fols. 301–312); as well as *Allemagne* 121, fols. 29–37, Servien (own hand minute) to king, July 7, 1648 (copy on fols. 38–49; and copy for Mazarin in *Allemagne* 117, fols. 335–348).

15. Turenne I, 127–130; La Court, 105–108; *Gazette* n° 125, August 20, 1648.

16. BNF *Ms. Baluze* 174 (*Carnet* 9), fols. 39–44. AAE CP *Allemagne* 109, fols. 146–149, Mazarin (Lionne minute) to Servien, August 14, 1648 (copy sent in *Allemagne* 121, fols. 337–341). After adding the passage at the bottom of the page, a secretary's hand (not Lionne) also inserted the addition on the margin of the minute. The extract from the copy sent, published in *LM* III, 173–181, is worth savoring *verbatim*.

17. BNF *Ms. Fr.* 4145, fols. 1–12, *Relation de la Bataille de Lens gaignee sur les Espagnols le xx d'Aoust MDCXLVIII par Louys de Bourbon prince de Condé Et escritte de Sa Main,* followed on fols. 13–14 by a list of French officer casualties; on fols. 15–21, Spanish officer prisoners; and on fol. 22, a letter from the Archduke Leopold to the Elector of Cologne [pub. in the *Gazettes* n°s 129 and 130, August 26 and 28, 1648, and in the *Revue militaire française* I (January, 1875) 105–125, with the list of French casualties.

18. For the Day of the Barricades, see Dubuisson I, 50–55; BNF *Ms. Fr.* 10273, pp. 93–105; *Ms. Baluze* 291, fols. 45–48; and AN U 336*, pp. 394–420 [pub. in *DPP* I, 246–260]; BNF *Ms. Fr.* 23319, fols. 127–159; JOURNAL, pp. 63–75; and ASVat *Francia* 96, fols. 309–310, Bagni deciphered copy, August 28, 1648. See also ASVen *Francia* 108, n° 31 I, Morosini (letter sent) to Senate, September 1, 1648 (transcript in BNF *Ms. It.* 1831, fols. 62–64). For Mazarin's account, which claims the queen agreed to let the *parlement* discuss the *rentes,* see Ass. Nat. Ms. 272, fols. 378–379, and the *Mem^{re}* (Lionne minute) *du Roy au Sr Servien Son Plenipot^{re} a l'assemblée generale,* August 28, 1648. The *Gazette* n° 131 of August 29 is even more dismissive of the "rumeur."

19. BNF *Ms. Baluze* 174 (*Carnet* 9), fol. 64; Ormesson I, 570–581; and Dubuisson I, 61–63. For the session of September 22, 1648, compare specifically AN *U* 336*, pp. 431–433 [pub. in *DPP* I, 267–268]; BNF *Ms. Fr.* 23319, fols. 176–179; JOURNAL, pp. 82–83; and NOUVEAU J., pp. 76–78; with the sanitized version in *U* 139*, pp. 594–604. See also Dubuisson I, 64; and ASVat *Francia* 96, fol. 320, Bagni (deciphered copy) to Panzirolo, September 18, 1648, and fols. 324–325, the newsletter covering events from September 18 to 24; ASVen *Francia* 108, nᵒˢ 38 II, 39 III, 40 I, 41 II, and 44 II, Morosini (letters sent) to Senate, September 15 (two letters), September 22 (two letters), and September 29, 1648 (transcripts in BNF *Ms. It.* 1831, fols. 77–84 and 89–90).

20. AAE CP *Allemagne* 121, fols. 426–433, Servien (own hand minute) to king, August 24, 1648 (copy on fols. 434–445); SRA *JOS* B II, Salvius (letter sent) to Johan Oxenstierna, August 18/28, 1648 [pub. in APW III C 4/2, 656–657]; AAE CP Allemagne 121, fols. 490–493, Servien (own hand minute) to Brienne, August 31, 1648 (copy on fols. 494–497); SRA *DG* 13, fols. 576–577, Salvius (letter sent) to Christina, August 21/31, 1648 [pub. in APW III C 4/2, 662–664]; AAE CP *Allemagne* 122, fols. 71 and 73–79, Servien (own hand minute) to king, September 7, 1648 (copy on fols. 80–91). See SRA *DG* 13, fols. 605–606, for a draft of the wording of the article on assistance. See Londorp VI, 345–346, for the city of Strasbourg's complaints against the treaty, and see VI, 346, for the Imperial princes' complaints against the French satisfactions, dated August 12/22, 1648.

21. HHSA RK *FrA* 92 XVI, fols. 500–502 and 505–509, Ferdinand (two letters sent) to Nassau and Volmar September 16, 1648 (duplicate of the second on fols. 518–522).

22. NOUVEAU J., pp. 81–99; ASVen *Francia* 108, nᵒ 44 II, Morosini (letter sent) to Senate, September 29, 1648 (transcript in BNF *Ms. It.* 1831, fols. 89–90, *Declaration . . . portant règlement sur le fait de la justice, police, finances, et soulagement des sujets de S.M . . . 22 octobre 1648, verifiée en Parlement le 24 octobre 1648* (Paris, 1648); Dubuisson I, 67–81; BNF *Ms. Fr.* 10273, fols. 115–118; and Talon, P&M, ser. 2, LXI, 288–343 or M&P, ser. 3 277–299.

23. HHSA RK FrA 90 II (Volmar Diary), September 30–October 3, 1648 [pub. in *APW* III C 2, 1144–1146]. See Volmar's deciphering of the second letter in HHSA RK *FrA* 92 XVI, fols. 510–511; AAE CP *Allemagne* 122, fols. 363–373, Servien (own hand minute) to king, October 6, 1648 (copy on fols. 374–390); *Allemagne* 122, fols. 426–430 and 439–444, Servien (own hand minutes) to king and to Mazarin, both of October 13, 1648 (copies on fols. 432–438 and 445–461); SRA *DG* 13, fols. 875–884, Johan Oxenstierna and Salvius to Christina, October 8/18, 1648 [pub. in *APW* II C 4/2,

730–738]; AAE CP *Allemagne* 122, fols. 439–444; *Allemagne* 122, fols. 486–492, Servien (own hand minute) to king, October 20, 1648 (copy on fols. 493–504); and *Allemagne* 122, fols. 544–546, Servien (a signed copy) to Anne, October 25, 1648. See the texts of the treaty both in Latin and badly translated in various languages on the Web: http://www.pax-westphalica.de/ [2006].

24. AAE CP *Allemagne* 122, fols. 612–616, Mazarin (letter sent) to Servien [pub. in *LM* III, 220–224].

25. For the speech of Aubry, compare AN *U* 336*, pp. 462–463 [pub. in *DPP* I, 285] with the sanitized version in *U* 139*, pp. 734–735. See also *"Le Courrier du Temps, Apportant Ce Qui Se Passe de Plus Secret en la Cour des Princes de l'Europe"* [Moreau: 825]. See Chavigny's *mémoire* in Ormesson II, 746–758, which the editor Chéruel (see pp. 745–746) dates for late 1649.

26. See any edition of Louix XIV's *Mémoires pour l'instruction du Dauphin* or, particularly, kindly refer to my own edition in English, *Louis XIV: Mémoires for the Instruction of the Dauphin* (London and New York, 1970). Please also see my "Louis XIV's *Mémoires pour l'histoire de la guerre de Hollande*," *French Historical Studies* VIII.1 (Spring, 1973) 29–50, and my *Louis XIV and the Origins of the Dutch War* (Cambridge and New York, 1988), all of which provide points of comparison to the present book.

Bibliography

Manuscript Sources

Austria

Österreichisches Staatsarchiv (Vienna)
    Allgemeines Verwaltungsarchiv
        Fürstlich Trauttmansdorffsches Zentral-Familienarchiv 108–111, 114–115, 124, 126
        Hofskammerarchiv
            Reichsakten 157
    Haus-, Hof- und- Staatsarchiv
        Geheime Staatsregistratur
            Repertorium N 95/68, 96/68
        Mainzer Erzkanzlerarchiv
            Friedensakten 9, 19, 25
        Österreichische Akten, Tyrol 20d–f
        Reichskanzlei
            Friedensakten 24c, 26, 35a, e, 46g, i, k, 47a–b, 48a–c, 49b, 50a–c, 51a–b, 52a–b, 52d, 53a, 54a, 54c, 55b, 90 I–III, 91, 92 I, III, V–VIII, X–XI, XVI, 94 III, 96 V–VI
        Staatskanzlei
            Friedensakten 1, 5, 7, 11

France

Archives Condé (Chantilly)
    Séries I 4, M 33, P 1
    Ms. 1086
Archives de la Guerre (Vincennes)
    A^1 78–80, 85–87, 89, 91–92, 95–96, 98–100
Archives des Affaires Etrangères (Paris)

Correspondance Politique
  Allemagne 5, 7–8, 10–18, 21, 23–24, 26–35, 37, 40–49, 51–57, 59–68, 75–90, 98–103, 107–108, 110–112, 116–123, *supplément* 5
  Autriche 13–16
  Bavière 1–2
  Brunswick-Hanovre 1
  Danemark 1–6
  Espagne, 14–15, 18–20, 23–28
  Grisons 3–9
  Hambourg 1
  Hesse-Cassel 1–3
  Hollande 8, 16–18, 20–27, 29–47
  Lorraine 9, 11, 13, 22, 32
  Mantoue 2, 5–7
  Modène 1
  Munster 1
  Naples 2
  Parme 1–2
  Pays Bas Espagnols 12, 14–30
  Pologne 2–10
  Portugal 1–3
  Rome 57–67, 94, 103, 105
  Sardaigne 4, 9–34, 40
  Saxe 1
  Suède 2–11
  Toscane 4–5
  Turquie 3–5
  Venise 43, 45–51, 53–55
Mémoires et Documents
  Allemagne 9
  France 245–248, 254, 259–264, 285–286, 782, 787, 805, 820–822, 830–837, 846–858, 860–861, 1415–1424bis, 1633–1638, 1706, 2163
Archives Nationales
  AB[xix] 2927
  K 1335–1336
  KK 1388–1389
  U 28, 136*–139*
  U 336*
Bibliothèque de l'Assemblée Nationale
  Mss. 168, 267, 272–279

Bibliothèque de l'Institut
  Mss. Godefroy 19–22, 83–87, 90–91, 160, 273–274, 283–284, 286,
    395, 482, 496, 512, 549
Bibliothèque Mazarine
  Mss. 2214–2236, 4409–4415
Bibliothèque Municipale, Rouen
  Ms. 3268 (Collection Leber 5776)
Bibliothèque Nationale de France
  Mss. Baluze 146–147, 163, 167–172, 174–175, 254–255, 291
  Mss. Cangé 60, 68
  Mss. Cinq Cents Colbert 2, 101, 103–104, 112–113
  Mss. Clairambault 383, 572–579, 600–611
  Mss. Dupuy 121, 616, 672, 738–739, 775
  Mss. Fr. 3701, 3768, 3784, 3855, 4092, 4145, 4220, 4414,
    5202–5203, 9225, 10205, 10212, 10273–10277, 10643–10646,
    10649, 15850–15864, 15870, 15884, 15914, 15935, 17861,
    17897–17900, 17906–17918, 17946–17956, 20984–20989,
    23319, 23527, 23565–23575, 23589–23590
  Mss. Italiens, 1802, 1820–1831
  Mélanges Colbert 27
Médiathèque d'Orléans *Ms.* 532 (419)

Germany

Giessen, Universitätsbibliothek
  Codex 200, 204, 206–210
Hessisches Staatsarchiv, Marburg
  4h 1694, 2121, 2137

Italy

Archivio di Stato di Torino
  Materie Politiche, Lettere Ministri
    Francia 44–52
    Munster 1–4
    Trattati 9–10
Archivio di Stato di Venezia
    Francia 81, 99–108
    Munster 1–8

Netherlands

Koninklijk Huisarchief, The Hague
  Nassau Papers
    A IV 1628: 15–18, 21, 36–38, 40–41, 56, 57
Nationaal Archief
  Staten Generaal (1576–1796)
    3243–3255 *Registers*
    4563–4565 *Registers en Indices*
    4853–4859 *Resolutiën*
    6714 *Bijlage Resoluties*
    6763–6771 *Liassen Vranckyck*
    8413 *Bijlagen*
    8449–8452 *French recueils*
    8453 *Négotiation de M^r d'Avaux à Osnaburg*
    12588.37 III, IV, 12588.47 I, II, 12588.56 II *Vervolg Loketkast*
  Staten van Holland (1572–1785)
    1374–1375 *Geheime Resoluties*

Portugal

Arquivo Nacional da Torre do Tombo, Conselho Geral do Santo
  Ofício: 1341–1343

Spain

Archivo General de Simancas
  Estado 2063, 2065–2066, 2250, 2254–2255, 2345–2350, 2353,
    2426–2429, 2433, 2471–2472
Archivo Histórico Nacional
  Estado 967, 2880
  Sección Nobleza, Ducado de Frìas 27/1–3, 33/1
Biblioteca del Palacio, Madrid
  Ms. 1817
Biblioteca Nacional
  Mss. 1026, 2377, 8747, 18200

Sweden

Riksarkivet
  Axel Oxenstiernas Samling A II, vol. 3

Diplomatica Germanica 1–15, 23
Johan Oxenstiernas Samling A I–II, B II
Kungliga Koncepter 1643–1648
Originaltraktater
Riksregistraturet 1636–1641, 1643–1645, 1645–1646 Svensk,
    1646–1647 Svensk

Vatican

Archivio Segreto
  Nunziatura di Francia 87–92, 92A–99
  Nunziatura di Paci 15–25
Biblioteca Apostolica Vaticana
  Codex Chisianus Latinus
    A I 1, 8 (1–20), 9, 14–18, 22, 24–25, 42, 45
    A III 69, 71
    Q III 57–58

Printed Sources

*Abhandelung Puncti Satisfactionis So von den Herrn Kay: unnd Schwedischen Abge-
sandten zu Osnabrug geschehen den 9/19 Martii 1648* (Vor den Minnenbrüder
in Loret, 1648).

*Accord Gemaeckt ende besloten Tusschen de Croon Vranckrijck . . . . ende de
Vereenighde Provintien . . . Over de Ligue Garentie, Ghedaen den 29 July 1647*
[Knuttel: 5487–5488].

Acta Pacis Westphalicae, ed. Konrad Repgen (Münster, 1962–).
  Serie I: Instruktionen.
    1 *Frankreich-Schweden-Kaiser,* ed. Fritz Dickmann *et al.* (1962).
  Serie II: Korrespondenzen
    Abteilung A: Die kaiserlischen Korrespondenzen
      1 1643–1644, ed. Wilhelm Engels (1969).
      2 1644–1645, ed. Wilhelm Engles (1976).
      3 1645–1646, ed. Karsten Ruppert (1985).
      4 1646, ed. Hubert Salm, Brigitte Wübbeke-Pflüger *et al.* (2001).
      5 1646–1647, ed. Antje Oschmann (1993).
    Abteilung B: Die französischen Korrespondenzen
      1 1644, ed. Ursula Irsigler (1979).
      2 1645, ed. Franz Bosbach (1986).
      3/1 1645–1646, ed. Elke Jarnut, Rita Bohlen *et al.* (1999).
      3/2 1646, ed. Elke Jarnut, Rita Bohlen *et al.* (1999).

4   1646, ed. Clivia Kelch-Rade, Anuschka Tischer, *et al.* (1999)

5/1   1646–1647, ed. Kriemhild Goronzy, Guido Braun *et al.* (2002).

5/2   1647, ed. Kriemhild Goronzy, Guido Braun *et al.* (2002).

6   1647, ed. Kriemhild Goronzy, Michael Rohrschneider, *et al.* (2004).

Abteilung C: Die schwedischen Korrespondenzen

1   1643–1645, ed. Ernst Manfred Wermter (1965).

2   1645–1646, ed. Wilhelm Kohl (1971).

3   1646–1647, ed. Gottfried Lorenz (1975).

4/1   1647–1648, ed. Wilhelm Kohl and Paul Nachtsheim (1994).

4/2   1648–1649, ed. Wilhelm Kohl and Paul Nachtsheim (1994).

Serie III: Protokolle, Verhandlungsakten, Diarien, Varia

Abteilung A: Protokolle

1/1   *Die Beratungen der kurfürstsliche Kurie: 1645–1647,* ed. Winfried Becker (1975).

3/1   *Die Beratungen des Fürstenrates in Osnabrück: 1645,* ed. Maria-Elizabeth Brunert (1998).

3/2   *Die Beratungen des Fürstenrates in Osnabrück: 1645–1646,* ed. Maria-Elizabeth Brunert (1998).

3/3   *Die Beratungen des Fürstenrates in Osnabrück: 1646,* ed. Maria-Elizabeth Brunert and Klaus Rosen (2001).

3/4   *Die Beratungen des Fürstenrates in Onabrück: 1646–1647,* ed. Maria-Elizabeth Brunert (2006).

3/5   *Die Beratungen des Fürstenrates in Onabrück: Mai–Juni 1648,* ed. Maria-Elizabeth Brunert (2006).

4/1   *Die Beratungen der katholischen Stände: 1645–1646,* ed. Fritz Wolff and Hildburg Schmidt-von Essen (1970).

6   *Die Beratungen der Städtekurie Osnabrück: 1645–1649,* ed. Günther Buchstab (1981).

Abteilung B: Verhandlungsakten

1/1   *Die Friedensverträge mit Frankreich und Schweden,* ed. Antje Oschmann (1999).

1/2   *Die Friedensverträge mit Frankreich und Schweden,* ed. Guido Braun *et al.* (2007).

1/3   *Die Friedensverträge mit Frankreich und Schweden,* ed. Antje Oschmann (2007).

Abteilung C: Diarien

1/1   *Diarium Chigi,* ed. Konrad Repgen (1984).

2/1   *Diarium Volmar: 1643–1646,* ed. Joachim Foerster and Roswitha Philippe (1994).

    2/2 *Diarium Volmar: 1647–1649*, ed. Joachim Foerster and Roswitha Philippe (1994).

    3/1 *Diarium Wartenberg: 1644–1646*, ed. Joachim Foerster (1987).

    3/2 *Diarium Wartenberg: 1647–1648*, ed. Joachim Foerster (1987).

    4   *Diarium Lamberg: 1645–1649*, ed. Herta Hageneder (1986).

  Abteilung D: Varia

    1   *Stadtmünsterlische Akten und Vermischtes*, ed. Helmut Lahrkamp (1964).

  Supplementa electronica

    1   *Die Westfälischen Friedensverträge vom 24. Oktober 1648. Texte und Übersetzungen:* http://www.pax-westphalica.de/ [2006].

Aitzema, Lieuwe van, *Verhael van de Nederlandsche Vreede-Handeling* (The Hague, 1650) 2 vols.

Antoine (garçon de chambre du Roy), *Journal de la maladie et mort de Louis XIII*, ed. Alfred Cramail (Fontainebleau, 1880).

Antwoordt Op 't Munsters Praetie, Anniantur Sed cave te ipsum (Dortrecht, 1646) [Knuttel: 5296 5296a, 5297a–b].

Aubery, Antoine, *Mémoires pour l'histoire du Cardinal Duc de Richelieu* (Paris, 1660) 2 vols.

Autentijc Extract Wt de Propositie van den Grave van Avaux Extra-ordinaris Ambassadeur . . . van Vranckryck: aengaende de Paus-gesinde hier te Lande. Gedaen in de Vergaderinge van de . . . Staten Generael in s'Graven-hage den 3 Martij 1644. Midtsgaders De Resolutie vn hare Ho: Mogende den selven dito daer over genomen ende aen de voorsz. Heere Ambassadeur gecommuniceert (Dortrecht, 1644) [Knuttel: 5106. See also Knuttel: 5107–1509].

Avaux, Claude de Mesmes, Count d', *Correspondance inédite du Comte d'Avaux*, ed. Auguste Boppe (Paris, 1887).

———, *Lettres de messieurs d'Avaux et Servien, ambassadeurs pour le Roy de France en Allemagne concernant leurs differents et leurs responses de part & d'autre en l'année 1644* (1650).

Avenel, Georges d', *Lettres, instructions diplomatiques et papiers d'état du Cardinal de Richelieu* (Paris, 1853–1877) 8 vols. Collection de documents inédits sur l'histoire de France, ser. 1.

Benedetti, Elpidio, *Raccolta di diverse memorie per scrivere la vita del Cardinale Giulio Mazarini Romano* (Lyon, n.d.).

Bignon, F., *Les portraictz au naturel avec les armoiries et blasons, noms et qualitez de Messieurs les plenipotentiaires assemblez à Munster et Osnaburg pour faire la paix générale* (Paris, 1648) [AAE Bibliothèque, Réserve T 31].

Brienne, Henri-Auguste de Loménie, Count de, *Mémoires du Comte de Brienne*. Collection des Mémoires relatifs à l'histoire de France, ed. Petitot and

Monmerqué (Paris, 1819–1829) ser. 2 XXXV–XXXVI, or in Nouvelle collection des mémoires pour servir à l'histoire de France, ed. Michaud and Poujoulat (Paris, 1836–1839) ser. 3, III.

———, *Response faite aux mémoires de Monsieur le Comte de la Chastre*, in *Recueil de diverses pièces curieuses pour servir à l'histoire* (1664).

Coleccion de documentos inéditos para la Historia de España ed. Feliciano de la Fuensanta del Valle *et al.* (Madrid, 1884–1885) LXIX, LXXVII, LXXX, LXXXII–LXXXIII, LXXXVI.

Commelyn, Johannes, *Histoire de la vie et actes mémorables de Fréderic-Henry de Nassau, prince d'Orange* (Amsterdam, 1656).

Condé, Prince de, "Relation officielle de la bataille de Lens, d'après les documents officiels du dépôt de la guerre," *Revue militaire française* I (January, 1875) 105–125.

Contarini, Alvise, *Relazione del Congresso di Munster,* ed. Nicola Papadopoli (Venice, 1864).

Declaration du Roy portant règlement sur le fait de la justice, police, finances, et soulagement des sujets de Sa Majesté, 22 octobre 1648 (Paris, 1648).

Dubuisson-Aubenay, François-Nicolas Baudot, *Journal des guerres civiles: 1648–1652,* ed. Gustave Saige (Paris, 1883) 2 vols.

Dumont, Jean, *Corps universel diplomatique du droit des gens* (Amsterdam, 1726–1731) 8 vols.

Escript Donné à Messieurs les Estats Generaux . . . par Monsieur l'Ambassadeur de France, le 4 Mars 1647 [Knuttel: 5456; in Dutch in Knuttel: 5457].

Estrades, Godefroy, Count d', *Correspondance authentique de Godefroy, Comte d'Estrades,* ed. Alexandre de Saint-Léger (Paris, 1924). Société de l'Histoire de France.

Extrait De l'Harangue du Comte d'Avaux, Ambassadeur Extra-ordinaire du Roy Tres-Chrestien Louys XIV Faite en l'Assemblée des Tres-haut & Puissants Messieurs, les Estats Generaux des Provinces Vnies, en la Haye le 3 du mois de Mars MDCXLIV (1644) [Knuttel in French: 5105; in Dutch: 5106–5109].

Ferrier, Jérémie, *Le Catholique d'Estat ou Discours politique des alliances du Roy Très Chrestien contre les calumnies des ennemis de son Estat* (Paris, 1625) (Rouen, 1625) (Paris, 1626).

Fin de la Guerre des Pays Bas aux Provinces qui sont encor sous l'obeissance d'Espagne, item La descouverte des Profondeurs d'Espagne cachées Sous ceste Proposition de Donner au Roy de France en mariage l'Infante d'Espagne avec Les dixsept Provinces des Pays-Bas en constitution de dot . . . En l'An de nostre Seigneur 1645. [Knuttel: 5185; in Dutch in Knuttel: 5314–5315; in German in Knuttel: 5316].

[Fouquet-Croissy, Antoine], *Le Courrier du Temps, Apportant Ce Qui Se Passe de Plus Secret en la Cour des Princes de l'Europe* [Moreau: 825].

Frantsch Praetie Sic vos non vobis (Münster 1646) [Knuttel: 5297–5299].

Frederick Henry, Prince of Orange, *Mémoires de Frédéric-Henri, prince d'Orange qui contiennent ses expéditions militaries depuis 1621 jusqu'a l'année 1646* (Amsterdam, 1733).

Gärtner, Carl Wilhelm, ed., *Westphälische Friedens-Cantzley, Darinnen die von Anno 1643 biß Anno 1648 bey denen Münster-und Osnabrückischen Friedens-Tractaten Geführte geheime Correspondence, ertheilte Instructiones, erstattete Relationes, und andere besondere Nachrichten enthalten* (Leipzig, 1731–1738) 9 vols.

Gazette de France (Paris, 1631–1792).

Gjörwell, Carl C., *Brev ifrån Svea-Rikes Canceller Grefve Axel Oxenstierna till Grefve Johan Oxenstierna . . . åren 1642–1649* (Stockholm, 1810–1819).

Gramont, Antoine, duc de, *Mémoires du Maréchal de Gramont*. Collection des mémoires relatifs à l'histoire de France, ed. Petitot and Monmerqué (Paris, 1819–1829) ser. 2, LVI–LVII, or in Nouvelle collection des mémoires pour servir à l'histoire de France, ed. Michaud and Poujoulat (Paris, 1836–1839) ser. 3, VII.

Groen van Prinsterer, Guillaume *et al.*, *Archives ou correspondance inédite de la maison d'Orange-Nassau* (Leiden and Utrecht, 1835–1915) 5 series, 25 vols.

Grotius, Hugo, *Hvgonis Grotii Epistolae ad Gallos, nunc primùm editae* (1648).

Guise, Henri, Duke de, *Mémoires du Duc de Guise*. Collection des mémoires relatifs à l'histoire de France, ed. Petitot and Monmerqué (Paris, 1819–1829) LV–LVI or in Nouvelle collection des mémoires pour servir à l'histoire de France, ed. Michaud and Poujoulat (Paris, 1836–1839) ser. 3, VII.

Haussonville, Gabriel Paul Othelin de Cleron, Count d', *Histoire de la réunion de la Lorraine à la France* (Paris, 1854–1859) 4 vols.

Hay du Chastelet, Paul, *Recueil de diverses pièces pour servir à l'histoire* (Paris, 1635, 1638, 1639, 1640, 1643).

Isambert, François-André, ed., *Recueil général des anciennes lois françaises depuis l'an 420 jusqu'à la revolution de 1789* (Paris, 1821–1833) 29 vols.

Jansenius, Cornelius, *Alexander Patricii Armacani, theologi Mars gallicus, seu de justicia armorum et foederum regis galiae libri duo* (1635, 1637, 1639).

———, *Le Mars François ou la guerre de France, en laquelle sont examinées les raisons de la justice prétendue des armes et des alliances du Roy de France, mises au jour par Alexandre Patricius Armacanus, théologien, et traduites de la troisième édition par C.H.D.P.D.E.T.B* (1637).

John IV, King of Portugal, *Cartas de el-rei D. João IV ao conde da Vidigueira (mãrques de Niza): embaixador em França*, ed. P. M. Laranjo Coelho (Lisbon, 1940–1942).

Joly, Claude, *Voyage fait à Munster, par M. Joly chanoine, de Paris, avec quelques lettres de M. Ogier prêtre et prédicateur* (Paris, 1670).

Journal contenant tout ce qui s'est fait et passé en la Cour du Parlement de Paris Toutes les Chambres assemblées sur le sujet des affaires du temps present (Paris, 1649).

Journal de ce qui s'est fait et passé au parlement sur les affaires du tems present, depuis le 13 mai 1648 jusqu'au 12 avril 1649 [1649].

Kort Verhael Aengaende 't versoeck der Heeren Ambassadeurs van Sijn Majesteyt van Vranckrijck, voor de Papisten hier te Lande Midtsgaders De Resolutien der Ho: Mo: Heeren Staten Generael der Vereenighde Nederlanden daer over genomen, ende aende voorsz Heeren Ambassadeurs gecommuniceert (Dortrecht, 1644) [Knuttel: 5107–5109].

Kybal, Vlastimil, and Incisa della Rocchetta, Giovanni, *La nunziatura di Fabio Chigi: 1640–1651* (Rome, 1943–1946) 1 vol. in two parts. Miscellanea della Reale deputazione Romana di storia patria, vols. XIV and XVI.

La Châtre, Edme, Count de Nançay, *Mémoires*. Collection des mémoires relatifs à l'histoire de France, ed. Petitot and Monmerqué (Paris, 1819–1829) ser. 2, LI, or in Nouvelle collection des mémoires pour servir à l'histoire de France, ed. Michaud and Poujoulat (Paris, 1836–1839) ser. 3, III.

[La Court, Henri Groulart de], *Mémoires de Monsieur D. . . . touchant les négociations du Traité de Paix fait à Munster en l'année mil six cens quarante-huit* (Cologne, 1674). Incorrectly attributed to D'Avaux.

La Rochefoucauld, François, duc de, *Mémoires de La Rochefoucauld,* Collection des mémoires relatifs à l'histoire de France, ed. Petitot and Monmerqué (Paris, 1819–1829) ser. 2, LI–LII, or in Nouvelle collection des mémoires pour servir à l'histoire de France, ed. Michaud and Poujoulat (Paris, 1836–1839) ser. 3, V.

Le Boindre, Jean, *Débats du parlement de Paris pendant la minorité de Louis XIV,* ed. Robert Descimon and Orest Ranum (Paris, 1997) 2 vols.

Le Clerc, Jean, ed., *Négociations secrètes touchant la paix de Munster et d'Osnabrug ou recueil général des préliminaries, instructions, lettres, mémoires etc. concernant ces négociations depuis leur commencement en 1642, jusqu'à leur conclusion en 1648, Avec les Depêches de Mr. de Vautorte, et autres Pièces au sujet du même Traité jusqu'en 1654 inclusivement* (The Hague, 1725–1726) 4 vols.

Leman, Auguste, *Recueil des Instructions générales aux nonces ordinaires de France de 1624 à 1634* (Lille and Paris, 1920). Mémoires et travaux publiés par des professeurs des Facultés catholiques de Lille, XV.

Lettre d'un Gentil-homme Venetien Escrite de Munster le 2 avril 1646 à un sien amy à Turin Traduite de l'Italien [Knuttel: 5300; in Dutch in 5301 and 5302].

Lettre Escripte de la Haye par un Gentilhomme François à un de ses amis à Paris, Avec Vn Escript donné à Messieurs les Estats Generaux . . . par Monsieur l'Ambassadeur de France [Knuttel: 5460–5461].

Loiseleur, Jules, and Baguenault de Puchesse, Gustave, *L'expédition du Duc de Guise à Naples, lettres et instructions diplomatiques de la cour de France:*

1647–1648, documents inédits (Paris, 1875). Mémoires de la Société archéologique de l'Orléanais, XIII.

Londorp, Michael Caspar, *Der Römischen Kayserlichen Majestät und des Heiligen Römischen Reichs Geist-und Weltlicher Stände Chur-und Fürsten, Grafen, Herren und Strändte Acta publica und schrifliche Handlungen* (Frankfurt am Main, 1668) 6 vols.

Longuerue, Louis Du Four, abbé de, *Recueil de pièces intéressantes pour l'histoire de France, et autres morceaux de littérature trouvés dans les papiers de M. l'abbé de Longuerue* (Geneva, 1769).

Louis XIV, *Mémoires for the Instruction of the Dauphin*, ed. Paul Sonnino (London and New York, 1970).

Mazarin, Jules, *Lettres du Cardinal Mazarin pendant son ministère*, ed. Adolphe Chéruel and Georges d'Avenel (Paris, 1872–1906) 9 vols. Collection de documents inédits sur l'histoire de France, ser 1.

Meiern, Johann Gottfried von, ed., *Acta Pacis Westphalicae publica, oder Westphälische Friedens-Handlungen und Geschichte in einem mit richtigen Urkunden bestärkten historischen Zusammenhang verfasser und beschrieben* (Hannover, 1734–1736) 6 vols.

Mémoires et négociations secrètes de la cour de France touchant la paix de Munster (Amsterdam, 1710) 3 vols.

Mercure François (Paris, 1605–1648) 25 vols.

Mignet, François, ed., *Négociations relatives à la succession d'Espagne sous Louis XIV* (Paris, 1835–1842) 4 vols. Collection de documents inédits sur l'histoire de France, ser. 1.

Modène, Esprit de Raimond de Mormoiron, Count de, *Mémoires du Comte de Modène sur la révolution de Naples de 1647* (Paris, 1827) 2 vols.

Montanus Arnoldus, *Leven en Bedrijf van Frederik-Hendrik, Prinse van Oranjen* (Amsterdam, 1652).

Montglat, François de Paule de Clermont, Marquis de, *Mémoires du Marquis de Montglat.* Collection des mémoires relatifs à l'histoire de France, ed. Petitot and Monmerqué (Paris 1819–1829) ser. 2, XLIX–LI, or in Nouvelle collection des mémoires pour servir à l'histoire de France, ed. Michaud and Poujoulat (Paris, 1836–1839) ser. 3, V.

Morbio, Carlo, *Epistolario inedito di Mazzarino* (Milan, 1842).

Morgues, Mathieu de, *Très humble, très véritable, et très importante Remonstrance au Roi* (1631).

Motteville, Françoise de, *Memoires de Madame de Motteville.* Collection des mémoires relatifs à l'histoire de France, ed. Petitot and Monmerqué (Paris, 1819–1829) ser. 2, XXXVI–XXXVII, or in Nouvelle collection des mémoires pour servir à l'histoire de France, ed. Michaud and Poujoulat (Paris, 1836–1839) ser. 2, X.

Munsters Praetie Deliberant Dum fingere nesciunt, Gedruct int Iaer ons Heeren 1646 [Knuttel: 5290–5295].

Nouveau Journal contenant tout ce qui s'est fait et passé aux Assemblées des Compagnies Souveraines du Parlement de Paris es années 1648 et 1649 Jusqu'à présent (Paris, 1649).

Ogier, François, *Actions publiques de François Ogier* (Paris, 1652–1655).

————, *Journal du congrès de Munster, par François Ogier, aumônier du Cte d'Avaux: 1643–1647,* ed. Auguste Boppe (Paris, 1893).

————, *Panégyrique du Comte d'Avaux* (Paris, 1650).

Olivares, Gaspar de Guzmán, Count-Duke de, *Memoriales y cartas del Conde-duque de Olivares,* ed. John H. Elliot and José F. de la Peña (Madrid, 1978–1981) 2 vols.

Ormesson, Olivier Lefèvre d', *Journal d'Olivier Lefèvre d'Ormesson, et extraits des Mémoires d'André Lefèvre d'Ormesson,* ed. Adolphe Chéruel (Paris, 1860–1861) 2 vols. Collection de Documents Inédits sur l'Histoire de France, ser. 3.

Oxenstierna, Axel, *Rikskansleren Axel Oxenstiernas skrifter och brefvexling, Utgifna af Kongl. vitterhets-historie-och artiqvitets-akademien* (Stockholm, 1888–1930) ser. 1, I–XI, XIII–XV, ser. 2, I–XII.

Pastoret, Amédée David, Marquis de, *Le Duc de Guise à Naples, ou mémoire sur les revolutions de ce royaume en 1647–1648* (Paris, 1825).

Poincten der Artijckulen, Ter Vergaderighe van de Hoog: Mog: Heeren Staten Generael Der Vereenichde Nederlanden gearresteert, Waer na De Heeren Plenipotentiarisen, ende Extraordinarij Ambassadeurs van desen Staet In het Tractaet van Vreden tot Mvnster, met die van den Coninck van Spanien hebben te verhandelen (Dortrecht, 1647) [Knuttel: 5430, 5430a–5432; in German in Knuttel: 5433; other publications in Dutch in Knuttel: 5434–5436].

Pontis, Louis de, *Mémoires du sieur de Pontis,* Collection des mémoires relatifs à l'histoire de France, ed. Petitot and Montmerqué (Paris, 1819–1829) ser. 2, XXXI–XXXII.

Praeliminaria Pacis Imperii, ed. Gustav Freytag (1648) 3 vols.

Priolo, Benjamin, *Ab excessu Ludovici xiii, de rebus gallicis historiarum libri XII* (Charleville, 1665).

Pulaski, Franciszek and Tomkiewicz, Ladislas, *La mission de Claude de Mesmes, Comte d'Avaux, Ambassadeur extraordinaire en Pologne: 1634–1636* (Paris, 1937).

Recueil de diverses pièces curieuses pour servir à l'histoire (Cologne, 1655/1666).

Recueil des Instructions données aux ambassadeurs et ministres de France depuis les Traités de Westphalie jusqu'à la Révolution française (Paris, 1884–).

Recueil de Tous les Traitez accordez en l'assemblée Generale, tenue à Munster & Osnabruck en Westphalie, pour la paix de la Chrestienté. Avec les Noms Et Qualitez de tous les Ambassadeurs & Plenipotentiaires qui ont assisté à ladite Assemblée. Imprimé sur les Originaux l'An de Salut 1650 [BNF M 14408: 6 I E12025].

Retz, Jean François Paul de Gondi de, *Oeuvres du Cardinal de Retz* (Paris, 1870–1896) 10 vols. Les grands écrivains de la France.

Richelieu, Armand Jean du Plessis de, *Lettres du Cardinal Duc de Richelieu, ou l'on voit la fine politique et le secret de ses plus grandes négociations* (Paris, 1695–1696) 2 vols.

————, *Lettres, instructions diplomatiques, et papiers d'etat du Cardinal de Richelieu,* ed. Georges d'Avenel (Paris, 1853–1877) 8 vols. Collection de documents inédits sur l'histoire de France, ser. 1.

————, *Mémoires du Cardinal de Richelieu,* in Collection des mémoires relatifs à l'histoire de France, ed. Petitot and Monmerqué (Paris, 1819–1829) ser. 2, XXII–XXX, or in Nouvelle collection des mémoires pour servir à l'histoire de France, ed. Michaud and Poujoulat (Paris, 1836–1839) ser. 2, VII–IX, or the incomplete but modern edition published by the Société de l'Histoire de France (1907–) 10 vols.

————, *Les papiers de Richelieu*
  section politique intéreure, correspondance et papiers d'état
  I   1624–1626, ed. Pierre Grillon (Paris, 1975).
  II   1627, ed. Pierre Grillon (Paris, 1977).
  III 1628, ed. Pierre Grillon (Paris, 1979).
       Index des tomes I, II, III, corrections et additions 1624–1628, ed. Pierre Grillon (Paris, 1980).
  IV   1629, ed. Pierre Grillon (Paris, 1980).
  V   1630, ed. Pierre Grillon (Paris, 1982).
  VI   1631, ed. Pierre Grillon (Paris, 1985).
  section politique extérieure, correspondance et papiers d'état
  I   Empire allemand (1616–1629) ed. Adolf Wild (Paris 1982).
  II   Empire allemand (1630–1635) ed. Anja Victorine Hartmann (Paris, 1997).
  III Empire allemand (1636–1642) ed. Anja Victorine Hartmann (Paris, 1999).
       Index des tomes I, II, III, ed. Aurelia Berger (Paris, 2003).

————, *Testament politique,* ed. Henri Desbordes (Amsterdam, 1688) or in Collection des mémoires relatifs à l'histoire de France, ed. Petitot and Monmerqué (Paris 1819–1829) ser. 2, XXXI, or in Nouvelle collection des mémoires pour servir à l'histoire de France, ed. Michaud and Poujoulat (Paris, 1836–1839) ser. 2, IX, or ed. by Louis André (Paris, 1947), or ed. by Françoise Hildesheimer for the Société de l'Histoire de France (Paris, 1995).

Saavedra Fajardo, Diego de, *Idea de un Principe Politico Christiano Representada en cien Empresas* (Munich, 1640).

Scotti, Ranuccio, *Correspondence du nonce en France Ranuccio Scotti,* ed. Pierre Blet (Rome, 1965).

Servien, Abel, *Harangue de M. le comte de La Roche Servient, conseill. du Roi en ses Conseils & son Ambass. Extraord. pour la Paix Generale, Faite à La Haye en l'assemblée de Mess. les Etats Généraux* (Paris, 1647). [Moreau: 1556; Knuttel: 5438, 5439. See also Knuttel: 5440–5442, 5442a, 5443–5444].

———, *Lettre de monsieur Servient . . . adressée à chacune des Provinces-Unies des Pays-Bas séparément, excepté la Hollande* (no date or place) [Moreau: 2040].

Siri, Vittorio, *Memorie recondite dall'anno 1601 sino al 1640* (Ronco, 1677–1679).

———, *Il Mercurio, o vero Historia de' correnti tempi: 1635–1655* (Casale, Lyon, Paris, Florence, 1644–1682) 15 vols.

Sousa Coutinho, Francisco de, *Correspondencia Diplomatica de Francisco de Sousa Coutinho durante a sua embaixada em Holanda,* ed. Edgar Prestge e Pedro de Azevedo (Coimbra and Lisbon, 1920–1955) 3 vols.

Svenska Riksrådets Protokoll, ed. Severin Bergh (Stockholm, 1906). Handlingar rörande Sveriges Historia, ser. 3, X–XII.

Sverges traktater med främmande magter jemte andra dit hörande handlingar, ed. O. S. Rydberg C. Hallendorf *et al.* (Stockholm, 1877–1934) 15 vols.

Talon, Omer, *Mémoires de Omer Talon,* Collection des mémoires relatifs à l'histoire de France, ed. Petitot and Monmerqué (Paris, 1819–1829) ser. 2, LX–LXIII, or in Nouvelle collection des mémoires pour servir à l'histoire de France, ed. Michaud and Poujoulat (Paris, 1836–1839) ser. 3, VI.

Tractaet van Vrede Beslooten den dertichsten Januarii deses tegenwoordigen Jaers sesthien hondert en ach en veertich binnen de Stadt van Munster in Westphalen tusschen den Doorluchtichsten en Grootmachtigen Prince Phillips de vierde Coninck van Hispanien etc ter eente ende de Hoogh Moogende Heeren Staten Generael vande Geunierrde Nederlanden ter andere zyde (The Hague, 1648) [Moreau in French: 3708; Knuttel in Dutch: 5733–5736, in French: 5737, and in Latin: 5738].

Traicté Et Articles De Paix Entre les Couronnes de France & D'Espagne, exhibez à Munster par Monseigneur le Duc de Longueville & Messieurs les Comtes D'Avaux et Servient, Ambassadeurs & Plenipotentiaires du Roy Tres-Chrestien, ès années 1646 & 1647 (1650) [Moreau: 3799].

Traités publics de la royale maison de Savoye avec les puissances étrangères depuis la paix de Château-Cambresis jusqu'à nos jours, publiés par ordre du roi et présentés à S.M par le comte Solar de la Marguerite (Turin, 1836–1861) 8 vols.

Tremblay, Joseph du, *Grand Mercy de la Chrestienté au Roy* (1625).

———, *Introduction à la vie spirituelle par une méthode facile d'oraison* (Paris, 1626).

Turenne, Henri de La Tour d'Auvergne, Viscount de, *Collection des lettres et mémoires trouvés dans les porte-feuilles du Maréchal de Turenne: pour servir de preuves et d'éclaircissemens à une partie de l'histoire de Louis XIV: et particulièrement a celles des campagnes du Général Français,* ed. Philippe-Henri de Grimoard (Paris, 1782).

————, *Mémoires du Maréchal de Turenne,* ed. Paul Marichal (Paris, 1909–1914) 2 vols. Société de l'Histoire de France.

Urkunden und Actenstücke zur Geschichte des Kurfürsten Friedrich Wilhelm von Brandenburg (Berlin, 1864–).

"Verhandlung der Pommerschen Gesandten auf dem Westphälischen Friedens-congreß, Siebente Abteilung," *Baltische Studien* XIV.2 (1852) 43–200.

Vertoogh Van Antoine De Brun, Raedt ende Ambassadeur van sijne Majesteyt van Spagnien tot bevordering der aengevangen Vrede-handelinge tot Munster, Aen hare Hog: Mog:de Heeren Staten Generael der vr\je Vereenigde Nederlanden, Schriftelijck gesonden uit Deventer den 11 February 1647, Wt het Fransch overgheset (Dortrecht 1647) [Knuttel: 5448–5451].

Waerachtich Verhael Vande Handelinghe Tot Mvnster, Tusschen de Majesteyten van Vranckrijck ende Spagnien, sedert dat de Pleinpotentiarijsen vande Heeren Staten Generael der Vereenighde Nederlanden als Middelaers daerinne sijn gebruyckt (Amsterdam, 1647) [Knuttel: 5428–5429].

Ziegler, Walter, ed. *Altbayern von 1550–1651: Dokumente zur Geschichte von Staat und Gesellschaft in Bayern,* Abt. 1, III, pts. 1–2 (Munich, 1992).

Secondary Sources

Ahnlund, Nils, *Gustav Adolf den store* (Stockholm, 1932) [translated by Michael Roberts] (New York, 1940).

————, et al., *Den Svenska utrikes politikens historia* (Stockholm, 1951–1961) 5 vols.

Aubery, Antoine, *Histoire du Cardinal Duc de Richelieu* (Paris, 1660).

————, *Histoire du Cardinal Mazarin* (Paris, 1688) 2 vols.

Aumale, Henri d'Orléans, Duke d', *Histoire des Princes de Condé pendant les XVIè et XVIIè siècles* (Paris, 1863–1896) 7 vols.

Avenel, Georges, Viscount d', *Richelieu et la monarchie absolue* (Paris, 1884–1895) 4 vols.

Barthold, Friedrich Wilhelm, *Geschichte des grossen deutschen Krieges vom Tode Gustav Adolfs ab mit besonderer Rücksicht auf Frankreich* (Stuttgart, 1842–1843) 2 vols.

Baudier, Michel, *Histoire du Maréchal de Toiras* (Paris, 1664).

Bayard, Françoise, Félix, Jöel, and Hamon, Philippe, *Dictionnaire des surientendants et contrôleurs généraux des finances du XVIᵉ siècle à la Révolution française de 1789* (Paris, 2000).

Bazzolini, Augusto, *Un Nunzio straordinario alla Corte di Francia nel secolo XVII* (Florence, 1882).

Bély, Lucien, and Richefort, Isabelle, *L'Europe des traités de Westphalie, Esprit de la diplomatie et diplomatie de l'esprit* (Paris, 2000).

Bibliographie des Mazarinades, ed. Célestin Moreau (Paris, 1850–1851) 3 vols. Société de l'Histoire de France.

Bierther, Kathrin, *Der Regensburger Reichstag von 1640–1641* (Kallmünz/Opf., 1971). Regensburger historische Forschungen, I.

Bohlen, Julius von, *Die Erwerbung Pommerns durch die Hohenzollern, Zur Erinnerung an die vor funfzig Jahren erfolgte Wiedervereinigung des ganzen Pommern unter die Herrschaft seines erlauchten Königshauses* (Berlin, 1868).

Bonney, Richard, *The King's Debts: Finance and Politics in France: 1589–1661* (Oxford, 1981).

Bougeant, Guillaume-Hyacinthe, *Histoire des guerres et des négociations qui précédèrent le Traité de Westphalie sous le règne de Louis XIII et le Ministère du Cardinal de Richelieu, et du Cardinal Mazarin Composée sur les Mémoires du Comte d'Avaux, Ambassadeur du Roi Très-Chrétien dans les Cours du Nord, en Allemagne & en Hollande, & Plénipotentiaire au Traité de Munster* (vol. I) and *Histoire du Traité de Westphalie ou des négotiations qui se firent à Munster et à Osnabrug pour établir la paix entre toutes les puissances de l'Europe Composée principalement sur les Mémoires de la Cour et des Plénipotentiaires de France* (vols. II and III) (Paris, 1727–1744) 3 vols. Also published in six volumes in 1744. Also published as *Histoire du traité de Westphalie ou des négociations qui se firent à Munster et à Osnabrug pour établir la paix entre toutes les puissances de l'Europe Composée principalement sur les Mémoires de la Cour et des Plénipotentiaires de France* (Paris, 1751) 6 vols.

Bouyer, Christian, *Michel Particelli d'Hémery* (Mémoire de Maîtrise, Paris-Sorbonne, 1970).

Braudel, Fernand, "Histoire et sciences sociales: la longue durée," *Annales E.S.C.* XIII.4 (October–December, 1958) 725–753.

Breucker, Gustav, *Die Abtretung Vorpommerns an Schweden und die Entschädigung Kurbrandenburgs* (Halle, 1879). Halle Abhandlungen zur neureren Geschichte, VIII.

Buisseret, David, *Henry IV* (London, 1984).

Castiglione, Valeriano, *Alla Maestà Christianissima di Luigi XIII il Giusto Rè di Francia, e di Navarra Per la Prosperità delle sue Armi* (n.d.).

Chaveriat, E., "D'Avaux et Servien," *Revue du Lyonnais,* ser. 5, IV (1888) 252–258.

Chéruel, Pierre Adolphe, "Les Carnets de Mazarin pendant la Fronde," *Revue historique* IV (May–August, 1877) 403–438.

———, *Histoire de France pendant la minorité de Louis XIV* (Paris, 1879–1880) 4 vols.

Chiala, Luigi, "Il Cardinale di Mazarino" (anonymous life of Cardinal Mazarin), *Rivista Contemporanea* IV (September–November, 1855) 539–584.

Church, William F., *Richelieu and Reason of State* (Princeton, N.J., 1972).

Cousin, Victor, "Des Carnets autographes du Cardinal Mazarin conservés à la Bibliothèque impériale," *Journal des Savants* (August, 1854) 457–470, (September, 1854) 521–547, (October, 1854) 600–626, (November, 1854) 687–719, (December, 1854) 753–773, (January, 1855) 19–42, (February, 1855) 84–103, (March, 1855) 161–184, (April, 1855) 217–242, (May, 1855) 304–324, (July, 1855) 430–447, (September, 1855) 525–545, (October, 1855) 622–637, (November, 1855) 703–719, (January, 1856) 48–60, (February, 1856) 105–119.

———, *La jeunesse de Madame de Longueville* (Brussels, 1853).

———, *La jeunesse de Mazarin* (Paris, 1865).

———, *Madame de Chevreuse et Madame de Hautefort* (Paris, 1856).

———, *Madame de Chevreuse, Nouvelles études sur les femmes illustres et la société du xviie siècle* (Paris, 1876).

Coville, Henri, *Etude sur Mazarin et ses démêlés avec le pape Innocent X* (Paris, 1914).

Croxton, Derek, *Peacemaking in Early Modern Europe: Cardinal Mazarin and the Congress of Westphalia: 1643–1648* (Selingsgrove and London, 1999).

———, "The Peace of Westphalia of 1648 and the Origins of Sovereignty," *International History Review* XXI (1999) 569–591.

Dedouvres, Louis, *Le Père Joseph polémiste: ses premiers écrits: 1623–1626* (Paris, 1895).

Dethan, Georges, *Gaston d'Orléans, conspirateur et prince charmant* (Paris, 1959).

———, *Mazarin et ses amis, étude sur la jeunesse du Cardinal d'après ses papiers conservés aux archives du Quai d'Orsay* (Paris, 1968) [translated by Stanley Baron as *The Young Mazarin*] (London, 1977).

———, *Mazarin, un homme de paix à l'âge baroque: 1602–1661* (Paris, 1981).

Dickmann, Fritz, *Der Westfälische Frieden* (Münster, 1959).

Dominguez Ortiz, A., *Crisis y Decadenzia de la España de los Austrias* (Barcelona, 1969).

Droysen, Gustav, *Gustaf Adolf* (Leipzig, 1869–1870).

Duchhardt, Heinz, ed., *Der Wetfälische Friede: Diplomatie politische Zäsur, kulturelles Umfeld Rezepttionsgeschichte* (Munich, 1998).

Dulong, Claude, *Anne d'Autriche, mère de Louis XIV* (Paris, 1980).

———, "Du Nouveau sur le Palais Mazarin: L'achat de l'hôtel Tubeuf par le Cardinal," *Bibliothèque de l'Ecole des Chartes* (CLIII, 1, 1995) 131–155.

Elliott, John. H., *The Count-Duke of Olivares, the statesman in an age of decline* (New Haven, Conn., 1986).

———, *Richelieu and Olivares* (Cambridge and New York, 1984).

Fagniez, Gustave, *Le père Joseph et Richelieu: 1577–1638* (Paris, 1894).

Fraga Iribane, Manuel, *Don Diego de Saavedra y Fajardo y la diplomacia de su época* (Madrid, 1955).

France, Bibliothèque Nationale, *Catalogue général des livres imprimés de la Bibliothèque nationale, Actes Royaux* (Paris, 1910–1960) 7 vols.

Gaudenzio, Claretta, *Storia della reggenza di Madama Cristina di Francia* (Turin, 1868–1869) 3 vols.

Giraffi, Alessandro, *Le Rivolutioni di Napoli* (Venice, 1647).

Green, Donald P. and Shapiro, Ian, *Pathologies of Rational Choice Theory: A Critique of Applications in Political Science* (New Haven, Conn., and London, 1994).

Griffet, Henri, *Histoire du règne de Louis XIII, roi de France et de Navarre* (Paris, 1758).

Guadet, Joseph, *Henry IV, sa vie, son oeuvre, ses écrits* (Paris, 1879).

Gualdo Priorato, Galeazzo, *Istoria del ministerio del cardinale Mazzarini, primo ministro di Francia* (Cologne, 1669) 3 vols. [French translation: Amsterdam, 1671].

Hammer-Purgstall, Joseph von, *Geschichte des osmanischen Reiches* (Pest, 1827–1835) 10 vols.

Hanotaux, Gabriel, and La Force, Augustin, Duke de, *Histoire du Cardinal Richelieu* (Paris, 1896–1967) 6 vols.

Hauser, Henri, *La pensée et l'action économique du Cardinal de Richelieu* (Paris, 1952).

Haussonville, Joseph, Count de, *Histoire de la réunion de la Lorraine à la France* (Paris, 1854–1859) 4 vols.

Henshall, Nicholas, *The Myth of Absolutism: Change and Continuity in Early Modern European Monarchy* (London and New York, 1992).

Jacob, Karl, *Die Erwerbung des Elsaß durch Frankreich im Westfälischen Frieden* (Strassburg, 1897).

Kettering, Alison McNeil, *Gerald ter Borsch and the Treaty of Münster* (The Hague, 1998).

Kleinman, Ruth, *Anne of Austria, Queen of France: 1601–1666* (Columbus, Ohio, 1985).

Lavisse, Ernest, *Histoire de France* (Paris, 1903–1911) 10 vols.

Le Laboureur, Jean, *Histoire du Maréchal de Guébriant contenant le recit de ce qui s'est passé en Allemagne dans les Guerres des Couronnes de France et de Suede et des Estats alliez contre la Maison d'Autriche. Avec l'histoire généalogique de la Maison du même Maréschal* (Paris, 1657).

Leman, Auguste, *Richelieu et Olivarès, leurs négociations secrètes de 1636 à 1642 pour le rétablissement de la paix* (Lille, 1938). Mémoires et travaux publiés par des professeurs des Facultés catholiques de Lille, XLIX.

———, *Urbain VIII et la rivalité de la France et de la maison d'Autriche* (Lille and Paris, 1920). Mémoires et travaux publiés par des professeurs des Facultés catholiques de Lille, XVI.

Lorentzen, Theodor, *Die Schwedische Armee im dreißigjährigen Kriege une ihre Abdankung* (Leipzig, 1894).

Lorenz, Gottfried, *Das Erzstift Bremen und der Administrator Friedrich während des Westfälischen Friedenskongresses. Ein Beitrag zur Geschichte des schwedisch-dänischen Machtkampfes im 17. Jahrhundert* (Münster, 1968). Schriftenreihe der Vereinigung zur Erforschung der Neueren Geschichte, IV.

Mentz, Georg, *Johann Philipp von Schönborn, Kurfürst von Mainz, Bischof von Würzburg und Worms: 1625–1673, Ein Beitrag zur Geschichte der siebzehnten Jahrhunderts* (Jena, 1896) 2 vols.

Mercenseffy, Grete, "Die Beziehungen der Höfe von Wien und Madrid während des dreissigjährigen Krieges," *Achiv für österreichische Geschichte* CXXI (1955) 1–91.

Merriman, Roger, *Six Contemporaneous Revolutions* (Hamden, Conn., and London) 1963.

Meyer, Johannes, *Kirchengeschichte Niedersachsens* (Göttingen, 1939).

Moote, A. Lloyd, *Louis XIII, the Just* (Berkeley, 1969).

————, *The Revolt of the Judges: The Parlement of Paris and the Fronde: 1643–1652* (Princeton, N.J., 1972).

Mousnier, Roland, *La vénalité des offices sous Henri IV et Louis XIII* (Rouen, 1945).

Netherlands, Koninklijke (Nationaal) Bibliotheek, *Catalogus van de pamflettenverzameling berustende in de Koninklijke bibliotheek*, ed., W. P. C. Knuttel (The Hague, 1889–1920) 9 vols.

Odhner, Clas Theodor, *Sveriges deltagande i Westfaliska fredskongressen och grunläggningen af det Svenska väldet i Tyskland* (Stockholm, 1875), Konig Vitterhets Historie och Antikvitets Akademiens Handlingar XXVII (1876) 37–370. German edition: *Die Politik Schwedens im Westphälischen Friedenskongress und die Gründung der schwedischen Herrschaft in Deutschland* (Gotha, 1877).

Palmer, Robert R., and Colton, Joel, *A History of the Modern World* 3rd ed. (New York, 1965).

Pastor, Ludwig von, *Geschichte der Päpste seit dem Ausgang des Mittelalters. Mit Benutzung des Päpstlichen Geheimarchives und vieler anderer Archive* (Freiburg in the Breisgau, 1899–1933 (16 vols). English edition: *The History of the Popes from the Close of the Middle Ages, drawn from the secret archives of the Vatican and other original sources* (London and St. Louis, 1924–1953) 40 vols.

Poelhekke, Jan Joseph, *Frederik Hendrik, Prins van Oranje; een biografisch drieluik* (Zutphen, 1978).

————, *De Vrede van Munster* (The Hague, 1948).

Quazza, Romolo, *La guerra per la successione di Mantova e del Monferrato: 1628–1631* (Mantua, 1926). Publicazioni della Reale Academia Virgiliana, ser. II, Miscellanea, 5–6.

Ranke, Leopold von, *Französische Geschichte* (Stuttgart and Tübingen, 1852–1855) 3 vols.

———, "Die grossen Mächte," *Historische-politische Zeitschrift* II (1833–1836) 1–51.

Ranum, Orest, *The Fronde: A French Revolution: 1648–1652* (New York, 1993).

———, *Richelieu and the Councillors of Louis XIII: a study of the secretaries of state and superintendents of finance in the ministry of Richelieu: 1635–1642* (Oxford, 1963).

Repgen, Konrad, "Chigi und Knöringen im Jahre 1645: Die Entstehung des Planes zum päpslichen Protest gegen den Westfälischen Frieden als quellenkundlisches und methodisches Problem," in *Dauer und Wandel der Geschichte: Festgabe für Kurt von Raumer* (Münster, 1966) 213–268.

———, "Fabio Chigis Instruction für den Westfälishen Friedenskongreß: Ein Beigrag zum kurialen Instructionwesen im Dreißigjährigen Krieg," *Römische Quartalschrift für Altertumskunde und Kirchengeschichte* XLVIII.1/2 (1953) 79–116.

———, "Die kaiserlich-französischen Satisfactionartikel vom 13 September 1646: ein befristetes Agreement," in *Der Westfälische Friede,* ed. Heinz Duchhardt (Munich, 1998) 175–216 (also in *Historische Zeitschrift* Beiheft 26).

———, "Der päpstische Protest gegen den Westfälischen Frieden und die Friedenspolitik Urbans VIII," *Historisches Jahrbuch* LXXV (1955) 94–122.

———, *Die Römische Kurie und der Westfälische Friede: Idee und Wirklichkeit des Papstums im 16. und 17. Jahrhundert* (Tübingen, 1962–1965) 2 vols. Bibliothek des Deutschen Historischen Instituts in Rom, XXIV–XXV.

———, "Uber den Zusammenhang von Verhandlungtechnik und Vertragsbegriffen, Die kaiserlichen Elsaß-Angebote vom 28 März und 14 April 1646 an Frankreich. Ein Versuch," in *Historische Klopfsignale für die Gegenwart* (Münster, 1974) 64–96.

Rapports et notices sur l'édition des Mémoires du Cardinal de Richelieu (Paris, 1905–1922) 7 vols. Société de l'Histoire de France.

Roberts, Michael, *Gustavus Adolphus: A History of Sweden: 1611–1632* (London, New York, and Toronto, 1958) 2 vols.

Rohrschneider, Michael, *Der gescheiterte Frieden von Münster: Spaniens Ringen mit Frankreich auf dem Westfälischen Friedenskongress: 1643–1649* (Münster, 2007). Schriftenreihe der Vereinigung zur Erforschung der Neueren Geschichte, XXX.

Rowen, Herbert H., *The King's State: Proprietary Dynasticism in Early Modern Europe* (New Brunswick, N.J., 1980).

Ruppert, Karsten, *Die kaiserliche Politik auf dem Westfälischen Friedenskongreß: 1643–1648* (Münster, 1979). Schriftenreihe der Vereinigung zur Erforschung der Neueren Geschichte, X.

Schneider, Bernd Christian, *Ius Reformandi: Die Entwicklung eines Staatskirchenrechts von seinen Anfängen bis zum Ende des Alten Reiches* (Tübingen, 2001). Beitrage zum evangelischen Kirchenrecht und zum Staatskirchenrecht LXVIII.

Schreiber, Renate, *Erzherzog Leopold Wilhelm. Kirche, Krieg und Kunst*, Diplomarbeit (Vienna, 1998).

Silvagni, Umberto, *Il Cardinale Mazzarino* (Rome, 1928).

Sonnino, Paul, "The Dating and Authorship of Louis XIV's *Mémoires*," *French Historical Studies* III.3 (Spring, 1964) 303–337.

———, "The Dating of Richelieu's *Testament politique*," *French History* XIX.2 (June 2005) 261–272.

———, "Dieu et la diplomatie dans l'espirit de Mazarin," *Revue d'histoire diplomatique* CXXI.3 (October–December, 2007) 193–204.

———, "Une documentation clé sur le congrès de Westphalie: Les papiers de Servien aux archives des Affaires étrangères," in *L'Europe des traités de Westphalie*, ed. Lucien Bély and Isabelle Richefort (Paris, 2000) 527–535.

———, "From D'Avaux to *dévot*: Politics and Religion in the Thirty Years War," *History* LXXXVII (April, 2002) 193–203.

———, *Louis XIV and the Origins of the Dutch War* (Cambridge and New York, 1988).

———, "Louis XIV's *Mémoires pour l'histoire de la guerre de Hollande*," *French Historical Studies* VIII.1 (Spring, 1973) 29–50.

———, "Prelude to the Fronde: The French Delegation at the Peace of Westphalia," in *Der Westfälische Friede*, ed. Heinz Duchhardt (Munich, 1998) 217–233 (also in *Historische Zeitschrift* Beiheft 26).

———, "What Kind of Idea is the Idea of Balance of Power?" in *The Transformation of European Politics 1763–1848: Episode or Model in European History?* ed. Peter Krüger and Paul W. Schröder (Münster, 2002) 63–76.

———, "A Young Person's Guide to Postmodernism." *Praesidium* 4.2 (Spring, 2004) 22–32.

Stradling, Robert A., *Europe and the Decline of Spain: A Study of the Spanish System: 1580–1720* (London, 1979).

Stüve, Carl, *Geschichte des Hochstifts Osnabrück bis zum Jahre 1508* (Jena, 1853–1882) 3 vols. [Reprinted: 1980].

Tallemant des Réaux, Gédéon, *Historiettes* (Paris, 1834–1836).

Tapié, Victor, *La France de Louis XIII et Richelieu* (Paris, 1967).

Tejera, Jose, *Saavedra Fajardo, sus pensiamentos, sus poesias, sus opiniones* (Madrid, 1884).

Teschke, Benno, *The Myth of 1648: Geopolitics and the Making of Modern International Relations* (London and New York, 2003).

Tessier, Jules, *Le Chevalier de Jant, Relations de la France avec le Portugal au temps de Mazarin* (Paris, 1877).

Tischer, Anuschka, *Französische Diplomatie und Diplomaten auf dem Westfälis-chen Friedenskongreß: Außenpolitik unter Richelieu und Mazarin* (Münster, 1999). Schriftenreihe der Vereinigung zur Erforschung der Neueren Geschichte, XXIX.

Treasure, Geoffrey, *Mazarin: The Crisis of Absolutism in France* (London, 1995).

Valfrey, Jules, *Hugues de Lionne: Ses ambassades en Italie: 1642–1656* (Paris, 1877).

Viti Mariani, Paolo, *La Spagna e la Santa Sede. Il matrimonio del Rè di Spagna D. Filippo IV con doã Maria Anna Archiduchessa d'Austria: 1645–1649* (Rome, 1899).

Voltaire, *Le Siècle de Louis XIV* (Geneva, 1768) 4 vols.

Waddington, Albert, *La République des Provinces-Unies: La France et les Pays-Bas Espagnols de 1630 à 1650* (Paris, 1895–1897) 2 vols.

Warmbrunn, Paul, *Zwei Konfessionen in einer Stadt. Das Zusammenleben von Katholiken und Protestanten in den paritätischen Reichstädten Augsburg, Bib-erach, Ravensburg und Dinkelsbühl von 1548 bis 1648* (Wiesbaden, 1983). Veröffentlichungen des Instituts für Europäische Geschichte Mainz. Abteilung für Abendländische Religionsgeschichte CXI.

Wedgwood, Cecilie V., *The Thirty Years War* (London, 1938).

Wicquefort, Abraham van, *Histoire des Provinces-Unies des Pais-Bas* (The Hague, 1719–1743) 2 vols.

Wolff, Fritz, *Corpus Evangelicorum und Corpus Catholicorum auf dem Westfälis-chen Friedenskongreß: Die Einfügung der konfessionnellen Ständeverbindungen in der Reichsverfassung* (Münster, 1966). Schriftenreihe der Vereinigung zur Erforschung der Neueren Geschichte V, 2.

Index

Acta Pacis Westphalicae, 17
Ager, 142
Aitzema, Lieuwe van, 1
Albret, Duke d', 90
Almighty. *See* God
Alsace, Upper and Lower, 8, 27, 38, 40–41, 60–61, 63, 66, 73–74, 77, 79, 82–84, 87, 89–90, 94–95, 100, 104, 140, 166, 170
Amalia Elizabeth, Landgravin of Hesse-Cassel, 25, 38, 43, 58, 67, 93, 96, 102, 120, 126, 132, 135, 147
Amiens, 80
Amsterdam, 3, 147
Anet, 126
Aniello, Tommaso (Masaniello), 135, 144
Anjou, Duke d', 53, 59, 89; conspiracies against, 126, 137
Annaliste movement, 4
Anne of Austria, Infanta of Spain, later Queen and Queen-regent of France, 1, 11–12, 18, 24, 29, 31–39, 43–44, 58, 60, 63–64, 68, 72–75, 78, 89–90, 112, 117, 121–122, 127, 134, 138, 140, 148, 150, 152–153, 155–156, 158, 160, 162, 164–165, 167–168; conspiracies against, 126, 137
Annese, Gennaro, 144, 147, 150
Answer to the Münster Chatterbox, 77
Antwerp, 63, 72, 83
Aragon, Ferdinand of. *See* Ferdinand of Aragon
Archivo General de Simancas, 7
Archivio Segreto del Vaticano, 8
Armentières, 59, 120, 130, 132
Arras, 26, 53
Artois, 27, 53, 78, 84, 163
Asti, 38

Aubry, 160
Auersperg, Count von, 35
Augsburg, Peace of, 62
Austria and Austrian(s), house of, 2, 10–12, 14, 16, 22–23, 27, 40–43, 61, 69, 76, 78–79, 82, 89, 95, 105; Anne of (*see* Anne of Austria); Archdukes of (*see* Innsbruck, Archdukes of; Leopold, Archduke); Don Juan of (*see* Don Juan of Austria). *See also* Hapsburg(s)
Autonomy, 92
Avaux, Claude de Mesmes, Count d':
background and emergence of, 20–21, 23–25, 27, 33, 34, 36; brother of (*see* Mesmes, President de); on France, 100; on Italy, 25, 147; on Portugal, 123; quarrels with Servien, 44, 48–53, 55–57, 92, 99, 112–113; return from Westphalia, 160; on Sweden, 24–25, 53, 56, 99, 112, 123–124, 126; on the Turks, 113
—characteristics and ideas of: his charm, 54; his flatteries, 69, 77, 93; his learning, 21, 45, 48, 99; his moderation, 25, 36, 43, 73, 79, 81–82, 99–100; his papers, 2, 7; his putative *Mémoires,* 9; his religion, 21, 24, 45, 64, 85, 120–121, 123; his scapegoating, 112–113; his skill, 21, 23–24, 27, 56, 96, 117
—on the Dutch, 85–86, 88; on their "interposition," 88, 91, 116
—in the Dutch Republic, 41–46; in Westphalia, 47–57, 64, 69, 70–71, 73, 77, 79, 81–82, 84–86, 88–89, 91–93, 96, 99–100, 108, 111–113, 115–118, 120–124, 127, 129–131, 135–138, 140, 146–147, 150–156, 158

Vincennes, 38, 160, 164
Viole, 165
Volmar, Dr., 62, 79, 82, 84, 161
Voltaire, 3, 45

Wallenstein, Imperial general, 13
Walsich, 76
Warnemünde, 67, 76
Weimarian army and Weimarians, 38, 73,
    83, 121, 131, 134, 140–141
Westphalia, 2, 28, 63, 95, 108, 136, 147;
    Congress and negotiations of, 1, 4–5, 37,
    39, 55, 80, 96, 128, 145, 166; Peace of,
    3–6, 8–9, 55, 88, 94, 101, 149; and rise of
    the state, 3–5, 8

William II, Prince of Orange, 116, 122, 132,
    142–143
Wismar, 60–61, 67, 76, 99, 102, 112
Wollin, 102, 117
Worms, 15, 38
Wrangel, 135, 139, 142, 161
Würtzburg, deputies of, 147

Ypres, 139, 160; Bishop of (*see* Jansen,
    Cornelius)

Zapata, Count, 35, 48
Zaragoza, 88, 103, 106
Zusmarshausen, 161

Harvard University Press is a member of Green Press Initiative
(greenpressinitiative.org), a nonprofit organization working to
help publishers and printers increase their use of recycled paper
and decrease their use of fiber derived from endangered forests.
This book was printed on 100% recycled paper containing
50% post-consumer waste and processed chlorine free.